W9-CAP-630

THE SEXUAL CENTURY

THE SEXUAL CENTURY

ETHEL SPECTOR PERSON, M.D.

YALE UNIVERSITY PRESS NEW HAVEN AND LONDON

Designed by Gregg Chase.
Set in Scala type by Keystone Typesetting, Inc., Orwigsburg, Pennsylvania.
Printed in the United States of America by Vail-Ballou Press, Binghamton, New York.

Person, Ethel Spector.
The sexual century / Ethel Spector Person.
p. cm.
Includes bibliographical references and index.
ISBN 0-300-07604-5 (alk. paper)
1. Sex role. 2. Sex discrimination against women. 3. Sex role—Psychological aspects. 4. Sex differences (Psychology) 5. Gender identity. I. Title.
HQ1075.P46 1999
305.3—dc21 99-34598
CIP

A catalogue record for this book is available from the British Library.

The paper in this book meets the guidelines for permanence and durability of the Committee on Production Guidelines for Book Longevity of the Council on Library Resources.

10 9 8 7 6 5 4 3 2 1

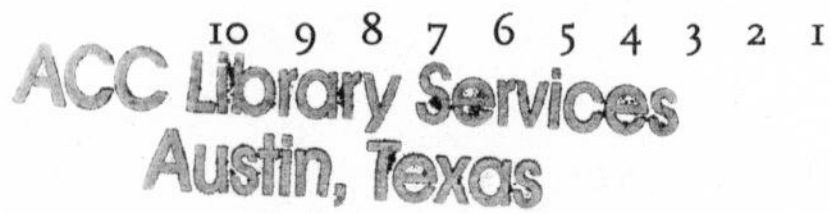

IN MEMORY OF LIONEL OVESEY

An intuitive and brilliant analyst, inspired and inspirational teacher, original and rigorous thinker, researcher in psychoanalysis before such research was fashionable, he was, to me, a friend, mentor, and collaborator in those days when men were said not to mentor women.

CONTENTS

xi
Acknowledgments

1
Introduction

PART I
Sex and Gender: General Considerations

ONE / 11
The Sexual Century (1998)
ETHEL S. PERSON

TWO / 31
Sexuality as the Mainstay of Identity: Psychoanalytic Perspectives (1980)
ETHEL S. PERSON

THREE / 55
Psychoanalytic Theories of Gender Identity (1983)
ETHEL S. PERSON AND LIONEL OVESEY

FOUR / 72
The Influence of Values in Psychoanalysis: The Case of Female Psychology (1983)
ETHEL S. PERSON

PART II
Cross-Gender Disorders

FIVE / 91
Gender Identity and Sexual Psychopathology in Men: A Psychodynamic Analysis of Homosexuality, Transsexualism, and Transvestism (1973)
LIONEL OVESEY AND ETHEL S. PERSON

SIX / 110
The Transsexual Syndrome in Males: Primary Transsexualism (1974)
ETHEL S. PERSON AND LIONEL OVESEY

SEVEN / 127
The Transsexual Syndrome in Males:
Secondary Transsexualism (1974)
ETHEL S. PERSON AND LIONEL OVESEY

EIGHT / 146
Transvestism: A Disorder of the Sense of Self (1976)
LIONEL OVESEY AND ETHEL S. PERSON

NINE / 161
Transvestism: New Perspectives (1978)
ETHEL S. PERSON AND LIONEL OVESEY

TEN / 178
Homosexual Cross-Dressers (1984)
ETHEL S. PERSON AND LIONEL OVESEY

ELEVEN / 194
Extreme Boyhood Femininity:
Isolated Finding or Pervasive Disorder? (1985)
SUSAN COATES AND ETHEL S. PERSON

PART III
Sex and Fantasy

TWELVE / 211
From Sexual Desire to Excitement:
The Role of Sexual Fantasy (1998)
ETHEL S. PERSON

THIRTEEN / 230
Gender Differences in Sexual Behaviors and Fantasies
in a College Population (1989)
ETHEL S. PERSON, NETTIE TERESTMAN, WAYNE A. MYERS,
EUGENE L. GOLDBERG, AND CAROL SALVADORI

FOURTEEN / 243
Associations Between Sexual Experiences and Fantasies in a
Nonpatient Population: A Preliminary Study (1992)
ETHEL S. PERSON, NETTIE TERESTMAN, WAYNE A. MYERS,
EUGENE L. GOLDBERG, AND MICHAEL BORENSTEIN

PART IV
Sex and Gender: Female Sexuality and Femininity and Male Sexuality and Masculinity

FIFTEEN / 259
The Erotic Transference in Women and in Men: Differences and Consequences (1985)
ETHEL S. PERSON

SIXTEEN / 278
Female Sexual Identity: The Impact of the Adolescent Experience (1985)
ETHEL S. PERSON

SEVENTEEN / 296
Some Mysteries of Gender: Rethinking Masculine Identifications in Heterosexual Women (1998)
ETHEL S. PERSON

EIGHTEEN / 316
Male Sexuality and Power (1986)
ETHEL S. PERSON

NINETEEN / 333
The Omni-Available Woman and Lesbian Sex: Two Fantasy Themes and Their Relationship to the Male Developmental Experience (1986)
ETHEL S. PERSON

PART V
The Impact of Culture

TWENTY / 347
Harry Benjamin and the Birth of a Shared Cultural Fantasy (1972/1997)
ETHEL S. PERSON

367
References

379
Index

ACKNOWLEDGMENTS

DR. LIONEL OVESEY (1915–1995), to whom this book is dedicated, will be remembered by future generations for his creative, cutting-edge psychoanalytic research and for his theoretical work in a number of interrelated areas. Whether by chance, psychic necessity, or design, his work—always ahead of its time—often generated controversy. This was true of his first project, a research study of the impact of culture on psyche. Invited to collaborate with Abram Kardiner, the topic they chose—the impact of oppression on blacks—was a product of Lionel's experience in the military. Stationed in the deep South in the 1940s, he had become sensitized to—and indignant about—the major proportions and implications of white racism. Their study, based on in-depth psychodynamic interviews with a nonpatient population, eventuated in a landmark book, *The Mark of Oppression: A Psychosexual Study of the American Negro*, published in 1951 (and reissued in 1963). Lionel himself regarded the book as a historic classic in the sense that it caught the psychological effects of oppression on a minority just before the advent of the black movement. But many "liberals" denounced the book *because* it called attention to psychological problems blacks suffered.

Risking criticism from a different quarter, Kardiner and Lionel, this time along with Aaron Karush, authored four papers (first published separately and then all together in 1966 as "A Methodological Study of Freudian Theory, I-IV") that constituted a major assault on the premise that libido theory was a sufficient theoretical framework for psychoanalysis. So doing, they predictably generated backlash from some psychoanalytic quarters. Nonetheless, their papers were among the pioneer critiques of instinct theory that have stood the test of time.

In the meantime, Lionel had begun to explore homosexuality and what he called pseudo-homosexuality, his first papers on these subjects appearing in 1954 and 1955. Once more into the fire. However, this time the negative reaction to Lionel's work was delayed. It was only in the late 1960s, with the advent of the gay liberation movement, when "studying" homosexuality had become politically suspect, that Lionel was sorely castigated. Nonetheless, when a thinker comes up with one important, original idea, he is generally guaranteed a place in intellectual history, and in studying homosexual imagery in heterosexual men, Lionel had come upon a major organizing insight. He observed that the homosexual dreams of heterosexuals were not fundamentally sexual but symbolized power, and he designated this imagery pseudo-homosexual. Building on this observation, he theorized how power impacts on sex and gender and, reciprocally, how sexual images are invoked to symbolize power issues; just as cigars or containers may symbolize the genitals, so, too, may the depiction of the genitals and sexual behaviors sometimes symbolize the acquisition or loss of power. His insight proved not only theoretically profound, but clinically useful, providing an interpretative route to help patients identify issues of powerlessness and of narcissistic injury.

Discerning that the symbolic equation of the penis with power was in part cultural, Lionel soon intuited that what women envied in men was primarily their power, not their penises, and that women suffered from cultural devaluation. He addressed these insights in an important paper "Masculine Aspirations in Women: An Adaptational Analysis" published in 1956. Noting the situation of women as a kind of oppressed group, he had within his conceptual grasp the essential insight that ultimately fueled the woman's movement fifteen years before that movement began to soar.

Over time, Lionel's interest turned more to general issues of sex and gender and I was privileged that he invited me to collaborate with him in writing a textbook on sex and gender.

My work on sex and gender grows organically out of my collaboration with Lionel, and many of my papers were co-authored with him. But we never got around to the textbook. In a sense this book is in lieu of the one that he and I intended to write together.

A methodical man, Lionel drew up an outline of all the subjects he thought we should cover in the textbook. Reading his proposed table of contents, we realized that neither of us had any first-hand experience with transsexualism or more than a fleeting exposure to transvestism. Lionel was adamant that we could not write a textbook without including these important subjects. Here, too, Lionel was prescient, recognizing the importance of understanding the relevance of these disorders to psychoanalytic theories long before gender-bending became such a popular topic. He insisted that we had to do the basic clinical research in order to know what we were talking about. There was no doubt of what the division of labor would be. I was going to have to find a population to study and to do the necessary interviews. And then we would theorize together and write alternating drafts. As it turned out, Lionel's timing was impeccable; we were to do our work together at the very moment when cross-gender phenomena began to explode into public consciousness.

In order to get the data that Lionel and I required—and Lionel was a psychoanalytic pioneer in the use of dynamically oriented interviews with nonpatients—I needed to find access to an at-the-time fluid sexual underground. I knew that if I could contact anyone with even fringe ties to the sexual underground it would serve as an introduction. I was lucky enough to have a connection to Harold Greenwald, who had written an important book on prostitutes (*The Call Girl: A Social and Psychoanalytic Study*, 1958), and he introduced me to some of the key players in the transsexual world. However, it was only with my introduction to Harry Benjamin, the "father" of transsexualism, and his then associate, Charles Ihlenfeld (who subsequently became a psychiatrist), that I was given essentially unlimited access to a large number of transsexuals. I used to sit in Harry Benjamin's office and interview his patients, most of whom were seeing him for hormone therapy. The work I did with Lionel would have been well nigh impossible without the cooperation of Harry Benjamin, who was hospitable to me despite his major bias against psychoanalysts. In fact, we became great friends.

Through Benjamin's good connections, I met a man I wrote about in my book *By Force of Fantasy*, there called Ed/Edna, who introduced me to transvestites and to the transvestitic network. He was a kind man and a good friend. Through him I was invited to transvestite parties throughout the Northeast, and it was at these events that I gained some of my deeper insights into the subjective meaning to transvestites of their participation in that world.

The homosexual scene was fairly well known to me. While many gays like to dress up as women from time to time, cross-dressing homosexuals (drag queens) are another matter. Through the underground cross-dressing network I was put in touch with "serious" cross-dressing homosexuals, who helped to make clear the differences in various kinds of cross-dressing behaviors—particularly those between transvestites (heterosexuals) and cross-dressing drag queens (homosexuals), though some individuals are in the borderland between the two categories.

Through these different sources, Lionel and I found the subjects through whose generous participation we came to understand some of the dynamics of the cross-gender disorders. Lionel and I established a true collaboration. Lionel interviewed many of our subjects. We discussed, argued, modified, co-invented and theorized, and jollied each other along. Through our work together I learned the virtues of collaboration.

My subsequent collaborations and interactions with scholars and thinkers from other disciplines have been indispensable in understanding sex and gender not just from a psychoanalytic perspective but from a socio-cultural one as well. Catherine Stimpson, now Dean of Graduate Studies at New York University, and I were both founding members of "Women in Society," a Columbia University seminar begun in 1974. It was thrilling to discuss papers in an interdisciplinary setting and to see how the various members responded differently to a paper depending on the parent discipline in which they had been trained. Catherine shortly thereafter became the founding editor of the journal

Signs: Women in Culture and Society. I joined her Editorial Board and suggested to her that we run an issue on sex. My paper "Sexuality as the Mainstay of Identity" (Chapter 2 in this book) was first published there. That issue, *On Women: Sex and Sexuality,* which I co-edited with Catherine, was subsequently published as a book in 1980 and remains in print. It brought together in one book the work of some leading feminists and psychoanalysts, at that time not commonplace.

I participated in a seminar on homosexuality at Columbia University (1975–1977), along with luminaries from both the department of English and the Columbia University Psychoanalytic Center. Several years later (1979–1980) I was invited to participate in a seminar, "Sexual Fraternities," at the New York Institute for the Humanities. Unlike the Columbia seminar, which was made up almost exclusively of heterosexuals, the Institute for the Humanities seminar was made up largely of homosexuals. The difference in the theoretical outlook of the two groups was striking to say the least and clearly made the point that the deeper insights sometimes come from those who have had some first-hand experience. But like autobiography and biography, both of which focus on the same phenomenon from different vantage points, important insights were garnered in both groups. (I sometimes think of psychotherapy as the task of helping a patient reconcile his autobiography with others' "biographical" perceptions of him.)

I participated in a Michel Foucault seminar at the New York Institute for the Humanities (1980–1981) given by Foucault himself. Though my acquaintance with Foucault was brief, it was significant from our first exchange. I had observed that naming gave relief to people who suffer from gender disorders, as was true in the history of many transsexuals, who would say "I was so glad to learn there are others like me." Foucault argued that naming was deeply constricting. I believe we were both right, and it is only cognizance of such a double perspective that gives depth perception to the broad field of sex and gender.

I was a consultant to Susan Coates's Childhood Gender Identity Project at St. Lukes-Roosevelt Hospital Center from 1983 to 1987. Susan was interested in my work with Lionel and used it in her initial formulation of boyhood femininity. She has gone on to develop a complex, impressive, and convincing model of boyhood femininity, the most outstanding model we have. Susan and I co-authored a paper on boyhood femininity that is included in this volume as Chapter 11.

Through "The Fantasy Project," which I established at the Columbia University Psychoanalytic Center for Training and Research, my co-investigators, Nettie Terestman, Wayne Meyers, and Eugene Goldberg, and associates Carol Salvadori and Michael Borenstein, and I were able to develop a questionnaire format to explore the relationship of sexual fantasy to sexual behavior and the sex differences in sexual fantasy. Our work was supported by grants from the Fund for Psychoanalytic Research of the American Psychoanalytic Association, 1982–1983, 1983–1984, and the Biomedical Research Grant of the New York Psychiatric Institute in 1983.

Special thanks go to several patients who have permitted me to use aspects of their life stories (heavily disguised) in a few papers, and to the many participants in my various research projects. I was very fortunate in that none of the subjects of my research raised any objection when they saw the published papers. The only "complaint" came from one of the drag queens I wrote about, who was mock offended that I had described "her" as attractive rather than as *very* attractive.

I was privileged in past years to discuss overlapping interests with the late Robert Stoller and the late Helen Singer Kaplan. My major intellectual home for thirty years has been the Columbia University Center for Psychoanalytic Training and Research, and it has been my good fortune that that institution has encompassed some distinguished theorists and first-rate critical minds. Among those who have impacted on me directly I include the late Sandor Rado and Abram Kardiner, who were both founders and directors of the Center, and, of course Lionel Ovesey. Three other directors of the Institute were particularly supportive of my work: the late George Daniels, the late John Weber, and George Goldman. I have also had the benefit of many conversations with Arnold Cooper, Willard Gaylin, Otto Kernberg, Ilene Lefcourt, Robert Michels, and Eleanor Schuker. In addition, Columbia has hosted either in the past or currently a number of other contributors to the field of sex and gender, among whom I would like to mention Stanley Coen, Jennifer Downey, Richard Friedman, Herbert Hendin, Richard Isay, Lila Kalinich, Wayne Meyers, Helen Myers, John Munder Ross, and Ralph Roughton. Both the Center and I have profited immensely from a series of supportive chairmen of Psychiatry at Columbia University, primary among them Lawrence Kolb and our current chair, Herbert Pardes, a true ecumenical in the field of psychiatry at a time when so few departments support both biological and psychological research.

In the preparation of this volume I have been well served by a brilliant editor, Gladys Topkis. She can change the depth of meaning of a whole page by inserting a single word. My manuscript editor, Margaret Otzel, proved to be both meticulous and patient, and I am grateful. My thanks go too to my assistant, Scott Martin, a graduate student in philosophy and education who I believe will one day make an important intellectual contribution in his field. Judy Mars, the librarian at the Columbia University Psychoanalytic Center, has been of invaluable help in locating articles and checking references. My husband, Stanley Diamond, has been supportive, as ever, and a wonderfully careful reader of my papers. And my sons, Louis and Lloyd Sherman, have paid me the honor of being supportive of me and proud of my work, as have my stepdaughters, Nancy Diamond and Jessica Diamond.

Many of the papers included in this volume have been previously published. There are deletions in the papers in order to eliminate repetition. (In some cases, repetitions have not been deleted insofar as they are critical to an argument not addressed in any of the other papers.) The papers have also been edited, changing a word or a passage in the service of clarity or felicity. I have added occasional footnotes (specified as "Footnote added, 1998") in order to update a passage or show its relevance to more current information or issues. But nothing substantive has been changed in any of the papers. The paper written in collaboration with Susan Coates has not been revised or edited, at her request.

I am grateful to the editors of the following journals and publishing houses for their permission to draw on these papers.

The University of Chicago Press for permission to reprint "Sexuality as the Mainstay of Identity: Psychoanalytic Perspectives" from *Signs: Journal of Women in Culture and Society*, vol. 5, no. 4, 605–630, copyright 1980 by the University of Chicago. All rights reserved.

The American Academy of Psychoanalysis for permission to reprint the following articles from *The Journal of the American Academy of Psychoanalysis:* "Psychoanalytic Theories of Gender Identity," 11 (2): 203–226, 1983; "Gender Identity and Sexual Psychopathology in Men," 1 (1): 53–72, 1973; "Transvestism: New Perspectives," 6 (3): 301–323, 1978; "Homosexual Cross-Dressers," 12 (2): 167–186, 1984; "Associations Between Sexual Experiences and Fantasies in a Non-Patient Population: A Preliminary Study," 20 (1): 75–90, 1992; and "The Erotic Transference in Women and in Men: Differences and Consequences," 13 (2): 159–180, 1985.

American Psychiatric Press for permission to reprint "The Influence of Values in Psychoanalysis: The Case of Female Psychology" from *Psychiatry Update*, ed. L. Grinspoon, 36–50, 1983.

The Association for the Advancement of Psychotherapy for permission to reprint the following articles from the *American Journal of Psychotherapy:* "The Transsexual Syndrome in Males: Part I. Primary Transsexualism," 28 (1): 4–20, 1974, and "The Transsexual Syndrome in Males: Part II. Secondary Transsexualism," 28 (1): 174–193, 1974.

Jason Aronson Inc. for permission to reprint "Transvestism: A Disorder of the Sense of Self" from the *International Journal of Psychoanalytic Psychotherapy*, 5: 219–236, 1976.

Waverly Press for permission to reprint "Extreme Boyhood Femininity:

Isolated Behavior or Pervasive Disorder?" from the *Journal of the American Academy of Child Psychiatry,* 24 (6): 702–709, 1985.

The *Journal of Sex and Marital Therapy* for permission to reprint "Gender Differences in Sexual Behaviors and Fantasies in a College Population" from the *Journal of Sex and Marital Therapy,* 15 (3): 187–198, 1989.

Greenwood Publishing Group, Inc., for permission to reprint "Female Sexual Identity: The Impact of the Adolescent Experience" from *Sexuality: New Perspectives,* ed. R. Friedman et al., 71–88, 1985.

Analytic Press for permission to reprint "Male Sexuality and Power" from *Psychoanalytic Inquiry,* 6 (1): 3–25, 1986.

The Association for Psychoanalytic Medicine for permission to reprint "The Omni-Available Woman and Lesbian Sex: Two Fantasy Themes and Their Relationship to the Male Developmental Experience" from *The Psychology of Men: New Psychoanalytic Perspectives,* eds. G. Fogel, F. Lane, and R. S. Liebert, New York: Basic Books, 71–94, 1986.

Though I have retained the copyright to "The Sexual Century," it has been published in *Revista de Psiquiatria da Sociedade de Psiquiatria do Rio Grande do Sul* (the Journal of the Psychiatric Society of Porto Alegre, Brazil), 20 (1), 1998.

In addition, "Some Mysteries of Gender," to which I have also retained the copyright, has been published in *Revista de Psicanálise da SPPA* (the Journal of the Psychoanalytical Society of Porto Alegre, Brazil), 5 (2): 173–193, 1998.

Introduction

MY INTEREST in sex and gender and in the symbolic meanings that attach to them began early in my professional life. One of my first analytic patients entered treatment because he was fearful that he would be unable to impregnate his wife. In the third week of the analysis he told me a dream in which his wife was pregnant. In his associations to the dream he revealed that she *was* pregnant, and that in fact he had already known this when he first came to see me! I reacted calmly, although I was worried, since it seemed to me almost delusional to enter treatment for a fictitious reason. But it soon became apparent that his "imaginary" reason for entering treatment was closely related to the real reason: his wife's conviction that he had major potency problems. This, too, turned out to be a fiction, but hers rather than his. I asked him what his potency problem was, and he answered that it was his inability to bring his wife to orgasm. As I inquired more about the nature of the sexual problem, it turned out that he could easily achieve and maintain an erection and perform intercourse for up to an hour! (This was at a time when the standard for male potency was the ability to maintain an erection for four strokes.) But this was not adequate for *her*.

The technical aspects of the sexual problem were easily addressed, to the satisfaction of both. But their shared fantasy preoccupation about his impotence led to the major issue in the analysis: his feelings of powerlessness. He was fortunate, and so was I, that his analysis proved to be successful in working through his sense of inadequacy in both the personal and professional arenas. This experience keyed me very early to the symbolic meaning of sex acts and the way we often understand the same word quite differently, perhaps particularly so in the sexual realm. For example, President Clinton does not define the recipient of fellatio as having engaged in sexual relations, whereas the Independent Counsel Kenneth Starr includes such "passive" participation in his definition of sexual relations.

This book is a selection of my papers on sex and gender, some co-authored, written over the past twenty-five years. The idea of collecting the papers in a single volume first occurred to me in the fall of 1997, on the occasion of my being invited by the Sociedade de Psiquiatria (SPRS) to give the keynote address at a conference on "Sexuality and Psychiatry" in Gramado, Brazil.[1] Writing that address, "The Sexual Century," I thought back on how radical the change in sexual mores had been over the past century and how this was reflected in psychoanalysis. I decided that it would be interesting to publish a number of my papers on sex and gender together since they too are on that trajectory of change. My own thinking over this past quarter century has deepened not only with the passage of time, new experiences, and new observations but in response to shifts within psychoanalysis and sexology and also in response to our culture's revamped notions of sex and gender.

Rather than arrange the papers in chronological order, I have ordered them according to topic. I have not included all my papers on the cross-gender disorders insofar as some of them, appearing in different venues, overlap too much. The papers chosen for publication are those that deal most directly with sex and gender. I have omitted papers that touch on sex or gender but are more about love than about sex, more about treatment issues than about gender, or more about specific issues such as work inhibitions or the conflicts between work and mothering than about broad considerations of gender.

Part I, "Sex and Gender: General Considerations," presents a general background and theoretical frame in which to conceptualize sex and gender. It opens with "The Sexual Century" (1998) an overview of how this century is distinguished not only by sexual-liberation movements but also by important technological and medical advances that have permitted greater sexual freedom without the fear of disease and pregnancy that plagued earlier generations, at least until the advent of the recent epidemics of genital herpes and AIDS. The past hundred years have constituted a major revolution not only in sexual practices but also in our knowledge about sex and gender and in our values as well. The chapter details the origins of sexology in the late nineteenth century in Germany and the explosion of the field in the United States in the twentieth century. It discusses the essential contributions of our leading sexologists. A major innovation that has revolutionized the way we think is the conceptualization of gender as separate from sexuality. Credit for this goes to the researcher John Money, who borrowed the term "gender" from its provenance in linguistics and introduced it into the medical and psychological literature. This is also the century of Freud, who taught us that sex has as much to do with the mind as with the genitals.

"Sexuality as the Mainstay of Identity: Psychoanalytic Perspectives" (1980) explores alternate paradigms within psychoanalysis about the nature of sexual motivation. It shows why sex has a privileged place in psychic development, even if we no longer view libido as a fixed sex drive. It criticizes the bias by which female sexuality is understood only in comparison to male sexuality, not

1. Afterward I was privileged to be a guest of the Sociedade Psicanalitica de Porto Alegre.

in its own right. "Psychoanalytic Theories of Gender Identity" (1983) reviews and critiques traditional theories of gender, including those of Sigmund Freud, Karen Horney, Ernest Jones, and those of more recent contributors, particularly Robert Stoller. It theorizes the independence-interdependence of gender identity and sexual identity. It asserts that femininity and masculinity are parallel constructs, that masculinity is not the natural state, as Freud argued, nor is femininity, as Stoller suggested. It proposes, rather, that gender role identity grows out of core gender identity and is decisively influenced by differences in object relations between the two sexes and in conformity to social norms. "The Influence of Values in Psychoanalysis: The Case of Female Psychology" (1983) touches on the biological and evolutionary biases in Freud's sexual theories and addresses the inevitable bias inherent in all studies of sex and gender, alerting us to the necessity of closely examining our own theories to look for our hidden assumptions and lines of reasoning. It details how theoretical biases against women corrupted the possibility of successful psychotherapy for many women.

Part II, "Cross-Gender Disorders," presents my clinical research papers and theoretical papers on transsexuals, transvestites, and homosexual cross-dressers, written in collaboration with Lionel Ovesey between 1973 and 1984. We were extremely fortunate in that we initiated our research project at a time when there was a burst of interest in sex and gender, generated not only by gay liberation and the women's movement but also by John Money's brilliant introduction of the distinction between sex and gender. This section also includes a paper on extreme boyhood femininity that I co-authored with Susan Coates in 1985.

The results of my work with Lionel Ovesey were both practical and theoretical. We developed a classification of transsexualism into primary and secondary transsexualism, which encompassed homosexual and transvestitic transsexualism. We were gratified that our classification was adopted in DSM-III. Using this classification, we were able to devise treatment recommendations based in part on the transsexual's history, that is—whether he was someone who had ever enjoyed his penis in either homosexual or heterosexual sex. One has to be much more cautious about recommending sex reassignment with secondary transsexuals—that is, men who had once functioned as homosexuals or transvestites and become transsexuals under stress. Beginning with our earliest paper in 1973 and explicit in our paper "Homosexual Cross-Dressers" (1984) is the now-current idea that homosexuality is not a single entity but is best referred to as the "homosexualities."

From the theoretical side, we argued that transsexualism ought to be conceptualized as a gender disorder rather than as a sexual disorder. We demonstrated the role of separation anxiety generated during the separation-individuation phase of infantile development as a primary factor in the etiology of transsexualism. This was an almost universal finding in our subjects; even so, we concluded that separation anxiety was a necessary but not sufficient condition in the etiology of transsexualism. We emphasized how the transsexual's willingness to part with his penis goes a long way toward demolishing the idea that castration anxiety is the central dynamic in cross-gender disorders. The need for a sense of safety and survival takes precedence over preservation of the penis.

We took our study into the field. We demonstrated how an understanding of some aspects of the internal life of transsexuals and particularly transvestites and cross-dressing homosexuals could best be grasped by reading the relevant pornography and by observing behavior and interactions at group meetings, parties, and drag balls, in a natural setting rather than hearing about them second-hand in an interview setting. In the field, one can see the enactment of fantasies of which the research subject may be unaware. In our paper "Transvestism: A Disorder of the Sense of Self" (1976) we were able to describe in great detail how initiation fantasies (the fantasy of initiation into cross-dressing by a woman, so frequently depicted in the transvestitic literature) were symbolically enacted at parties. Our field work provided information about the importance of shared fantasies in establishing emotional bonds between transvestites and made visible some of the derivatives of preconscious and unconscious wishes that are otherwise hard to elicit. We showed how exposure to a sexual network and first-hand knowledge of other transvestites' enactments (whether of dressing or of body modifications) sometimes tips the balance to enactment, but alternatively may provide sufficient vicarious gratification so that the pressure for enactment is diminished. This early work in the field of cross-gender disorders demonstrates how fantasy sometimes acts as substitute gratification, sometimes as the prelude to enactment; it is organically connected to my current thinking on the role of conscious fantasy in everyday life (Person, 1995). (Once, in the 1970s, when Lionel and I presented this work, we were criticized by a very eminent psychoanalyst as sullying our psychoanalytic work with anthropology. But we were pleased to be linked with anthropology. We recognized early on that field work, questionnaire studies, and all kinds of explorations were necessary to develop an in-depth understanding of sex and gender.)

We found that the overall imaginative life was somewhat constricted in transsexuals and in many transvestites as well. What this means is that the fantasy/wish decision to become a woman becomes so urgent that other imaginative material is essentially crowded out. Why this is often so and why it is less frequent in homosexual cross-dressers is elaborated in our paper "Homosexual Cross-Dressers" (1984). This imaginative limitation, of course, is one reason that psychoanalytically oriented psychotherapy is very difficult with some patients who suffer cross-gender disorders.

Emphasis on separation anxiety in the genesis of the cross-dressing disorders was validated to a large degree by Susan Coates in her work with feminine little boys. The paper we co-authored, "Extreme Boyhood Femininity: Isolated Behavior or Pervasive Disorder?" (1985), shows that separation anxiety plays a role in the genesis of femininity in the majority of these children but is not the single factor. Coates and I also noted the difficulty in translating from a population of effeminate boys to an adult population, insofar as the future sexual and gender patterns of effeminate boys cannot be definitively predicted. Some will turn out to be homosexual, others (relatively few) may become transvestites or transsexuals, and some will become heterosexual.

Part III, "Sex and Fantasy," is devoted to a discussion of sexual desire, fantasy, and enactment. In "From Erotic Desire to Sexual Excitement: The Role of Sexual Fantasy" (1998), I review the relatively scant psychoanalytic literature on sexual excitement and discuss how sexual desire can be conceptualized. Very important to the issue of sexual desire is what triggers it, and how desire is mediated by fantasy. In order to understand desire—or its lack—one must explore the question of how sex recruits nonsexual themes to sexual fantasies and the issue of sexual boredom. "Gender Differences in Sexual Behaviors and Fantasies in a College Population" (1989) was written in collaboration with my co-investigators in the Fantasy Project at the Columbia University Psychoanalytic Center. It analyzes data gathered in a questionnaire study of university students in 1982–1983. Our findings did not altogether tally with popular beliefs about sex differences. For example, our study offered little support to the contention that women are masochistic. In fact, both sexes reported the same level of masochistic fantasies. The study did reveal fantasies of domination and sadism in a significant minority of men. These and other findings are reported in detail in the paper.

The second paper from the Fantasy Project, "Associations Between Sexual Experiences and Fantasies in a Nonpatient Population: A Preliminary Study" (1992), was designed to answer a specific question that would be hard to research in any but the sexual sphere. That question is what the relationship is between conscious fantasy and behavior—that is, are fantasies used as a substitute gratification or do they act as a prelude to behavior? Or both? (The reason the sexual sphere offers the best research opportunity is that we can assume the near-universality of sexual fantasies and behaviors, an assumption not warranted in most other realms of activity.) Our major finding was that erotic fantasies cannot be viewed as compensation for lack of sexual experience. We concluded that "the earliest psychoanalytic model of wish fulfillment providing gratification for the individual suffering from a state of deprivation does not appear to be applicable when one is dealing with the sexuality of young adult subjects. One interpretation of the data is that sexually uninhibited individuals engage in more activities and produce a greater range of fantasies, whereas sexually inhibited individuals suppress both behavior and fantasy. Another possible interpretation is that reality experiences may serve as a stimulant (or source) of the material for fantasy." These findings led me, in later work, to explore how fantasy was so often predictive of behavior (See *By Force of Fantasy: How We Live Our Lives.*)

Part IV, "Sex and Gender: Female Sexuality and Feminity and Male Sexuality and Masculinity," addresses differences in the developmental experiences and cultural expectations of men and women that predispose them to different gender and sexual patterns. "The Erotic Transference in Women and in Men: Differences and Consequences" (1985) describes some important differences in the sexual and erotic feelings men and women develop toward their therapists, and therefore provides an introduction to sexual and gender differences in men and women. "Female Sexual Identity: The Impact of the Adolescent Experience" (1985) makes the important distinction that in sex one is both the desiring subject and someone else's desired object. This duality makes the definition of sexual identity necessarily complicated and elusive. I suggest that the male more often overidentifies as subject, the female as object, and that this choice may lead to a marred sexual identity for both. In the case of the female it may predispose to value being chosen over the enjoyment of sex per se. Coupled with the predominant mode of female induction into masturbation (as compared with boys), the result may be a relative female hyposexuality. This paper also touches on some issues of power in sexual interactions with men. "Some Mysteries of Gender: Rethinking Masculine Identifications in Heterosexual Women" (1998) addresses the important issue of cross-gender identifications in heterosexual women, including an analysis of the source of these masculine identifications and the various reasons that heterosexuality is not impacted. Despite the overabundance of papers on penis envy, the issue of cross-gender identifications in heterosexual women has not been much discussed in the literature. This paper distinguishes between the way culture may suppress paternal (nonconflictual) identifications and the way some cross-gender identifications are by their nature conflictual. It expresses what I believe are the limits to the "fluidity" of desires and identities so frequently touted as the ideal in postmodernist theory.

"Male Sexuality and Power" (1986) looks at the basic fault lines in the development of male sexuality. It explores the popular belief that male sexuality is innately aggressive and sadistic. It gives case examples in which issues of power and control enter into sex and love relationships. It suggests that there are specific problems inherent in male development that predispose men to sexual anxieties, later counteracted by fantasies (and their behavioral enactments) of power and control over the female sex object. "The Omni-Available Woman and Lesbian Sex: Two Fantasy Themes and Their Relationship to the Male Developmental Experience" (1986) uses two common fantasy preoccupations of men to explore further the nature of male sexuality. Fantasies of the omni-available woman reveal not only the pressing desire for female availability but the simultaneous desire to erase any one woman's individuality or importance. Fantasies of lesbian sex are related to the sometimes transient episode of transvestitic impulses in adolescence, which are parallel with the transient homosexual impulses so commonly seen then. Explorations of both the omni-available woman fantasy and the lesbian sex fantasy emphasize the male sense of inadequacy in relation to the mother and fear of her, this in addition to the castration anxiety vis-à-vis the father that has been more commonly posited as the decisive factor in male sexuality. A kind of shared phallic narcissism, embodied by the male cultural ego ideal of macho sexuality, is invoked to obscure the underlying anxieties many men experience.

Part V, "The Impact of Culture," addresses the way a particular historical mind-set and set of circumstances impact on the way we understand sex and gender. "Harry Benjamin and the Birth of a Shared Cultural Fantasy" (1972/1997) is a paper I wrote concurrent with my friendship with him, which he asked that I publish after his death. I have updated the paper to show how his "discovery" of transsexualism launched a major shared fantasy. Beginning as a longevity doctor, one who worked to help his patients avoid some of the indignities of aging, he became a doctor who helped his patients jump over the apparent irreversibility of their sex. This he was able to do because of his intellectual antecedents in the context of the cultural assumptions of the 1960s and 1970s.

The chapters in this volume touch on themes that have been central to my thinking. They raise the question of how we know what we know, and the impossibility of escaping bias. They emphasize the necessity of viewing the development of sex and gender in men and women as parallel phenomena; neither sex is ultimately privileged. The theme of fantasy runs throughout my work; it is the thread that connects my interest in the cross-gender disorders with my interest in how fantasy is embedded in sexual desire and romantic yearning (Person, 1988). The way power finds expression in sex and love is also a theme found in much of my work. I have become increasingly uncertain of first causes and of the precursors that determine sexual choice or gender attributes. I suspect they may *never* be fully explicated. I am certain that most homosexuals do not suffer any sexual disorder (or no more so than heterosexuals). But I believe that the cross-gender disorders *are* disorders; that is, they are correlated with personal distress and conflict that are not all the result of social stigmatization. In other words, not all unusual sexual or gender characteristics are merely variations. Thus, while I am touched by all the various liberation movements, I don't agree with the premise that the problem is always with the culture's strictures. Consider, for example, pedophilia. Nor do I believe in the postmodernist value of fluidity as a goal to be pursued in and of itself. Although there are genuine bisexuals among us, this need not become the standard to which we should all aspire. Overall, I consider gender role more potentially fluid than either sexual preferences or core gender identity.

Finally, what unites many of my papers is the idea that no aspect of human development can be understood exclusively in terms of intrapsychic development. Studying sex and gender in the twentieth century makes it abundantly clear that the way sex and gender develop and are experienced and expressed are the result not only of nature and nurture (which refer to biology and early life experiences) but also of the impact of the larger culture, its unspoken values and biases, and its pressures to conformity.

PART I

Sex and Gender: General Considerations

1

The Sexual Century

1998

ETHEL S. PERSON

WHILE VICTORIANS "dressed" their piano legs so as not to offend anyone's sense of propriety, today it is considered acceptable to expose legs, breasts, and buttocks on beaches, in discos, and in centerfolds. This is but one small example of the startling changes that have transpired over the past hundred years in sexual modesty and in the public expression of sexuality if not in sexual practices. It's safe to assume that few sexual acts have been discovered for the first time in the twentieth century, though the number of practitioners of different kinds of sexual acts has undoubtedly increased. What has changed most is how we think about sex. In the nineteenth century, Princess Diana would have been shunned for having had an extramarital affair, divorcing her husband, and then becoming involved in another much-publicized sexual relationship. Now, those very same acts in conjunction with her glamour and her good works have made her sympathetic and even heroic to millions, indeed hundreds of millions, of people, with the result that there was a massive outpouring of grief and love in response to her death in a car crash in August 1997.

Over the course of the twentieth century, sexual liberation has limped and lurched, but in a direction that has transformed the way most of us regard our bodies and live our sexual lives. Wide era-to-era swings between sexual suppression and sexual exuberance have been noted by historians of sex. However, the current changes go beyond the ideology of sexual liberation to include altered ideas about masculinity and femininity, heterosexuality and homosexuality. These changes in attitudes and behavior are of such magnitude, and appear to be so irreversible, so destined to leave their mark on all subsequent eras, that we are justified in calling this the "sexual century."[1]

Sexual liberation is the product of the ideology of self-fulfillment coupled with medical advances that have made sex safer, less likely to have unwanted consequences. These medical breakthroughs include the discovery of sulfanilamides in 1921 and of penicillin in 1929, both of which were effective in counteracting venereal diseases (though penicillin was first produced in large amounts only beginning in World War II), and approval by the Food and Drug Administration (FDA) of the birth control pill Enovid in 1960. Although the ideology of sexual liberation had its antecedents earlier in the century—in the first wave of feminism, the free love movement, and the flapper era—it came into full flower through the rhetoric of sexual liberation and gay liberation in the 1960s, the new women's movement of the 1970s, and more recently through the sadomasochist liberation movement, which though relatively small has nonetheless become the inspiration for the widespread practices of tattooing and piercing. The women's movement mandated a re-evaluation of gender roles—that is, femininity and masculinity. Gender-bending, the adoption of cross-gender traits or even the assumption of total cross-gender identities, has entered the mainstream. Nowadays transvestites and transsexuals are often celebrated as icons of liberation despite the fact that so many of them experience extreme psychic discomfort.

Some contemporary observers see the sexual revolution as having foundered by the mid-1980s, felled by genital herpes and the AIDS virus. It is true that some of the more visible excesses of the 1960s and 1970s—wife swapping, orgies, rampant promiscuity—have contracted, under pressure not just from health threats but from the anti-pornography forces (among them adherents of the religious right and feminists as well), critics of the negative impact on children of divorce (because sexual liberation is often blamed for the rising divorce rate), and the current recognition of and opposition to spousal abuse and child abuse (which includes sexual abuse) (Heidenry, 1997, pp. 296–299, 309–317). Nonetheless there persists a trend to sexual openness dramatically different from the Victorian ethos.

What really marks this as the sexual century is more than the liberalization of sexual practices; it is the changes in the way we think about sex. Describing the twentieth-century reaction against Victorianism as "sexual modernism," intellectual historian Paul Robinson (1976) demonstrated how major

1. Robert Christgau named the twentieth century the sexual century in a review of the book *What Wild Ecstasy* by John Heidenry. Christgau says "Some thirty years into the so-called sexual revolution, near the end of what might well be designated the sexual century, veterans of its intricate physical skirmishes and pitched rhetorical battles are left with one question: Just how important is sex, anyway?" See "The Pleasure Seekers: A Survey of the Issues and Players in the World of Modern Sex" in *The New York Times Book Review,* April 27, 1997, p. 26.

modernist sex reformers, researchers, and theorists effected this sea change in contemporary attitudes. Unlike Victorian sexologists who were proponents of sexual repression, the current practitioners are "sexual enthusiasts" (Robinson's term, p. 3). They have espoused tolerance for pluralism in sexual practices, legitimization of some common behaviors previously considered deviant (particularly homosexual sex and masturbation), and recognition of the sexual desires and capacities of women. In doing so, they have challenged the idea that the aim of sex is primarily procreation. Modern theorists point out that most acts of heterosexual intercourse do not lead to reproduction, nor is reproduction the only primary function of sex. To Robinson, removing sexuality from the institutional context of marriage and reproduction is the very core of modernism in sex. Once sex was delinked from procreation, the whole range of sexual acts could be looked at from a different perspective.

What Freud added to the ongoing reappraisal of sex was the insight that what people did was not identical with their unconscious motives and fantasies. In studying fantasy, Freud discovered the diversity of desires that fuel our behaviors. This means that the behavioral observations on which the studies of the sexologists were based were not sufficient to fully explain the layering of motives that impels specific sexual behaviors.

Freud also posited a sexual force, libido, and elevated it to the central position in human development. *Libido* is usually considered synonymous with sexual energy or instinct.[2] In Freud's scheme, it is generated within the body and propels itself toward discharge. As such, it acts as a stimulus on consciousness, where it is transformed into a wish. Fulfillment of the wish leads to the reduction of tensions and thereby to pleasure. Freud's notion of instinct suggests both a tension to be discharged and the mode by which the discharge takes place. In this sense, Freud's description of libido belongs to what has been called an "essentialist" point of view.

Taking the essentialist position quite literally, the Freudian Marxists Norman Brown, 1959, and Herbert Marcuse, 1955, among others, promulgated the idea that sexual liberation, which they equated with lifting the repression barrier and freeing all our sexual impulses including polymorphous perverse elements, would express our truest nature. In their view, sexuality was too often repressed by an onerous culture, but its expression was essential to fully lived lives. Contrary to Freud's belief that the conflict between sex and culture is inevitable, the liberationists contend that education can undo the pernicious effects of repression, which is mainly the result of learned prejudices. However, the connections between sex and culture have proved more complex than

2. Freud suggested that it is "that force by which the sexual instinct is represented in the mind" (Freud, quoted by Jones, 1955, Vol. 2, p. 282).

Freud's first formulations, and surely more complex than their bastardization in popular culture.

In contrast to Freud's essentialist assumptions, sociologists and theorists from women's studies and queer theory have articulated what I will call the constructionist view of sex and gender (see Weeks, 1984, pp. 28–30). They propose that sexuality and gender are not the products of nature alone but are molded by historical and social forces. The explicit idea that part of the sex/gender package is socially programmed goes back to the 1950s, for example, in John Money's contention that gender develops in accord with the sex to which the newborn is assigned rather than with any biological propensity.[3] It was also expressed in the early work of sociologists John Gagnon and William Simon on sexual scripting (1973). However, it is Michel Foucault's groundbreaking work on the history of sex that is generally credited with the major turn to constructionism in modern sexual theory (see Foucault, 1979). More recently, queer theory and women's studies have addressed questions about sexual politics, about the relationship of patriarchal values to power issues in male-female sexual relationships, and about the complex relationships among sexual preference, self-identity, and choice (Weeks, 1984).

Although sexuality is a biological force, grounded in the anatomy, physiology, and hormonal secretions of the human body, nonetheless, each individual's sexual practices and attitudes are shaped and colored by cultural attitudes and directives. These are themselves powerfully affected not only by medical advances but by the studies of the sexologists and sexual theorists. This century's sexologists and theorists have revolutionized the way we conceptualize sex and gender and also how we regard what we do.

In turn, our theorists of sexuality are themselves impacted on by the changing *zeitgeist*. What appears at first glance to be neutral science is shaped by cultural values, almost to the same degree as was true of nineteenth-century sexologists but to diametrically opposite effect. Twentieth-century sex researchers, reformers, and liberationists, like the rest of us, are necessarily influenced by the cultural biases and prejudices that prevail about sex, the high valuation this century and this culture have accorded individual freedom, and their personal sexual predilections as well.

In what follows, I will give a brief overview of how sexual attitudes, medical breakthroughs, and the work of the sexologists, psychoanalysts, and sociologists in conjunction with theories generated in the context of sexual minorities have interacted to change both what we do sexually and how we think about it.

3. Even earlier, sexologists and sociologists had pointed out that part of the sex/gender package was socially programmed. This idea is already implicit and explicit in the work of Havelock Ellis.

Sexologists and Sex Reformers

The move to sexual modernism can be traced to the very beginnings of the scientific study of sex in the 1870s, although at first liberalization was mixed in with more traditional values (Sulloway, 1979, chap. 8). In those early days, little attention was paid to "normal" sex, with the exception of the biology of reproduction. Deviance, rather than normality, was the focus.

Most of the early work emerged in the German-speaking world. One of the first phenomena on which the sexologists trained their eyes, bringing to it what they believed to be a medical rather than a moral perspective, was homosexuality (Sulloway, Chap. 8). Earlier in the nineteenth century, sexual deviance had been classified with crime (and even poverty) as a sign of a hereditary, degenerative failure. Carl Heinrich Ulrichs (1862–1895), a homosexual lawyer, propounded a new theory that the homosexual was not criminal or insane but "a female soul in a male body," the result of an error in embryonic differentiation (Sulloway, p. 281). (This was a crossover idea from the then revolutionary studies taking place in embryology, and it stands as a good example of how a scientific breakthrough in one field can inspire new ideas in an apparently unrelated field.)

Richard Krafft-Ebing (1840–1902), professor of psychiatry at the University of Vienna, "the true founder of modern sexual pathology" according to the sexologist Iwan Bloch (quoted in Sulloway, p. 279) was influenced by Ulrichs. Krafft-Ebing came to believe that homosexuals had failed to move beyond the stage of fetal bisexuality because of genetic flaws. Although this idea was not original with him, he was influential in changing the approach to homosexuality from moral and legal condemnation to medical concern. (It is perhaps ironic that the medical model of homosexuality, which posited homosexuality as a disease in order to protect homosexuals, has come to be resented just as much as the legal one it replaced, which saw it as a crime.) Unlike Ulrichs's position, Krafft-Ebing's sympathetic stance was shaped not by any personal identification as a sexual "deviant" but by the example and mentoring of his maternal grandfather, a criminal lawyer, known as "the last hope of the damned," who defended homosexuals in the mid-nineteenth century (Sulloway, p. 280).

During the same period in which homosexuality began to be regarded in a more tolerant light, thanks to the new theories of the sexologists, masturbation continued to be maligned. In the scientific community, it was widely believed to result in depletion and insanity—lifelong degenerative effects that were clinically documented to the satisfaction of most of the medical profession. In essence, masturbation was pathologized (Marcus, 1964).

By the turn of the century, the narrow interest in deviance and reproductive physiology had gradually given way to a broad interest in "normal" sexuality. Originating in part from the burgeoning psychiatric concern with concepts of normality, the study of normal sexuality nonetheless had deeper roots in the contemporary fascination with deviance. The study of such perversions as sexual sadism and sexual masochism made it clear that the domain of sexuality extended beyond the genitals. This insight enlarged the scientific imagination, forcing scientists to distinguish between sexuality and procreation, and the idea of erotogenic zones other than the genitals entered the literature.

It was in the context of these expanding views of sexuality that Sigmund Freud (1856–1939) proposed the first psychological view of sexuality, a theory that describes sex at the interface between the body and the mind, establishes the sexual instinct as composite in nature, demonstrates childhood sexuality, and delineates the fantasy life linked to sexual desire. Freud's psychological view became immensely influential during World War II, particularly in the United States, in part because of the mass influx of analysts as a result of Hitler's rise to power (Bullough, 1994, pp. 91, 148).

Sex historian Vern Bullough argues that "a major result of [the] rising influence of Freudian ideas . . . was to make Americans more conscious and less reticent about sexuality, since simply to read Freud was to become aware of sexuality" (p. 149). Perhaps it is no accident, then, that the leading sex researchers and reformers of the twentieth century have been mostly American. Even if they were never accorded quite the same intellectual status as Freud, from a practical point of view, they were extremely influential in changing the way we regard sex and the way we engage in it.

While observers might include different names on their lists of the most influential sexologists of the twentieth century, most such lists would include Havelock Ellis, Alfred Kinsey, William Masters and Virginia Johnson, and John Money. I would add to that list Harry Benjamin (see Chapter 20). And any list of important reformers would have to include Margaret Sanger, as well as several scientists in the field of reproductive biology without whose work Sanger's mission would never have been fulfilled.

Among the sexologists, the Englishman Henry Havelock Ellis (1859–1939) has been described as the first of the yea-sayers, a major endorser of all kinds of sexual practices (Brecher, 1969, p. 3). According to Ellis's autobiography (1939), he decided early in life to devote himself to the scientific study of sex in order to "spare the youth in future generations the trouble and perplexity which this ignorance had caused me" (p. ix). Ellis was referring to his preoccupation with and fear about nocturnal emissions. Keeping to his youthful vow, he embraced a medical education, familiarizing himself with a voluminous literature on sex in many languages. Over the course of thirteen years

(1897–1910), he published his *Studies in the Psychology of Sex,* which originally encompassed six volumes. Well aware of the significance of his work, he wrote in his autobiography that on completion of the project, he felt as Gibbon must have felt when he completed his monumental *History*. "The work that I was born to do is done," he recorded in his diary (1939, p. 432).

Although much of that work is a compilation of others' insights and views, it has nonetheless been central to the field of sexology. Robinson, for example, considers Ellis the most important figure in the emergence of the modern sexual ethos and believes that his work "established the basic moral categories for nearly all subsequent sexual theorizing," (Robinson, p. 3). Ellis gathered information from diverse sources to arrive at some very modernist assumptions. Drawing on a large database, he insisted that homosexuality was congenital and therefore must be distinguished from neuropathic degeneration. If homosexuality was the *only* mark of degeneration, he argued, it would be circular to attribute its cause to degeneration. Ellis also tried to rescue masturbation from being labeled a vice, although he did have one reservation: he feared it might have the potential for separating sexuality from love. In attempting to legitimize more diverse expressions of sexuality, Ellis invoked anthropology and cultural history to demonstrate how different cultural attitudes toward sex affect sexual practices.

Alfred Kinsey (1894–1956), biologist and student of gall wasps turned sexologist, initiated a large interview study in 1938 that documented "who does what, when and with whom" (Brecher, 1969, p. 104). Kinsey and his associates published the first phase of their results in *Sexual Behavior in the Human Male* (1948). The product of a decade's work, it was groundbreaking in its large scale statistical studies and revolutionary in that it viewed any single sexual "outlet" as equivalent in "value" to any other. It thus implicitly blurred the distinction between homosexual and heterosexual. More important, it undermined this distinction by explicitly stating that the source of sexual stimulation, in this case homosexual behavior, should not be taken as descriptive of the individuals themselves. Although previous studies had revealed that approximately 4 percent of the male population was exclusively homosexual, Kinsey reported that 37 percent of adult males had had at least one homosexual experience to orgasm in adolescence or thereafter and that fully 50 percent had responded to homoerotic stimuli. The discovery that the practice of homosexual behavior was so widespread both shocked the public and made it impossible to view homosexual acts as restricted to a tiny deviant minority. The famous Kinsey Scale, which rates all individuals on a seven-point homosexual-heterosexual progression, from zero (completely heterosexual) to six (completely homosexual), further "normalized" homosexuality by putting it on a continuum with accepted sexual behavior. For homosexuals, Kinsey's work provided validation that, among other influences, would help pave the way for gay liberation some years later.

Other Kinsey Report statistics that shocked the public stated that 30 to 45 percent of the men in his sample had had extramarital sex and that 70 percent had patronized prostitutes. There is no doubt that his statistics demonstrating the extremely widespread practice of masturbation helped destigmatize it. Kinsey and his co-workers published a comparable study of women five years later (Kinsey et al., 1953).

William H. Masters (b. 1915) and Virginia E. Johnson (b. 1925) studied the human sexual-response cycle in the laboratory and later introduced sex therapy as a new discipline. Their study of sexual physiology lasted from 1954 to 1966, in the course of which they observed more than ten thousand orgasms in men and women under laboratory conditions. These orgasms were achieved with manual or mechanical masturbation, "artificial coition" with a transparent probe, sexual intercourse with the woman on the top or on the bottom, and stimulation of the breasts alone without genital contact. They described four successive levels or phases of arousal: excitement, plateau, orgasm, and resolution (Masters and Johnson, 1966).

The writer John Heidenry suggests that the videotape Masters and Johnson made of a female orgasm in 1958 changed forever the way we understand female sexuality (1997, pp. 17–19). That film showed that clitoral self-stimulation caused the woman to have an orgasm that resulted in contractions within her vagina, a sequencing replicated many times in different women. The public dissemination of this information was later incorporated into the rhetoric of the women's movement and paved the way for a major shift in female sexual behavior. (What made women open to this information was the legalization of the birth control pill in 1960, in roughly the same time frame as Masters and Johnson's findings.) Many women were able to undo the mental set through which they had suppressed or rejected their own sexuality, so that they could expect to enjoy as much sexual pleasure as men, understand the role of clitoral stimulation in arousal and orgasm, value orgasms, and insist on adequate stimulation by their partners.

Because he was a clinician, Masters knew that many people suffered from a variety of sexual inadequacies and problems. Beginning in 1959, when they initiated a therapy program to help couples suffering from sexual problems, Masters and Johnson soon discovered that premature ejaculation, impotence, and frigidity were much more commonly the result of psychological than of physiological factors. Consequently, they expanded their interest from the physiology to the psychology of sexual inadequacy and designed a sex-therapy program—the very first—to counter psychological problems. As a result, many people learned rather simple techniques and strategies that helped them overcome a range of garden variety sexual problems (Masters and Johnson, 1970). The implications of Masters and Johnson's work were largely profemininist, with a bias toward achieving adequate sexual functioning in heterosexual couples. Later on they undertook to study homosexuals as well, but their work focuses less on homosexuality than does that of the other major sexologists of this century.

In 1955, the sex researcher John Money (b. 1921) and his associates, through their pioneering studies of intersexed patients,[4] made an extremely important distinction between biological sex and gender (Money et al., 1955a,b; Money, 1973). They demonstrated that the first and crucial step in gender differentiation was self-designation by the child as female or male, in accordance with the sex of assignment.[5] They also established that gender differentiation, usually irreversible by eighteen months, was complete by about four and a half years. In order to distinguish sex roles (masculinity and femininity) from erotic activities, Money originated the term "gender role." Later he distinguished "gender identity" from "gender role." Unlike Freud, who saw the motor of sexual differentiation as the child's recognition of the anatomical sex difference, Money saw the sex of assignment and subsequent social compliance as the driving force in the acquisition of gender. (And here is one major precursor of the current emphasis on constructionism.)

Money, more than other sexologists, emphasized the important role of fantasy in sex. For him the diagnosis of homosexuality depended on the sex of the person one was able to fall in love with. Sexuality has its own diverse elements: sexual object choice, sexual fantasy, eroticization, desire, and conscious sexual identity. Money was astute enough to raise the question not only of what one did but of whom one thought about while one was doing it.

Harry Benjamin (1885–1978), one of the famous longevity doctors who administered hormones to preserve sexual activity and youthfulness, became known as the father of transsexualism. In contrast to Money, who showed how rearing impacted on gender, Benjamin identified a group of people who, despite their normal biology and what he judged to be the normal circumstances of their early lives, grew up desiring to be members of the opposite sex. He conferred on this group a new diagnosis, transsexualism, and opened up a major debate about its etiology. Benjamin, a German expatriate living in the United States, revived the biological explanation of Ulrichs that a female soul

4. In intersexed patients, the different components of biological sex do not match. So, for example, an infant who is genetically male may have such a severe hypospadia (the urethral opening displaced to the base of the penile shaft) as to make the infant appear female. There are also a number of patients in whom there are variations in the chromosome patterns; they are not XX or XY.

5. For an update on this concept, see Person, "Some Mysteries of Gender: Masculine Identifications in Heterosexual Women," this volume.

might be trapped in a male body, or vice versa. No stranger to hormone therapy, he initiated hormonal treatment to bring the body into more accord with the psyche. Through his identification of a new group of patients, Benjamin indirectly paved the way for the later psychoanalytic interest in the origins of cross-gender identifications (particularly in the work of Stoller [1968a, 1975b] and of Person and Ovesey [1974a,b,c, 1978, 1984]).

A close look at the lives of our leading sexologists shows that they have been either explicitly or secretly liberationist and that a few of them possess a natural sympathy for those who were "deviant" or aberrant by virtue of their own sexual predispositions. Havelock Ellis had a fascination with watching women urinate.[6] Kinsey, too, appears to have been motivated not only by the imperatives of science but by a belief in the liberalization of sex. That Kinsey, despite his conventional Midwestern appearance and commitment to his marriage (apparently a happy one) and his four children, was bisexual, and, at least in later years, masochistic is only now finding its way into print.[7] Like many other prominent sexologists, he had an immense collection of erotica. Late in his career, he began filming sexual encounters of his own staff (Jones, 1997, pp. 99–113). I discuss Harry Benjamin's personal predilection to tolerance in Chapter 20. At the same time that I have suggested that some psychological predilection makes some of us more liberationist than others, let me quickly add that extreme sexual conservatives have as many psychological predilections to account for their views as do the liberationists. While no branch of science can ultimately be value-free, this may be particularly true of the field of sexology for self-evident reasons; we all have one or another kind of bias whatever our sexual predilections and preferences.

Ellis and Benjamin explicitly and Kinsey implicitly had a dual mission—not only to explore the field scientifically but to liberalize it so that other people might not suffer from either internal distress or public stigmatization. In this they were successful, as a series of legal decisions and administrative judgments show. In 1957, the Supreme Court of the United States narrowed the legal definition of obscenity, expanding the umbrella of constitutional protection to cover a broader range of works portraying sex in the arts. In 1961, Illinois was the first state to repeal its sodomy statutes. And in 1973, the

6. Robinson (1976, p. 38) quotes Arthur Calder-Marshall to the effect that Ellis "was impotent most of his life and a urolagnist as well." Ellis himself revealed his fascination with urination in his autobiography. His own explanation was that his urolagnia resulted from seeing his nurse urinate in a public park: he "heard a mysterious sound as of a stream of water descending to the earth" (Ellis, 1939).

7. Kinsey's masochistic practice was to insert into his urethra a small rod or wire and simultaneously twist a cord around his testicles (Jones, 1997, pp. 99–113). My guess is that he may have been enacting a feminine identification, in which the urethral opening was a vagina, and the testicles symbolically castrated. The evidence for his masochism is clear cut.

American Psychiatric Association, on the basis of a membership vote, removed homosexuality from the category of psychopathology.

Although the work of all the sexologists I have discussed has been the target of some criticisms and revisions, their major findings have stood the test of time. Taken together, their pioneer studies in sexology have provided (1) a delineation of the frequent variations in sexual behavior, particularly establishing how widespread homosexual practices are; (2) studies of masturbation establishing that almost all males and many females masturbate, with no negative sequelae; (3) new information about the physiology of sexual arousal and discharge (establishing among other things the robustness of female sexuality); and (4) a clear distinction between gender and sexuality. This new knowledge has fueled not only the destigmatization of masturbation and homosexuality but also sexual liberation for women and recognition of the broad range of variations in masculinity and femininity.

The work of birth control reformers and scientists was just as far reaching in its impact as that of the sexologists, and perhaps more so. Margaret Sanger (1879–1966) founded the birth control movement in the United States in the 1920s. This was ultimately a prerequisite to sexual liberation and to greater sexual freedom for women. In 1917, Sanger was arrested and jailed for distributing contraceptives to immigrant women from a Brooklyn storefront. By the 1920s and 1930s, her name had become virtually synonymous with the birth control cause. While the movement sputtered during the Depression and World War II, primarily because of powerful Catholic opposition, Sanger never gave up her mission (Chesler, 1992).

In 1951 Sanger met Dr. Gregory Pincus, who had been carrying out extensive work in fertility, and encouraged him to develop a contraceptive pill. This he did, synthesizing estrogen and progesterone. Pincus then enlisted Dr. John Rock, chief of gynecology and obstetrics at the Harvard Medical School, to carry out clinical trials with humans.

Dr. John Rock was the first scientist to fertilize a human egg in a test tube and among the first to freeze sperm cells. He administered Pincus's powerful new synthetic version of progesterone to several women and then, because birth control was still illegal in Massachusetts, conducted a series of clinical trials with a new pill in Puerto Rico, where birth control had been legalized in 1937. Following a double-blind study in Puerto Rico, the FDA approved the birth control pill (Enovid) in 1960 (Bullough, 1994, pp. 193–195).

In 1965, in *Griswold v. Connecticut,* the Supreme Court ruled that the private use of contraception merited constitutional protection—another instance of the courts giving sanction to the new views of sexuality pioneered in the century. In 1973, in *Roe v. Wade,* the Supreme Court voted to legalize abortion, invoking a woman's right to privacy (though this ruling continues to be challenged).

As these and other legal decisions and public-policy initiatives show, the work of the birth control reformers and the development of an effective contraceptive have been crucial complements to that of the sex researchers in helping to change both the legal and the social environment in which we now live our sexual lives.

Freud's Psychoanalytic Studies of Sex

Although many sexologists achieved great prominence within their lifetimes and are still remembered for the magnitude of their contributions—Krafft-Ebing and Havelock Ellis, in particular—few have been accorded enduring status as preeminent intellectual theorists. Freud, who radically changed our ideas and attitudes about sex, was the first student of sex to be given serious attention by contemporary intellectual historians (Robinson, 1976). As Robinson points out, Freud achieved such prominence precisely because he was not just a sexologist or a sexual theorist; his sexual theories were not primarily in the service of sexual liberalization but formed the core of a larger psychological theory. Freud connected fantasy and the inner life of the mind with sexual behavior.[8] In the wake of Freud's pioneering studies, the primary importance of sex to both psyche and culture became obvious, and sexual studies, theories, and theorists assumed a new position of importance in intellectual discourse.

Freud's discovery of the laws governing unconscious mental life and the significance of infantile sexuality (expounded in *The Interpretation of Dreams* [1900] and *Three Essays On Sexuality* [1905], respectively) are generally regarded as his most profoundly original insights. It is said that Freud "'discovered' what he admitted every nursemaid already knew about: the sexuality of children" (Mitchell, 1974, p. 17). Not just nursemaids but a number of sexologists should be given priority for the observation that sexuality did not first emerge in adolescence as the natural consequence of the maturation of the sex organs, but had a long antecedent history in childhood. Although Freud's theories were continuous with previous theories (for example, as regards his emphasis on bisexuality and erotogenic zones), his revolutionary contribution was to demonstrate that infantile sexual development has profound consequences for the adult's erotic life and character structure.

Because my subject here is sexuality, I will focus my discussion of Freud on *Three Essays*. Steven Marcus, literary critic and professor of English at

8. Freud also afforded us an intellectual tool with which to understand and relate diverse phenomena such as neurosis, normal personality development, and some aspects of culture.

Columbia University, pointed out how Freud used an essentially Darwinian or evolutionary model to demonstrate the component nature of the sexual instinct: "Like Darwin, Freud is concerned with the 'variations' in form and structure that the sexual instinct takes, and he is interested in arranging or classifying these 'variations' in such a way that both their resemblances and differences be rendered in full account" (1975, p. 519). Freud's use of Darwinian insights is, of course, another major example of how new insights in one area of science provide new ways of perceiving and organizing data in other fields.

Freud discerned that minor perverse elements are frequently present in the lives of both neurotic and healthy people.[9] By suggesting that elements of both perversions and neuroses occur as minor strains in healthy people, Freud concluded that he had demonstrated a "connected series." This finding led him to propose that perverse wishes are normal components in the development of the sexual instinct. Conversely, the nature of the sexual preference in perversions can be understood as only one element in the composition of the sexual instinct—an element that has not undergone the repression that would have resulted in its being subsumed into conventional "mature" sexuality. Although Freud himself never viewed homosexuality as perverse per se, psychoanalysis in general absorbed the valuations of "normal" and "perverse" sexuality explicit in the science and culture of the day.

Observing the diverse practices in perversions, Freud introduced an important distinction between the object and the aim of the sexual instinct. The *object* is defined as that person toward whom the sexual activity is directed, whereas the *aim* is that activity toward which the drive is directed. The distinction between object and aim enabled Freud to further document the fact that the sexual instinct is made up of component parts.[10]

To demonstrate the origin of the component parts of sexuality, Freud turned to an exploration of childhood sexuality and erotogenic zones. His liberating insight, following the lead of several nineteenth-century sexologists, was to see evidence of early sexuality and infantile perverse behavior as the rule rather than the exception, as normal rather than pathological. It was in this context that he demonstrated that sexuality was broader than genitality

9. Freud's insights and theories on sexuality evolved through the years. Freud's first sexual theory—the seduction theory—originated in his work with female hysterics in the 1880s and 1890s. Freud's subsequent renunciation of the seduction theory represented a major turning point in his thinking, and many Freudian scholars believe that it was crucial to the development of psychoanalytic thinking insofar as it shifted the focus from real experience to fantasy. Only within the past few decades has there been an attack on Freud's motivation for such a shift. But it seems clear that it was only after he had abandoned the seduction theory that he became able to envision the importance of the spontaneous sexual manifestations of infantile sexual life and of sexual fantasies.

10. Kinsey, too, used the distinction between object and aim to destigmatize homosexuality. His did this by focusing on the aim rather than on the object.

alone: "the excitations from all these sources are not combined; but each follows its own separate aim, which is merely the attainment of a certain sort of pleasure. In childhood, therefore, the sexual instinct is not unified and is at first without an object, that is, autoerotic" (1905, pp. 32–33).

Through the discovery of the composite nature of the sexual instinct, the universal disposition to bisexuality, and the childhood condition of polymorphous perversion, Freud introduced the idea that normal sexuality was precarious and difficult to achieve. In fact, he suggested that without cultural repression the sexuality of a much greater number of persons would be "perverse."

As has already been mentioned, this last idea was picked up by a number of sexual liberationists, who believed that society caused the individual to repress sexuality to his or her grave detriment and that that repression must be undone. Norman Brown, in *Life Against Death: The Psychoanalytic Meaning of History* (1959), and Herbert Marcuse, in *Eros and Civilization* (1955), interpreted Freud's findings variously as a plea to ease the sexual repression of childhood, to tolerate the perversions, and even to liberate and embrace one's own polymorphous perverse sexuality. Doing so, they argued, would cure not only individual people but society too. Thus, the liberationists contend that education can undo the pernicious effects of repression, itself mainly the result of learned prejudices.

Freud's own vision of sexuality was not ultimately hopeful, and he did not reach the same conclusions as his revisionist followers. While Freud advocated some sexual reform, he was convinced of the inevitability as well as the necessity of sexual repression if man was to function as a social animal. For Freud, there was an inevitable conflict between instinctual life, by which he meant sexual life, and civilization. This is the heart of his tragic vision, most fully elaborated in *Civilization and Its Discontents* (1933a). Freud also believed that cultural pursuits depended on sexual sublimation.

Like much of the work of the sexologists, Freud's work too, has been the target of serious and substantial criticism. Nonetheless, his basic contributions have remained indispensable to any understanding of the relationships among psyche, sex, and gender.

New Formulations in Psychoanalysis

Just as Freud was responsive to the science of his day, so too are subsequent generations of analysts and scholars. During the past several decades, there has been a re-evaluation within psychoanalysis of the validity of three long-standing polarities: (1) masculine and feminine, (2) heterosexual and homosexual, and (3) normal and abnormal/perverse.[11] Although the newer theories employ Freud's pivotal insights, they depart widely from his initial formulations.

Gender: In addition to creating a psychological theory of sex, Freud was also the first to explain femininity in psychological rather than in biological terms (1930). So doing, he paradoxically proposed both an essentialist theory of masculinity and a constructionist theory of femininity. (Man is born, but woman is made.)

Freud's gender theory ultimately proved untenable because it has become apparent that gender attributes are not "natural" in boys, compensatory in girls (presumed by Freud to be initiated by the trauma of the discovery of the sex difference). Girls and boys begin to diverge in behavior, mannerisms, and interests as early as twelve to eighteen months of age, long before their discovery of the anatomic distinction. It is here that the work of Money and his colleagues in demonstrating that the first and crucial step in gender differentiation is the child's self-designation as male or female is particularly pertinent. Gender identity, which refers to the distinction between masculinity and femininity, develops in correspondence to core gender. Consequently, gender precedes sexuality in development and organizes sexuality, not the reverse, as Freud had theorized (see Person and Ovesey, 1983). However, some current work shows that prenatal hormones do contribute to aspects of gender identity, to the nature of object choice, and perhaps even in some instances to core gender identity (Money, Schwartz, and Davis, 1984; Friedman and Downey, 1995; Diamond and Sigmundson, 1997).

Moreover, recent investigations show that gender identity is not just dichotomous, masculine and feminine. Like biological sex, and like the sexual impulse, gender has many different configurations, mandating that we speak of the masculinities and femininities (and sometimes of mosaic patterns) and not simply of masculinity and femininity (Chodorow, 1994).

Heterosexuality and Homosexuality: In her classic paper "Compulsory Heterosexuality and Lesbian Existence" (1980), the poet and feminist Adrienne Rich attacked our culture's assumptions about the "normative" status of heterosexuality by recognizing that heterosexuality, like homosexuality, represents a narrowing of sexual possibilities.[12] In retrospect, the requirement of sexologists and psychoanalysts that an etiological explanation be provided for homosexuality but not for heterosexuality is clearly indefensible. Just as

11. Important critiques of the biological determinism that underlies the assumption of only two normative modes of development, male and female, have been made not only by analysts but by contributors from the academy and by feminist, gay and lesbian theorists.

12. I am very pleased that this paper was first published in a book I co-edited with Catharine Stimpson (Stimpson and Person, 1980).

Freud's idea that masculinity was the norm while femininity had to be explained now appears illogical, so, too, does the idea that homosexuality and not heterosexuality requires explanation.

Chodorow (1994) points out that traditional psychoanalytic theory assumes that we automatically identify with the same-sex parent—a phenomenon regarded as so inevitable that it requires no "motivational explanation"—and, further, that once this identification is made, we "normally" eroticize the opposite-sex parent. Given Freud's insight that there is a bisexual tendency in all of us, Chodorow argues that no matter where one falls in the continuum from heterosexuality to bisexuality to homosexuality, we might logically assume that there is a developmental history to account for it. There cannot be a simple "normative" oedipal complex—only one supraordinate pathway of development for boys and one for girls. The ultimate etiology of sexual preference is unknown, and we are left with the puzzle of why heterosexuality is the most usual outcome. Certainly our impulse to conformity must play a role.

We now know that homosexuals may or may not be perverse, and heterosexuals, too. Just as we have a more complex notion of biological sex and of gender, so, too, do we require a much more complex theory of sexuality than the one we now have. Bell and Weinberg (1978) proposed a "typology of homosexualities" (this idea was presaged in the work of Ovesey [1969], Ovesey and Person [1973], Person [1975], and Socarides [1978]. There is now a consensus that there are not just homosexuals and heterosexuals, but a variety of homosexualities and of heterosexualities too. And some people self-identify as bisexual.

Perversion: After Freud, the psychoanalyst-sexologist who has perhaps contributed most to a deeper understanding of perversion is Robert Stoller. Based on his observation of the way sexuality so often gets fused with aggression, Stoller's chief contribution (1975a) may have been to describe perversion as the erotic form of hatred. Stoller's work can be read as an elaboration of Freud's idea that there is an intrinsic dark side to sexuality, one that sets a natural limit to the liberalization of sexual practices.

Constructionism (Constructivism)

Constructionism, which has been called the non-essentialist theory of sex, is the theory that sex is not simply the expression of a biological force but that the form it takes is socially constructed. Jeffrey Weeks, a major constructionist and historian of sex, writes that "the critique of essentialism . . . has been very useful in casting light on hidden but controlling assumptions, and in opening up the sexual field to new questions, about history, power, meanings, diversity, choice, and so on" (1986, p. 113). In this I concur.

For example, the study of the history of homosexuality sheds light on the intersection of psyche and culture. Freud made a particularly valuable contribution to historical relativity when he pointed out that "the most striking distinction between the erotic life of antiquity and our own no doubt lies in the fact that the ancients laid the stress upon the instinct itself, whereas we emphasize its object" (Freud, 1905 [in a footnote added in 1910], p. 149). What this means is that for the ancients it was what you did—whether you were active or passive—and not with whom you did it, whether man or woman—that defined acceptability. Consequently, same-sex sex among men had a very different meaning in antiquity than it does today.

Even though homosexual behavior has undoubtedly always been with us, the self-concept of *being* homosexual is relatively new. That homosexuals now self-identify as homosexual has central significance not only to psychoanalysts but to historians and sociologists as well. While the phrase "coming out" refers to the public acknowledgment of one's homosexuality, there is an analogous internal "coming out." An individual comes to construct an identity as homosexual out of his or her sexual tendency. Although this process now seems almost inevitable, nonetheless a cognitive category of sexual identity must preexist in order for a homosexual-behaving person to self-identify as a homosexual person. Historians point out that homosexual self-identification probably did not occur as such before the nineteenth century. Weeks (1979) suggests that by the mid-nineteenth century a distinctive male homosexual subculture had emerged, much like the contemporary one, with a "distinctive argot and 'style.'" Boswell (1980) has pointed to a gay subculture with its own literature and argot in the eleventh and twelfth century. Participation in such a subculture shapes the homosexual identity.

Questions of why the category "homosexual" emerged, what the psychological ramifications are of identification within the subculture, what functions it serves for society at large, and the meaning of the profound homophobia such self-labeling invokes in others have become the basis for major inquiries in both sociology and history. These analyses make significant contributions to understanding the way homosexuals' identities evolve, particularly through mutual interaction within the subculture.

Even so, sociological and historical analyses that rely solely on a constructionist or a scripting frame of reference are unable to account for the origins and divergence of homosexual and heterosexual trajectories. Therefore, it still remains for neuropsychiatrists, psychoanalysts, and developmental psychologists to theorize the origins of sexual object choice.

Moreover, some of the extreme constructionists seem to believe that anything constructed can be reconstructed. Therefore they describe each individual's sex and gender as capable of embracing a dizzying multitude of possibilities, reversals, and new choices. The problem that must still be accounted for is the stability in personality structure. What psychoanalytic theory provides is the concept of psychic structure that becomes relatively stable in the course of development, with change coming much more slowly than might be assumed from the constructionist position.

What's now happening in informed theories in many disciplines is that attempts are being made to integrate the essentialist and constructionist points of view without doing damage to either. What is critical to this venture is that investigators and thinkers plumb hard to explore their personal biases as well as the biases inherent within their particular discipline.

Overall, the major changes in contemporary sexual attitudes and behaviors have had important effects in three different but often overlapping areas: (1) diminishing sexual repression, (2) introducing new ideas about female sexuality, which have in turn effected a re-evaluation of male sexuality and of the basic nature of femininity and masculinity, and (3) acceptance of some practices that were previously thought of as pathological, among them masturbation and, to a large degree, homosexuality as well. But sexual liberation was showing signs of contraction, evident even before the advent of AIDS. One major problem is that utopian expectations of sexual pleasure of an unprecedented nature proved illusory. Conflicts about sexual preferences in sexual acts and their frequency and duration did not automatically disappear. While more people have undoubtedly achieved greater sexual pleasure, others have been bitterly disappointed.

Paul Robinson has a keen understanding of some of the underlying tensions in the modern sexual tradition. Writing in 1976, he located this tension in the division between a romantic past, whose repressions we hoped to rid ourselves of, and a deromanticized future, whose emotional emptiness we fear even as we anticipate its greater freedom. This might be read as a reiteration of Rollo May's formulation of love without sex in the nineteenth century versus sex without love in the twentieth.

In addition, a very serious impediment to the continuing liberalization of sex is the linkage of sexual impulses with aggression. It is of note, of course, that Kinsey, Masters and Johnson, and most of the other sexual modernists did not choose to study the perversions and stopped short of any analysis of sadomasochism. Without looking at aggressive or antisocial impulses in sexuality—the dark side of erotic desire—one would be hard put to understand the past historical swings between the liberalization and the repression of sexuality.

Our intuitive knowledge of the anarchic nature of sexual desire may constitute the cultural brakes through which a limit is set to the liberalization of sex.

What of the present? Two different kinds of concerns about sexuality are in the forefront of public consciousness. On the one hand, the AIDS epidemic and the resurgence of sexually contagious diseases have sparked a campaign to reduce sexual behavior among teenagers. This campaign appears to have been successful in part. A recent study shows an increase in abstinence in both male and female high-school students.[13] At the same time, a major national debate on sexual harassment has surfaced that focuses on the abuse of power in the service of sex in the workplace and political arena. Sexual abuse of the young in schools and houses of worship has also drawn wide attention.

Diverse opinions regarding important sex and gender issues have begun to emerge in different pockets of public life and include the question of homosexuality in the military, the relevance of politicians being "outed" in extramarital relationships of one or another kind, the glass ceiling for women, and the debate about whether leadership and power should or can be effectively exercised in the same way by men and women.

What of the future? Just as the trend to sexual liberation has undergone a slowdown since the 1970s, the field of sexology has also arrived at a kind of pause. There is fundamental work in process, however, that will undoubtedly change our concepts of gender role identity and our sexual and affectional patterns in the next several decades. The work I refer to is the ongoing manipulation of reproductive techniques, which may eventually have an even larger impact on the way we come to view gender and heterosexuality and homosexuality than the birth control technologies had on sexual liberation and particularly on the sexual liberation of women.

Currently, it is possible for a birth mother to be impregnated by an already fertilized egg in which the egg and sperm may come from different sources (for example, from the parents-to-be or from individuals who will have no further role in the future of the child-to-be). Implementation of an artificial womb looms in the not too distant future. There is already an ongoing debate on the implications of manipulating sperm so as to favor the birth of a girl or a boy. And what of genetic manipulation to facilitate one or another trait?

If two eggs can be merged to form a zygote, as may have already occurred, what will the impact be on how we view sex and gender? Several people have already sounded the alarm about the diminishing importance of men or the "redundant male" (the title of a book by Cherfas and Gribbon, 1984). Even leaving out the looming question of cloning, what will happen if two sperm,

13. This study refers to sexual intercourse. For example, "teenage boys reporting they had intercourse dropped from 57 percent in 1991 to 49 percent in 1997. For girls the figure dropped from 50.8 to 47 percent" ("Poll Shows . . ." *New York Times*, September 18, 1998, p. A26).

courtesy of some still to-be-developed chromosomal transfer of an x chromosome, may also be merged to form a zygote?

While sexual liberation freed the sexual act from the threat of reproduction, the reproductive technologies will free reproduction from the necessity of sex. What such reproductive technological innovations, if put into practice, will do to our beliefs about sex and gender and to our sexual practices is an interesting question. My own belief is that, among other things, they will serve to further legitimate homosexuality, since gays and lesbians will be able to have natural children and form families comparable to those of heterosexuals.

Even if the unconscious is timeless (as it may or may not be), our patterns of expressing sex and gender have changed as a result of gay liberation, feminism, the pill, the separation of sex from procreation, the work of the sex researchers and psychoanalysts, and the political pressure of various sexual minorities. With such further social and scientific changes as will undoubtedly take place, we should expect that the shaping and enactment of our drives, wishes and fantasies, the fundamental *matériel* of the Freudian unconscious, may surface in ever new incarnations. Although unconscious impulses and wishes may sometimes emerge and swamp conscious ones, they in turn bear the imprint of the preconscious and conscious attitudes and beliefs that permeate the ever changing *zeitgeist*. The traffic between culture and psyche is always two-way, if not round-trip.

2

Sexuality as the Mainstay of Identity: Psychoanalytic Perspectives

1980

ETHEL S. PERSON

IT HAS long been recognized that certain conventions—the double standard, the cult of virginity, and the requirement that female sexuality find expression solely within monogamous heterosexual marriages—control and inhibit female sexuality. Whatever their origins might be, these conventions are major supports for male dominance and patriarchy. Consequently, various feminist critiques have proposed one or another new prescription for sexuality as a part of a general restructuring of society.

However, it is difficult to formulate such prescriptions without a large theory of sexuality. The aim of this chapter is to evaluate psychoanalytic paradigms, themselves in transition, in order to see what they imply for a contextual theory of female sexuality. Two popular assumptions will be challenged: (1) that sexuality is an innate force that achieves ideal expression when free from cultural inhibitions; and (2) that female sexuality is inhibited (hyposexual), whereas male sexuality represents the norm. On the contrary, I argue that all individuals internalize their culture, which shapes both their experience of desire and their expression of sexuality. If female sexuality is now inhibited, male sexuality is driven and cannot serve as a model. Sexuality must be understood not only in terms of its source but also in its relationship to the maintenance of identity.

Theories About the Nature of Sexual Motivation

Although the terms "sex" and "sexual" appear to be self-explanatory, they are difficult to define because sexual life in humans has so evolved that sex is not identical to the mechanism of reproduction. Sex refers to four separate, but related, physical-psychological sets of data: (1) biological sex, defined by six anatomical and physiological characteristics: chromosomes, gonads, internal genitalia, external genitalia, hormones, and secondary sexual characteristics; (2) gender, composed of core gender identity (the sense "I am female" or "I am male"), gender role identity (the sense "I am feminine" or "I am masculine"), and gender role behavior; (3) sexual behavior, overt and fantasied, expressed in both choice of object and nature of activity; and (4) reproduction (Money, Hampson, and Hampson, 1955b, 1956; J. G. Hampson, 1955; Stoller, 1968a; Ovesey and Person, 1973). However, the term "sexual," as used in everyday speech, refers almost exclusively to sexual behavior, not only pleasurable genital activity and its associated fantasies but any other sensual experience that has erotic meaning for the individual.

Theories about the nature of sexuality are, in general, theories of sexual motivation—why people initiate or respond to erotic activity. They usually address the source of sexual desire and arousal. Beach (1956) states the problem: "Since no animal mates in order to reproduce, but animals must mate in the service of species survival, we are faced with the problem of identifying the source of reward or positive reinforcement which impels individuals to copulate" (p. 299). Sexual arousal may occur with direct genital stimulation, but arousal often occurs without it. The reasons an individual becomes aroused or initiates sexual activity may appear, at first glance, to be self-evident because sex is so integral to life and so highly valued in contemporary culture. Yet there is little agreement concerning the source of sexual motivation.

An adequate theory of sexual motivation must offer explanations for the following aspects of sexuality: (1) the motor force behind the desire to initiate sexual behavior; (2) the immense strength of the sexual impulse as it is sometimes subjectively experienced; (3) the absence, avoidance, or inhibition of sexuality and the variable intensity of sexual desires; (4) the diversity of erotic stimuli and situations that trigger sexual arousal in different individuals (e.g., heterosexual, homosexual, or inanimate objects); (5) the existence of a "sex print"—that is, the restriction of an individual's erotic responses to limited stimuli (for example, being "turned on" to only one thing, such as a shoe, or to several); (6) the confluence of sexual and nonsexual meanings in both sexual and nonsexual behavior; and (7) the cultural preoccupation with sexuality. In sum, a sexual theory must account for both the power and the plasticity of sex.

There are now two major paradigms for the source of sexual motivation in humans. Freud's libido theory, essentially a biological theory that postulates a fixed sexual drive has been dominant for more than fifty years. However, some theorists follow Beach's lead, postulating an appetitional theory of sexual motivation in opposition to the libidinal or drive theory. While the second paradigm acknowledges a neural reflex for orgasmic release, the occasion for sexual arousal is viewed as learned or conditioned rather than biological.

Profoundly different implications attach to the two paradigms. The drive or libidinal model describes a tension that must be discharged or converted via sublimation, neurosis, or perversion. The appetitional model posits the pursuit of pleasure as the motive force for sexuality. This difference in focus reflects a current dichotomy in theories of behavior. Although there is a formal consensus that a mind-body split is untenable, interpretations of behavior are increasingly polarized in the direction of either biological determinism or cultural contingency, so much so that belief in the existential self as the locus of choice has almost vanished. In libido theory, sexuality is both a motor force in culture and an innate force with which culture must contend. The dichotomy posed is whether sexuality is a creator of culture or is itself created by culture.

Although less fully articulated, a third paradigm exists that remedies some of the problems inherent in the first two. An amalgam of Freud's psychological theory of sexuality and object-relations theory, it places the appetitional component in a developmental motivational context. Rather than view libido as controling interpersonal relations, it emphasizes the way in which early object relations shape the experience of desire. Each of the three paradigms must be judged in terms of its usefulness in explaining the different aspects of sexuality described previously. In addition, each paradigm has different implications for the way we view both female and male sexuality.

THE LIBIDO THEORY OF SEXUAL MOTIVATION

"Libido" is a term that is rarely defined in the psychoanalytic literature. Freud suggested that it was "that force by which the sexual instinct is represented in the mind" (quoted by Jones, 1955, vol. 2, p. 282). He considered it the equivalent of sexual longing. At times, he used the term as synonymous with sexual excitation, which led him to speculate that many different organs contributed sexual tension to sexual instinct.

In Freud's theory (Freud, 1908c, 1920b, chaps. 20, 21), drive is generated within the body and propels itself toward discharge; as such, it is outside the realm of consciousness, though it acts as a stimulus on consciousness, where it is transformed into a wish. The fulfillment of the wish leads to the reduction of tensions and thereby to pleasure. Freud's notion of instinct both implies a tension to be discharged and suggests the mode by which this discharge takes place. Libido is considered an energy that has direction (some specific aim to accomplish), object (the instrument by which the aim is to be fulfilled), different intensities, and the capacity for transformation into equivalences, such as neurotic symptoms. Psychosexual development unfolds in accordance with maturation. All psychic development derives from a biologically scheduled unfolding of libido. From the polymorphous condition of infancy, libido moves through a series of preordained, orderly stages (oral, anal, phallic, oedipal), each attached to an erotogenic zone and, after latency, subsumed into genital sexuality. Sexuality, then, is distinguished from genitality. It refers to sensual, pleasurable gratification from specific body zones, using thumb sucking as a prototype. Freud's theory is both a physical energic theory, because libido is viewed as an energy, and a biological theory, because each stage of sexuality is intrinsically connected to a stage of biological development.

However, a psychological theory is superimposed upon the biophysical theory. Freud described two purely psychological events that interact with the deployment of libido and are crucial to development: first, the child's discovery of anatomic distinction with her or his subsequent reaction to that discovery; and second, the entrance into the oedipal stage. The psychological aspects of his theory will be amplified later when we turn to the third paradigm of sexual motivation. In this theory, there is only one kind of libido: masculine. Perhaps because of constitutional endowment or because the path of libidinal development in women is so circuitous, the relative attenuation of sexuality in women is considered a foregone conclusion (Freud, 1908c, 1933b).

CRITIQUE OF LIBIDO THEORY

Despite its enormous heuristic value, particularly for understanding the apparent centrality of sexuality to mental life and for collating a vast array of clinical data, the concept of libido has been critically evaluated in a number of disciplines. Feminist critiques point out the masculine bias implicit in any theory that takes male development as the norm and female development as a deficit model of male development. Psychoanalysts have argued that Freud's concept of instinct is based on a pre-Mendelian model. Some analysts claim that Freud uses the concept of instinct to mean just drive (or motivational source) and not inherited patterns for discharge since he uses the word for drive (*Trieb*) rather than instinct. Although these two meanings may appear blurred, Ernest Jones (1955) suggests that "on the whole the word *Trieb* in Freud's writings more often means 'instinct' in our sense . . . which definitely implies an inborn and inherited character" (vol. 2, p. 317). But there are serious objections even to the narrower concept of instinct.

One of the earliest, most comprehensive, and most forceful critiques was by Kardiner, Karush, and Ovesey (1959), who point out that libido has two different sets of connotations: an appetitive component and an energic component. With regard to the first, Kardiner and colleagues regard sex as a physiologic need, like that for food, water, oxygen, and warmth. Their quarrel with Freud is that he not only postulates libido as the subjective perception of the sexual need but also contends that the "behavior which brings gratification is also held to be instinctual" (p. 502). In their view, "The goals of such needs [for food, sex, etc.] are not learned, and one may, if he wishes, call them 'instinctual' " (p. 503). But, they maintain, the route to satisfaction of those needs is learned. Insofar as the infant needs the breast (mother) to satisfy its hunger, that need is a learned association. Kardiner and colleagues are unable to concede that there is an "inborn need either for a sexual object in general or for a sexual object of a particular gender" (p. 507).

As for the energic connotation of libido theory, Freud holds that libido is a transmutable energy, which can be moved from one body zone to another and from one sexual object to another and which can be transformed into anxiety, symptoms, and so forth. However, as Kardiner and colleagues have pointed out, libido is a hypothetical construct, derived from nineteenth-century physics as a model. Libido cannot be observed; it is used to "explain" different intensities of behavior and as such is tautological. The assumption of libido as the life force is totally unproved.

Kubie (1948), among others, raises questions about the one point that Kardiner and colleagues are willing to concede to Freud's theory of libido; that is, the equivalence of sex and hunger. The need for water and for metabolites is manifest through the subjective experience of thirst and hunger and is mediated through a demonstrable disequilibrium in homeostatic processes. Therefore, in the case of thirst and hunger, one is able to formulate the mediating link between body process, on one hand, and "felt" need, on the other. Freud's organic sexual excitation, the biological substratum of libido, has yet to be established.

There have been several attempts to identify some homeostatic disequilibrium that might account for sexual need and is analogous to the mechanisms that account for the need for food and water. If one considers male sexuality, pressure on the seminal vesicles has been proposed as the motor force of sexual desire. However, this model of male sexuality, which we might term the "elimination" model, has been discredited as too limited (Beach, 1956); it cannot account for childhood sexuality, continued desire in castrates, or a number of other special cases. Nor has it been possible to correlate arousal with specific hormone levels (Hardy, 1964). There is some evidence, however, that arousability, if not arousal, is dependent on hormone level (Whalen,

1966). Hormones act on sexuality in at least two ways: indirectly through their role in dimorphic development (and, some say, in the genesis of the male or female brain), as well as directly on arousability.

Attempts to locate the source of some homeostatic disequilibrium to account for sexual need have thus far failed. In part, Freud's analogy of sexual need to hunger is intrinsically poor, based on the individual's subjective sense of need, often experienced as peremptory. But in hunger and thirst, arousal occurs at fairly regular intervals and is relatively predictable and autonomous. Furthermore, only the satisfaction of the appetite is socially prescribed, not the need itself. Contrast this with sexuality, in which arousal itself is prohibited in many circumstances—for example, if it is attached to an incestuous object. Thus, one might guess that the biological and psychological mechanisms that underlie the regulation of sexuality differ from the regulatory mechanisms of those other appetites with which sexuality is compared.

In sum, the concept of instinct applied to human sexuality is outdated. Even in animal studies it has been replaced by the concept of "innate" behavior conceptualized in terms of the release and inhibition of specific physiological mechanisms. In the lower mammals sex is considered "stereotypic" rather than "instinctive." As one moves up the evolutionary scale, sex is no longer predominantly controlled by reflex and endocrine mechanisms. In humans, sexual behavior appears to depend more on learning and experience and less on hormonal and genetic contributions. As Ford and Beach put it, "the human male does not have to learn how to fill his penis with blood so that it becomes erect and rigid, but he may have to learn how to copulate" (1951, pp. 178–79). Such a concept does not deny the importance of biological factors in the organization and expression of sexual behavior; it does suggest that sexuality is subject to great variability and even disruption on the basis of experience. With the current spate of biological research, it is still possible to speculate that the biological basis for sexual drive will be revealed.[1] But the burden of proof must fall on proponents of instinct theory since several viable alternate theories can account for sexual appetite and sexual motivation.

THE APPETITIONAL THEORY OF SEXUAL MOTIVATION

This theory, too, is biological insofar as it acknowledges the individual's innate or biological capacity for physiological sexual arousal and discharge. However, it emphasizes different origins of the motivation for sexuality than libido theory does. As proposed by Hardy (1964), sexual motivation represents one special case of principles common to motives generally (pp. 4–6) In summary,

1. No one doubts that there are neurophysiologic and neuropharmacologic underpinnings in sexuality. The question in dispute is the initiating event for arousal. Current works that focus on the biology of sexuality are Gorski, 1974; Heath, 1972; MacLean, 1975.

a motive derives from a learned expectation of affective change (e.g., pleasure or the avoidance of pain or fear). Because local stimulation of the genitals and genital climax are pleasurable, the quest for sexual discharge will become associated with the pleasure of genital stimulation and serve as a cue for sexual arousal even in the absence of direct stimulation. Hardy further postulates that various stimuli become linked to sexual arousal or avoidance on the basis of cultural prescriptions and sanctions. Female hyposexuality would be viewed as a product of cultural inhibition. This schema for sexual motivation, whether explicitly labeled an appetitional theory or not, provides the theoretical base for formulations that focus on historical contingency and culture in the genesis of sexual fantasy, patterns of arousal, and behavior. Such theories emphasize the social sources of sexuality, whereas in libido theory sexuality is viewed as biophysical in source.

The most forceful argument for the social origins of sexual motivation is presented by Gagnon and Simon in their classic work, *Sexual Conduct: The Social Origins of Sexual Development* (1973). They argue that Freud, like other post-Romantic innovators, transferred the image of the contest of the individual against the state to the arena of sexuality, with a contest between the instinctual aims of the individual and his repressive culture or parents. They view the "unproven assumption. . . . of the 'power' of the psychosexual drive" as the major obstacle to understanding sexuality (p. 15). According to Freud, sexual arousal is natural; according to Gagnon and Simon, the physiological concomitants of excitement are not necessarily recognized as such until they are appropriately identified. The latter idea dovetails with Schacter and Singer's (1962) demonstration that external events influence the individual's interpretation of physiological change. In other words, the conscious interpretation of a biologic event is subject to variation, depending on cultural input. More and more analyses of sexuality emphasize historical contingency. Take, for example, Foucault's *History of Sexuality*, in which the title itself throws down the gauntlet to the biological determinists. "Sexuality must not be thought of as a kind of natural given which power tries to hold in check, or as an obscure domain which knowledge tries to uncover. It is the name that can be given to a historical construct" (p. 105). Foucault focuses on the relationship of power and social control to the construction of sexuality, which took on its modern form in the eighteenth century. Such a construction renders the content of sexuality.

CRITIQUE OF THE APPETITIONAL THEORY

While the appetitional theory is adequate to explain arousal, diversity of sexual stimuli, and even sexual inhibition, it offers no basis for understanding either the peremptory nature of sexuality or its symbolic valences. Theories that emphasize social origins are extremely useful in pointing to cross-cultural and historical variations in the deployment of sexuality and in challenging the concept of sexuality as instinctive and biologically mandated. However, within the terms of their own assumption, they do not offer adequate insight into mechanisms that mediate between culture and individual subjectivity. This is, of course, the same objection that has been raised against the interpersonal school of psychoanalysis, in which the simplistic assumption is so often made that subjectivity simply mirrors what is exterior. A theoretical formulation is required that can address the problem of how family, society, and culture are reflected in individual psychological development. This task was first undertaken in adaptational theory, particularly in the work of Kardiner (1939) and Rado (1956), and more recently in object relations theory.

TOWARD A NEW PARADIGM: FREUD'S PSYCHOLOGICAL THEORY AND OBJECT RELATIONS THEORY

Despite the shortcomings of libido theory, it will not be readily replaced until an alternate paradigm emerges that can "explain" the same data. Such a paradigm in fact exists within psychoanalysis. It is in large part a distillate of Freud's work, omitting the emphasis on sex as instinct but postulating a developmental sequence by which sex comes to have central significance in personality, with particular focus on the interrelationship between the capacity for sensuality and the development of object relations. It offers great flexibility and coherence in integrating biology and social reality.

As George Klein (1976) makes clear in an essay on "Freud's Two Theories of Sexuality," it is more than plausible to preserve the importance of sexuality in the etiology of neurosis and in motivation in general without adhering to a drive-discharge or libido theory. He elaborates this position in a closely reasoned argument in which he suggests that Freud really proposed two theories of sexuality: the libido theory and what he calls Freud's clinical theory. (I prefer to call it Freud's psychological theory to distinguish it from his biological theory.) Klein finds it unlikely that Freud himself believed he had formulated two different theories, and some Freud scholars may have the same difficulty. The suspicion does emerge, as one reads Klein's paper, that he may be introducing new twists and attributing them to Freud in the hopes of avoiding controversy.

Yet there is within the body of Freud's work a theory of sexual behavior that does not depend on accepting libido as a necessary construct. It allows the correlation of insights from psychoanalytic theory with those from cognitive theory and affective theory (on which the appetitional theory is based). Klein states, "In the clinical theory, sexuality is viewed as an appetitive activity within a reticulum of motivational meanings rather than the manifestations of linear force impelling itself against a barrier" (p. 21). He points out that Freud correctly identified sensual pleasure as the shared factor in different sexual experiences, both infantile and adult, nongenital and genital. This pleasure is different from the removal of unpleasure; it is primary because it comes from the direct stimulation of dermal surfaces.[2] (This argument is congruent with Hardy's.) From Klein's point of view, Freud's major contribution to the theory of sexuality was his discovery that nongenital, infantile sexuality was in emotional continuity with genital sexuality. Both the capacity for sensual pleasure and the means of eliciting it undergo serial development. In clinical (or psychological) theory, this "is a guided process, one in which societal sanctions, values, and encouragement are vital. . . . From this premise . . . Freud evolved a conception of how this development is affected by a person's symbolized record of interpersonal encounters through which he has been sensually aroused" (p. 21).

In object relations theory, the close interrelationship between infantile sexuality and early object relations is definitive for mental life. The earliest bonding between mother (or surrogate) and child takes place in the experiential context of the tactile-sensual modality. In fact, it has been demonstrated that physical skin contact between infant and caretaker is critical to the infant's emotional and cognitive development.[3] Lichtenstein (1977) has raised the question of the evolutionary purpose of pregenital sexuality (nonprocreative sexuality); it may be precisely to promote bonding between the infant and significant others. Thus, sexuality will always carry the affective connotations of early object relations. "As development occurs, the conceptual scope or sensual experience comes to include representations of the actions and relationships through which the pleasure is won or thwarted, of restraint and controls, and of self-related meanings" (Klein, 1976, p. 27). Because sensual pleasure is the vehicle of object relationships in the real world, sexuality expresses an enormous variety of motives, predominantly dependent or hostile.[4] Or sexuality may be used in the service of stabilizing one's sense of self, assuaging anxiety, or restoring self-esteem.

Furthermore, because sensuality arises directly from body surfaces that have other functions as well, sensual experience will by its very nature be symbolically interlocked with nonsensual activities or aims. The force of sexuality exists precisely because it is linked with other motives. Klein (1976) suggests that it is neither the need nor the wish for sensual experience that motivates an individual toward sexual behavior but, rather, "manifestations of

2. It is this aspect of sensuality that accounts for the pleasure in foreplay. In drive theory with its emphasis on pleasure as the outcome of tension reduction, there is no adequate explanation for forepleasure, a problem that Willhelm Reich ingeniously tried to solve.

3. These conclusions are demonstrated in the work of René Spitz, 1945, 1946; see also Dowling, 1969, and Ross, 1979.

4. The psychoanalytic formulation of nonsexual motives in sexual behavior was made in the mid-1950s in a significant series of papers by Lionel Ovesey; see particularly, "The Pseudohomosexual Anxiety," *Psychiatry* 18 (1955): 17–25, and "Masculine Aspirations in Women," *Psychiatry* 19 (1956): 341–351.

the cognitive schemata in a state of continued or repetitive activation" (p. 28). The clearest expression of this union of sexual and nonsexual motives is found in those clinical instances in which an individual feels driven by sexual desire (e.g., any bout of compulsive sexuality such as episodic fetishism). Don Juan is not just in search of sex.

In sum, object relations theory attempts to formulate ways in which the experience of the external world is internalized, not just in the organization of perception and affective relationships but in the very creation of subjectivity. While all psychoanalytic theory acknowledges the internalization of external values and prohibitions in the formation of ego ideal and superego, there is more emphasis in object-relations theory on the way subjectivity (fantasies, wishes) is influenced by the experiential. More than an amalgam of object need tied to pleasure, sexuality reflects desire, which depends on fantasy. The substance of fantasy itself draws on experience.

CRITIQUE OF THE PSYCHOLOGICAL AND OBJECT RELATIONS THEORY OF SEXUALITY

This theory, too, has its limitations. It is useful in unraveling certain clinical phenomena, but because of all the special conditions that mediate the shape of internalizations (affect, perception, maturational stage, conflict, etc.), the theory is not predictive. So, for example, object relations theory *alone* cannot account for the division of the world into two genders, a division that has such profound consequences for the shape of individual desire.

Once we establish the possibility that the nature of sexuality owes more to culture than to biology, it is difficult to justify the claim that sexual inhibition, by definition, does violence to the individual. If we are to sustain the conviction that the expression of sexuality is crucial to autonomous personality development, we must make explicit those mechanisms (in distinction to drive discharge) that account for the central importance of sexuality in psychological life. We must consider its function in personality development, its meaning and value to the individual, and, above all, the relationship between sexuality and the consolidation of identity. It is in these contexts that we may be better able to understand the implications of inhibited sexuality for women.

The Function and Value of Sexuality

At the simplest level, the function of sexuality is to obtain sexual discharge or pleasure or experience ecstasy (Lichtenstein, 1970). Orgasm has been described as a biological opiate, offering relief of pregenital as well as genital tension, strengthening the ego, regression in the service of the ego, and so forth (Ross, 1970). But the function of sexuality extends beyond either the pursuit of pleasure or the remediation of discomfort. First, self-stimulation in infancy provides sensual pleasure independent of reliance on external objects. The ability to produce orgasm at will, through masturbation, lends itself to a sense of self-sufficiency and power in the adolescent. Consequently, the development of a sense of autonomy (characterized by the ability to function independent of external objects) may be developmentally linked to masturbation. Second, sexuality may symbolize union with the loved object; it may be the primary vehicle for the expression of intimacy in a culture in which so many other expressions of physicality are proscribed. One analyst (Fairbairn, 1952) has gone so far as to suggest that the sex "drive" is primarily object seeking rather than pleasure seeking. At the very least, sexuality is intertwined with object relations and may become the vehicle for the expression of love, hostility, or dependency.

But while the "beneficent effects of orgastic experiences" (Ross, 1970, p. 267) are widely documented, the primacy of sexual development in personality is no longer taken for granted. This is the case even among analysts who subscribe to the libido theory of sexuality. It has been found impossible to correlate genitality and orgasmic competence with overall personality maturation; there is even less correlation among women than among men (Ross, 1970; Deutsch, 1964; Lichtenstein, 1970). On the basis of Hartmann's work, sexuality is considered no more than one among three to five variables in personality development. Given the findings of ego psychology, it is not possible to see personality maturation as the dependent variable, sexuality as the independent one (Ross, p. 281; Lichtenstein, p. 269). In the case of "perversions," the "perverse" symptom represents sexuality as it has been filtered through a distortion in object relations, rather than a sexual fixation that disturbs object relations (Person and Ovesey, 1974a,b, 1978).

Even though analysts have downgraded the theoretical importance of sexuality, they still believe that sex maintains a unique position in psychic development. If sexual development is not the independent variable in psychosexual development, what is the justification for claiming that it is the leading variable? There is an assumption in psychoanalysis, sometimes tacit, sometimes explicit, that sexuality is linked to identity. Many individuals corroborate this psychoanalytic assumption and report that they experience their sexuality as self-defining. If sexuality does not have a "nature," as libido theory suggests, one is left with the task of explaining the experiential testimony that sex is the "core."

SEXUALITY AND IDENTITY

Eissler (1958a,b) and Lichtenstein (1977) explicitly suggest a direct link between sexuality and identity. Eissler (1958a) says that "orgasm (aside from the biological aspects) when viewed in its relationship to the ego must contain a meaning and function beyond the attainment of physical pleasure and the reduction of tension" (p. 237). He suggests that orgasm serves the ego function of the affirmation of personal existence. But the capacity for orgasm appears relatively late in development. Consequently, Lichtenstein (1977) suggests that all libidinal gratification serves the same function early in development that orgasm does later and that "the very core of a person's being fully himself profoundly depends on the affirmation of the conviction of his existence as incontrovertible truth" (p. 313). He believes that non-procreative sexuality serves the evolutionary purpose of establishing a "primary identity." While psychoanalytic theory customarily derives the emergence of identity from early object relations (the separation-individuation phase) and from the infant's development of body image, Lichtenstein proposes that both identity and sexual theme are transformations of the infant's perception of its instrumental use by mother. He conceives of this process as a version of "imprinting."

Against the proposition that sexuality is a cornerstone of identity, we have the historian's contention that self-identification in the modern sense of a conscious sense of self may not apply to earlier historical epochs at all, let alone a self-identification based on sexual practice. In contrast to Lichtenstein's position, and in view of the historical variability of the sense of self as separate, it seems to me that in contemporary culture, sexuality is nearly always, but not invariably, linked to identity. That the linkage is not invariable is a salient point, particularly in reference to the difference between female sexuality and male sexuality. When sexuality does play a large role in identity it is through the mediating structure of gender and "sex prints."

GENDER

There is contemporary agreement (with the significant exception of one major study) that gender differentiation is prephallic, observable by the end of the first year of life and immutable by the third year.[5] The first and crucial step in psychosexual development and gender differentiation arises in the early years of life, most often in agreement with the parental designation of the child's sex. This self-designation, defined by the term "core gender," may have unconscious as well as conscious components. Gender plays an organizing role in psychic structure similar to other modalities of cognition such as space, time, causation, and self-object differentiation. Why core gender is of such crucial importance in organizing personality is still an open question. Put another

5. See Susan Baker, "Biological Influences on Human Sex and Gender" for the one exception: Imperato-McGinley's work on the 5-reductase deficit of male pseudohermaphroditism. *Signs: Journal of Women in Culture and Society*, 6:1 (1980).

way, the question is why only two gender possibilities exist.[6] This question has been pointedly raised by Fineman (1979), who suggests that the fixity of *two* gender roles seems to confirm Freud's "penile semantics." Less provocatively, one might say that the knowledge that there are two categories of beings permeates mental life even before knowledge of a sex difference as such exists. Since gender roles and behaviors in fact exist on a gradient, I would assume that their organization into two genders, which correspond to the two sexes, offers some cognitive advantage (the ready division into two opposites such as like and different, self and other).

Gender orders sexuality. Why else do those few genetic males misdiagnosed as females and reared as females grow up dreaming the dreams of women? Gender launches the individual into a particular psychosexual pathway; it is decisive for the shape of the oedipal configuration, which is a crucial event in acculturation. In addition, socialization into passivity or activity, subordination or autonomy, is decisive for the way sexuality (sensuality) is experienced and for the fantasies that attach to it. Thus, gender training, not just the previous record of sensual experience, molds sexuality.

Sexuality, in turn, may be a mainstay for gender. Insofar as sexuality is a major component in the maintenance of gender, it is crucial to identity. There is a wealth of clinical evidence to suggest that, in this culture, genital sexual activity is a prominent feature in the maintenance of masculine gender but a variable feature in feminine gender. Thus an impotent man always feels that his masculinity, not just his sexuality, is threatened. In men, gender appears to "lean" on sexuality. It is impossible to locate a physically intact man who has never achieved orgasm by any route whatsoever who does not have significant psychopathology. In males, the need for sexual performance is so great that performance anxiety is the leading cause of secondary impotence. The vast array of male "perversion" (in both types and numbers), in contrast to perversion in women, may be testimony to the male need to preserve sexuality against long odds. In contrast, whether or not a woman is orgasmic has few implications for personality organization. Put another way, there is a difference between men and women in the primacy of sexuality, at least in this culture. In women, gender identity and self-worth can be consolidated by other means.

This difference in the relationship between genital sexuality and gender is, I believe, the single most telling distinction between female and male

6. However, social scientists have an increasing awareness that some cultures employ a third category, e.g., the berdache categories among some traditional Native American societies. See, e.g., G. Herdt, ed., 1994, *Third Sex, Third Gender: Beyond Social Dimorphism in Culture and History*, New York: Zone Books. (Footnote added, 1998.)

sexuality. Whatever the causes of the difference, it means that while women may suffer the consequences of sexual inhibition, sexual expression is not critical to personality development. Many women have the capacity to abstain from sex without negative psychological consequences. (The problem for women is that they are often denied the legal right of sexual refusal.) In men, there is such a rigid link between sexual expression and gender that their sexuality often appears driven rather than liberated.

SEX PRINT

The relationship between sexuality and identity is mediated not only through gender but also through what I have called the "sex print."[7] The sex print is an individual's erotic signature. It signifies that the individual's sexual potentiality is progressively narrowed between infancy and adulthood. This phenomenon has been alluded to by sexologists and analysts of markedly different persuasions. In Freud, the polymorphous perverse infant-child is metamorphosed into the heterosexual adult through psychosexual maturation and under the aegis of the family. Eissler (1958a), while remarking on "perversions," noted that "biological knowledge has little value when it is observed that the pleasure premium is unconditionally tied to a rigid individual pattern. . . . Despite many other available channels for gratification the physical demand remains ungratified" (p. 236–37). It is clear that this description applies to nearly all individuals, obligatory heterosexuals, obligatory homosexuals, and so on. The sex print conveys more than just preference for a sexual object; it is an individualized script that elicits erotic desire. It also refers to the strong preference for specific erotic techniques, though this aspect of the sex print may prove to have a strong biological predisposition. Tripp (1975) notes that "people and lower animals both end up with sharply specific sex patterns, though in man these vary enormously from one individual to the next" (p. 17).

From the subjective point of view the sex print is experienced as sexual "preference." Because it is revealed rather than chosen, sexual preference is felt to be deep rooted and deriving from one's nature. To the degree that an individual utilizes sexuality (for pleasure, for adaptation, as the resolution of unconscious conflict) and to the degree that sexuality is valued, one's sexual "nature" will be experienced as more or less central to personality. To the extent that an individual's sex print "deviates" from the culture's prescription for sexuality, it may be experienced as even more central to identity (at least in this culture). So, for example, many transsexuals and transvestites report both relief and a sense of personality consolidation when "I found out what I am," when "I found out there were others like me" (Person and Ovesey, 1974a).

7. I use "sex print" in the sense of fingerprint—i.e., it is unchangeable and unique. I do not mean to imply anything about its origins by this term, and it has no reference to imprinting.

Although sexual preference represents the narrowing of sexual potential, it is not experienced that way by most people. To some degree this is because sex printing is more pronounced (i.e., the script is more rigid) in the perversions, less pronounced in both heterosexuality and homosexuality. Furthermore, each individual usually has a cluster of effective erotic stimuli or fantasies so that it is possible to focus on one's own diversity rather than circumscription. It is also true that, within limits, one can add to one's effective sexual repertoire. Then, too, many people can perform effectively in many different situations, although without the subjective experience of excitement. Most important, heterosexuals have always had the advantage of viewing their sexuality as natural.

Even so, the sense of one's sexuality as bedrock derives not only from the shape of pleasure but also from the fact that the same erotic stimuli remain effective. So, for example, it is difficult for most heterosexuals to become bisexual even when they consciously make the effort, out of intellectual or political conviction. In therapy, change in sexual orientation or even in sexual attitude (e.g., the insistence that a partner be "superior" in intellectual achievement) is achieved only with great difficulty and sometimes not at all. In some homosexual male patients who enter treatment in order to change their sexual orientation, it has been reported that the effective obstacle to change is not the inability to have intercourse with women or the preference for sex with men, but the unwillingness to give up a homosexual "identity."

The mechanism of sex printing is obscure, despite the obvious advantage in eliminating certain situations as sexual (some mechanism for the control of sexuality occurs in every species). Freud uses the explanatory concepts of repression, maturation, and fixation; however, his explanation depends on accepting the psychosexual stages of libido as inborn. Tripp (1975) suggests a neurological basis, nature unspecified, to account for the fact that each individual "loses his initial diversity of responses as his sexual interests become even more narrowed down to specific channels of expression" (p. 19). Social sanction is often cited as the vector that socializes individuals toward obligatory heterosexuality. This explanation does not suffice. First, if sex printing were simply learned or conditioned, it could be readily unlearned or deconditioned. We have, in the relative irreversibility of sex print, the same problem as in the conceptualization of gender: the puzzle of why "learned" behavior is apparently irreversible. This form of "learning" is connected with the process of identity formation. The inability to describe the mechanism of this connection has led some theorists to the arbitrary and unwarranted assumption that imprinting occurs in humans. Second, the critical question is not why some patterns are strongly eroticized but, rather, why other erotic scripts are aversive. Third, social sanction cannot be used to explain sex printing in those individuals whose preferences depart from the conventional ones.

In sum, for the individual, both gender and sex print carry the subjective impression of being part of the private self, immune to external demands, autonomous. In this sense, they appear to be part of the private realm, distinct from the public one. The importance attached to one's sexual "identity" may be even greater in a culture like ours, in which stabilizing features, such as rigid class distinction or geographical rootedness, are missing and cannot anchor personality. In other words, sexual identity draws its significance from individual development and as the repository of desire but becomes more important as other self-identifying features in the culture are attenuated.

Relevance of Sexual Paradigms to Issues of Female Sexuality

Sexual paradigms have relevance for at least three feminist concerns: (1) the importance of sexuality to individual development; (2) the relationship among sexuality, power, and dependency; and (3) the relationship of sexual liberation to the women's movement.

SEXUALITY AND INDIVIDUAL DEVELOPMENT

It is, in a sense, easier to prescribe for sexuality in some version of utopia than to grapple with intrinsic ambivalences attached to the expression of female sexuality in this culture. There are essentially two problematic areas in female sexuality: masochism and inhibition of sexuality. The issue of masochism has been dealt with extensively; a number of authors have demonstrated that masochism, insofar as it is a common part of female fantasy life, is secondary to the power relationships that exist in patriarchal society and is not intrinsic to female psychosexual development per se (see, e.g., Ovesey, 1956; Person, 1974).

Inhibition of sexuality has not received the same theoretical attention accorded masochism. Female sexual inhibition really refers to three separate orders of phenomena: (1) inhibitions of assertiveness that take place in an interpersonal context; (2) inhibition of sex per se as manifest by an inhibition of desire, arousal, or orgasm; and (3) low sexual "drive." The first set of inhibitions has little to do with sexuality; it is most often based on deference to the male and fear of him and includes such behaviors as "faking" orgasm, not insisting on adequate stimulation, assuming that male orgasm terminates a sexual encounter, and paying excessive attention to pleasing rather than to being pleasured. This set of inhibitions is usually easily resolved when a woman achieves greater assertiveness and a sense of autonomy. In fact, many so-called frigid women turn out to have no substantive problems with the achievement of arousal or orgasm; they suffer from either ignorance about what constitutes appropriate stimulation or interpersonal intimidation. True female sexual inhibition refers to inhibition of desire, arousal, or orgasm, which arises out of psychological conflicts. Primarily, then, since most women are capable of orgasm, female sexual inhibition refers to low female "drive." So-called low drive is manifest in the low rates of female adolescent masturbation, the tendency to tie sexuality to intimacy, and the ability to tolerate anorgasmia. Here the tacit assumption is that male sexuality constitutes the norm and that women perform at a deficit.

The most striking difference between the sexes in the behavioral manifestations of sexuality occurs in adolescence. Induction into genital sexuality is of particular importance.[8] For some individuals sexual activity begins prior to adolescence; according to Kinsey, one-fifth of his male sample and one-tenth of his female sample experienced orgasm prior to age twelve (Gagnon and Simon, 1973, p. 55). For most individuals, though, sexuality emerges during adolescence under the impact of two factors: the hormonal shifts of puberty cause bodily changes that focus attention on emerging sexuality and may even result in spontaneous arousal and orgasm; next, social life is increasingly organized around disparate patterns of male and female interests and behaviors, which include imitations (rehearsals) of adult forms of social and sexual interaction.

In males, adolescence is characterized by the beginning of overt sexual activity and ejaculation. For most females, menstruation is the key event; for males, ejaculation. Menstruation may tend to inhibit sexual exploration, both for symbolic reasons and because it carries the threat of pregnancy. Whatever the reason, sex becomes organized differently for the two sexes. In males, Kinsey found that more than 80 percent masturbated to orgasm by age fifteen, whereas only 20 percent of females had. This discrepancy was still apparent in data collected twenty years later (Gagnon and Simon, 1973, p. 55). Thus masturbation in females is more erratic than it is in males; in females only about two-thirds ever masturbate to orgasm, and, of those, half discover masturbation after having been introduced to orgasm in an interpersonal context. Explanations for the low level of female masturbation vary, but from the clinical point of view it is very significant. As has been noted previously, a male who has not achieved orgasm by either masturbation or coitus by the age of twenty almost certainly suffers from significant sexual psychopathology, whereas no such conclusion can be drawn in the case of an anorgasmic female.

What consequences flow from these differences? It is generally assumed that the low rate of female masturbation reflects a problem. The advantages of the expression of sensuality and of genital sexuality in development are self-evident. The sense of autonomy is tied, at least subjectively, to the expression

8. This account is drawn from a superb section on adolescent sexuality by Gagnon and Simon, 1973.

of sexuality in many individuals, and there is evidence in the clinical literature that masturbation in adolescent girls is related to high self-esteem and to the subsequent pursuit of career goals (Maslow, 1942, 1939). But it is unlikely that masturbation itself is so beneficial; more likely general assertiveness plays some role in the exploration of both sexuality and role experimentation.

Low masturbation is not a problem per se; it is a problem only insofar as it reflects the female experience of sexuality as reactive rather than autonomous. Neither anorgasmia nor abstention necessarily bodes ill for women. There is no correlation between achievement of orgasm and mental health in women. Part of the confusion about the importance of sexuality is that the importance of sensual-erotic pleasure is not separated from the importance of orgasm. While orgasm does not seem crucial to the achievement of high levels of personality integration in women, the absence of the capacity for sensual pleasure does not bode well for either sex.[9] Part of the confusion stems from the fact that any discrepancy between female and male sexuality is viewed as problematic for females. The male model of sexuality, with its emphasis on orgasm and on sexuality as performance and achievement, is used as the sexual standard for both sexes. Consequently, hand in hand with the preoccupation with "sexual liberation," we see an almost fanatic preoccupation with the achievement of orgasm, multiple orgasms, and "vaginal orgasms." The absence of a focus on genitality in some women may reflect the psychobiographical fact that genitality (in contrast to sensuality) was never invoked.

In the individual woman, relative or absolute disinterest in genital sexuality does not constitute evidence for repression provided that there is some capacity for sensual gratification. Genitality and orgasm do not seem to be crucial to psychological development in women. There are alternate routes for achieving autonomy and consolidating gender. This is not to deny that previously "frigid" women may experience ego expansion when they achieve orgasm for the first time or that many women clinically have significant areas of repressed sexuality. Nor is it to deny that many people achieve their greatest sense of intimacy and union through sexuality. Rather, I argue that one must demonstrate repression rather than assume it, that periodic asexuality and anorgasmia seem consonant with mature ego development in women, and that one should not dictate a tyranny of active sexuality as critical to female liberation.

The degree to which the difference between women and men in the primacy of genital sexuality represents a biological or cultural divergence is an open question. On one hand, as Gagnon and Simon point out, female capacity

9. In this regard, see Ruth Moulton's (1966) interesting observation that aversion to having the breasts touched correlated with poor therapeutic results in her treatment sample of "frigid" women.

for orgasm does not predict the rate of orgasm, thus suggesting the primacy of the cultural input. On the other hand, the frequency of spontaneous ejaculation in adolescent males almost insures the integration of genital sexuality into their psychosexual development and fantasy life, while the paucity of spontaneous orgasm in females may, in turn, be viewed as biological or cultural, pending evidence to establish one or the other position.[10]

Whatever the causes, in this culture there is a relative "muting of female erotic impulsivity," in Dorothy Dinnerstein's (1976) phrase. In libido theory, inhibition of female sexuality is understood as the result of either the circuitous path of libidinal development in females or diminished constitutional endowment. From the culturist perspective, it is the product of selective strictures. While it is undoubtedly true that direct cultural proscriptions influence attitudes, such strictures are not usually decisive in psychological life. Take, for example, the widespread occurrence of male adolescent masturbation in the Victorian era; while the strictures against masturbation were influential, they did not deter the entire male adolescent population.

It is probably more to the point that socialization for girls occurs in such a way that the record of internalized object relations will support the cultural bias. Fear of pregnancy (or fear of the pill) acts in the same direction. Female psychosexual development is only currently being reformulated.[11] One root of low "drive" is in the particular configuration of the female oedipal constellation. The girl finds her erotic rival the source of dependent gratification, a situation that intensifies her oedipal rivalry. Furthermore, the fact that their first erotic object is homosexual may lead some women to repress their earliest experiences of sensuality (this may be one reason some women regard certain sexual acts as shameful). It is only within the context of the specific female oedipal constellation that other psychological contributions to muted erotic sensibility can be understood. It is probable that females start life with as much sensual-erotic potential as males, but certain inhibitions implicit in female object relations countervail, inhibitions solidified by cultural biases and realistic consequences.

Emphasis on the inhibition of female sexuality has almost precluded discussions about the quality of male sexuality, which often seems compulsive in the guise of liberated sexuality. Although both sexes may display inhibited sexuality (e.g., orgasmic inhibition in women, impotence in men), among men one more often sees compulsive sexuality, and not just among men who

10. Ford and Beach (1951) claim that in all human societies that have been studied, "males are more likely than females to stimulate their own sexual organs" (p. 242). In both lower mammals and female primates, there is relatively little masturbation. Consequently, Ford and Beach support an "evolutionary" or biological component. With the same data available, Gagnon and Simon form a cultural interpretation.

11. Dinnerstein's *The Mermaid and the Minotaur* (1976) is the most systematic exposition of this point of view to date. However, her account is hampered somewhat by her completely ahistorical perspective.

have sexual "problems." What stokes male sexuality to this extent? Not libido, but rather the curious phenomenon by which sexuality consolidates and confirms gender. While it is unclear why this linkage occurs in men and not usually in women, the meaning of sexuality to men and the ways it is used are clear. First, sexuality represents domination; witness the widespread rape, control, and transgressive fantasies among men. Consequently, anxiety about any threat to masculine power can be assuaged by sexual encounter. Second, dependency needs can be disguised as sexual; this is especially important for men who are denied any legitimate outlets for dependency gratification. Third, reassurance against castration anxiety should never be underestimated as the motivation for a sexual encounter, particularly in such a competitive culture as ours. Fourth, the need to overcome a primary female identification (as is fostered by the custom of female monopoly of child care) may lead to an overvaluation of the penis and sexuality. In other words, relative gender fragility in men fosters excessive reliance on sexuality. Men appear to engage more in sex for sex's sake (sex shorn of interpersonal meaning) than women do, yet sex carries many hidden symbolic valences for men. One can conclude that it is just as meaningful to talk about male hypersexuality as it is to talk about female hyposexuality.

Given the current liberal climate of thinking about sexuality, there is a danger, not so much of an antierotic attitude, but of insisting too much on the expression of sexuality as the sine qua non of mental health and self-actualization. It is extremely difficult to separate ourselves from the current cultural standards and to judge how highly we should value the expression of sexuality per se. If one does not adhere to a belief in drive theory, one must question whether the overriding emphasis placed on sexuality is inevitable or even desirable. In any neutral discussion, one would have to weigh not just the developmental advantages of active sexuality but also the adaptive advantages of the capacity for abstinence, repression, or suppression. This is particularly true because of the difference between women and men in developmental and adult sexual patterns: it has been too easily assumed that the male pattern of sexuality is freer, beneficial, and more desirable. The way in which sexuality is integrated into personality has greater meaning than the rate of orgasm.

SEXUALITY, POWER, AND DEPENDENCY

Feminist analyses have verified the psychoanalytic insight that sexuality reflects multiple motives. Sexual fantasies are tied to both nonsexual motives, which arise from individual experience, and personality styles that stem from gender-role training. The nonsexual, nonaffectionate motives most often expressed are power and dependency motives. This is true of both actual behavior and dream images and fantasies. It is precisely because sexuality is so often the vehicle for the expression of power relations that sexuality is by its very nature a subject for political inquiry. Obviously, from the feminist and sexual liberationist points of view, the freeing of sexuality from other contaminating motivation is highly desirable. All three paradigms of sexual motivation described previously acknowledge the confluence of sexual and nonsexual motives in sexual and nonsexual behavior. What is extremely interesting, and somewhat paradoxical, is that in libido theory it is theoretically possible to experience sex uncontaminated by other considerations provided that one is able to dissolve cultural inhibitions and individual conflicts. This hope is at the heart of Wilhelm Reich's and Norman O. Brown's cultural prescriptions.

By contrast, in the third paradigm, the meaning of sexuality will always be linked to nonsexual meaning because of the infantile intertwining of sensuality and object relations and because sensual-sexual parts of the body (e.g., the mouth in sucking) have multiple meanings and functions in development. Sex qua sex, without these other meanings, is an impossibility. Sex will always be permeated with meanings that attach to individual and social parameters. In particular, because sensuality develops in the relatively dependent, helpless child, with the earliest gratification attached to powerful adults, it is unlikely that sexuality will ever be completely free of submission-dominance connotations. At the same time, it is possible that being female will not necessarily carry submissive connotations. In other words, the limitations to sexual "liberation," meaning liberation from power contaminants, reside not in the biological nature of sexuality, or in cultural and political arrangements, and certainly not in the sex difference, but in the universal condition of infantile dependence. It may be that the consequences of infantile dependence form the substance of tragedy; such a suspicion, of course, echoes Freud's pessimistic assessment of the human condition.

SEXUAL LIBERATION

While we might expect to be able to predict which groups would favor a historical analysis of sexuality and which a biological one, one is very frequently surprised. For example, one group of feminists postulates a feminine libido (as a version of biological substratum) as opposed to a masculine libido but may view the feminine as superior (Cixous, 1979). Some advocates of the rights of sexual minorities have utilized a "by nature" or congenital argument to justify their demands, yet many homosexuals favor a cultural analysis. With the development of the gay rights movement, the theoretical focus among gays has shifted from the causes of homosexuality to the causes of prejudice against it. Interest in this latter question parallels (and may be instrumental in) the heightened interest in historical and cultural variations of sexual practice and attitudes toward sexuality.

Despite the recent focus on the historical forces that shape sexuality and despite the extremely cogent criticisms of libido conceptualized as drive, Freud's paradigm remains paramount. While it is easy to understand that historical contingency limits our choices and opportunities, it is more difficult to accept the proposition that historical contingency forms a substantial part of the sexual self. We still tend to regard sexuality, as it exists, as representing human nature uncorrupted by social institutions. Take, for example, the enormous influence of the ideology of the sexual liberation movement.

It is a tenet of "sexual liberation" that society has caused individuals to repress their sexuality to their grave detriment. Such a belief is based on the assumption that sexuality is natural, an essence that seeks a particular expression out of its own nature, and, furthermore, that repression of sexuality stunts the personality. In other words, sexual liberation draws on Freud's libido theory and on the theories of some Freudian revisionists (Brown, Marcuse) as its intellectual rationale. It is surprising how many people who consider themselves anti-Freudian or antipsychoanalytic agree fundamentally with the postulates of libido theory. Sexual liberation is strikingly espoused by several groups that have little else in common; one might even say that they border on hostility toward one another, as illustrated in the differences in assumptions among gay, S-M, and mainstream liberationists; feminists; pornography advocates; and practitioners in the sex therapy industry.

Sexual liberation is not the same as female liberation, an observation feminists have been making for years (e.g., Millett, 1970). It is clear from object-relations theory that sexuality is the vehicle for the expression of nonsexual motives. In this culture there may be a basic contradiction between sexual liberation and personal liberation (or autonomy) for women insofar as sexuality as constructed expresses dependent or masochistic trends. Sexuality, even when abundantly expressed, in contrast to repressed sexuality, cannot be liberated as long as women have to define themselves vicariously through their relationship to men.[12] Sexuality then carries the inevitable distortions implicit in psychosexual development and the connotations of instrumental use as the major modality for securing a self-defining sexual liaison. Sexuality takes on too much meaning as interpersonal "glue," too little meaning as pleasure or self-expression.

If one is not an advocate of libido theory, one must take seriously the alternate proposition that sexuality as experienced is not as autonomous, independent, or natural as one subjectively feels it to be. The sexuality so often liberated is a product of sexist conditioning rather than the true individual core

12. Sexual liberation is often confused with sexual activity. Autobiographies such as Evelyn Keyes's *Scarlett O'Hara's Younger Sister: My Lively Life In and Out of Hollywood* (1977) inadvertently make this point abundantly clear.

that sexuality is so often assumed to be. From a feminist point of view, sexual liberation can be a conservative force in society insofar as it enshrines the status quo as bedrock. Any radical social critique must consider the possibility that "id" itself, in part the repository of wishes, is not insulated from culture, although once consolidated, it may be largely immutable in any one individual. The feminist movement must deal not just with personal liberation but also with the institutions that shape desire.

Reserve about sexual liberation as a political movement can conflict with enthusiasm for individual sexuality. On the one hand, it can be conceded that sexuality is plastic, not exclusively dictated by "nature"; on the other hand, the individual's sexuality is not endlessly plastic. Once subjectivity and sexuality are consolidated in the course of individual development, they are as nature to the individual, not to be changed lightly or easily. Thus a healthy respect for eroticism as it is experienced is in order.

In sum, then, sexual liberation, while important and even crucial to some individuals, has significant limitations as social critique and political policy. At its worst, sexual liberation is part of the cult of individuality which demands only legitimization of the expression of the individual's needs, what appears to be her raw "impulse" life, against the demands of society without considering a political reordering of the social order itself. Achievement of the conditions necessary to female autonomy is a precondition for authentic sexual liberation.

Conclusion

Many psychoanalytic theorists currently view sexuality as a motivational system that derives not from drive but from the psychological record of sensual experience integrated through a series of object relations. While the object relations theory of sexuality does not preclude adherence to a drive theory of sexuality, it renders it superfluous. Even in this revised formulation, sexuality still appears to maintain a unique position in psychic development. In particular, sexuality is related to identity formation through the mediating structures of gender and sex print. One of the crucial differences between female and male sexuality is the invariable dependence of gender identity on sexuality in males, a dependence not invariably found in females. The mechanism of this association is unclear but may be related to the female monopoly of child care.

Theories of sexuality have relevance to issues of female sexuality and feminist theory in several ways. Female sexual inhibition or low female sexual "drive" reflects partly cultural intimidation, partly developmental issues. We must avoid using male sexuality as the norm; just as females may be hyposexual, male sexuality frequently appears to be driven rather than liberated. Male sexuality is often driven by the need to express dominance symbolically. While it may be difficult to "liberate" sexuality from power contaminants, it will represent an advance when dominance is not automatically linked with male sexuality, submission with female sexuality.

Although sexuality is experienced as autonomous, part of the self uncorrupted by social institutions, the fantasies attached to desire reflect interiorization from the culture. Therefore, some problematic aspects of sexuality are not immutable. Interiorization is not a singular reflection of cultural values. It occurs in the context of self and object relations. Sexual reform depends not just on attitudinal change regarding sexuality but on significant changes in child rearing and away from the stereotypic rendering of sex roles. Real sexual liberation will come from female liberation, not the other way around.

3

Psychoanalytic Theories of Gender Identity

1983

ETHEL S. PERSON AND LIONEL OVESEY

FOR MANY years, there was essentially no interest in the origins and development of femininity and masculinity. They were simply assumed to correspond by nature to the two biological sexes, despite their historical and cross-cultural variability. The insight that the existence of personality differences between the sexes required explanation was a major intellectual leap. Freud must be credited with that insight, for psychoanalysis was the first comprehensive personality theory that attempted to explain the origins of what we now call gender.

Historically, there have been three psychoanalytic formulations that have attempted to account for the origins of gender: Freud's original concepts; an early oppositional view, stated most clearly by Karen Horney and Ernest Jones; and, more recently, a new theory proposed by Robert Stoller. The first two antedate the conceptualization of sex and gender as separate, though interrelated, entities, while Stoller's formulation makes use of this distinction.

Freud postulated that masculinity was the natural state from which the girl retreated into femininity upon the fateful discovery that she had no penis (Freud, 1924a, 1925, 1931, 1933b). Although Freud's theory clarified a wealth of material about gender, it was primarily referable to oedipal and postoedipal development.

His formulations evoked a strong critique, particularly from Horney (1924, 1926, 1932, 1933) and Jones (1927, 1933, 1935), who proposed an alternative formulation. In contradistinction to Freud's belief that femininity represented thwarted masculinity, they suggested that both femininity and masculinity predated the phallic phase and that each derived separately from innate predispositions. Therefore, femininity and masculinity had prephallic, hence preoedipal, origins.

Stoller (1974, 1975a, 1976) proposed a state of primary femininity in both sexes which he called protofemininity, a remnant of the child's primary identification with its mother. In his view, the content of masculinity represents the male need to overcome a primary feminine identification. In Freudian terms, this would be a kind of reaction-formation.

The purpose of this chapter is threefold: first, to evaluate Freud's original theory of gender identity and the criticisms leveled against it by early writers; second, to review Greenson's concept of disidentification and Stoller's hypothesis of protofemininity, to which it gives rise; and third, to examine how the insights of contemporary psychoanalysis, gained from ego psychology and object relations theory, contribute to our understanding of gender identity, both normal and pathological. These considerations focus our attention on the ways in which gender and sexual development influence each other. Most importantly, we will demonstrate that Freud's paradigm, in which sex orders gender, has been superseded by the opposite paradigm, not yet fully articulated, in which gender orders sex.

History of Definitions of Gender Identity

It was not until 1955 that Money and his associates derived the distinction between sex and gender from their pioneering studies of hermaphroditism (Money et al., 1955a,b; 1956). They demonstrated that the first and crucial step in gender differentiation was self-designation by the child as female or male in accordance with the sex of assignment and rearing. In the same work, they also established that gender differentiation, usually irreversible by eighteen months, was complete by about four and a half years.

In order not to confuse the sex of the genitalia and erotic activities with nongenital and nonerotic sex roles and activities prescribed culturally and historically, Money and his associates (1955a) originated the term "gender role." They defined it as "all those things that a person says or does to disclose himself or herself as having the status of a boy or man, girl or woman, respectively. It includes, but is not restricted to, sexuality in the sense of eroticism. Gender role is appraised in relation to the following: general mannerisms, deportment and demeanor; spontaneous topics of talk in unprompted conversation and casual comment; content of dreams, daydreams, and fantasies; replies to oblique inquiries and projective tests; evidence of erotic practices; and, finally, the person's own replies to direct inquiry."

Money intended the term gender role to be all-inclusive, as defined above. To his chagrin, it failed of this purpose. Years later, Money (1973) gave a good-humored historical account of the introduction of this term and what happened to it:

> In this definition, it was my ivory tower ideal that "all those things that a person says and does to disclose himself or herself as having the status of boy or man, girl or woman, respectively," would unite what the observer perceives and records with what the person knows and feels about himself or herself. In this way one's gender role as self-experienced would be the same as one's gender identity, and there would be no need for two terms. But such an easy circumvention of the mind-body split did not win easy acceptance. Though the term *gender role* immediately was adopted into the scientific language, the term *gender identity* was soon there too—the role belonging to behavior and empirically observable; the identity belonging to the mind and inferentially construed.

To resolve this confusion, Money (1965) wrote the following definition of gender identity and its relationship to gender role:

> The sameness, unity, and persistence of one's individuality as male or female (or ambivalent), in greater or lesser degree, especially as experienced in self-awareness and behavior. Gender identity is the private experience of gender role, and gender role is the public expression of gender identity.

Stoller (1968a), in order to sharpen the distinction between femaleness and maleness (sex) and femininity and masculinity (gender), originated the term "core gender identity," meaning self-identification as female or male. Drawing on the earlier definitions of Money and Stoller, we altered the term gender role to "gender role identity," to make it parallel to core gender identity, thus reflecting on sight the fact that gender role, too, is a form of identification (Ovesey and Person, 1973).

We defined gender identity generically as composed of core gender identity and gender role identity. In this context, core gender identity, the female-male polarity, reflects a biological self-image and can be defined as an individual's self-designation of biological femaleness or maleness. It is the sense of belonging biologically to one sex or the other; that is, the conviction: "I am female" or "I am male." In contrast, gender role identity, the feminine-masculine polarity, reflects a psychological self-image and can be defined as an individual's self-evaluation of psychological femaleness or maleness, the sense of femininity or masculinity; that is, the belief: "I am feminine" or "I am masculine" as measured against societal standards for feminine or masculine behavior.

Freud's Gender Theory

Despite his vast output, only four of Freud's papers dealt predominantly with sexual differences, and these appeared late in his career (Freud, 1924a, 1925, 1931, 1933b). Freud believed that prephallic development was essentially congruent for both sexes. Development diverged only with the child's discovery that boys had penises and girls did not. He derived his theory of femininity and masculinity, what we now call gender role identity, from the contrast between the behavior of the two sexes after that discovery.

Freud believed it was natural that the boy's phallic striving should attach to his mother, who had been his libidinal object since infancy. The Oedipus complex, consisting of a tender attachment to mother and a hostile rivalry with his father, represented the natural outcome of libidinal development. It was only in the context of the Oedipus complex that the boy's earlier perception of the sexual distinction took on meaning. He now surmised, on the basis of his prior experience of loss of the breast and of feces, that his penis might be the price of his libidinal cathexis to his mother. The boy chose the narcissistic cathexis of his penis over the libidinal cathexis of his mother, renounced her, and identified with his father. Thus, it was castration anxiety that resolved the Oedipus complex and led to superego formation, the internalization of paternal authority.[1]

Although the boy's masculinity was enhanced by his identification with his father, it originated in innate active (or masculine) strivings toward his mother. In this sense, Freud viewed masculinity as the innate or natural gender.

Freud believed that, in contrast to the boy, the girl responded to the discovery of the sexual distinction with the assumption that she had been castrated, whereupon she accepted the notion of clitoral inferiority and for the rest of her life suffered from penis envy. The girl held her mother, who sent her into the world so insufficiently equipped, as responsible for her lack of a penis. Therefore, in order to acquire a penis, she renounced her mother as a love object and turned libidinally to her father. Later, when she learned that her castration was irreparable, she wished to have her father's baby in compensation. Thus, in the boy castration anxiety resolved the Oedipus complex, whereas in the girl castration anxiety ushered in the Oedipus complex.

1. Freud, in *The Ego and the Id* (1923), suggested the model of melancholia, in which the individual identifies with a lost object, as a prototype of superego formation. But there is a distinction between the melancholia model and the model of superego formation. In superego formation, the boy identifies not with the renounced, or lost, libidinal object (his mother) but with his competition (the father).

Freud was never able to formulate a satisfactory hypothesis for the ultimate disposition of the Oedipus complex in women. He believed that in males, the Oedipus complex was normally resolved and the superego became its heir. Not so in females, though, in fairness to Freud, he did admit that his insight into these developmental processes in girls was "unsatisfactory, incomplete and vague" (Freud, 1924a). Nevertheless, on balance, he seemed to feel that total dissolution of the Oedipus complex in women was unlikely because it was extremely difficult to give up the two wishes, to possess the father's penis and have the father's child. To the degree that conscience was formed, it was not out of castration anxiety but out of fear of loss of love. In Freud's psychology, penis envy or the masculinity complex was at the center of the female psyche, whereas castration anxiety was central in the male.

Freud believed that the reaction to the discovery of the sexual distinction was decisive not only for female sexual development but also for the development of those personality traits he associated with femaleness: passivity, masochism, and narcissism. The little girl, once she recognized that she could never be masculine, retreated into femininity as an expression of her inherent inferiority. Consequently, femininity derived from the psychological ramifications of a single, momentous, and traumatic perception: the girl's discovery of her anatomic difference from boys, a difference viewed as inadequacy.

Horney and Jones: An Alternate Theory

Even in the 1920s and 1930s not all analysts agreed with Freud's formulations on women. A lively debate on femininity appeared in the psychoanalytic literature in which Freud, on one side, and Horney and Jones, on the other, were the major protagonists.[2]

Horney's was the more original contribution, Jones's confirmatory of her findings. Horney's theoretical dispute with Freud is not generally well understood; current assessments of her views on female development overemphasize her sociological explanations. This misinterpretation of Horney stems from her later fame as a culturist. The essence of the argument was how penis envy ought to be regarded and whether femininity was primarily a retreat from thwarted masculinity or was independent and autonomous. In contrast to Freud, Horney and Jones proposed that femininity was primary, not derivative, and that it antedated the phallic phase and was innate.

In her papers on female psychology, written early in her career, Horney took issue with Freud on three major interrelated points: (1) the cause of the

2. See Fliegel (1973) for a more detailed account.

girl's turn from mother to father, (2) the nature of female genital awareness, and (3) the genesis of penis envy.

It is self-evident that in the usual course of development, the girl does, in fact, substitute the father for the mother as the libidinal object. In the Freudian exposition, the girl turned to her father in search of the penis her mother denied her. In contrast, Horney attributed heterosexual object choice to innate femininity, itself grounded in female biology and awareness of the vagina, not to disappointment at lack of a penis. The future culturist was at that point in her career very much a biologist.

Jones (1935) supported Horney's contention. He suggested that the girl's Oedipus complex—that is, her erotic attachment to her father—developed directly out of innate femininity:

> This view seems to me more in accord with the ascertainable facts, and also intrinsically more probable, than one which would regard her femininity to be the result of an external experience [viewing the penis]. To my mind, on the contrary, her femininity develops progressively from the inner promptings of an instinctual constitution. In short, I do not see a woman . . . as an "homme manqué," as a permanently disappointed creature struggling to console herself with secondary substitutes alien to her nature. The ultimate question is whether a woman is born or made.

Thus, in the opinion of both Jones and Horney, heterosexual desire was innate. The girl desired the penis libidinally and not narcissistically.

The claim for innate femininity and innate heterosexual object choice was linked to biology and the small girl's awareness of her vagina. Horney suggested that the frequency of rape fantasies and fears of vaginal injury demonstrated awareness of the vagina, albeit an awareness frequently repressed later in development. Freud denied that the small girl was aware of her vagina. He believed the girl's leading organ was her clitoris and explained her renunciation of the clitoris as a consequence of penis envy. In Horney's view, the little girl's main concern was with what she had, not with what she didn't have. She was primarily concerned with her vagina, the space within her body, not with the little boy's penis.

Horney agreed with Freud that penis envy was an invariable finding in little girls and confirmed his discovery of penis envy and masculine strivings in the analyses of adult women, but she differed in explaining their origins. For Horney, penis envy was not the cause of the girl's turn to her father but the result of a defensive flight from libidinal and oedipal desires and identification with the abandoned object. Thus, she turned Freud's argument on its head. In essence, she substituted an object relations analysis for the masculinity complex in women in the place of an explanation grounded in penis envy as an existential fact of female life.[3]

The Fate of the Freud-Horney Debate

As Fliegel (1973) pointed out, the differences raised in the debate over the origins of femininity were never really resolved: the objections to Freud's position simply disappeared from subsequent literature. Mitchell (1974) concluded that there was a crystallization of two opposite positions "and that within psychoanalysis little momentous has been added since." Both Fliegel and Mitchell traced the contours of the debate, but neither could explain why the subject dropped out of any psychoanalytic dialogue for so many years, only to be renewed in the 1970s.

Contemporary observers confirm Horney's and Jones's contention that female and male behavior is discrepant at a very early age, prior to the child's awareness of the anatomic sexual difference, but have held that their explanations, as well as Freud's, are too narrowly derived. Blind children, boys with congenital absence of the penis (Stoller, 1968a), and girls with congenital absence of the vagina (Stoller, 1968a) have all been observed to differentiate along gender lines corresponding to their biological sex. These observations prove that gender differentiation cannot be primarily derivative from body awareness or perception of the sexual distinction.

Horney's and Jones's formulations, like Freud's, give too much priority to perceptions of genitals and genital sensations. They linked gender identity almost exclusively to body ego. Freud's original question, "What is the effect on the girl's mental life of the discovery that the clitoris is an inferior penis?" was replaced by the questions "Is the little girl aware of her vagina?" and, if so, "What are the consequences for mental life of this awareness?" But as Kleeman (1976) says, "Genital sensations and genital self-stimulation contribute to core gender identity . . . but I do not believe that this genital sensation and awareness normally act as major organizer[s] of behavior."

3. She suggested (1926) that the term "primary penis envy" should be applied to penis envy demonstrable in childhood and based simply on the anatomic difference between the sexes. She attributed it to envy of the male child's mode of urination. Primary penis envy was a universal but transient stage in which the girl was said to be at a realistic disadvantage because she lacked the narcissistic, exhibitionistic component of urination. This stage was without substantive consequences for subsequent female development.

Horney derived the adult masculinity complex, which she called the "flight from womanhood," from the Oedipus complex, not childhood penis envy. She found "that the girls and women whose desire to be men is often so glaringly evident have at the very onset of life passed through a phase of extremely strong father fixation."

When the girl renounced her ties to her father, she identified with him instead. The major difference between the female and male oedipal resolutions is that the female identifies with the abandoned object, whereas the boy does not; instead, he strengthens his tie to the father. Ironically, Horney is more faithful to Freud's model of melancholia in discussing oedipal resolution than Freud himself was.

Paradoxically, Horney, the culturist, attributed gender to innate heterosexuality. For her and for Jones, femininity and masculinity were created in nature and correspond to biology. In contrast, Freud posited that masculinity was created in nature while femininity was "born" of psychological despair.[4] Horney and Jones emphasized, as did Freud, that there was a particular problem in female development, but to them the problematic area shifted conceptually from penis envy to dread of being a woman.

Stoller, like Horney and Jones, posits gender consciousness as integral to emerging self-consciousness. But he fails to maintain masculinity and femininity as parallel constructs. He reverses Freud's assumption of masculinity as the natural state, arguing that for both sexes, the first gendered state is femininity, not masculinity.

Stoller's Gender Theory

Well aware that gender identification precedes the child's discovery of the sexual distinction, Stoller looks for the roots of gender in the period of infancy. He ascribes primary femininity, "protofemininity," to the earliest phase of life and views it as an integral part of emerging identity in both sexes. This raises a special problem for boys, who must disidentify so they may achieve an appropriate masculine identity.

DISIDENTIFICATION

The concept of disidentification derived from Greenson's therapy with a five-and-a-half-year-old boy whom Greenson believed to be a "transsexual transvestite."[5] Greenson (1966) had the felicitous insight that the boy confused the wish to *have* the mother with the wish to *become* the mother. Thus, he inferred that the wish for an ongoing affective tie to the mother was expressed by the assumption of a female identification. He regarded the boy's interest in his mother's clothes as both "a failure of individuation and a defense against separation anxiety." Basing his formulations primarily on the work of Greenacre (1958) and Jacobson (1964), he observed that gender identification was only one aspect of identity in general: "in early infancy both girls and boys form a primitive symbiotic-identification with the mother's person. . . . This results in

4. Mitchell (1974) claims that Freud posits "man and woman are *made* in culture." Chodorow (1980) points out that "Freud holds the inconsistent and sexist position that man is born whereas woman is made." Both Mitchell and Chodorow recognize Horney's biological stance despite her culturist overlay.

5. It is doubtful that this child, Lance, was on the transsexual-transvestite continuum at all, as Greenson believed, since so many of his personality characteristics (interest in make-up, role diffusion, theatricality) resemble those one obtains retrospectively in histories from effeminate homosexuals, not from transsexuals or transvestites (see Person and Ovesey, 1974a,b).

the formation of a symbiotic relationship with the mother. . . . The next step . . . is the differentiation of self-representation from object-relationships."

In focusing on the formation of gender identity, Greenson suggested that four factors were of crucial significance: (1) awareness of anatomical and physiological structures in oneself; (2) sex of assignment; (3) a so-called biological force, inferred also by Stoller (1968a), which only rarely was strong enough to counteract the first two factors; and (4) in the boy, the necessity for disidentification from the mother and the establishment of a new identification with the father. This fourth factor, disidentification, made gender identity more precarious developmentally for boys than for girls. The boy's continuing identification with the mother might impede the consolidation of male gender identity, whereas it facilitated the establishment of female gender identity in the girl.

The actual process of disidentification was only briefly described. Greenson suggested that it was "a special problem because the boy must attempt to renounce the pleasures and security-giving closeness that identification with the mothering person affords, and he must form an identification with the less accessible father." He stressed that both parents must facilitate the counter-identification, the mother by allowing and promoting it, the father by providing the boy with "motives" for identifying with him. Thus, he focused on the role of parental behavior in insuring that the process was a success. As far as intrapsychic factors in the boy were concerned, Greenson singled out envy of the opposite sex as a major obstacle to this process, hence particularly destructive to the consolidation of male gender identity. The reason for this, he suggested, was "that envy is one of the main driving forces in man's wish to be a woman and originates in the early envy all children feel towards the mother" (Greenson, 1968). It is important to note that in Greenson's formulation, any failure in the process of disidentification was understood in terms of motivation and defense.

PROTOFEMININITY

Stoller believed that the boy must overcome his identification with his mother in order to achieve masculinity. He charged that Freud erred twice in giving the advantage to males in psychosexual development (Stoller, 1974): "first . . . he assumed as a biological given that maleness was the firmer, more natural state (which, as we have noted, present-day research contradicts). The second was that he said the male is off to a healthier start because his relationship with his mother is by definition heterosexual." Instead, as Stoller (1975a) saw it: "While it is true that the infant boy's first love object is his mother, there is an earlier phase in which he is merged with her before she exists as a separate object; that is, he has not yet distinguished his own body and psyche as different from hers—and she is a female with a feminine gender identity. It is possible, then, that the boy does not start heterosexual as Freud presumed, but rather that he must separate himself from his mother's female body and femininity and experience a process of individuation into masculinity." To put this another way, the boy must overcome his identification with his mother and identify with his father in order to achieve masculinity. This is in contrast to Freudian gender theory, where the major problem is the girl's switch in love object from mother to father.

At the same time, the girl benefits from this primary femininity (Stoller, 1976): "There is a conflict built into the sense of maleness that females are spared; core gender identity in males is not, as I have mistakenly said, quite so immutable. It always carries with it the urge to regress to an original oneness with mother."

In this view, the bedrock of feminine identification means that all men must struggle to overcome a feminine identification. Men, therefore, in general, are more susceptible to problems in gender identity than women; in particular, they suffer more from cross-gender disorders. Insofar as protofemininity is a "normal" developmental stage for both sexes, many attributes of masculinity, such as "a preoccupation with being strong and independent, untender, cruel, polygamous, misogynous, perverse . . . may be reactive to the male's fear of a regressive pull to that early symbiotic merger with the mother" (Stoller, 1976).

How, precisely, does protofemininity come about? Stoller viewed the early environment of the infant as "feminine" simply because it is bounded by the mother-child symbiosis. In order to account for early intrapsychic femininity, he fell back on imprinting, a mechanism he had proposed as the etiological agent in male transsexualism (Stoller, 1968a): "our theory must also make room for other nonmental mechanisms (i.e., not motivated by the individual) by which the outside reality also is emplaced within." Thus, Stoller suggested that it is imprinting that insures that the bedrock gender identification in all infants, male as well as female, is initially female.

CRITIQUE

While Horney and Jones were right in giving the same weight to "primary" femininity as to masculinity, to designate both as "innate" and derive them from innate heterosexuality is to obscure the complex development of both gender and sexuality. Stoller, by proposing a stage of protofemininity, apparently solved the problem of the origins of primary femininity but offered no parallel construction for primary masculinity. As Kleeman (1976) pointed out, "Psychoanalytic theory of *primary identification* leaves unanswered why a normal three-year-old boy is clearly a boy even though his contact has been largely with a female adult." Furthermore, there is no evidence that the symbiotic state that exists prior to self-object differentiation is one of primary identification that confers gender behavior or gender identity on the infant.

However, Stoller's theories have been accorded some plausibility because they seem, at first blush, to explain certain prominent features of cross-gender disorders. In order to understand fully the limitations of Stoller's theory of primary femininity, we must turn to a consideration of psychoanalytic theories of gender disorders, both Stoller's and our own (Ovesey and Person, 1973).

Psychoanalytic Theories of Cross-Gender Disorders

Sexologists of different theoretical persuasions agree that cross-gender identity problems as manifested in transsexualism, transvestism, and homosexuality occur more frequently among males than females. Male-to-female transsexuals exceed female-to-male in the ratio of four to one, transvestites (fetishistic heterosexual cross-dressers) are exclusively (or almost exclusively) male, and effeminate male homosexual cross-dressers, at least in terms of both clinical and social visibility, numerically far exceed their masculine female counterparts. Cross-gender identity problems not only predominate in males but occur earlier. Femininity in boys may be seen as early as a year; masculinity in girls is hardly ever noted before three to four years of age. Femininity in boys almost always has consequences for development, but this is not true for masculinity in girls. Explanations for this differential in sex ratio have varied, but one factor stands out. There are significant consequences for gender development depending on whether the child's primary caretaker is of the same or the opposite sex (Greenson, 1968; Person, 1974).

There are essentially two psychoanalytic explanations for this discrepancy in the sex incidence of cross-gender disorders. Stoller argues that the male and the female have fundamentally different underlying tasks; the boy must disidentify from mother while the girl need not. He argues that this makes the boy more vulnerable to gender disorders. In contrast, we take disidentification to be the same process as separation-individuation. Consequently, we argue that both sexes must disidentify; otherwise, the outcome is autism. The underlying task for both sexes is separation-individuation, and it is equally difficult for both. However, when separation-individuation is disrupted, the intrapsychic reparative maneuvers the child undertakes have different consequences for males and females. If either the male or the female child experiences enough disruption in the separation-individuation phase, he or she may be left with borderline features. But in the male, borderline personality may be complicated by gender aberrations, the source of which we will elaborate later. First, we will address the serious limitations of Stoller's theoretical model.

Stoller confronted the problem of establishing evidence for a protofeminine phase in both sexes by turning to his work on male transsexuals. He saw male transsexuals as a natural "experiment" that demonstrates protofemininity in both sexes. Thus, his formulation of the etiology of transsexualism is crucial to his theory of protofemininity. He argued that transsexualism is "*a keystone for understanding the development of masculinity and femininity in all people*" (Stoller, 1974, see also 1976).[6]

Stoller believed that if the mother extends a blissful symbiosis with her infant son too long, the result is femininity in the little boy, the extreme case of which is transsexualism. He regarded this femininity as the product of the imprinting of femininity on the malleable infant's unresisting protopsyche and unfinished central nervous system. Imprinting produces a conflict-free feminine core gender identity, so that the little boy feels himself to be female despite demonstrable male anatomy. Stoller's argument, then, is that the femininity one sees in male transsexuals demonstrates the feminizing effects of the infantile "biopsychic" environment, one that we do not usually see in normal development but can infer.

Yet, his hypothesis is significantly flawed in both its data base and the inferred mechanism of imprinting. Stoller himself acknowledged the most serious problem in his general theory, that of the data base for establishing a protofeminine phase. According to Stoller, the "behavioral surface" of the infant's femininity, whether the infant is female or male, is not evident before the age of one year. By that time the earlier hypothesized feminine state in boys may be covered over by masculinity, so that the earlier phase "will never be manifested to an observer." If the gender markers denoting masculinity and femininity do not appear before the age of one year, there is no observable evidence for Stoller's assertion of a protofeminine state in normal boys—or girls, for that matter. In other words, he has no data base.

But even in male transsexuals, there is no data base to establish primary femininity. Femininity does not appear earlier than one year of age (in most reported cases of boyhood femininity or effeminacy, the boys are three to four years of age). Therefore, one cannot observe "protofemininity" even in those boys destined to have a cross-gender disorder. Stoller offered no explanation for this delay in the manifestations of the hypothetical imprinting.

6. Stoller does not consider it paradoxical that he establishes primary femininity in women by arguing from data collected on male transsexuals (Stoller, 1976). This line of reasoning is reminiscent of the peculiarity in Freud's description of female masochism, originally formulated only as it occurs in men (Freud, 1924).

Implicit in his formulation is a conceptual confusion between observable behavior and subjective identity. His model suggests that identity will be revealed in behavior and, conversely that feminine behavior reveals a feminine identification. But it is precisely the discovery of the frequent discrepancy between self-identity and behavior that is so revealing in the study of transsexualism. The "failure to individuate," as a model, does not adequately distinguish between the genesis of feminine behavior, on the one hand, and the genesis of feminine identity, on the other. Often they don't coincide.[7]

As regards the proposed mechanism of imprinting, there are three major objections.[8] First, there is no evidence of imprinting in humans. Second, imprinting as an ethological concept accounts for object choice, not identity. The ducklings followed Lorenz; we do not know how they self-identified. Even if imprinting existed as a mechanism for the transmission of "femininity," behavioral attributes, not identity, would be imprinted. Third, there is the question of what Stoller believed was being imprinted; in other words, what constitutes the mother's femininity that is hypothetically placed within the child's unconscious. While it is true that the infant's primary caretaker is usually genitally female, the fact of sex does not suggest what feminine characteristics may permeate the biopsychic environment. Paradoxically, Stoller seemed at this juncture to confuse sex and gender, a distinction he otherwise rightly emphasized.

Most important as a critique of Stoller's theory is the question many investigators raise about his etiological explanation of transsexualism and his insistence that it is nonconflictual. Most psychodynamically oriented psychiatrists and psychologists find clinical evidence for a conflictual basis for transsexualism (Golosow and Weitzman, 1969; Ovesey and Person, 1973; Person and Ovesey, 1974a,b). Stoller, in contrast to Greenson, stressed nonconflictual rather than conflictual elements in the genesis of femininity in boys and men. Consequently, he disregarded Greenson's adaptational and motivational approach. His theory appears to be continuous with Greenson's, but in reality breaks with it conceptually. Stoller's theory of imprinting, implying a fixed female core gender, cannot account for the fluctuation of the transsexual wish in any one patient or for those patients in whom the wish first appears in adulthood; a conflictual motivational hypothesis easily addresses these issues.

7. The original concept of disidentification derived from a study of Lance, who displayed both feminine behavior and female identifications. But in transvestites, identity, not behavior, may be feminine. Take, for example, the common observation that transvestites often engage in traditionally supermasculine pursuits (mountain climbing, piloting, etc.), despite a strong feminine identification. In contrast, in some homosexuals, behavior may be feminine or effeminate, while core gender identity seldom is. One needs a model that is capable of explaining the frequent discrepancies between behavior and identity.

8. Stoller acknowledged only indirectly the many apt critiques the concept of imprinting has invoked. In an appendix (1979), he suggested substituting the word "fixing," which frees one from misusing the concept "imprinting," but he changed only the word, not the concept.

In contrast to Stoller's theories, we (Ovesey and Person, 1973; Person and Ovesey, 1974a,b) have proposed that the transsexual's femininity is derived from fantasies of symbiotic merger with his mother as a defense against separation anxiety. We have demonstrated that in transsexuals, core gender identity is ambiguous, not unambiguously female. This ambiguity, when there are no physical or biological abnormalities, is the outcome of conflict, usually engendered during the phase of separation-individuation, with subsequent distortions in self-representation and object relations.

Both girls and boys must separate and individuate; that is, they must disidentify, if we must use that term. Girls and boys are probably equally susceptible to disruptions in the process of separation-individuation with resultant separation anxiety. Both girls and boys may resort to the fantasy of merger with the mother in order to be, to have, or to be the same as she is in the service of mastering that separation anxiety. In both sexes, the perpetuation of these merger fantasies disrupts the sense of self and object relations as well as certain ego functions. Such difficulties in separation-individuation are equally serious in the two sexes, often resulting in a borderline organization of personality.

But in boys, such merger fantasies may, in addition, be accompanied by a gender marker. When the merger fantasy persists (or is reinvoked) after cognitive awareness or imitative motor behavior has emerged, ambiguous core gender and cross-gender behavior and identification may appear.[9] Insofar as male gender is tenuous, castration anxiety will be experienced more intensely; thereby merger fantasies cause further (secondary) disruption to personality development. For these reasons, the merger fantasy leads to the higher incidence of cross-gender disorders among males—transsexualism, transvestism, and cross-dressing homosexuality.[10] In all these disorders, there is evidence of ambiguous core gender.

9. Just as in males, in females, too, merger fantasies may be enacted. In fact, one of the most frequent clinical findings in women is the patient's complaint that she speaks with the voice of her mother or acts like her mother (eloquently described by Friday, 1977). Such behavior, generally subsumed under the rubric "negative identification," is threatening to the sense of separateness but does not carry gender connotations, as it may (or may not) in males.

10. Yet merger fantasies are not in themselves predictive of the nature or extent of psychopathology. Separation anxiety and merger fantasies occur intermittently as normal phenomena during the separation-individuation phase of infantile development, and they are widespread findings in many psychiatric disorders, particularly in the borderline range of psychopathology. It is extremely important to emphasize, as we have done elsewhere, that even in the presence of pervasive merger fantasies, not every male will display cross-gender characteristics (Person and Ovesey, 1974a,b,c). Among borderline males, there is usually no ambiguity of core gender identity or gender role identity despite the prevalence of merger fantasies. Although most patients with full-blown cross-gender disorders do have borderline features, they are distinguished from other borderline patients by impairment of both core gender identity and gender role identity. The merger fantasy appears to be a necessary but not sufficient condition to produce ambiguous core gender identity and cross-gender behavior. It is the merger fantasy, not the prolongation of a hypothetical and unproved protofeminine state, that is central to the genesis of the cross-gender disorders, although the fantasy per se cannot be considered the sole etiological factor.

In sum then, our formulation is markedly different from Stoller's. He suggested that separation-individuation is per se more difficult for males, who begin with a female identification and who must disidentify. We do not believe that separation-individuation is intrinsically more difficult for males, as Stoller suggests, or for females, as Chodorow (1978) suggests. But, when conflicts arise in separation-individuation, they are adaptively resolved in a way that has different consequences for the two sexes.

Toward a Psychoanalytic Theory of Gender

As already noted, many observers have confirmed that female behavior and male behavior are discrepant within the first years of life, before the child knows the sexual difference. Because the roots of gender differentiation precede the phallic period, Freud's gender theory cannot be correct.

For Freud, masculinity is the more natural state; for Stoller, femininity. In fact, for Stoller, femininity is built into earliest unconsciousness in both sexes. But if one cannot demonstrate Stoller's contention that a protofeminine state exists, based solely on his work with transsexuals, then one is not justified in assuming that the natural state is feminine. If we cannot accept his model of transsexualism, there is no evidence whatsoever to support a hypothetical protofeminine state. The assertion that it regularly occurs in both sexes (or either) is completely unproved; consequently, Stoller's theory of gender is purely speculative.

We agree with Horney (1924, 1926, 1932, 1933) and Jones (1927, 1933, 1935) that femininity and masculinity must be viewed as parallel constructs, but their assertion that gender derives from innate heterosexuality is incorrect, insofar as sexual object choice appears to be acquired rather than innate.

Money and his colleagues demonstrated that the first and crucial step in gender differentiation is the self-designation by the child as male or female; this designation arises in agreement with the sex of assignment and has unconscious as well as conscious components. Most investigators agree that gender differentiation is observable by the end of the first year of life and, under normal circumstances, is immutable by the third (with the exception of one major study; see Imperato-McGinley, 1979). Core gender derives from nonconflictual learning experience, not from conflict.[11] Core gender identity, once established, locates the appropriate object for imitation and identification.[12]

11. Stoller made this point in his studies on primary femininity in women, but his argument that protofemininity occurs in both sexes confuses his contribution and detracts from consideration of both "primary" femininity *and* masculinity.

12. Why core gender is of such crucial importance in organizing personality is still an open question. But it

The original analytic emphasis on genital sensations and genital self-stimulation, the discovery of the sexual distinction, castration anxiety, penis envy, and the Oedipus complex as constituent elements of gender has not been abolished, but these factors are now regarded as superimposed upon earlier influences in gender differentiation. They are all easily identified in contemporary analyses. Although they are no longer deemed the bedrock of gender, clinically they remain the central focus.[13] Freud's contention that the oedipal period is crucial to the divergent development of gender is correct. But, in fact, his account tacitly assumes that the child has already achieved an appropriate core gender identity.

Early object relations are different in the two sexes and decisively influence certain attributes of femininity and masculinity. These are operative in those preoedipal identifications and fantasies that emerge as soon as the infant has differentiated self from object. It is only by learning their gender and identifying with the "appropriate" parent that children are launched into the oedipal period.[14] *In this sense, one can say that gender precedes sexuality in development and organizes sexuality, not the reverse* (Person, 1980).

To say that gender orders sexuality is not to detract from the autonomous qualities of sexuality, such as intensity, or from interactions between sexuality and gender. Our formulation emphasizes that gender, itself the result of postnatal events, organizes object choice (Baker, 1981) and sexual fantasies. This point of view is affirmed by various intersex and pseudohermaphroditic studies. For example, Money (1965), discussing eroticism among AGS (adrenogenital syndrome) women exposed to elevated prenatal androgens, treated and untreated, says: "the imagery of the erotic thoughts and desires is all suitably feminine in keeping with the sex of rearing and the psychosexual identity. The unfeminine aspect of the experience applies only to the threshold and the frequency of arousal, and to the amount of sexual initiation that it might engender."[15] What happens in fetally virilized genetic females unambiguously

---

does play an organizing role in psychic structure. The question is really why only two gender possibilities exist. This question has been eloquently raised by Fineman (1979), who suggests that the "fixity of two gender roles seems to confirm Freud's penile semantics."

13. The central psychodynamic conflicts that emerge during analyses are gender-discrepant. Freud's formulation of male psychodynamics has stood the test of time much better than his formulation of female development. And, indeed, most contemporary observers would echo Freud in placing castration anxiety at the heart of the male psyche. When we turn to women, it seems unlikely that penis envy is the central conflict. Instead, what we see clinically is an array of dynamics more variable than that among males. Discussing superego formation, Freud emphasized fear of loss of love as central. We find this far more prevalent in neurotic conflicts among women than penis envy.

14. I have added quotation marks to the word "appropriate." Looking back, I see our statement as inadverently restricted to heterosexuals. Boys who identify as feminine will identify more with the mother resulting in a higher incidence of homosexual object choices, and girls who identify more with a male figure will be more likely to be lesbians. (Footnote added, 1998.)

15. In later publications, Money reported a higher incidence of homosexuals among this population. See Person (1993) in this volume. (Footnote added, 1998.)

reared as males? Money and Dalery (1977) reported a sample who turned out to have normal male gender identity and heterosexuality (i.e., they chose females as sexual objects). Consequently, most psychoendocrinologists hypothesize that gender identity is determined by rearing and not by innate factors, although certain gender behaviors are influenced by innate factors (prenatal hormone environment), and that sexual orientation is most likely determined by rearing (Baker, 1981).

In sum, there is no evidence that the original (or natural) gender state is masculine, as proposed by Freud, feminine, as suggested by Stoller, or innate, as proposed by Horney and Jones. Normal core gender identity arises from the sex of assignment and rearing. It is nonconflictual and is cognitively and experientially constructed. On the other hand, gender role identity, both normal and aberrant, is shaped by body, ego, socialization, and sex-discrepant object relations. Unlike normal core gender identity, it represents a psychological achievement and is fraught with psychological conflict.

Can psychoanalysis, the science of conflict, provide a comprehensive theory of gender identity? No, it cannot, since it can play no part in explaining the origin of conflict-free normal core gender identity.[16] However, as we have demonstrated in this chapter, psychoanalytic theory can sharply illuminate those aberrations of core gender identity that stem developmentally from conflicts during the separation-individuation phase and produce gender ambiguity. Similarly, psychoanalytic theory is essential for the understanding of both normal and aberrant gender role identity.

16. We have been asked how we can propose a psychoanalytic theory of gender disorder when we raise doubts about the existence of a viable psychoanalytic theory of gender identity. There are two answers to that question. First, we do not believe that psychoanalytic theory must be taken in its narrowest sense, as the science of conflict. But, if we accept the narrow definition, we would still have to rely on psychoanalytic theory to conceptualize cross-gender disorders. An analogous example will make the point; although learning is an autonomous ego function, many learning problems (obviously excluding learning disabilities) are conflict-derived.

4

The Influence of Values in Psychoanalysis: The Case of Female Psychology

1983

ETHEL S. PERSON

AT THE heart of the psychoanalytic enterprise is the purpose of examining the ways in which thoughts and behaviors, beliefs, preferences, and values are influenced by unconscious mental processes. Psychoanalysis is a discipline that fosters skepticism about the apparent meaning of surface phenomena, thereby challenging the certainty of either revealed or objective truth, the first (religion) explicitly and the second (science) implicitly. Like philosophy, psychoanalysis alerts us that we must look for the values and ideology underlying any body of knowledge, including psychoanalysis itself.

No cultural enterprise is value free, including science. Science values objective knowledge. Objectivity is fundamental to the pursuit of science, as is evident in the historical fact that science is an achievement of Western culture, not an autonomous development in every culture. Yet, as Kuhn (1962) has pointed out, scientific research is based on beliefs about the nature of the world. Although these beliefs appear to be objective and truthful, they may be superseded when new findings or anomalies arise to contradict the existing set of beliefs, assumptions, or traditions. Thus, despite its objectivity, science is both the product of cultural values and a contributor to the cultural evolution of values. According to Hogan and Emler (1978), "Science supports the myth of developmental progress. Innovation, experiment, the rebuilding of theory, all these are justified because they will make things better . . . the extraordinary success of science in the modern era has contributed to the influential position of individualism and rationalism" (p. 486).

A similarly complex relationship exists between cultural values and psychoanalysis. Psychoanalysis, beginning with Freud's assumptions, embodies values central to Western culture. Chief among these are an interest in the individual and his or her welfare and a commitment to self-knowledge as an end in itself. Rieff (1961) claimed that "Freud created the masterwork of the century, a psychology that . . . unriddled—to use Emerson's prophetic catalogue of subjects considered inexplicable in his day—'language, sleep, madness, dreams, beasts, sex' " (p. xx). By insisting that nothing human was alien to him, Freud revealed a commitment to the worth of the individual, no matter how marginal or mad. Freud's work is thus an integral part of an intellectual tradition that elevates individualism to an ideology.

In turn, psychoanalysis has given a distinctive shape to intellectual life in the twentieth century. According to Rieff, "Freud's doctrine, created piecemeal and fortunately never integrated into one systematic statement, has changed the course of Western intellectual history; moreover, it has contributed as much as doctrine possibly can to the correction of our standards of conduct" (p. xx). Indeed, some psychiatrists and critics of culture have raised the objection that individuals living in an era of declining objective moral authority attempt to substitute the goals of mental health and normalcy for a comprehensive moral system (Rieff, 1966; Morgenthau and Person, 1978; Gross, 1978). Psychoanalysis and values, then, like science and values, ply a two-way street.

This discussion is meant to emphasize the fact that no *cultural* enterprise can be value free. A cultural enterprise must, by definition, be value laden and embody a set of beliefs. Values are not always easily separated from prejudice and bias. Values may be generally defined as highly abstracted ideas about what is good or bad, right or wrong, desirable or undesirable. Prejudice and bias carry a particularly pejorative connotation. To be prejudiced or biased means to judge without adequate knowledge or examination and to come to a premature conclusion, usually unfavorable. Therefore, it is important to distinguish the values that are implicit in the context and framework of any cultural enterprise from the values and prejudices that contaminate the applications or the theoretical assumptions of an enterprise.

In psychoanalysis, as in the other behavioral sciences, observations and hypotheses are inevitably distorted by historical bias and sometimes, more pervasively, by values buried in major theoretical assumptions. As Macklin (1973) has pointed out, values are implicit in psychoanalysis in at least three ways. Values are held by the patient, values are held by the therapist, and values are implicit or explicit in the theory. As long as those values coincide, they go virtually unnoticed. Cultural biases become most apparent during times of social change, times when they no longer coincide.

Freud sincerely but mistakenly believed that analysts could be ethically neutral and that the observations of analysis were value free. Freud himself, however, offers an example of the influence of bias in his own beliefs about the nature of femininity.

Under the impact of changing cultural norms, we have become aware of the existence of sexism in all the psychotherapies, including psychoanalysis, and the theoretical justifications for sexism in fundamental psychoanalytic assumptions. Changing prescriptions and changing concepts of the female role(s), as well as the persistence of outdated theories, have led us to scrutinize value biases implicit in practice and theory.

In this chapter I describe changes in the definition of normative femininity and in psychoanalytic formulations of female psychology. Reformulations of female development seem to have lagged unduly, given the considerable countervailing data and the serious critiques of early formulations. As I will demonstrate, the reasons for this lag illustrate the methodological problems and the value biases in psychoanalytic theory making that transcend the special case. The chapter explores a dual concept of values, examining some of the perversions of values (biases, prejudices) that have developed and also reviewing the beliefs and commitments (general values) that underlie psychoanalytic formulations. By focusing on one example, I demonstrate how new data, both from psychoanalysis and from other fields, have forced a reexamination of the methodology of psychoanalysis and of the values embedded in its major theoretical assumptions.

Sexism and Changing Goals in Therapy

Many feminist scholars and mental health professionals have used the theme of sexism in psychotherapy to illustrate the value bias underlying therapeutic decisions and practices and theoretical formulations. The concept of "normalcy" or appropriate femininity necessarily colors the assessment of both pathology and treatment goals. According to Broverman and colleagues (1970), mental health professionals, rather than challenge gender stereotypes, shared popular biases. Dependency and passivity were seen as normal female qualities and assertiveness and independence as normal male qualities. Accordingly, mental health professionals attributed role dissatisfaction in women to psychopathology. The debate about normal female development and femininity relates to the more general debate in psychiatry about the distinction between difference (or deviation) and mental illness. Arguments about "what women want" and whether these goals reflect health or neurosis are analogous in form to arguments about homosexuality or political dissidence.

Because psychoanalytic theory proposes mental health norms, it also implies therapeutic goals. This is true regardless of what one proposes as the primary mental health objective—genital maturity, motherhood as the ultimate resolution of penis envy, the cult of true femininity, mature object relations, or generativity. For clinicians, knowledge of this existential dilemma, what has been called the dual descriptive-normative role of theory (Macklin, 1973), translates into vexing clinical problems. Clinicians no longer have the certainty of fixed, external definitions of abnormality and mental health, previously conceptualized as mature genitality or as the achievement of gender-appropriate behavior. And the therapeutic community stands charged "with fostering traditional gender roles, stereotyping of women, biased expectations and devaluation of women, sexist use of theoretical constructs, and responding to women as sex objects, including seduction" (Vaughter, 1976, p. 140).

WHAT WOMEN WANT: CHANGING TREATMENT GOALS

Analysts disagree strongly about whether the nature of psychological illness has changed or whether we have simply developed a new language for describing old problems. Some classes of clinical problems do seem virtually unchanged, such as the biologically derived mental illnesses. But a decisive shift has occurred in the problems of living that patients predominantly complain about and in the goals they seek.

Attitudinal changes toward sex, gender, and pair-bonding implicit in the sexual revolution, the women's movement, and the crisis of the family have complex and contradictory implications for opportunity and security in women's lives. With the changing definitions of femininity, women have assumed greater latitude in their lives; the modern woman does not entirely resemble her more traditional counterpart. Many goals have changed radically, while some remain the same. In any case, we can no longer be dogmatic about the appropriate choices in women's life trajectories. A greater range of plausible and acceptable adaptations exists, stemming from the dramatic changes that have taken place in the cultural milieu. Whatever the major presenting symptom, newer treatment goals, insofar as they are articulated, are cast in terms of making possible a woman's individual enhancement in the professional, sexual, or relational sphere. The emerging pattern is one of activity and achievement, not one of passive acceptance, and while underlying conflicts may be the same, different adaptive resolutions are sought.

Increasingly, women are seeking treatment as an explicit aid to their search for autonomy and self-realization, and they believe that the vehicle for this search is their professional or creative achievement. This stands in marked contrast to goals commonly stated twenty years ago. At that time, such ambitions were often believed to represent masculine aspirations and hence to be misguided. Penis envy and its attendant anxieties were considered to lie at the heart of a woman's work problems. Today, the goal is to work through any inhibition of assertion or achievement motivation.

Women today are also seeking greater sexual fulfillment. They are looking for new modes of interpersonal relationships, different from the more traditional role in which submissiveness and ingratiation were deemed so integral to their "femininity." Today, women place increasing value on egalitarian relations, and this extends to the therapy situation. Many more women seek female therapists in order to avoid the stereotypical relationship in which a young and helpless female patient is dependent on an older and authoritative male.

Some goals, of course, are not at all new. Women are still motivated toward stable affiliative relations, as are men. Many seek treatment because they are unable to form a permanent relationship, while others seek it to help them through the breakup of a marriage, a deteriorating relationship, or the stresses that accrue from the breakdown of the family.

Shifting goals highlight the intrinsic problem in the dual descriptive and normative roles of theory. The serious potential for therapeutic bias in goal setting is sometimes underestimated. Take, for example, Barglow and Schaefer's (1976) response to a hypothetical question raised by Marmor (1973) about treating Ibsen's Nora. Should an analyst interpret her penis envy and rejection of a normal female role, or should he encourage her healthy rebellion? Barglow and Schaefer disavow the dilemma, asking, "Are these really psychoanalytic problems? Psychoanalysis, after all, is not an ideology (the critics to the contrary), but professes to be a science" (p. 322). In my opinion, Marmor was right, and Barglow and Schaefer have missed the point: an analyst's response (countertransference) must be permeated by his or her world view. Preferences and beliefs influence the therapist's judgment and may thereby slant interpretations or therapeutic emphasis.

Therapists communicate their values not primarily with directives but with silences, questions, and the very rhythms and cadences of the therapeutic hour. Sometimes, though, their directives are explicit. I have seen this in consultation and treatment with any number of women, particularly those now in their fifties and sixties. Many of these women were directly advised by analysts and psychiatrists that their feminine obligation, destiny, or duty lay in preserving the marriage, in not threatening their husbands, in modulating their own sexuality, and so forth. Parenthetically, former patients in this age group bear the most hostility to psychiatry. While such inappropriate direct interventions are manifestations of countertransference reactions, the underlying theory has enabled clinicians to remain blind to them. In other words, although these countertransference reactions were individually derived and not theoretically mandated, they were culturally and theoretically reinforced.

Furthermore, psychoanalysts may have tended to be more prescriptive with women than with men because of their shared countertransference response toward women. For example, Chodorow (1978) has pointed out the prescriptive quality in Freud's discussion of female psychology: the little girl "must," "has to," and so on. Finally, at a time when dependency was more consonant with the female role, women may have sought such interventions transferentially with more insistence than male patients.

An Overview of Changing Theories

Freud essentially used only a single concept, penis envy, to explain the development of sexuality, normal gender development, and neurotic conflict in women. By ascribing femininity solely to the outcome of thwarted masculinity, his theory doomed women to infantilism and immaturity relative to men. Contemporary psychoanalysis, in contrast, takes a systems approach. Most important, theories of normal sexual development, of the acquisition of femininity (gender), and of the predominant neurotic conflicts have now been revised.

The following sections discuss the changing theories in these areas in broad strokes. A review of changes in these formulations highlights the faulty methodology and the underlying ideology that for so long locked the old ideas into place. Many other aspects of female psychology must be omitted here because of space limitations. Despite the importance of changes in conceptions about conscience and morality (Schafer, 1974; Gilligan, 1982) and about early object relations (Chodorow, 1978), for instance, the review cannot extend to these areas.

CHANGING THEORIES OF SEXUALITY

It was a tenet of Freudian theory that female sexuality must necessarily be somewhat debilitated or hyposexual, given the need to switch both object and organ. According to Freud, penis envy was decisive in sexual development, as well as in neurotic conflict and the development of femininity. Penis envy was responsible for the girl's turn away from her mother (renouncing the clitoris) and toward her father (to get a penis from him). This double switch was believed to result in a diminished libido. This theory appeared to be substantiated by the inability of many women patients to achieve orgasm. Clara Thompson (1950) was among the first to reassess the apparent problem of female sexuality. She believed that the major sexual dilemma for women was not penis envy but acknowledging their own sexuality in this culture. Her insight proved prophetic.

It is in the area of sexuality that the most radical changes have occurred, both in women's expectations and in psychoanalytic theory. The continuing role of clitoral eroticism in adult women, as demonstrated by Masters and Johnson (1966) and others, has led to a repudiation of Freud's theory of a clitoral-vaginal transfer, hypothetically triggered by the young girl's sense of clitoral inferiority and eventually in a debilitated sexuality. No one today holds that true femininity depends on achieving vaginal orgasms. And female sexuality is no longer viewed as debilitated; it is now viewed as actively robust.

Along with rhetoric, actual sexual practices have also changed. Female sexuality has been liberated in two ways. First, it has been freed from ignorance. That maximal sexual pleasure in orgasm depends on adequate clitoral stimulation and is not an automatic outcome of heterosexual coitus was a crucial insight. Coupled with significant changes in sexual behavior, this knowledge has permitted more women to find sexual fulfillment than ever before, a major benefit of the scientific studies of sex.

Second, sexuality has been freed from an exclusive focus on male preferences and from the traditional idea of female submissiveness in relationships. As we have seen, female sexual inhibition was often based on deference to and fear of the male. In many women, these sexual inhibitions begin to resolve themselves when women achieved greater assertiveness and a sense of autonomy. This would not be possible, however, without a significant redefinition of the female-male bond. In fact, many so-called frigid women have no substantive problems with achievement of either arousal or orgasm. They suffer instead from ignorance about what constitutes appropriate stimulation or from interpersonal intimidation.

Somewhat surprisingly, many psychiatrists persist in minimizing the effect of the sexual revolution on women. Frequently, they argue that we see changes only in behavior and that unconscious wishes and conflicts remain unchanged. This argument ignores the psychological function of orgasm per se, its power to reaffirm the "incontrovertible truth" of the reality of personal existence (Lichtenstein, 1961; see also Eissler, 1958a; Person, 1980). Liberated sexual behavior among women thus may open new potentialities that, while sexual in nature, transcend the sexual. Sexual achievement has almost unequivocally benefited women, not only proffering sexual gratification but often serving as a cornerstone for increased self-esteem.

It would be erroneous, however, to dismiss the historical suppression of female sexuality as solely cultural in its origin. The critical developmental and psychoanalytic question is why the female erotic impulse has been vulnerable to suppression across so many different historical and cultural circumstances (Person, 1980). So, despite systemic cultural suppression of masturbation—for example, warnings to boys and girls in the Victorian era that masturbation causes blindness or insanity—sexuality in boys was not totally suppressed, as many boys continued to masturbate, although fearful of the consequences. In contrast, the fact that so many middle- and upper-class Victorian girls suffered more complete sexual repression of masturbation and grew up with either the eradication or dimunition of the pleasure of intercourse or a complete antipathy to sex suggests a difference in male sexuality and female sexuality. It may be that female sexuality is more vulnerable to suppression. (This difference in sexuality may have offered some adaptive advantage to women in ages long past.)

CHANGING THEORIES OF GENDER IDENTITY

Gender identity has also been systematically reevaluated. There is a growing psychoanalytic consensus that classical formulations fail to theorize the acquisition of core gender identity ("I am female/male") and gender identity (femininity/masculinity) in accordance with the facts of development. Anatomical differences, while important, are no longer seen as determining per se. According to Howell (1981), "It is the study of gender identity that has offered the most important correction to Freud's theory of feminine development" (p. 16).

Freud derived his theory of masculinity and femininity, what we now call gender role identity, from the contrast between the behavior of the two sexes after the child's discovery of the anatomical distinction that boys have penises while girls do not. He suggested that on discovering the sexual distinction, the little girl was overcome by clitoral inferiority and penis envy and hence developed the compensatory characteristics of passivity, masochism, narcissism, and dependency. He also believed that the treatment of women was inherently limited because the cause of their problems, genital inferiority, was essentially incurable.

Such a theory is intrinsically odd, because it should be apparent to even a casual observer that girls and boys begin to diverge in behavior, mannerisms, and interests by twelve to eighteen months of age. Freud's formulation underscores the danger of deriving developmental theories from adult analyses without validation from child observations. Horney (1924, 1926, 1932, 1933) and Jones (1927, 1933) strongly challenged Freud's theories, proposing that femininity was primary, not derivative, and that it antedated the phallic phase and was innate. Horney attributed heterosexual object choice to innate femininity, itself grounded in female biology and awareness of the vagina, not in disappointment over lacking a penis. Jones supported Horney's contention. As he put it, "The ultimate question is whether a woman is born or made" (Jones, 1935, p. 273). Thus, in the opinions of both Jones and Horney, heterosexual desire was innate. The girl desired the penis libidinally, not narcissistically. Contemporary theorists confirm Horney's and Jones's observations that gender differerntiation is preoedipal. But current research strongly suggests that sexual object choice is acquired, not innate.

Money and his colleagues (1955a,b, 1956) demonstrated that the first and crucial step in gender differentiation is the child's self-designation as male or female, which evolves according to the sex of assignment and has unconscious as well as conscious components. Most theorists today believe that the developmental lines of gender precede those of sexuality, a complete reversal of Freud's original formulations.

This change in theoretical formulation has manifold implications for therapy, and many of these have been achieved without being made explicit. The concept of normative femininity is freed from the stereotypes of passivity, masochism, dependency, and narcissism. The content of femininity is now regarded as multidetermined, with significant input from cultural prescriptions. Femininity and masculinity are seen as parallel constructs, removing any theoretical reason to posit inherent restrictions on women's creativity and autonomy. Consequently, modern theory does not view female prospects as intrinsically dim.

However, a critical developmental and psychoanalytic question remains, one that cannot be reduced to a simple cultural perspective. The question concerns the universal polarity of gender role(s) that exists despite the plasticity of the content of those roles. A theory is required that integrates object relations, the symbolic investment of the genitals, and sexual differences, along with the cultural perspective.

Differences in gender role are now attributed to diverse antecedents that include biological differences, learning, power relations, scripting, socialization, sex-discrepant expectations that shape fantasies, and cultural myths, in addition to the standard psychoanalytic emphasis on body awareness, sexual distinction, and the vagaries of the Oedipus complex.

CHANGING VIEWS ON THE CENTRALITY OF PENIS ENVY

Feminists have complained bitterly about the damage done by propagation of the penis envy doctrine as the irreducible dynamic in female mental life. They have raised the suspicion that it is not women who are fixated on penis envy but psychoanalysis. While analysts of different theoretical persuasions ascribe varying significance to penis envy as an operative dynamic, few stress it to the same degree that Freud or Deutsch did. Many analysts have since reevaluated the data and come to different conclusions.

According to Blum (1976), "Though very important and ubiquitous, penis envy can no longer be regarded, if it ever was, as the major organizer of femininity. . . . To derive femininity mainly from penis envy would be developmental distortion and reductionism" (p. 186). Although Phyllis Tyson (1982) believes that the awareness of anatomical differences may function as a "psychic organizer," she has argued echoing Blum, that "we must look to the early identifications with the idealized mother-ego ideal in order to understand the greater portion of the feminine personality organization" (p. 77). And Lerner (1980) has written, "Today's analyst is less quick to label women's aggressive, ambitious, and competitive strivings as 'masculine' or to interpret them a priori as a manifestation of penis envy" (p. 39).

While Freud put penis envy at the center of the female's neurotic conflicts, today one hears much more, and much more to the point, about conflicts over fear of loss of love or over excessive dependency needs. First alluded to by Freud (1924), the fear of loss of love belongs with a cluster of traits that are particularly characteristic of women in Western cultures: dependency needs, fear of interdependence, fear of abandonment, unreconstructed longing for love relationships with a man, and fear of being alone. These problems are viewed not as bedrock, replacing penis envy as a core, but as preoccupations in the minds of contemporary women. They may, however, be rooted in early female object relations, socialization, or a combination of factors. And to some degree, they may reflect the individual's response to the external situation. Many analysts and psychologists have come to recognize the need to distinguish contextual responses from internalized stable personality traits.

Values and Theory Making

Recent changes in practice and theory are of inestimable practical benefit to women. From the vantage point of psychoanalysis as an intellectual and scientific discipline, however, we would risk trivializing the theoretical failures of Freud and his followers if we were to restrict our interests solely to correcting the inaccuracies and misperceptions related to the special case of female development. Thus, while we may applaud various corrections in our theories of female psychology, we must also confront the reasons why penis envy for so long retained its power as a monolithic explanation and why sexuality and femininity were essentially seen as meager and distorted. Some have insisted that these early formulations reveal the severe limitations of psychoanalytic theorizing. The emphasis here is on *theorizing* rather than on *theory*, because the whole psychoanalytic enterprise has been challenged, not just one tenet of psychoanalytic theory. The specific questions concern how these theories have persisted for so long and what their persistence reveals both of faulty methodology and of value biases. As the following discussion illustrates, they have persisted for at least three reasons: misogyny, the lack of a requirement for verification in psychoanalytic theorizing, and the underlying biological assumptions in psychoanalysis.

FREUD'S PATRIARCHAL BIAS

Under the impact of changing social values, feminist scholars and analysts have come to insist that Freud wrote from the patriarchal stance typical of his cultural milieu. Because he viewed female development simply as a variant of male development, he failed to achieve a comprehensive or accurate description and theory. Furthermore, they argue, his theoretical biases were automatically translated into therapeutic biases and had profound negative impacts on women patients. Freud not only viewed women as powerless but also saw them as lacking essential special capacities and a powerful unique sexuality. Penis envy as doctrine, focusing as it does on female inadequacy, coincided with the traditional perception of the woman as powerless, inferior, and subordinate. A number of feminist writers pointed this out, eloquently challenging the analytic formulation of the origins of "femininity." Theories of female psychosexual development have, in the past, been misused as justifications for women's subordinate positions in society.

Horney (1926) literally charted Freud's bias. She drew a close parallel between a small boy's ideas about sexual differences and psychoanalytic ideas about feminine development. Doing so, Horney was among the first to raise the possibility that Freud's insistence on the centrality of penis envy was related to the male's envy of the female, particularly of her capacity for motherhood. In a remark that Rohrbaugh (1979) has also quoted, Millett (1970) made an interesting and relevant observation: "Freudian logic has succeeded in converting childbirth, an impressive female accomplishment, and the only function its rationale permits her, into nothing more than a hunt for a male organ" (p. 185).

The charge that Freud's psychology of women is infused by patriarchal values has not been restricted to feminists. Consider, for example, Schafer's (1974) objection: "Freud's ideas on the development and psychological characteristics of girls and women, though laden with rich clinical and theoretical discoveries and achievements, appeared to have been significantly flawed by the influence of traditional patriarchal and evolutionary values. This influence is evident in certain questionable presuppositions, logical errors and inconsistencies, suspensions of intensive inquiry, underemphasis on certain developmental variables, and confusions of observations, definitions, and value preferences" (p. 483). Freud's beliefs mirrored those of his culture. His systematic distortion alerts us to the danger of using common sense corroborated by cultural consensus to confirm scientific theory. Value bias lulls us into theoretical complacency.

THE LACK OF SYSTEMATIC VERIFICATION IN PSYCHOANALYTIC THEORY

Psychoanalytic data are subject to a variety of interpretations. Therapists of different persuasions encounter the same underlying data from the couch: symbols, dream content, fantasies, and so forth. Yet Freudians, Jungians, culturists, and others use these data to verify their theories, thereby revealing the inadequacy of the couch as the sole source of data for verifying theory.

Biases in perception and interpretation occur all the time. The fact that they persist and become codified in psychoanalytic theory reflects a methodological problem in psychoanalytic theorizing. Misperception does not usually or necessarily take the form of distorting the symbols of conflict. Nor is it based on thin air. Misperception can occur from paying selective inattention to data or incorrectly weighing their significance. A random fantasy is different from an organizing fantasy. Most commonly, bias is reflected in a misinterpretation of the meaning of the data. On the one hand, the analyst may view attempted conflict resolution as symptomatic rather than adaptive, in accordance with his or her subjective values. On the other hand, the analyst may interpret certain symbols as being causal, eradicable, or intrinsic rather than as being secondary, maladaptive attempts at conflict resolution.

Grossman and Stewart (1976) have illustrated the latter distortion in their paper "Penis envy: from childhood wish to developmental metaphor." They presented two clinical examples of analyses in which the interpretation of penis envy, apparently grounded in clinical data, "*had an organizing effect, but not a therapeutic one*" (p. 194). In both examples, the interpretation of penis envy was close enough to the data of the analyses that the women accepted the interpretation and used it to rationalize and consolidate their real pathological constellations. Thus, penis envy is often a symbolic condensation that conceals significant underlying conflicts. As Blum (1976) stated, "It is necessary to theoretically distinguish between penis envy as a dynamic issue and as a developmental influence" (p. 186). Freud himself made a peculiar jump from patients' clinical fantasies about castration to his developmental hypothesis about the little girl's discovery of "the fact of castration." His confusion between fantasy and the reality precluded his investigation of the meaning of castration fantasies.

One must distinguish between the meaning of clinical themes and developmental causality (Person, 1974). Meaning can be separated from assumptions of continuity insofar as the latter imply a causal chain. Many analysts have criticized assumptions of continuity and causality that are routinely made in psychoanalysis, along with the other historical sciences such as history, evolution, and developmental psychology. However, it would be inaccurate to claim that psychoanalysis is simply a science of meaning and therefore does not belong to the natural sciences. Psychoanalysis is a natural science insofar as it deals with the composition of self-sustaining characteristics of current mental organization. Thus it addresses the schemata of meaning and their association with affect in a horizontal segment of time (see Modell, 1978). It is out of the correspondence between meaning sets and affects that we generate psychoanalytic hypotheses.

Klerman (1982) made an apt observation that is worth echoing here. Psychoanalysis has been rich in generating hypotheses but has not been sufficiently committed to their verification. This case study regarding the psychology of women clearly illustrates the dangers of theorizing developmental processes without seeking validation from nonanalytic data. To hold to theories without such validation is to invite contamination by value biases.

THE BIOLOGICAL ASSUMPTIONS OF PSYCHOANALYSIS

While misogyny has been posited as responsible for certain inaccuracies in early psychoanalytic theories about women, it does not account adequately for their persistence in the presence of countervailing data. An explanation based on Freud's misogyny is too narrow if his misogyny is seen as emanating solely from simple historical bias. The question really is whether his misogyny is incidental to the basic assumptions of psychoanalysis or is intimately related to the structure of the ideas Freud generated. To the degree that we raise this question, we must move beyond an examination of susceptibility to a particular value bias in psychoanalysis and consider that biases may be even more broadly based in their underlying assumptions.

In 1961, Rieff raised exactly this point: "A denial of the Freudian psychology of women cannot depend on historical reductions of Freud's own psychology. . . . His misogyny, like that of his predecessors, is more than prejudice; it has a vital intellectual function in his system. . . . And just as sympathetic expositors of Schopenhauer and Nietzsche want to dismiss these philosophers' views on women as idiosyncratic and philosophically irrelevant, so the neo-Freudians (led by eminent women analysts like Karen Horney) would like to omit that part of Freud's work as mere culture-prejudice, maintaining that much of the remaining doctrine can be realigned without damage" (pp. 199–200).

In general, Freud was able to use criticism from both his followers and his defectors by integrating it into his theories. For example, Adler's concepts of masculine protest and power strivings are regarded as having been catalytic in Freud's consideration of aggression. On the other hand, despite cogent contemporary criticisms of his theories of female development (e.g., Horney,

1924, 1926, 1932, 1933; Jones, 1927, 1933, 1935), Freud never revised these theories. Later criticisms met the same fate at the hands of Freud's followers. Although Clara Thompson (1943) clearly stated that women envy men at least in part because of women's subordinate position in culture, she had no impact on mainstream psychoanalytic theories about women. Ovesey's observations on the devaluation of women (1956), Moulton's work on primary and secondary penis envy (1973), as well as the work of others, all now well regarded, were originally viewed as merely culturist. Thus, Freud and his followers never really confronted or resolved Freud's schema of female development, and the argument about the critical factors in female development remained dormant until the 1970s.

During the 1970s, women's expectations were radically altered, and feminists have been extremely vocal in their protests against psychoanalytic theories about women. Parallel with changing cultural directives about appropriate goals and the content of "femininity," psychoanalytic theories about the development of women were fundamentally revised. This is not to say, however, that psychoanalytic theory changed in direct response to the women's movement. Indeed, many of the criticisms leveled against psychoanalysis in the 1970s were the same as those raised by an earlier generation of feminists and dissident analysts. The pertinent question, then, is why psychoanalysis has become more receptive to the same critiques.

The delay in incorporating these critiques can only indicate the vital function of the misogyny underlying the psychoanalytic theories. Alluding to Freud's problem in theorizing the psychology of women, Schafer (1974) has stated that "it . . . was introduced into Freud's theorizing, and thus his comparative view of men and women, by his adhering to a biological, evolutionary model for his psychology. . . . This model requires a teleological view of the propagation of the species. . . . One observes in this entire line of thought the operation of an implicit but powerful *evolutionary value system*. According to this value system, nature has its procreative plan, and it is better for people to be 'natural' and not defy 'natural order' " (pp. 468–469). Rohrbaugh (1979) has raised the same question about Freud's theory, provocatively asking whether psychoanalysis can exist without penis envy. She believes that the concept of penis envy is embedded in Freud's insistence on a framework of biologically unfolding psychosexual stages and that his theory cannot account adequately for input from the familial, social, or cultural context.

Although Freud's clinical studies reveal a broad perspective, what has been referred to as his psychological theory or his metapsychology rested on reducing mental processes to biology and on minimizing the influences of experience and learning. By adhering to a strictly instinctual frame of reference, his theory could not offer an adequate means of understanding the influences on female development of early object relations, the prephallic development of personality, or the subordinate societal role of women. In effect, Freud was unable to theorize adequately the interface between individual psychology and cultural injunction.

TOWARD A PARADIGM SHIFT

Retrospectively, it appears that psychoanalysis was unable to encompass early criticisms about theories of female development until it had developed the ability to theorize the intersection between individual psychology and the cultural milieu. Analysts had objected to the theories of the interpersonal school because they implied that subjectivity simply mirrored the external world. Thus, they viewed the critiques of classical formulations of female development as largely culturist. These analysts were unwilling to embrace a perspective that seemed to undermine their hard-won recognition of the importance of intrapsychic and unconscious factors. Only recently have the theoretical assumptions of psychoanalysis been enlarged to the point that the earlier criticisms could be assimilated. Before this could happen, the question of whether "the unconscious has a history," in Marcus's (1982) phrase, had to be addressed. More narrowly, this question relates to the way in which external reality is internalized and so organizes individual psychology. What was required, then, was a shift away from a theory which posited that development was exclusively the preordained outcome of libidinal development—that is, a shift away from reducing mental processes to biology—and a shift toward a theory that focused on object relations and internalization as the major psychic organizers. Bias regarding women could apparently not be fully recognized or acknowledged before a more general paradigm shift had occurred.

There is today a growing consensus that libido theory, taken alone, provides an inadequate explanation of human development. While the basic constructs of psychoanalysis (motivation, the importance of childhood experiences, unconscious mental processes, and so forth) are still viable and are almost universally accepted, some tenets of metapsychology have been challenged. Given the studies of ego psychology, Ross (1970) and Lichtenstein (1970) have suggested that personality maturation can no longer be seen as the sole dependent variable and sexuality as the sole independent one. Sexuality is considered one independent variable among others, although it is still regarded as the leading one by some theorists. Object relations theory attempts to formulate those ways in which the experience of the external world is internalized, not just in the organization of perception and affective relationships, but in the very creation of subjectivity. While all psychoanalytic theory acknowledges the internalization of external values and prohibitions in the formation of the ego ideal and superego, object relations theory places more emphasis on the way subjectivity (fantasies, wishes) and the formation of ego are influenced by the experiential. Even sexuality, so clearly grounded in biology, is embedded in meaning and cannot be understood without reference to culture. Individuals internalize aspects of their interpersonal world, albeit in a way that is distorted by infantile mental processes and fantasies. This internalization shapes both their experience of desire and their expression of sexuality (Person, 1980).

Summary

The case of female psychology stands as a cautionary tale. Not only does it demonstrate the impact of historical bias on scientific assumptions but, more important, it lays bare some underlying assumptions in early psychoanalytic theories. This special case, in which theories appeared to be verified by clinical data, reveals methodological problems specific to the field of psychoanalysis. The temptation to confuse the symbols and meanings uncovered in analysis with developmental causality is readily apparent. Such confusion causes us to risk mistaking the accidents of historical contingency for eternal underlying truths. Consequently, the case of female psychology encourages us to distinguish systematically between the contingent and the universal. It reveals the impact of beliefs and value biases on both patients and analysts. It forces us to refine our scientific paradigms, first to acknowledge the inevitable dual descriptive-normative role of any psychoanalytic theory (Macklin, 1973), and second to separate hypothesis generating from hypothesis testing (Klerman, 1982).

Finally, the case of female psychology leads us to reexamine certain underlying psychoanalytic assumptions. As I have argued here, misogyny may be too narrow an explanation for Freud's misunderstanding of women. Freud's misunderstanding and misogyny have broader meaning than simple cultural prejudice. His scheme of female psychosexual development betrays a biological bias that leads to an overemphasis on genitals and reproduction and that lacks an appropriate theoretical scaffolding to support a full understanding of the manifold influences in personality development. It is indeed ironic that in attempting to avoid culturist reductionism, Freud mistook Victorian femininity for eternal femininity.

Given its recent theoretical developments, psychoanalysis can now encompass the issues raised by the study of female psychology. We have made significant revisions in theory. We will no doubt revise the revisions, on the basis of new insights that cast light on our current blind spots. The acknowledgment that values are pervasive in psychoanalysis, as in other scientific disciplines, should not discourage us. Psychoanalysis as a theory and a methodology is constantly evolving, and this, indeed, is what distinguishes it from blind ideology.

PART II

Cross-Gender Disorders

5

Gender Identity and Sexual Psychopathology in Men: A Psychodynamic Analysis of Homosexuality, Transsexualism, and Transvestism

1973

LIONEL OVESEY AND ETHEL S. PERSON

IN THE 1960s and 1970s, a burgeoning interest in gender and in the problems of gender identity began to emerge. Among the pioneers in this field, one in particular stands out. Through the study of hermaphroditism and other forms of sexual variation, John Money and his associates (1955a,b, 1968a) clearly established that the primary determinants of gender identity are psychological. Another worker prominent in this field is researcher Robert Stoller (1968a), a psychoanalyst who has concentrated mainly on the developmental dynamics of transsexuals and transvestites. In this chapter, we will first define gender identity and describe how it develops, drawing heavily on the concepts of Money and Stoller. Next, we will describe the psychodynamics of gender identity in biologically normal heterosexual males. In so doing, we will review the concept of pseudohomosexuality (Ovesey, 1969), which illuminates the unconscious integration of conflicts about gender role. Finally, we will demonstrate the psychodynamic interrelationships between gender identity and sexual psychopathology in three disorders: homosexuality,[1] transsexualism, and transvestism. In each of these disorders biologic sex is

1. As will become apparent in subsequent papers, I no longer regard homosexuality as a singular entity but have come to refer to the "homosexualities." However, certain types of homosexuality do present as disorders as do certain types of heterosexuality. (Footnote added, 1998.)

normal but gender identity and sexual behavior are markedly aberrant. We will provide a psychodynamic analysis of the symptoms and propose a hypothesis of the developmental origins of each disorder.

Gender identity refers to a person's self-designation as male or female and as masculine or feminine. These two categories are commonly known as core gender identity and gender identity, respectively. We find the latter term confusing because it is not clearly differentiated from the former. Instead of gender identity, therefore, we will use the term "gender role identity." Core gender identity, the male-female polarity, reflects a biological self-image and can be defined as an individual's self-designation as biologically male or female. It is the sense of belonging biologically to one sex or the other—that is, the conviction "I am a male" or "I am a female." Gender role identity, the masculine-feminine polarity, reflects a psychological self-image and can be defined as an individual's self-evaluation of psychological maleness or femaleness. It is the sense of masculinity or femininity—that is, the belief "I am masculine," or "I am feminine," as measured against societal standards for masculine or feminine behavior.

The development of core gender identity is decisively influenced in the earliest years of life by gender assignment, the sexual designation of the child by the physician and parents. For all practical purposes, gender assignment at birth is based on the appearance of the external genitalia. In fact, misassignments can occur only when the external genitalia are incongruent with other attributes of biologic sex. After gender is assigned, the parents relate to the child either as boy or as girl, and rearing proceeds accordingly. The child's awareness of this core gender identity is already visible to the observer in the first year of life and is fully developed by age three. If gender assignment is definite and the parents display no ambiguity, even where the genitalia themselves are ambiguous, core gender identity will be normal. Even if the person feels anatomically flawed and has problems with gender role identity, core gender identity will remain firm. On the other hand, if there is parental ambiguity about gender assignment, this will lead to ambiguous core gender identity. Subsequently, if gender is definitively assigned and parental ambiguity ends, the child's core gender identity is consolidated either as male or as female.[2]

Gender role identity of necessity reflects gender assignment and hence includes core gender identity. However, it is a much more complicated self-representation. As we have seen, core gender identity is established early in childhood and thereafter remains a fixed entity. It is a static self-representation,

2. For a more current formulation of gender assignment in intersexuality, see Chapters 1 and 17 in this volume. See also Meyer-Bahlburg, "Gender Assignment in Intersexuality," 1998. (Footnote added, 1998.)

a classification. Gender role identity, on the other hand, continues to develop well into adulthood. Furthermore, once established, it does not remain firm but fluctuates throughout life. It is a dynamic, or functional, self-representation, a measurement of performance, varying with the person's capacity at any one time to behave in accordance with the prescribed gender role. It emerges gradually as the child responds to societal directives. These are mediated at first within the family, by the parents, and later by the extrafamilial society itself.

Three major components can be distinguished in gender role identity, each with masculine and feminine connotations: (1) core gender identity; (2) sexual behavior, overt and fantasied, expressed in both choice of object and nature of activity; and (3) culturally determined and institutionalized nonsexual attributes and behavior, such as physical appearance, dress, mannerisms, speech, emotional responsiveness, aggressiveness, and countless others too many to enumerate. These items are continuously monitored, consciously and unconsciously, for masculinity or femininity in a never-ending process of self-validation. Self-confidence and self-esteem ebb and flow with this process as the person fails or succeeds in meeting role requirements.

Disturbances of gender role identity are widespread in psychopathology. This is true for both sexual and nonsexual disorders. In contrast, disturbances of core gender identity are very limited in number and, with one exception, occur only when biologic sex is defective. The single exception is transsexualism, a sexual disorder in which biologic sex is completely normal but core gender identity appears to be reversed, for reasons that are unclear (we will consider some possible explanations later). In all other sexual disorders, core gender identity remains intact. Thus, for example, male homosexuals may believe their masculinity is impaired,[3] but they do not doubt their intrinsic maleness. The same can be said of transvestites, exhibitionists, fetishists, and so on: their gender role identity is disturbed, but their core gender identity is normal.

Pathological disturbances of gender role identity stem from unconscious conflicts about gender role. These conflicts are culturally derived from institutions that categorize behavior as either "masculine" or "feminine." In our male-oriented society the position of women is devalued, and status accrues to men solely by virtue of the fact that they are men. The polarities of masculinity and femininity are identified respectively with positive and negative value judgments. Masculinity represents strength, dominance, superiority; femininity represents weakness, submissiveness, inferiority. The former is equated with success, the latter with failure. These values are stereotypes that express

3. I believe this to be less true today, when the social stigmatization has declined, at least in parts of the country, and gay liberation has acted to repair damaged self-esteem. (Footnote added, 1998.)

the historical prejudices of males in our culture. It is true that they are currently under militant attack and in the process of long-needed change. Nevertheless, men and women alike still use these stereotypes in evaluating many aspects of behavior, their own as well as others'. For this reason, in neurotic conflicts about gender role, the same unconscious symbols are used by both sexes. The sexes differ in the psychodynamic integration of these symbols, however, because of differences in anatomy, biological function, and culturally assigned gender roles.

Generally speaking, in men, pathological disturbances in gender role identity result from failures in masculine performance. The unconscious symbol par excellence for such performance, sexual or nonsexual, is the penis. Phallic size, integrity, and ability to function are repeatedly invoked as symbols of masculine assertion. Success or failure, as the case may be, is measured in terms of phallic power or phallic weakness. Thus, failures in the masculine role in any area of behavior—sexual, social, or vocational—are often unconsciously represented through a symbolic equation: *I am a failure as a man = I am castrated = I am a woman (I am effeminate) = I am a homosexual.* The final idea in this chain inevitably gives rise in heterosexual men to anxiety about being homosexual, as in reality these men are not. Their self-designated homosexuality is not a true homosexuality at all but simply reflects the self-assertive failure. It is a symbolic homosexuality, a "pseudohomosexuality," and the associated anxiety can be designated "pseudohomosexual anxiety" (Ovesey, 1969).

Psychodynamically, the equation we have cited is the central constellation in disturbances of gender role identity in men. How a man handles this equation not only differentiates health from neurosis but also contributes significantly to symptom formation, should neurosis be the choice. In the relatively healthy male, unencumbered by neurosis, the ideas in this equation are not of much consequence. The anxiety they generate is kept to a minimum and hence is readily surmounted. In such cases, the problem can be realistically confronted and effectively resolved. In neurotic males, however, the superimposition of the equation on pre-existent inhibitions of assertion can have serious repercussions.

Thus, men who suffer from pseudohomosexual anxiety at times of self-assertive crises are subject to paranoid fears of homosexual attack, usually in the form of anal rape. Such fears are especially prominent when the "masculine" failure results from a competitive defeat. The same social stereotypes that are used to define hierarchal relationships between men and women are also used to define competitive relationships between men. Power struggles, therefore, are perceived in terms of dominance or submission. The former is assigned a masculine value, the latter a feminine value. Victory is then associated with masculinity, defeat with femininity. Hence, in any competition, the weaker male may unconsciously see himself as castrated and forced to submit as a homosexual to the stronger male.

A clinical example will demonstrate the unhappy effects of a competitive defeat on a susceptible male. The patient was a twenty-eight-year-old, married, fully heterosexual medical resident undergoing psychoanalysis for an obsessive personality disorder. He was hypercompetitive, overconscientious, perfectionistic, and preoccupied with ambition, status, and achievement. In his last year of residency, he aspired to be the chief medical resident, but the position was given to someone else. The patient responded with a depression and promptly had a nightmare:

> He was in a proctologist's office lying prone in a jackknife position on an examining table. He was fully clothed, but his trousers and shorts were pulled down and his bare buttocks were exposed. His victorious rival approached with a sigmoidoscope and suddenly without warning or lubrication jammed it forcibly into his anus. The patient screamed in pain and leaped off the table. He yanked out the instrument and staggered to the door, bleeding profusely from the rectum.

After reporting the dream, he remarked, "Boy, he really reamed me out!" He then wondered whether he was a latent homosexual. His anxiety, however, was strictly a pseudohomosexual anxiety since the anal assault symbolized his competitive defeat and in no way reflected an erotic homosexual wish. The word "reamed," of course, is a folk-term that symbolically substitutes homosexual rape for ignominious defeat. "Fucked," "screwed" "buggered," and "shafted" are similar terms of the same genre.

In disturbances of gender role identity, where the anxiety is very great, the neurotic male may not be able to cope realistically with his failures. In these circumstances, he may attempt to retrieve his flagging masculinity by failing back on the unconscious fantasies of magical repair laid down in infancy and early childhood. Instead of incorporating the breast, however, the patient relies on incorporating the penis. In heterosexual males, the inevitable byproduct of such a reparative move is a pseudohomosexual anxiety. Here are two examples, previously published (Karush and Ovesey, 1961), in which both patients were heterosexual males who used homosexual imagery in the service of dependency. The first example demonstrates the oral route for phallic incorporation:

A young man enmeshed in a hostile dependent transference complained that the analyst was not solving his problems. He compared him bitterly to his mother, who rejected him and never provided for his needs. In this setting, he had the following dream:

> He saw a penis and performed fellatio. There was an orgasm and a huge gush of milk that looked thin, like skim milk. Next he was talking to a psychoanalyst who told him he saw fifteen to thirty patients a day. He was amazed at the doctor's capacity and his large income.

The patient experienced no erotic arousal but awoke with an intense pseudohomosexual anxiety. The dream dramatizes his dissatisfaction with the therapist's ministrations. In the wish to be fed by the therapist and thus to acquire his strength, he identifies him with his mother. The therapist's penis functions as the mother's breast and gives him milk, but the milk is of poor quality. It is skim milk, from which the richest portion has been removed. In other words, he feels as deprived by the therapist as by his mother, and he is no better off now than he was before. The underlying envy of the therapist therefore continues unabated in the second part of the dream.

The next example demonstrates the anal route for phallic incorporation. The penis is not used as a feeding organ but symbolizes the omnipotent power of the donor. The patient was a dependent man engaged in a competitive effort to expand his business. He was fearful that he would fail and repeatedly sought reassurance from the therapist, who of course could not guarantee his success. The patient thereupon resorted to a magical solution that he revealed in a dream:

> He felt ill and went to a hospital. The office of the physician resembled the office of the therapist. The doctor examined him and told him he needed an injection. He was put on a couch, face down. The doctor filled a huge syringe and plunged the needle into his buttock. He felt excruciating pain and then found his penis swelling to an enormous size. He stood up and began to urinate. The stream emerged with such great force and in such gargantuan quantities that it swept everything before it and flooded the whole hospital. He felt immense pride in his power, but awoke in a state of anxiety.

Here, as in the previous example, there was no erotic arousal. His anxiety therefore was interpreted as a pseudohomosexual anxiety.

Incorporative fantasies are most common in passive-submissive males. They are more likely to accept the feminine connotations of their dependent strivings than to defend their masculinity by struggling against them. More paranoid, power-driven males, however, find passivity intolerable and rely on power rather than dependency to retrieve their masculinity. Instead of phallic incorporation, therefore, they force other men to submit as homosexuals, orally and anally, to their domination. In this way, they enhance their masculine image at the expense of their victims' weakness. They may succeed temporarily in creating an illusion of relative masculinity, but in the end the effort is doomed to failure. The fantasied act, albeit symbolic, is still perceived as homosexual and hence intensifies the very anxiety it is designed to alleviate.

Disorders of Gender Identity

There are three major disorders of gender identity in which the gender disturbance is overt: homosexuality,[4] transsexualism, and transvestism. All three occur in association with sexual psychopathology, and it has been customary in psychiatry to designate them as sexual disorders. We feel this designation is too narrow since it downgrades the gender component. Obviously, all three disorders are both sexual and gender disorders, existing always in combination and never in isolation. In our opinion, they are best understood as neuroses, and we propose to conceptualize them as such. From our studies, however, we would not group all of them together. Psychodynamically, they can be separated by weighting the motivational significance of their two components—sex and gender identity. Once this is done, homosexuality can be classified primarily as a sexual disorder[5] in which the gender disorder is secondary, and transsexualism can be classified in the reverse direction, primarily as a gender disorder in which the sexual disorder is secondary. In transvestism the two components are about equally weighted.

Before we can conceptualize these disorders in psychodynamic terms, we must first define neurosis. We will use an adaptational definition. It is a core definition, somewhat simplistic, but it catches the essence of the neurotic process and will suffice as a working definition for our purposes. Neurosis is an impairment of function by anxiety due to unconscious fantasies of imagined danger. The fantasies arise developmentally in a family setting where there is parental intimidation of self-assertion in any area of behavior, nonsexual and sexual. The child then imagines that certain dangers will accrue if he attempts to satisfy his needs. He therefore becomes afraid and to a variable degree withdraws from the activities in question. The symptoms of the neurosis represent attempts by the patient to defend himself against these unconsciously perceived imagined dangers and, if possible, to salvage some satisfaction for the need that has been impounded.

In nonsexual psychopathology, the earliest neurosis is derived from sepa-

4. This statement should be limited to extreme effeminate or habitual cross-dressing homosexuals. Most of what follows in regard to the theorization of the psychodynamics of homosexuality refers to those groups. (Footnote added, 1998.)

5. As previously indicated, I no longer regard homosexuality as a sexual disorder, though homosexuality, like heterosexuality, has specific dynamics. But note that I do not regard dynamics as synonymous with etiology. (Footnote added, 1998.)

ration anxiety, occurring in the pregenital period of development. The unconscious fantasy of imagined danger here is the fact of separation itself, which is perceived as a threat to survival and hence equated with death. Under such circumstances, the insecure child attempts to perpetuate his dependency. He inhibits self-assertion and invokes various mechanisms, conscious and unconscious, to maintain the tie to his mother. In our clinical experience, dependency is a nuclear conflict in the major gender disorders. Homosexuals, transsexuals, and transvestites alike all suffer from unresolved separation anxiety. In consequence, their assertion is inhibited, and their sense of masculinity is deflated.

The nonsexual aspects of the three disorders fit easily into the same conceptual framework, even though in each the dependency conflict is resolved in a different way. We are not so fortunate, however, when it comes to the sexual aspects. Homosexuality and transvestism can be conceptualized psychodynamically in traditional psychoanalytic terms, but transsexualism will not fit into such a scheme. It requires separate treatment, and we will deal with it later in this paper (see also Chapters 6 and 7). The discussion that immediately follows, therefore, is applicable in general to all the sexual disorders, including homosexuality and transvestism, but not to transsexualism.

In sexual psychopathology, the unconscious fantasies of imagined danger that block the normal expression of the sexual impulse are essentially the same in all men. What differs is the choice of symptom. The key fantasies are (1) death, castration, and homosexual attack from the competitive male, originally the father; and (2) entrapment, engulfment, castration, and death during intercourse by the "vagina dentata" of the female, originally the mother. Clinically, these destructive fantasies are rarely separated from one another except through the work of psychoanalysis; instead, they are fused in a conglomerate way and are usually experienced as total annihilation or, in more psychoanalytic terminology, as "ego dissolution." Developmentally, they have their roots in preoedipal parental intimidations but are elaborated and intensified as the child struggles through the oedipal period. They are largely dissipated in the normal resolution of the Oedipus complex and subsequently do little harm. However, if the intimidations are too severe the Oedipus complex is not resolved, and the punitive fantasies persist. Should this occur, the child continues to misperceive his sexual impulses as transgressions and is unable to surmount his fears; instead, in various ways, he inhibits his sexual impulses.

In psychoanalytic theory, the central role in the genesis of the sexual disorders is traditionally assigned to the castration component of the conglomerate anxiety, and the symptoms are understood, therefore, primarily as various ways of allaying castration anxiety. On this basis, sexual symptoms fall readily into two groups, and the sexual disorders can be classified accordingly as pleasure inhibitors or pleasure facilitators. In the first group, in order to achieve protection against castration anxiety, the symptom impairs the sexual capacity, either partially or totally. This is what happens in impotence and frigidity. In the second group, the symptom becomes the precondition—by allaying the castration anxiety—for erotic arousal and release of the neurotically impounded sexual impulse. This is what happens, for example, in exhibitionism, where the viewer's recognition reassures the patient that he does in fact possess a penis, and in masochism, where the patient suffers a token punishment in advance of sexual pleasure. Homosexuality falls in the category of pleasure facilitators; transvestism straddles the classification with symptoms in both categories; transsexualism has different dynamics, but in terms of classification belongs with the pleasure inhibitors.

Psychodynamically, therefore, the sexual disorders can be conceptualized primarily as attempts to ward off lethal retaliation for normal sexual expression. They are, first and foremost, pathological forms of sexuality that make use of pathological ways of achieving or preventing sexual satisfaction. Secondarily, however, the sexual disorders intensify pre-existing doubts about masculinity and hence aggravate concomitant disturbances of gender role identity. The doubts have preoedipal beginnings, but their main impetus comes later, from the faulty resolution of the Oedipus complex. It is at this time that sexuality is inhibited and the chosen symptom is laid down. Simultaneously, the retaliatory fears inhibit assertion and foster dependency, leading to reparative measures either in fantasy or in behavior. These measures are designed not only to allay castration anxiety but also, as we have seen, to bolster flagging gender role identity.

In the three major gender disorders, where the reparative measures are acted out, the sexual conflict and the gender conflict are intermingled, and the final symptomatic configuration reflects both. Let us examine the psychodynamic interrelationships between sex and gender as they are manifested in males in homosexuality, transvestism, and transsexualism.

HOMOSEXUALITY

In male homosexuality, the patient protects himself from retaliatory fears by diverting his sexual impulses to a homosexual object. It is not at all clear why a homosexual object is deemed safer than a heterosexual one, but it is certainly true in clinical practice that the confirmed homosexual is inordinately fearful of women as sexual objects.[6] In fact, the reversal of the object choice is no

6. Whatever the etiology of homosexuality, this description is valid, though the reaction to the female genitals is often experienced as distaste rather than fear. Some homosexuals have no negative reaction to the female genital but feel uncertain about how to have sex unless two penises are involved. What our early

simple diversion; it would be more accurate to say that the male homosexual in turning toward men literally flees from women. Seen in this light, male homosexuality as a neurotic symptom can be understood narrowly as a phobic avoidance of the female genital. The revulsion experienced by so many homosexuals toward the vagina lends credence to this view.

How are we to account for the specific choice of symptom in this disorder? We suspect that psychodynamically the answer lies in the intensity of the vagina dentata fantasy in male homosexuals, which is far greater than in heterosexuals suffering from other sexual disorders. A developmental basis for our hypothesis is provided by family studies which show that male homosexuality is fostered in a family constellation where the boy is caught between an overpowering, seductive, intimate mother and an emotionally detached, hostile, rejecting father (Bieber et al., 1962). We would expect the son of such a mother not only to have a great deal of separation anxiety but simultaneously to fear that she will devour him should he attempt to hold onto her. Thus, dependency on the mother, instead of sustaining life, is associated with loss of ego identity and death. It is this fear of engulfment and annihilation by the mother as a dependency object that is mobilized by erotic interest in the mother during the oedipal phase and displaced to her vagina.

Through the male object, the homosexual not only allays his castration anxiety but also solves the problem of dependency and retrieves his masculinity. The sexual motivation, therefore, rarely exists in isolation but is usually combined with the nonsexual motivations of dependency and power. These pseudohomosexual motivations express the associated conflict of gender role identity and operate psychodynamically in the homosexual exactly as they do in the heterosexual; except, of course, that the reparative fantasies are not confined to the imagination but are acted out. Not only do the two pseudohomosexual motivations enhance the motive force of the homosexual motivation; their relative strengths determine the psychosocial structure of the homosexual relationship, as well as the physical mechanics of the homosexual act.

Thus, the gender disturbance in male homosexuality falls along a feminine-masculine gradient. At one extreme are the homosexuals who assume a feminine identification, more or less accept themselves as homosexuals, and usually show little interest in change. The typical family constellation reported by Bieber and his coworkers (1962) is most likely to be found in this group. They see themselves as weak, tend toward passivity, and have little faith in their capacity to meet masculine requirements. They give up competition with other men and take refuge in submission. The dependency motivation is

formulation omits is the similar distaste or fear the heterosexual male feels on exposure to another man's penis in a potentially sexual situation. (Footnote added, 1998.)

very strong in them, so they must struggle particularly hard against engulfment by the mother. They protect themselves from maternal annihilation by transferring their dependency needs to a male object. For them, the major adventitious purpose of the homosexual act is dependency gratification; therefore, they prefer either to perform fellatio on their partner or to be anally mounted by him. In this manner, magically, through incorporation of their father's penis, they also repair their deficient masculinity. The most extreme examples of such homosexuals are the cross-dressers, the so-called queens, who dramatize their "feminine" traits as much as possible, short of castration, in order to attract the stronger, more "masculine" male.

At the other end of the feminine-masculine gradient is the homosexual who assumes a masculine identification, rejects his homosexuality, and is often interested in becoming a full heterosexual. The typical family constellation reported by Bieber and his coworkers (1962) is less apt to be found in this group. The mother is less frightening and the father more threatening; consequently, the son fears the vagina less and defeat by male competitors more. He too is dependent, but he is more assertive than his feminine counterpart, and his dependency needs are not as pressing. He abhors passivity because of its "feminine" connotation, tends to be combative, and struggles to prove that he is "masculine." The power motivation is very strong in him, and he tries to redeem his masculine failure through a compensatory domination of weaker partners. He seeks men who will submit to him orally or anally but often refuses to accept the reverse role. In this way, he not only satisfies himself sexually but also enhances his deflated masculinity by making a woman out of his partner. The homosexual act itself is a confession of masculine failure, yet in this instance it is used paradoxically to confirm masculinity. We apply the label "paradoxical homosexuality" to cases of this kind. They fall at the extreme end of the gradient and comprise the bulk of the hypermasculine homosexuals, the so-called closet queens. They are the "muscle men," invariably paranoid in personality, who at times introduce aggression, even to the point of violence, into the homosexual act.

Here are two clinical examples of hypermasculine or paradoxical homosexuality. In the first example, the patient's preferred homosexual activity was to sit on his partner's chest, masturbate himself, and ejaculate into the partner's face. The victim's indignity was the patient's masculine triumph. Occasionally, the patient would satisfy his partner by masturbating him too, but more often he would add insult to injury by refusing further involvement. In the second example, the patient practiced a somewhat different variation, but on the same theme. He wrestled with his partner until he pinned him down. Then, as the partner lay helpless, he placed his knees on his shoulders, grabbed the partner's penis and masturbated him to climax. To him, the partner's ejaculation was the ultimate token of his submission. In the process, he became erotically aroused but rarely permitted himself to have an orgasm. To do so he felt would reduce him to the weaker man's level and thus place his own masculinity in jeopardy.

We see, then, that cross-dressing, submissive, effeminate homosexuals and aggressive, dominant, hypermasculine homosexuals are at opposite ends of the gender gradient. The great majority of homosexuals, however, fall between the two extremes. In some cases, the feminine identification is more prominent; in other cases, the masculine identification is more prominent. In many instances the identification vacillates from femininity to masculinity and then back again within the same person depending on the stress experienced in meeting the requirements of the masculine role.

TRANSVESTISM

The term "transvestism"[7] literally means cross-dressing. In psychiatry, however, the term is used not only phenomenologically but also diagnostically. Transvestism is traditionally defined as heterosexual cross-dressing, where the clothing is used fetishistically for sexual arousal. The transvestite's heterosexuality differentiates him from the homosexual drag queen, and his male core gender identity differentiates him from the transsexual; the fetishism differentiates him from both. This definition is accurate as far as it goes, but in our opinion it is incomplete. The transvestite uses female clothing not only fetishistically but also nonfetishistically, to relieve anxiety about gender role identity.

Developmentally, transvestism originates after object differentiation has taken place and a sense of maleness has been consolidated. The cross-dressing typically begins in childhood or adolescence and is accompanied by sexual arousal. Most often the child himself initiates the cross-dressing; occasionally, it is initiated by the mother, a sister, or some other female relative or acquaintance. The initial experience may involve partial or total cross-dressing; should it be the former, it eventually progresses to totality. In either case, a favored article of clothing, or a few articles in combination, become erotic in themselves and may be used habitually as fetishes, first in masturbation, later in intercourse. The fetishistic mechanism can be understood psychodynamically as a flight from the woman, originally the mother. Sexual interest is symbolically displaced to an inanimate object, which is less dangerous, and hence permits sexual release. The fetish therefore both arouses and defends, and, to the extent that it is incorporated into sexual intercourse, it lessens the threat from the woman.

7. This is a preliminary report of a study still in progress (see Chapter 7). We have conceptualized the psychodynamics within an adaptational frame of reference. For other psychoanalytic studies see Fenichel (1930), Segal (1965), and Stoller (1968a).

The use of female clothing to relieve gender tension is nonfetishistic and is distinct from the sexual act. Transvestites periodically cross-dress and frequently pass in public disguised as women. Unlike the transsexuals, these patients not only acknowledge their manhood but tend to be extremely competitive with other men. In consequence, they often seek hypermasculine jobs—pilot, scuba diver, policeman—in which they function exceedingly well. Nonetheless, the impulse to don female garb is overwhelming and irresistible, particularly after a vocational crisis that demands great assertiveness.

Clinically, transvestites exist on a continuum from nonmasochistic to masochistic. Both extremes have fetishistic and nonfetishistic cross-dressing in common. The masochistic transvestites, however, during masturbation or intercourse, also submit to bondage and whipping at the hands of the woman, either in fantasy or in reality. The extremes differ markedly in their family constellations and developmental histories; hence, in their psychodynamics and symptomatic presentations. This difference is also apparent in transvestitic pornography, which divides sharply along nonmasochistic and masochistic lines. For purposes of clarity, we will discuss the two types separately in their most divergent forms.

Nonmasochistic transvestism: In these patients the mother is generally warm and supportive, the father distant and threatening, often verbally abusive, at times physically so. As in homosexuality and transsexualism, the mother turns to the son for gratifications not forthcoming from her marriage. She is seductive in her closeness to the boy, but at the same time encourages his cross-dressing, either covertly or overtly; that is, she accepts it without protest or, less commonly, actively participates in it. The father maintains his distance and fails to intervene with the mother in behalf of his son. This lack of intervention is the characteristic feature of the father-son relationship in transvestism, both nonmasochistic and masochistic.

We suspect that the mother is using the son to gratify herself sexually but represses her real interest by denying his masculinity. The child, for his part, interprets the mother's approval of his cross-dressing somewhat differently. He is gratified by the intimacy but guilt-ridden. He assumes that the mother wishes to disguise him as a girl in order to placate the father, whom he has supplanted. In other words, he sees his mother as a co-conspirator in the attempt both to gratify him and to protect him from the father's wrath. At bottom, of course, the boy's distortion is based on his need to preserve the mother as a dependency object. In fantasy, the nonmasochistic transvestite typically pines for a warm and intimate relationship with his mother or sister while dressed as a woman. He acts out this fantasy in his search for a wife: he seeks a woman like his mother or sister, who will also teach him to dress and apply make up.

The belief in the efficacy of disguise, then, derives from a specific mother-son interaction. A successful resolution of the Oedipus complex is not possible in such a family setting, The mother is too intimate, and her behavior greatly intensifies the son's oedipal rivalry with the father. Nevertheless, sexual performance as such is usually not compromised, though transvestites frequently show dampened sexual drive. The use of fetishism blurs the maternal image and enables the patient to surmount his sexual anxiety. In bed with a woman he functions reasonably well; at least, disorders of potency do not seem to be much of a problem in transvestism. Clinically, the sexual inhibition is overshadowed by the inhibition of nonsexual masculine assertion. The patient is locked into an endless struggle for power with other men. The competition is perceived as violent aggression, and the patient wards off retaliation, death, castration, and homosexual attack by donning female attire.

All transvestites resort to total cross-dressing periodically, especially in response to severe anxiety about assertive demands. Generally, however, anxiety about masculine assertion is chronic, and most transvestites require prophylactic measures short of full female regalia to contain it. For this reason, many transvestites carry photographs of themselves dressed as women. The photographs are mini-symbols of cross-dressing and magically provide some protection at all times. In a similar vein, some transvestites may continuously wear a female garment, such as women's underpants, when dressed outwardly as males. In nonsexual situations, the underpants are secretly protective, but when the patient gets into bed with a woman the underpants become sexually stimulating.

The female clothes magically protect him in three ways: (1) They symbolize the mother as a transitional object; thus he perpetuates his dependency and continues to rely on her for protection; (2) they symbolize an autocastration, a token submission to his male competitors, which wards off retaliation; and (3) they disguise his masculinity and serve to disarm his rivals. The clothes conceal his penis, the symbol of masculine power, and deny his hostile intent. He therefore feels safe because his rivals do not know that he is secretly plotting their demise. He avoids detection by passing as a woman, which makes it possible for him to risk assertion and thus validate himself as a man. Indeed, the successful deception not only allays retaliatory anxiety but even confers on the patient an inflated sense of masculinity. In his own mind, the transvestite is Superman in drag!

All these themes are reflected in the pornographic literature designed for this group. A typical story follows: Mr. X, a traveling salesman, is incorrectly identified by the Mafia as a runaway mobster. Several representatives of the Mafia are assigned to trap him in a hotel room and rub him out. Mr. X, though naked, manages to escape and runs into another room in the same hotel.

There he encounters a beautiful young woman who agrees to help him. She suggests that he can escape only by dressing in her clothes (fortunately, Mr. X and the girl are the same size). She makes him up, does his hair, lays out his wardrobe, and teaches him how to walk like a woman. The escape is achieved, and the pair realize that they have fallen in love. Mr. X proposes marriage but acknowledges that he is so taken with wearing female clothes that he is not sure he can give them up. The girl reassures him, saying she had always wanted a husband and a sister in one package, and they live happily ever after.

Masochistic transvestism: Here, as stated before, to facilitate sexual arousal, the patient not only uses fetishism but also submits masochistically to bondage and whipping. The family constellation in many respects seems to be the reverse of that in nonmasochistic transvestism. The mother emerges as an angry, destructive, domineering woman who shows little if any warmth toward her son. In this group, cross-dressing by the mother tends to be punitive, in contrast to the supportive, conspiratorial cross-dressing by the mother in nonmasochistic transvestism. The father, from our data, cannot as yet be described with equal clarity. He is a shadowy figure, distant, emotionally detached, in a house dominated by a woman. He, too, fails to protect his son from the mother.

The parents' marriage is an unhappy combination. The mother takes out her frustrations on the son. We assume that she displaces onto him much of the fury she feels toward the father. She is a "castrating" woman and systematically feminizes the boy through subjugation, occasionally by cross-dressing him. In the process, she also stimulates him erotically, which, like the castration, must be her unconscious intent. Thus, early in life, the boy is forced into dependency on a hostile "phallic" mother from whom he never escapes. Here again, the Oedipus complex cannot be successfully resolved. The image of the mother contaminates all subsequent female objects, and the father in the guise of other men remains a competitive threat.

Nonsexually, in both masochistic and nonmasochistic transvestism the female clothes symbolize a transitional object, a token submission, and a disguise. These are the gender components of the conflict, and their main purpose is to bolster masculinity. A crucial difference in the nature of the transitional object distinguishes the two types of transvestism. The nonmasochistic transvestite identifies with a supportive mother who protects him from castration by his male competitors and thus preserves his penis; the masochistic transvestite identifies with a phallic mother who endows him with phallic power and thus undoes his castration. In this sense, identification with the phallic mother is identification with the aggressor. Consequently, the masochistic transvestite's personality may appear hyperaggressive, but in fact his underlying self-image remains that of a castrated male.

Sexually, the masochistic transvestite is confronted with a double threat: the competitive male and the dominating female. The latter is by far the more threatening, and the patient's sexual symptoms are designed primarily to provide protection against castration by the woman partner. We can only assume that the gender components themselves, through cross-dressing, dispose of the male threat. The defenses against the female, however, are more complicated. They consist of three mechanisms: fetishism, token submission, and masochism. The first, fetishism, we have already described. The second, token submission, is acted out through cross-dressing, as it is with the male, except here he appeases the dangerous woman who may then be approached sexually. The third mechanism, masochism, is more punitive. The patient submits to bondage and beating. In this way, he expiates his guilt for desiring the woman by paying for his pleasure in advance. Once punishment has been inflicted and his conscience assuaged, the woman grants him her sexual favors.

All these mechanisms show up in the pornography of the transvestite. The differences between the masochistic and nonmasochistic transvestites in the pornography they prefer are very striking, reflecting, of course, the contrasting mother-son relationships. In the masochistic transvestite's pornography, a woman seduces a man into cross-dressing. Her motive, however, is not to befriend him, let alone save his life, as in the nonmasochistic version, but rather to dominate and humiliate him. The woman is depicted not as sweet, kind, and sisterly but as a malevolent, big-breasted, tightly corseted, booted "phallic" woman, often holding a whip. She forces the man into "femininity" by cross-dressing him; then she holds him in bondage and beats him. The man protests, but only feebly, since in reality he is a willing victim and seeks to be subjugated.

TRANSSEXUALISM

Transsexualism[8] as a clinical entity was first delineated by Harry Benjamin (1953, 1954, 1966), who also gave the syndrome its name. We define a transsexual behaviorally as a biologically normal person who insistently requests hormonal and surgical sex reassignment. The etiology of transsexualism is much disputed. Benjamin (1966) postulates an endocrine etiology despite the absence of laboratory confirmation. Money (1970) theorizes that the most likely etiology is an "extremely tenacious critical period effect in the gender-identity differentiation of a child with a particular but as yet unspecifiable vulnerability." Stoller (1968a) postulates an "imprinting" mechanism that derives from a specific familial situation. Still others (Golosow and Weitzman, 1969; Weitzman, Shamoian, and Golosow, 1970; Socarides, 1970) postulate a

8. This is a preliminary report of a completed study by Person and Ovesey, "The Transsexual Syndrome in Males" (Chapters 6 and 7 in this volume).

psychological etiology with the developmental roots of origin antedating genital sexuality. We side with this last, psychological hypothesis.

Stoller attributes male transsexualism to a characteristic mother-infant relationship occurring within a disturbed marital setting. In his sample, the mothers were generally unhappy people with underlying depression and a deep sense of emptiness. They lived in loveless, essentially sexless marriages with emotionally withdrawn, often physically absent husbands. However, they did not seek extramarital involvements but instead turned to their infant sons for fulfillment. They kept the child in constant physical contact with them, always carrying, holding, or touching him.

According to Stoller, this mother-son symbiosis in the early years of life produces a female core gender identity by a nonconflictual, nondynamic learning process akin to imprinting in lower animals. Any subsequent personality disturbance derives primarily, not from intrapsychic conflict, but from societal demands that are incongruent with the person's core gender identity. There are two critical objections to Stoller's formulation: first, there is no certain evidence that imprinting in the ethological sense exists in human beings as it does in lower animals; and second, some transsexuals say that their symptoms first appeared under stress in adolescence, or even in adulthood.

The male transsexual is defined by most workers as having a female core gender identity. From our experience, it seems more accurate to say that transsexuals have an ambiguous core gender identity. Although the presenting complaint may be the stereotyped, "I am a female soul trapped in a male body," this statement represents an adaptive maneuver to resolve the ambiguity rather than a strong conviction. It is true that there is a history of gender discomfort, abhorrence of certain masculine activities, preoccupation with feminine activities, and early cross-dressing accompanied by emotional relief. Nevertheless, the fantasies of childhood and adolescence are cast in the form of a wish, not a conviction; for example, "I would like to be a girl," not "I am a girl." The conviction crystalizes out rather abruptly when the patient learns of the existence of transsexualism. Patients commonly speak of their great confusion as to what they were—heterosexual, homosexual, transvestite—until they learned about transsexualism, usually through an account of the life of Christine Jorgensen (1967).

This distinction between an ambiguous and a female core gender identity is a central issue in understanding transsexualism. It argues against Stoller's theory of nonconflictual imprinting and permits the disorder to be conceptualized psychodynamically in conflictual terms as a neurosis. In our opinion, transsexualism originates in extreme separation anxiety occurring early in life, before object differentiation has been accomplished. To alleviate the anxiety, the child resorts to a fantasy of symbiotic fusion with the mother. In this way, mother and child become one and the danger of separation is nullified. We believe that this reparative fantasy is the psychodynamic basis for transsexualism in the male and that the transsexual phenomena can be understood clinically as attempts to ward off threats to psychic fusion with the mother.

Thus, in the transsexual's unconscious mind, he literally becomes the mother and, to sustain this fantasy, he attempts to reverse his core gender identity from male to female. Although this is a highly theoretical formulation, it is solidly rooted in current psychoanalytic concepts about early child development (Greenacre, 1958; Jacobson, 1964; Mahler, 1968). It is also supported by clinical evidence from adult transsexuals. The memory attached to the first experience of cross-dressing in the mother's clothes is almost invariably the same: "I felt very warm, very comfortable. . . . I had company, I felt wanted." This memory is very different from the transvestite's first cross-dressing experience, which is often accompanied by sexual excitation. For the transsexual, the mother's clothes are a symbolic representation of the pregenital mother. Wearing them, he reestablishes the early symbiotic relationship with her. It is no surprise, therefore, that a frequent adult transsexual fantasy is of mothering, particularly mothering a girl child.

Let us turn now to the relative asexuality of transsexuals and their abhorrence of homosexuality. The "true" transsexual before surgical sex reassignment frequently has no sexual experience other than masturbation. Some do not even masturbate but obtain sexual release solely through nocturnal emissions. Masturbation is usually performed in a mechanistic, dissociated way, either with no fantasy at all or with a vague heterosexual fantasy in which the patient sees himself as a woman. In either case, the pleasure yield seems minimal, at times almost to the point of anhedonia. The main component of this asexuality is a specific self-loathing of male physical characteristics—not just the genitalia—but all other aspects of maleness as well, such as hair distribution, musculature, fat distribution, absence of breasts, etc.

The penis, of course, is the most significant of all the male insignia. The patient's willingness, or rather eagerness, to part with his penis is the sine qua non of transsexualism. The transsexual does not suffer from castration anxiety; on the contrary, he suffers from anxiety unless he is castrated. We have noted that the transsexual impulse is progressive. The actual loathing of the male insignia may occur late in childhood but more typically appears in adolescence or early adulthood, and is itself a progressive phenomenon. The male insignia, particularly the penis, block the credibility of womanhood; that is, they give the lie to the psychic fusion with the mother. For the same reason, the transsexual indignantly rejects homosexuality, which one might otherwise anticipate would be his chief sexual outlet. Were he to accept homosexuality he would perforce acknowledge that he was male.

Not only does the ambiguous core gender identity result in asexuality; it also impairs gender role identity and undermines masculine behavior. In other words, transsexuals not only feel confusion about core gender identity but progressively perform badly as little boys. One hears a history of displeasure in sports and roughhousing and a preference for girls' activities. In adolescence, they become cognizant of their lack of interest in the other sex and increasingly notice the discrepancy in their development from that of normal boys. We believe that the poor performance in the masculine role tips the ambiguous core gender identity toward resolution in a female identity. In this sense, the male insignia represent a demand for masculine performance, a demand that cannot be met. The self-loathing is focused on the male insignia, thereby preserving a modicum of self-esteem for the fantasied other self—that is, the "female" self.

In summary, then, in male transsexuals, the security motivation takes priority over sexuality. In our view, the primary threat to the transsexual does not emanate from the retaliation implicit in an oedipal configuration but is the threat to survival from early maternal abandonment. The predominant reparative fantasy is symbiotic merger with the mother to insure security. By strict definition, therefore, transsexualism is not primarily a sexual disorder but a disturbance of core gender identity that results in severe impairment of gender role identity. Sexuality by and large drops out or is expressed in heterosexual fantasies, in which the patient preserves his security by assuming the female identity. In other words, sexuality is largely sacrificed to consolidation of cross-gender identification and thus to security needs.

In this chapter, we first delineated disorders of gender identity from sexual psychopathology. In so doing we constructed a psychodynamic framework within which the two disorders could be conceptualized, either singly or together. We then utilized the framework to demonstrate the psychodynamic interrelationships between gender identity and sexual psychopathology in homosexuality, transvestism, and transsexualism. In each of these disorders, we subjected the symptoms to a psychodynamic analysis and proposed a developmental hypothesis for their origin. We believe our theoretical framework will prove equally useful in conceptualizing other disorders in which both sex and gender play significant roles.

6

The Transsexual Syndrome in Males: Primary Transsexualism

1974

ETHEL S. PERSON AND LIONEL OVESEY

TRANSSEXUALS FALL into two groups: primary and secondary. The former are transsexuals throughout the course of their development; the latter are effeminate homosexuals and transvestites who become transsexuals under stress. In this chapter we delineate the syndrome of primary transsexualism. We present clinical examples and discuss gender identity, family history, childhood development, clinical course, and personality structure. In the following chapter we discuss secondary transsexualism.

In a previous paper (Ovesey and Person, 1973 [Chapter 5 in this book]), we established a theoretical framework in which we demonstrated the psychodynamic interrelationships between gender identity and sexual psychopathology in homosexuality, transsexualism, and transvestism. In this chapter, we examine male transsexualism in more detail. We define transsexualism as the wish in biologically normal persons for hormonal and surgical sex reassignment. We demonstrate, first, that the transsexual wish is the nucleus of a transsexual syndrome, and, second, that the transsexual syndrome in males is not a unitary disorder but a final common pathway for patients who otherwise differ markedly in family history, developmental history, psychodynamic patterning, personality structure, and clinical course. The differentiation of these patients is not of solely academic interest; it is of crucial importance for the psychiatrist who must evaluate applicants for sex reassignment.

We are in agreement with others (Stoller, 1968a,b; Segal, 1965; Socarides,

1968, 1970; Golosow and Weitzman, 1969; Gershman, 1970; Weitzman, Shamoian, and Golosow, 1970) that transsexualism, transvestism, and effeminate homosexuality have their origin in the preoedipal period. We proposed in our initial paper (Ovesey and Person, 1973) that all three disorders stem from unresolved separation anxiety during the separation-individuation phase of infantile development.[1] In point of time, we suggested that they originated along a developmental gradient: transsexualism first, transvestism and effeminate homosexuality later. The symptomatic distortions of gender and sex in the three disorders reflect different ways of handling separation anxiety at progressive levels of maturation.

Thus, as we see it, in male transsexualism, the child resorts to a reparative fantasy of symbiotic fusion with the mother to counter separation anxiety. In this way, mother and child become one and the anxiety is allayed, but the cost is an ambiguous core gender identity (sense of maleness). We infer that this fantasy is laid down before the child is three years old (normally, core gender identity is firmly established by that age). The ambiguous core gender identity also impedes sexual development and in most transsexuals leads to relative asexuality.

In contrast to transsexualism, separation anxiety in transvestism and effeminate homosexuality is allayed not by symbiotic fusion with the mother but by resort to transitional and part-objects. These mechanisms are not as primitive as symbiosis and do not become available to the infant until he has moved further along on the separation-individuation gradient. The mechanisms may become operant before the age of three, but their major effects come later, since there is little ambiguity about core gender identity either in the transvestite or in the effeminate homosexual; to the contrary, core gender identity in both is predominantly male. Gender role identity, however, is markedly disturbed.[2]

Classification

The stages of maturation along a developmental gradient are not neatly compartmentalized but overlap. In consequence, under conditions of stress, the

1. See Mahler (1972) for an excellent summary of the separation-individuation process. Mahler dates the principal psychologic achievements of this process to the period from about the fourth or fifth to the thirtieth or thirty-sixth month of age.

2. In transvestism, the female clothes represent the mother as a transitional object and hence confer maternal protection. They are also used sexually as fetishistic defenses against oedipal anxiety. In effeminate homosexuality, the boy would like to maintain the dependent tie to the mother but fears engulfment and annihilation. In the Oedipus complex, this fear is eventually transferred to the vagina, and the homosexual solves both his sexual and dependency problems by changing the sexual object. In his case, therefore, the separation anxiety is allayed through the pseudohomosexual components (Ovesey, 1969) of the homosexual act. His partner's penis is equated with the mother's breast and is incorporated orally or anally as a part-object.

transsexual impulse may arise defensively as a regressive phenomenon in some effeminate homosexuals and transvestites. Clinically, therefore, there are three prototypic histories in patients who seek sex reassignment, and transsexuals can be classified in accordance with these prototypes. We have divided them into two groups, which we have designated primary and secondary transsexuals.

Developmentally, the primary transsexuals progress toward a transsexual resolution of their gender and sexual problems without significant deviation either heterosexually or homosexually. Behaviorally, therefore, they are primarily transsexuals from the beginning and throughout the course of their development. In them, the transsexual impulse is insistent and progressive, and usually they cannot rest until they reach their objective. In the second group are those patients who gravitate toward transsexualism only after sustained periods of active homosexuality or transvestism. Behaviorally, therefore, they are primarily homosexuals or transvestites, and only secondarily do they become transsexuals. In them, the transsexual impulse may be either transient and fluctuating or insistent and progressive. In the latter case, it may eventually become a full-blown transsexual syndrome. In summary, then, we can classify transsexualism clinically under the following headings:

I. Primary transsexualism
II. Secondary transsexualism
    A. Homosexual transsexualism
    B. Transvestitic transsexualism[3]

In our clinical experience, the great majority of male transsexuals will fit easily into this classification. A few patients, however, will straddle two, or even all three of the categories, and in their clinical course be mixtures of transsexualism, transvestism, and homosexuality. They will have transitory episodes of each, shifting from one to the other, before they ultimately embark on the final transsexual resolution. We have concluded from a study of female transsexuals that there is no female equivalent of primary male transsexualism. In our opinion, the transsexual syndrome in women develops only in homosexuals with a masculine gender role identity. Female transsexualism, therefore, can be classified as another form of secondary (homosexual) transsexualism.

This chapter is based on a psychiatric study of twenty transsexual patients in various stages of hormonal and surgical treatment. Ten were primary and ten were secondary transsexuals. The latter broke down into five homosexual and five transvestitic transsexuals. All the patients were volunteers referred by Dr. Harry Benjamin's office and The Erickson Educational Foundation, both

3. The terms "homosexual transsexualism" and "transvestitic transsexualism" have previously been used by Money (1970–71).

clearing houses for patients seeking sex reassignment. The patients were studied in psychiatric interviews. Five patients were seen in single interviews only; fifteen were seen approximately once a week for several weeks, then irregularly for periods ranging from a few months to as long as two years. All patients were first seen by Dr. Person, who also conducted all ongoing interviews. Selected patients in each category were seen in consultation by Dr. Ovesey.

The numerical breakdown of our sample is not statistically significant. We chose to study more primary transsexuals than either homosexual or transvestitic transsexuals because we wished to establish beyond a doubt that primary transsexualism is a distinct diagnostic entity, separate from both homosexual and transvestitic transsexualism. Sulcov (1973), in a study of sixty-five consecutive applicants for sex reassignment, classified them as follows: homosexual transsexuals 52 percent; "asexual isolates" (primary transsexuals in our classification) 18 percent; transvestitic transsexuals 18 percent; unclassified 12 percent. The median age of those classified as transsexuals was the following: homosexual transsexuals twenty-two, primary transsexuals twenty-four, transvestitic transsexuals forty.

Gender Identity in Transsexualism

The presenting complaint of the transsexual, both primary and secondary, is usually a variant of the plea, "I am a female soul trapped in a male body." The patient claims that this was a lifelong conviction, although he at no time denies the anatomic reality of his maleness. Stoller (1968a) accepts this claim and attributes the patient's conviction to a female core gender identity laid down within the first three years of life. We find ourselves in disagreement with Stoller. We question the transsexual's conviction of femaleness, as well as its life-long duration. We also question Stoller's hypothesis that transsexuals have a female core gender identity.

Whether or not the transsexual's conviction of femaleness is truly a conviction is, of course, a matter of interpretation. Clinically, he appears confused about gender identity, and his conviction seems an attempt to resolve this confusion rather than a true conviction. (In this chapter, we use the term "conviction" to express the patient's representation of his feelings, not our interpretation of them.) In our opinion, the transsexual does not succeed fully either in denying that he is male or in accepting that he is female. On this basis, we believe it would be more accurate to say that transsexuals have an ambiguous core gender identity. The ambiguity derives from the unconscious fantasy used by transsexuals to allay separation anxiety: namely, symbiotic fusion with the mother. Our hypothesis is bolstered by the fact that the conviction has an evolutionary history; that is, it does not spring ready-made into the child's head. Furthermore, the evolutionary process is not the same in all transsexuals. Its course in primary transsexuals is very different from that in secondary transsexuals, and the ambiguity is far greater in the former than in the latter.

The primary transsexual in childhood has no major defense against separation anxiety other than this fantasy, which markedly inhibits masculine behavior; hence, the primary transsexual has undiluted gender discomfort that becomes progressively more severe as he grows older. Not until late adolescence or early adulthood, when he learns of the existence of transsexualism, does he get any relief. Only then does he resolve the ambiguity through a transsexual identity and sex reassignment. The secondary transsexuals, on the other hand, are perhaps more successful in alleviating gender discomfort. They usually resolve the ambiguity somewhat earlier by dealing with the separation anxiety either as transvestites or as homosexuals. The defenses in these disorders tip the ambiguity toward a male core gender identity. As long as these defenses work, the patients maintain some semblance of emotional balance. However, under conditions of severe stress, when their tenuous masculinity is threatened, they may regress to transsexualism and seek a reversal of core gender identity.

It would be helpful here to review the autobiography of Christine Jorgensen (1967), the "ur" transsexual. Emotionally withdrawn, Jorgensen as a child was asexual but was regarded as a sissy. In our classification, he was a primary transsexual. At the termination of his army service, Jorgensen speculated on his initial confusion about gender identity: "I was underdeveloped physically and sexually. I was extremely effeminate. My emotions were either those of a woman or a homosexual. I believed my thoughts and responses were more often womanly than manly. But at that point, I was completely unaware of the many combinations of masculinity and femininity, aside from homosexuality, that exist side by side in the world" (1967, p. 43).

In 1948, at the age of twenty-two, he read a newspaper article about the work of a prominent endocrinologist who had experimented with the masculinization of a chicken and the return to vigor of a castrated rooster. At first, Jorgensen considered masculinization, but he finally opted for feminization. He described himself at the time to a doctor: "I've tried for more than twenty years to conform to the traditions of society. I've tried to fit myself into a world that's divided into men and women . . . to live and feel like a man, but I've been a total failure at it. I've only succeeded in living the life of a near recluse, completely unable to adjust" (p. 73).

In *The Male Hormone* by de Kruif, Jorgensen read a statement that profoundly impressed him: "Chemically, all of us are both man and woman because our bodies make both male and female hormones, and primarily it's an excess of testosterone that makes us men and an excess of female hormones that makes us women; and the chemical difference between testosterone and estradiol is merely a matter of four atoms of hydrogen and one of carbon" (1945, p. 79).

He began to medicate himself with estradiol. Soon thereafter he found a sympathetic physician with whom he discussed "certain historical cases" of sex conversion reported in medical journals, presumably of pseudohermaphrodites. The quotes above reveal that Jorgensen's conclusions about his gender identity (pseudohermaphroditic, but truly female) were achieved via a perusal of the medical literature and not simply from some inner process. Jorgensen's ingenuity lay in forging his identity; the term "transsexualism" was subsequently coined by Benjamin (1953). Today, many transsexuals conclude as did Jorgensen that there is some chemical imbalance that causes their problem, but this has become a much easier conclusion since Christine Jorgensen did the spadework for them.

Primary Transsexualism

Case 1. A. appears as a tall, quiet, shy, striking-looking blonde woman in her early twenties.[4] In fact, she is a thirty-year-old transsexual. She has been taking hormones for two years and has been living as a woman since her orchiectomy eight months ago. The remaining sex conversion surgery will be scheduled when financially possible. She has a receding hairline, which she masks by wearing her hair forward. The beard is not visible but is still palpable; she must have electrolysis for another year. She feels comfortable as a woman in every social situation, except at the beach, where she is afraid her male genital will show. She is not psychologically minded and in the interviews had difficulty remembering her early years. Nevertheless, she tried hard to cooperate, focused on trying to remember dreams and fantasies, and was very proud when she could. The relationship with the interviewer became very meaningful to her, and she has stayed in contact on a flexible basis since the termination of her regular sessions.

Except for a two-year period between the ages of seven and nine, A. lived with his mother until they broke with each other over the orchiectomy and A.'s assumption of the female identity. The mother is now fifty-eight years old. There is an older brother, thirty-two, who is married and the father of two sons.

4. In the two clinical examples that follow we have used the convention of referring to the patient as male prior to assumption of the female role and as female after the assumption of the female role.

The parents were divorced when A. was two, and the father has had no contact with the boys thereafter. He died when A. was seven. A. has no memory of him.

A. was never close to her mother, though she feels she loves her. The mother is undemonstrative but will respond with affection if A. takes the initiative. She is described as strong-minded and stubborn but easily hurt and quick to tears. She worked as a saleswoman from the time she was divorced, leaving the boys with a neighbor until she came home. A. had pneumonia when he was two and was hospitalized for three weeks. As a child, he was very lonely and spent many hours by himself watching television. He was introverted and shy, not very assertive, and gave no trouble to anyone. In the early years, he relied on his brother, who was his "Lord Protector." A. has read Stoller's book (1968a) and insists that her mother "in no way" resembles the mothers of Stoller's transsexual patients. (See discussion under *Family History*.)

A.'s mother always had "beaus." Her longest romance was with D., who was something of a father-surrogate to A. The romance ended when A. was six. A few months later, the mother left the boys with relatives and went to live in another town. In her two-year absence, between A.'s seventh and ninth years, A. started dressing in women's clothes. The experience was always accompanied by a sense of warmth and well-being but was totally nonerotic. When he was ten, his mother discovered his cross-dressing and severely berated him. He did not cross-dress again until several months prior to his surgery. However, he always wanted to be a girl and had fantasies of mothering a girl child. This is a common fantasy among transsexuals, first noted by Money (1968b). We interpret the fantasy as an attempt to mother oneself through identification with the child.

A. was not in the least effeminate as a child but was acutely aware of his difference from other boys and felt profoundly isolated. Until he was twelve he had frequent nightmares of being chased by a monster, and he wet his bed well into his teens. He was always mildly anorexic until he began hormone therapy. At puberty and for many years thereafter, he made consistent attempts to "be a man," even though in personality he was nonassertive, overaccommodating, and fearful of arguments, lest they become violent. He went out for football, lifted weights, and became a drag car racer. Manifestly, he was very successful in these endeavors, but inwardly they brought no relief. He used obsessive preoccupation, first with playing football, later with mechanics, to hide his loneliness and depression, both from himself and from others. He had many friends with whom he shared activities, but he revealed himself to no one. Nonetheless, many people used him as a confidant, respecting his judgment and discretion. He bound people to himself by endlessly doing favors—running errands, lending money, fixing appliances, and always being available. After college, he worked for many years, productively, for an engineering firm.

His sexual life consisted of infrequent masturbation, usually without any fantasy; occasionally, he fantasized about being a woman having intercourse with an unidentified man. He never developed a romantic interest in either men or women. As his friends married, he became friends with the couples. Often, he was the confidant of the wives and ultimately of the children, with whom he felt most at ease. He always saw the desired relationship between the sexes from a woman's point of view, but his attitudes were somewhat conventional; for example, men always had to open doors for women and light their cigarettes. He disapproved of a male friend's infidelity and identified with his wife. A. has followed these rules of etiquette both as a man and as a woman. As for homosexuality, A. believes that one should not be judgmental, but she would find it personally abhorrent and unnatural.

In essence, then, with the exception of his asexuality, A. made a good behavioral adaptation as a man. He was even able to maintain platonic dating relationships and was much sought after by women. At the same time, in his inner life, he felt estranged, lonely, anxious, and depressed. Were there no such thing as sex-conversion therapy, A. believes that he would have been able to maintain such a life indefinitely, but it would have remained joyless and empty.

As time went on, his depression deepened. His friends became progressively more involved in their family lives, and A. felt more and more excluded. Amid mounting social pressure to get married, he was totally unable to desire or initiate sex with a woman. With the years, it became more of a burden to sustain his masculinity, and his interest in mechanics and racing cars waned. He began to suffer an increasing sense of oddness, and life seemed less and less worth living. He had heard of Christine Jorgensen some time during college and thought that her experience might apply to him. He began to read all the literature on transsexualism, and his preoccupation with sex reassignment gradually took on obsessive proportions. He started saving his money and began treatment as previously described. Shortly thereafter, he resigned from the engineering firm, resumed cross-dressing, and began to live and work full time as a woman. Currently, A. is employed as a file clerk, a step down vocationally, but a price A. is willing to pay.

After adopting the woman's role, A. has experienced some remarkable changes, both in feeling and in behavior. The mild anorexia has disappeared, and A., previously a heavy smoker, has totally given up cigarettes. She reports a greater ease and sense of well-being. She particularly stresses her increased ability to be assertive. She is now able to make demands on others instead of constantly doing favors for them. She no longer lets people take advantage of her but has learned to protect herself. Her propensity for obsessive preoccupation remains, but the content has shifted to the practical realities of being a woman—accumulating money for the operation, shopping for clothes, making new girlfriends, learning how to use make-up, and so forth. A. has been asked out by men, but she is too embarrassed about her beard and penis to risk it. She feels once these last signs of maleness are gone, she will have no difficulty finding men.

Case 2. B., now twenty-nine years old, has been followed for two years. When first seen, she had been receiving hormone therapy for a year and was undergoing epilation, but she still lived, worked, and dressed as a man. One year ago she underwent sex reassignment surgery and subsequently has lived full time as a woman.

B. comes from an unstable family background. Her mother was a "good" woman who provided essential care, but in a distant way. She and B. were never close. She knew nothing of B.'s inner life, nor did she ever show any interest in it. The father, a traveling salesman, was away a great deal. His visits home, however, were not happy occasions. He paid little attention to B. and there were frequent angry confrontations with the mother. He had a "nervous breakdown" when B. was six and has been in a mental hospital ever since. There is a younger brother, now twenty-five, who is married and has children.

As an infant, B. suffered from severe bouts of asthma. He was hospitalized for three weeks at nine months of age and again for four weeks at fourteen months. The condition then stabilized, and he required hospitalization only one more time, when he was four years old. According to his mother, there was a real question of his very survival during the first year and a half of his life. He was obese ever since he could remember and remained markedly overweight until the first year of hormone treatment between the ages of twenty-six and twenty-seven during which he lost 100 pounds. He was a lonely child and had no playmates except for his brother and his brother's friends. He engaged in boys' activities with them, but with a private sense of distaste. He was not considered effeminate but was perceived as "fat and nervous." He spent most of his time alone, watching television and thinking his own thoughts.

He began to cross-dress at the age of four. He first tried one of his mother's dresses, which he would have preferred, but it was so large that he got lost in it. Snugness was important to him, so for a few years, until he grew bigger, he settled for her underpants. The feeling accompanying the cross-dressing was always one of "warmth," never erotic. He often stayed home from church on Sundays so that he could wear his mother's clothes. He remembers by the age of twelve lying in bed longing to be a girl. He prayed to be discovered by his mother or grandfather so that they would share his secret and help him with his burden. Eventually, of course, they did discover him. He told them the truth, that he preferred to be a girl, but they refused to listen and brushed him off with the comment, "It will pass. Just don't do it any more." A misfit among boys, he prided himself solely on his "breasts," which were unusually large because he was so fat. He had no sexual outlet other than very occasional masturbation unaccompanied by fantasies.

B. did well academically. In the second year of college, he read a newspaper of a famous transsexual, a female impersonator. Slowly, he began to believe that this syndrome described his plight. He dropped out of school and confronted his mother, who again denied the problem. He became very depressed, made a serious suicide attempt, and was hospitalized. The psychiatrist was unsympathetic, thought he was psychotic, and treated him with electric shock.

Released, he tried once more to be a man. He gave up cross-dressing, got a good job as a computer operator, and spent all his spare time as a drag car racer. The effort was unsuccessful. No matter how busy he made himself, he could not suppress the wish to be a woman. One day, when racing, he became aware again of his suicidal impulses, this time the wish to drive the car off the road. Fearful that he would kill himself, he began to save money and secretly made plans for hormone therapy and sex reassignment.

One month before surgery, well epilated and big-breasted, B. began to dress full time as a woman. Almost immediately he attracted a bisexual male with whom he had a sexual affair. This was his first sexual encounter with another person. The two had intrafemoral intercourse with B. in the female position. He imagined himself to be a woman and thus did not consider the act to be truly homosexual. The ease with which he attracted a man proved to be a harbinger of the future. The change in personality since reassignment has been quite startling. The withdrawn, shy, unattractive, dowdy, acneiform young man has metamorphosized into a forceful, lively, humorous, attractive young woman.

Within two months after the operation, B. had two proposals of marriage, the first from an elderly transvestite, which she refused, the second from a six-foot, seven-inch construction worker, which she accepted. We were fortunate in being able to interview both men. The successful suitor was a bisexual who had previously been married and was a father. He stated that he had always been behaviorally heterosexual except for a single brief homosexual relationship. He maintained that he looked upon B. as a real woman, no different in his eyes from any other. At the time of this writing, he and B. are living together and plan to marry as soon as his divorce becomes final. B. describes sex as pleasurable and claims that she is orgastic.[5] The pairing of transvestites

5. Some years later, it turned out that the successful suitor was a closet transvestite, who become more interested in B.'s night gowns than in B., and B. ultimately left him. (Footnote added, 1998.)

and operated transsexuals was noted by Guze (1968). We know of three such marriages.

Family History. From observations of male transsexuals, Stoller (1968b) delineated a characteristic mother-son interaction within a disturbed marital setting. The crucial factor is an "excessive, blissful physical and emotional closeness between mother and infant, extended for years and uninterrupted by other siblings" (p. 169). Thus, according to Stoller: The mothers "have given their infant sons a blissful closeness in which all wishes are granted, especially, unhappily, the wish to remain a part of mother's body" (p. 167). The mothers were generally unhappy people with underlying depression and a deep sense of emptiness, who lived in loveless, essentially sexless marriages. The fathers were emotionally detached, passive and/or feminine, and often physically absent, particularly during the transsexual's early years.

Our series of ten primary transsexuals do not bear out the crucial factor, the characteristic mother-son interaction. However, we relied solely on reports from the subjects, without any primary data from the mothers. Even so, the historical accounts we obtained were so uniform that it is difficult for us to reconcile them with Stoller's findings. In no instance did we elicit a history consonant with a state of "blissful closeness" between mother and child. When several patients were pressed to comment on the infantile experience as described by Stoller, each insisted that it would have been impossible, because nothing in the mother's personality indicated any potential for close-binding behavior, physical or emotional.

In all ten of our subjects, when they described their mothers, there was one key feature that never varied: the mothers dutifully provided routine care, often in the face of harsh realities, but were insensitive to the child's emotional needs. This was stated in a variety of ways by different patients, but the meaning was always the same: "She was oblivious to my depression and loneliness." "She was too preoccupied with her own troubles to know what was happening with me." "She was strong-willed and stubborn; she never listened." "She would always try to help, but so many things got left unsaid." Essentially, the mother was responsive to the child's needs as she saw them, not as he experienced them. In our sample, therefore, mother and son were not excessively close but rather excessively distant. The fathers, however, as viewed by our subjects, were very much like those reported by Stoller.

We have already postulated that early separation anxiety is a necessary precondition in the development of transsexualism. In this connection, it is of interest to note that half of our primary transsexuals, five out of ten, gave a history of physical separation from the mother within the first four years of life. In each instance, the separation was necessitated by the child's hospitalization for illness. Separation anxiety, of course, can be produced by a variety of causes. In our series of primary transsexuals, it seemed to arise from a deficit in the quality of empathic mothering, often in association with a real separation precipitated by the child's illness.

Developmental History and Clinical Course. Several workers (Stoller, 1968a; Money, 1968b]; Green, 1968a) have reported that transsexual patients showed an early displeasure in boyish pursuits, concomitantly with a preference for girls' activities and for girls as playmates. Many were mothers' helpers and derived pleasure from housekeeping. According to these workers, effeminate behavior was common, and the patients were often called sissies by their peers. Our findings for primary transsexuals are at some variance with these reports, particularly in regard to effeminacy.

In our series of ten primary transsexuals, nine showed no evidence of effeminacy in childhood. They were identified by their peers as boys and were never referred to as sissies. At school, they participated in rough-and-tumble behavior when required, but with an inner sense of abhorrence. As far as we can make out, they did not engage in girls' activities or play with girls any more than normal boys did. Some helped out with housework, but as a necessary chore, not because it was especially pleasurable. Only one of the ten was effeminate and dubbed a sissy in his boyhood. He avoided boyish pursuits, preferred girls' activities, and had girls as playmates. This one transsexual, effeminate in mannerisms, was also emotionally withdrawn and asexual, both characteristic findings in primary transsexualism. We have therefore classified him as such, though actually he would fall on a continuum between primary and secondary (homosexual) transsexualism.

All ten of our primary transsexuals were socially withdrawn and spent most of their time after school by themselves at home. They read, watched television, occupied themselves with hobbies, or just sat, stewing in anxiety and depression. In effect, they were childhood loners with few age-mate companions of either sex, an observation also made by Pomeroy (1968). As children, our patients were envious of girls and fantasized being girls, but none actually believed that he was a girl. To summarize, then, in his childhood, the primary transsexual is not effeminate, but he feels either abhorrence or discomfort in boyish activities. This creates a feeling of difference and estrangement from other children, both boys and girls. The result is a chronic sense of isolation, the inner experience of every primary transsexual in our series.

Stoller (1968a) has described three boys, first seen between the ages of four and five, who in their characteristics resembled adult male transsexuals he had previously studied. They were extremely effeminate, cross-dressed in their mothers' clothes, wished to be girls, and insisted that when they grew up they would become women. On this basis, Stoller diagnosed them as cases of childhood transsexualism and suggested that they could become adult transsexuals. All three boys had very emotionally expressive, theatrical personalities, described by Stoller as follows: "It is interesting to note that all three of these boys are considered to be extremely creative by their families, teachers, and other observers. All have a remarkable precocity with regard to painting, dancing, costumes, designing of clothes, acting, hair-dressing, story-telling, and love of music" (1968a, p. 94).

Here again, Stoller's findings are at variance with ours. The differences between these three boys and our primary transsexuals are startling. Our patients were neither effeminate nor theatrical; if anything, they were at the opposite end of the personality spectrum. How are we to account for these discrepancies in findings? Why are our observations of mother-son interaction, childhood masculinity, and personality structure exactly the opposite of those reported by Stoller and other workers in this field? We believe the answer lies in their failure to distinguish sufficiently between primary and secondary transsexuals, who have different childhood histories and hence different personalities as adults. To us, Stoller's histories sound very much like those Bieber and his associates (1962) obtained from adolescent homosexuals, including the cross-dressing. If, in fact, Stoller's three boys grow up to be transsexuals, we predict that they will first pass through a homosexual period; that is, they will be secondary (homosexual) transsexuals.

In our sample, as he advances through childhood, the primary transsexual becomes increasingly aware of the difference between himself and other boys. This difference is sharply defined in adolescence, when most boys become sexually aware of girls and homosexual boys become sexually aware of other boys. The primary transsexual, however, does neither; instead, he is essentially asexual and shows little sexual interest in either sex. Most often, he has no sexual experience other than masturbation, and even the masturbation is infrequent. Seven of our ten subjects masturbated less frequently than once a month. Masturbation was usually performed in a mechanistic, dissociated way, either with no fantasy at all or with a vague heterosexual fantasy in which the patient saw himself as a woman. The fantasies were impersonal, and the partner was usually a stylized man rather than a real person. The pleasure yield was minimal, at times almost to the point of anhedonia.

A major component of this asexuality in all of our primary transsexuals was a specific self-loathing of male physical characteristics. The loathing typically began in late adolescence and was a progressive phenomenon. It encompassed not only the genitalia but all other aspects of maleness as well, such as fat distribution, musculature, hair distribution, absence of breasts, and so forth. The penis, of course, is the most significant of all the male insignia. The willingness, or rather eagerness, to part with the penis is the sine qua non of primary transsexualism. Secondary transsexuals are also willing, but not quite so eager.

The male insignia, particularly the penis, block the credibility of womanhood; that is, they give the lie to the psychic fusion with the mother. They also represent a demand for masculine performance, a demand that cannot be met. The self-loathing is focused on the male insignia, thereby preserving a modicum of self-esteem for the fantasized other self—that is, the "female" self. For the same reasons, the primary transsexual indignantly rejects homosexuality; were he to accept it, he would perforce acknowledge he was male.

There is a uniform history of childhood cross-dressing in our sample of ten primary transsexuals. All ten began to cross-dress sometime between the ages of three and ten, usually in the mother's clothes. All preferred outer garments, most often a dress, occasionally a slip, sometimes both. A few tried on undergarments but did not sustain much interest. Undergarments, of course, are more intimate apparel and, as such, more sexual in their connotation. The cross-dressing in all ten was surreptitious. Typically, in early adolescence, the practice evoked shame and was voluntarily abandoned as unmasculine, then resumed openly on a full-time basis after the transsexual resolution. In contrast, cessation of cross-dressing is infrequent in secondary transsexuals, both homosexual and transvestitic.

In the primary transsexual, the memory attached to the first experience of cross-dressing is invariably the same: "I felt very warm, very comfortable." . . . "I had company." . . . "I felt relieved." . . . "I felt wanted." This experience is very different from the transvestite's initial experience, which is often erotic and, if not, later becomes so. The primary transsexual never relates to the clothing fetishistically, nor does texture have the same intrinsic interest for him that it has for the transvestite. In our opinion, the primary transsexual's response to women's clothing reflects solely the alleviation of separation anxiety. We interpret his cross-dressing, therefore, as symbolic fulfillment of the unconscious wish for symbiotic fusion with the mother.

Primary transsexuals when first seen may be dressed as either men or women. In our sample, those who presented as men showed none of the characteristics of exaggerated femininity associated with effeminate homosexuality. They were conservative in dress and subdued in manner, the very antithesis of flamboyance or even style. They claimed to have no interest in male attire and were reluctant to call attention to themselves as men. Those who presented as women gave a much different impression. Not only did they pay more attention to dress, but mannerisms, voice, and posture were more animated. The overall effect, however, was still on the conservative side, especially in comparison with effeminate homosexual cross-dressers.

In postadolescence, the primary transsexual often makes "one last effort" to be a man in order to resolve the confusion he feels and to overcome his sense of isolation. This effort usually involves an all-out immersion in some activity commonly regarded as distinctly masculine. For example, the patient may join the army or go out for football. Two of our patients devoted years to drag car racing. Often the patient enters into the selected activity with monomaniacal zeal in order to crowd out all doubts about his masculinity, along with associated thoughts and feelings. When this "last effort" fails, as it inevitably does, the patient becomes even more isolated, anxious, and depressed. Ashamed, confused, with no outlet for intimate conversation or even confession, he begins a quest for some explanation of his distress. He avidly reads the psychologic and sexual literature, searching for clues to define his real nature to himself. Eventually, he stumbles on an account of transsexualism, usually about Christine Jorgensen (1967). Finding there are others similar to him becomes a great relief and for many Christine Jorgensen's autobiography has become their "Bible." Not only do they find relief, they find a new scenario for possible resolution.

Although there is a history of gender discomfort, the fantasies of childhood and adolescence are cast in the form of a wish, not a conviction; for example, "I would like to be a girl," not "I am a girl." The conviction, "I am a female soul," usually crystallizes out rather abruptly in late adolescence or early adulthood when the patient learns of the existence of transsexualism. Patients commonly speak of being greatly confused as to what they are—heterosexual, homosexual, transvestite—until they learn of transsexualism. This revelation, with its attendant explanation, offers relief, first of all, by giving the patient an identity. Thus, one patient, referred by the Erickson Educational Foundation, stated his reason for contacting us: "I want to be a transsexual."

Secondly, the literature on transsexualism offers a medical vehicle for a fantasy—the wish to be a woman—to be converted into a reality.[6] It is at this point that the wish hardens into the conviction that the patient is indeed a woman trapped in a man's body. Many physicians, upon hearing that the patient believes he is a woman, automatically assume that the patient is psychotic. However, since the patient is presented with medical evidence that the condition *does* exist, his subsequent belief that he is a woman does not fulfill the criteria for classification as a delusion. In point of fact, the vast majority of transsexuals are not psychotic.

Personality Inventory. The description that follows applies to patients prior

6. This insight is probably the beginning of my conceptualization of the shared cultural fantasy (Person, 1995). (Footnote added, 1998.)

to conversion therapy. We found very little variation in the personalities of our primary transsexuals; to know one was almost literally to know all. We have already commented extensively on their ambiguous core gender identity and their relative asexuality. Another feature was their uniformly low aptitude for psychologic insight. We found it difficult to elicit dreams, and in those few that were reported associations were meager and accompanied by considerable denial. Fantasies were more available, mostly stereotypic female fantasies lacking in both imagination and color. Except in masturbation, they were usually asexual and focused mainly on the romantic aspects of male-female relationships.

Depression, most often experienced as loneliness, was another characteristic feature. The depression was not guilty, self-accusatory, or angry, but was essentially an empty depression. The patients described their lives as men historically and in the present as sad, lonely, empty, and colorless. Suicidal ideation and suicide attempts were frequent. Six of the ten men admitted suicidal preoccupation, and two had made actual suicide attempts. The depression could perhaps be attributed mainly to failure in the masculine role with subsequent anxiety and loss of self-esteem. Our clinical impression, however, is that these patients were describing an ongoing depressive core, intensified by current stress but not caused by it. In their histories, there are frequent occurrences of thumbsucking, enuresis, and eating disorders, either anorexia or overweight. We believe these childhood symptoms, as well as the depression, are related to early separation anxiety.

There is a schizoid quality to the primary transsexual's personality. As previously described, his childhood is characterized by isolate behavior. Nonetheless, by adolescence or adulthood, some of these patients had acquired the knack for friendly but not intimate asexual relationships with both men and women. A great deal of time is spent with others, but feelings are not ordinarily alluded to. The patient is ingratiating and makes himself indispensable in a variety of ways; however, his friends are totally unaware of the transsexual problem or of his mental agony. These friendships, as experienced by the patient, have a symbiotic coloring, but typically he withholds a full commitment, as though anticipating rejection.

As a group, we found the primary transsexuals extremely gentle and self-effacing. Assertiveness was seriously crippled, though it survived enough in the work area to allow adequate and, on occasion, even outstanding performance. Energy and creativity, if present, were expressed in solitary pursuits and hobbies, often with obsessive thoroughness. These patients were always pliant and agreeable in their relationships with others unless thwarted in their demands for sex reassignment. In these circumstances, they became stubborn, strong-willed, and intractable. Otherwise, they were generally incapable of manifest anger.

Mental life, before and after surgery, is characterized by obsessive preoccupation with gender-related items. The obsessive form remains throughout; only the content changes. Thus, in childhood, the primary transsexual is obsessed with being a girl. In adolescence, he is obsessed with "one last effort" to be a man. In adulthood, before surgery, he is obsessed with sex conversion. His waking hours are filled with plans to get enough money for the operation and with learning how to be a woman. After surgery, he is first obsessed with the anatomical results, then centers on how to be more feminine both in appearance and in behavior.

The endless striving for perfection in the feminine role may lead to further surgery, usually facial plastic procedures or breast augmentation. In fact, one might say that the preoccupation with making "one last effort" as a man gives way to a preoccupation with fitting into the feminine norm. It is our impression that gender ease is never fully established. However, we have not seen subjects five or ten years postconversion, so that it remains theoretically possible that obsessive preoccupation with gender eventually recedes.

In sum, then, primary transsexuals are schizoid-obsessive, socially withdrawn, asexual, unassertive, and out of touch with anger. Underlying this personality, they have a typical borderline syndrome characterized by separation anxiety, empty depression, a sense of void, oral dependency, defective self-identity, and impaired object relations with absence of trust and fear of intimacy (Kernberg, 1967; Grinker, Werble, and Drye, 1968; Masterson, 1972). In our opinion, they most closely resemble a subgroup of the borderline syndrome that Grinker calls "the adaptive, affectless, defended, 'as if' persons" (Grinker, Werble, and Drye, 1968, p. 87). Unlike other borderline patients, however, primary transsexuals are distinguished by severe impairment of both core gender identity and of gender role identity from earliest childhood.

7

The Transsexual Syndrome in Males: Secondary Transsexualism

1974

ETHEL S. PERSON AND LIONEL OVESEY

SECONDARY TRANSSEXUALISM is defined as transsexualism that develops in homosexuals and transvestites regressively, under conditions of stress. Homosexual and transvestitic secondary transsexuals are distinguished from each other and both from primary transsexuals. Primary transsexuals, as we have seen, are essentially asexual and progress toward a transsexual resolution without significant deviation, whether heterosexual or homosexual. In them, the transsexual impulse is insistent and progressive, and usually they cannot rest until they reach their objective. Secondary transsexuals are effeminate homosexuals and transvestites who gravitate toward transsexualism only after sustained periods of active homosexuality or transvestism. In them, the transsexual impulse may be a transient symptom or may harden into a full-blown transsexual syndrome.

Although our study is based on ten applicants for sex reassignment, five homosexual transsexuals and five transvestitic transsexuals, our discussion draws on our much wider clinical experience with effeminate homosexuals and transvestites, many of whom have transsexual impulses but do not seek sex reassignment.

Homosexual Transsexualism

The vast majority of male homosexuals lack the propensity for a transsexual regression. The propensity exists almost entirely in cross-dressing effeminate homosexuals who comprise a very small segment of the homosexual population.[1] As we noted in Chapter 5, they fall into two subgroups: passive effeminate homosexuals and the more aggressive, though equally effeminate, drag queens. These two subgroups have similarities as well as differences in personality and psychodynamics. In the two clinical examples that follow, we will describe a typical patient in each subgroup.

Case 1. C. is a fat, effeminate 32-year-old man who lives with his parents. He is compliant, nonassertive, and unable to mobilize much anger. Despite these inhibitions, he is engaging, affectively responsive, and easy to talk to. His adaptive competence is of a very low order. Although extremely bright and articulate, he failed to complete high school, dropping out in his senior year. He has worked only a total of two years in his entire life. His mother has always slipped him money, while both pretend to the father that he is working. There is one sister, now twenty-five who is married. C. has been an exclusive homosexual as far back as he can remember. He now wants sex reassignment so that he can marry his current lover and live with him as his wife.

C. and his mother are bound together in a mutually interdependent relationship, each unable to let go of the other. As we would expect, he is markedly ambivalent about her. A sampling of his comments, culled from the interviews, follows: "I once loved my mother passionately, but I went through a period of hating her. She destroyed my life. . . . She was always very physical and smothered me with kisses. We used to see each other naked all the time. . . . She's either totally giving or totally selfish. She never ate until my sister and I had enough. . . . I have never been able to move away for fear of hurting her."

The mother and father have never gotten along. The father makes good money but gambles it away, so money has always been a problem. According to C., the father was ungiving and a tyrant at home, but generous to everyone else. The mother has always manipulated the father by lying to him and, C. suspects, by withholding sex. He doubts that they have had any sex life for many years. After C. was born, the father began gradually to absent himself from the family, and by the time C. reached adolescence, the father was seldom present. C. does not know for certain whether this was volitional withdrawal or whether he was pushed out by the mother, but the arrangement seemed perfectly acceptable to both.

We interviewed C.'s mother, who confirmed the familial history. She rationalized her lifelong intrusiveness into her son's life by predicating it on his physical frailty, a total fiction. She had always known of C.'s homosexuality and fully accepted it, but she refused to acknowledge his wish for a sex change. We

1. Rarely, a cross-dressing, noneffeminate homosexual will apply for sex reassignment. These patients fall on a gradient between primary transsexualism and homosexual transsexualism.

found her psychologic aptitude nonexistent. She was almost impossible to interview because of her incessant hysterical pleas that we help her boy and save him from the surgeons. As she saw it, his sole problem was his inability to work. It was clear to us that her underlying motivation was to keep C. at home with her.

C. was an effeminate child. He played with girls and pursued girlish interests. He cross-dressed regularly with parental approval from early childhood until the age of fifteen. The cross-dressing was theatrical and used to enhance C.'s fantasies of being a girl. It was never erotic, as in the transvestite, nor did it provide a feeling of comfort, as in the primary transsexual. His parents thought it so amusing that they often asked him to entertain. Once, when he was seven, they took him to relatives for Easter dinner dressed as a girl.

C. began a very active and pleasurable sex life when he was twelve. He engaged in various homosexual activities with peers, older boys, and adults. His sexual preference is passive anal intercourse, although he will reluctantly engage in other sexual transactions in order to please a partner. In such circumstances, he is capable of assuming the active role, but he does not enjoy it. His sexual relationships have been mostly transient contacts with partners picked up while cruising. Prior to his present involvement, he had only one long-term affair. This occurred ten years ago and lasted for one year. C. was so upset when the affair ended that he became suicidal and had to be hospitalized.

After his release, he hung around with a drag crowd for about six months. Once again he cross-dressed, but only in public to be seen, never in private. Initially, he felt secure in the group, liked the feeling of fooling people, and dreamed of "high drag." This was obviously an adaptive maneuver to compensate for the loss of his lover, but it failed because he had neither the physical attributes nor the money to be a successful drag queen. He received no narcissistic reinforcement as a woman since he lacked beauty, and the masculine homosexuals whom he was really after paid little attention to him since most of them wanted another man, not a drag queen. Thoroughly discouraged, C. gave up drag and returned to his previous existence, with its characteristic cruising.

For a time, in search of a new lover, he was extremely promiscuous. Gradually, as the years passed, he became disenchanted with gay life. He was not meeting the right people, he was getting the wrong responses, and he was picking up repeats. He began to gain weight, and although he is only five feet, eight inches tall, he now weighs over 200 pounds. His sex life diminished markedly, and his infrequent attempts were marred by erectile failures. In the interviews, he lamented his plight: "I feel inadequate as a homosexual. I can't do the bathroom thing any more. If someone is hypermasculine, I tremble with fear; if swish I don't like it. I have gotten too fat and I'm losing my hair."

Whenever pressure mounted, he wheedled money from his mother and traveled. Last year he went to Spain and met a presumed heterosexual with whom he lived. He engaged in face-to-face intrafemoral intercourse with this lover and fantasized himself as a woman. For the first time in his life he began to think seriously of sex reassignment: "I've known about transsexualism since Jorgensen. I could relate to this guy in Spain better if I were female. He wants me to stay in the house and play the whole thing, be subservient." He believes he is willing to forego sexual pleasure in order to live as a woman with this man. He is still hesitant, however, because he is skeptical that the lover will, in fact, marry him. At the same time, he is loath to give up life with his mother, since she so completely caters both to his dependency needs and to his passivity.

Case 2. D. is a very attractive twenty-two-year-old drag queen. He is a fashion designer on New York's Seventh Avenue, where he works dressed as a man, but he frequently hustles as a woman, presumably to make money to support his art school tuition. He belongs to the gay liberation movement and devotes considerable time to homosexual causes. Away from work, he is a member of a network of drag queens, all of whom, like D., are active hustlers. He has been taking hormones for two years in order to enhance his impersonation of a woman, but he has never before sought sex reassignment. Now, however, in the wake of an abortive love affair, he is pursuing a transsexual resolution.

D. lives with his parents, a brother one year younger, and a sister three years younger, in a lower-middle-class ethnic neighborhood. The father is a foreman in a factory. He has a reputation as a street fighter and, according to D., has always been "extraordinary violent" both in and out of the home. D. and his brother were frequently beaten, though the brother, who was more defiant, bore the brunt of it. The sister for the most part was spared. The father has not hit D. in a while and is described as mellowed, but D. is still terrified of him. He openly states that he hates his father and would like to see him dead, though he concedes that his father "adores" him.

In early childhood, before the age of four, D. had repeated bouts of broncho-pneumonia. On several occasions he required hospitalization. His mother has told him that more than once she believed it was "curtains" for him. D. describes his mother as very devoted but not overtly affectionate. She did not shower the children with kisses, but neither was she cold. D. likes his mother but is not especially close to her. The mother and both siblings know of D.'s homosexuality and seemingly accept it. They do not know, however, that he is a drag queen and a hustler. The father is totally ignorant of D.'s private life.

As a child, D. was fat, and he remained so until he started taking hormones two years ago. Since then he has lost forty pounds. He was always effeminate and preferred playing with girls. Although outwardly lively and gregarious, inwardly he felt lonely and spent hours by himself reading avidly. He became consciously aware of his homosexuality at the age of thirteen, when he read Krafft-Ebing. In adolescence, he switched his major interest from books to movies and became a "movie freak." His fantasy life is extremely rich and draws on books and the screen for heroines, with whom he identifies.

He began cross-dressing secretly at home in his own room when he was a child. He was never discovered, and to this day no one in the family knows about it. As in the case of C., the cross-dressing was not erotic and was not used directly to relieve anxiety; rather, it was the stimulus for fantasies of D. himself in theatrical female roles. He became progressively involved in full drag and the queen circuit beginning when he was eighteen. He gave up dressing in private at that time and now dresses only to go into public to be seen as a woman.

D. "came out" when he was sixteen under the auspices of an older homosexual with whom he fell in love. He was initially both active and passive in anal intercourse but soon came to prefer the passive role. His interest in sexuality diminished as his interest in drag increased. According to D., the diminution antedated his use of hormones, but since he has been taking medication, his sexual drive has all but disappeared. He rarely gets aroused and has no interest in orgasm; in fact, he states he has not had an ejaculation for two years. Occasionally, he has passive anal intercourse with a homosexual partner, not for sexual satisfaction but to feel the penetration, which gives him a sense of security. At present, however, his sexual activity consists primarily of performing fellatio in parked cars on the heterosexual men he hustles. He claims that these "tricks" believe him to be a woman and praise him highly for his services. Sexually, he feels nothing. He gets his "kicks" from fooling the men and through their attention. And, of course, he likes the money.

D. desires a "love relationship" with a "real" man. He has an underlying chronic depression and believes that only through such a relationship would he find relief. In reality, however, he has been in love three times, always with homosexuals. Each affair terminated in what D. construed as a rejection. Each time he became acutely depressed and felt suicidal, though he never actually made a suicide attempt. He suspects that he may have been instrumental in maneuvering all three rejections.

He has two fantasized modes of combating his depression. In the first fantasy, he identifies with Marilyn Monroe, who killed herself with sleeping pills. He glorifies her "vulnerability" and argues that the completely beautiful life is tragic. In this frame of mind, he courts rejection and romanticizes his suicidal ideation. In the second fantasy, he identifies with the Dowager Empress of China, a woman of immense power, who is said to have forced visitors to perform cunnilingus in token of their submission. He then concentrates on gay political activism or, alternately, on concocting lavish costumes for the competitions at drag queen balls. His personality shows alternating evidence of the double identification; thus, he may appear either as passive and ingratiating or haughty and somewhat paranoid. In spite of his "vulnerability," he is quite aggressive, usually with words, but on at least one occasion with a knife. Whether vulnerable or aggressive, however, he is always emotionally labile, expressive, and theatrical.

His current depression and concomitant wish for sex reassignment stem from two failures as a homosexual. D. was involved for three months in making a dress for a ball. He lost the competition and felt extremely disappointed. Shortly thereafter, he fell in love with an apparently hypermasculine homosexual. During their first sexual encounter, it emerged that his lover not only preferred the passive role in anal intercourse but was horrified that D. had breasts. After this experience, D. concluded that a homosexual adaptation was impossible for a queen and that his best hope for securing a "real" man lay in undergoing sex conversion. Whether or not this wish will persist, only time will tell.

Family History. There are three typical family constellations retrospectively reported by homosexual transsexuals. The same three, of course, are reported by effeminate homosexuals, from whom homosexual transsexuals derive. The father is either passive or hostile and, in most instances, though not all, emotionally absent. The distinguishing parameter is the quality of the mothering, which may be symbiotic, intrusive, or hostile. These are predominant patterns, but they are not exclusive; that is, they can exist in variable combinations. In some instances, the mother may not easily fit into any of the three categories.

The *symbiotic mother* has been described by Masterson as the typical mother of the borderline patient (1972). Although Masterson was not in this work dealing with either effeminate homosexuals or transsexuals, his description corresponds exactly to one pattern of mothering that emerged in our studies. The mother herself is borderline. As a child, she too experienced abandonment depression and an inability to separate. In her role as mother, she relives her infantile experience and attempts to cling to the child to fill her emptiness. Clinging behavior is the hallmark of this type of mother, and, unconsciously, she may regard the child as either her own mother or herself. Stoller, as we have seen, has described a similar mother-son interaction in the three effeminate boys whom he diagnosed as possible childhood transsexuals (Stoller, 1968a).

The *intrusive mother* is the configuration reported by Bieber in his study of male homosexuality (Bieber, 1962). Such a mother is overpowering and invasive, causing the son to fear engulfment and annihilation. This mother is more differentiated than the symbiotic mother. She does not wish to preserve a mother-son symbiosis in which the two roles are diffused; rather, she aims to make the son dependent. Her motivation is various; it may represent a phobic anxiety for the son's survival or the intrusion may be motivated by a special need to derogate maleness.

The *hostile mother* is physically and emotionally abrasive. In this pattern, the son makes a hostile identification with his mother in order to preserve his security needs, but his personality is invariably more paranoid than in the two previous instances.

Developmental History and Clinical Course. Homosexual transsexuals are effeminate at all times, from early childhood to adulthood. As children, they generally prefer girls as playmates, avoid boyish pursuits, and serve as mother's helpers. All fantasize about being girls, especially while cross-dressing, but core gender identity is essentially male. Ambiguity, when present, is far less pronounced than in primary transsexuals. Despite the early effeminacy, no adult homosexual transsexual has ever reported to us that as a child he actually believed he was a girl or that he would grow up to be a woman. Even postoperatively, we have never seen a homosexual transsexual who believed in his femaleness to the same extent as the primary transsexuals.

Cross-dressing begins in childhood, usually well before puberty. It is occasionally reported to cause relaxation, but more typically the clothes are used for narcissistic gratification. Later, after puberty, they are also used to attract male sexual partners. The theatrical potential of impersonation is realized early. Interest in make-up is precocious compared with other transsexual patients. Cross-gender fantasies are frequently tied to identifications with movie actresses, particularly among drag queens. The homosexual cross-dresser wants to be noticed. To this end, he wears colorful, flamboyant clothing, often to the point of caricature, especially at drag queen balls.

The initial self-identification, often made in preadolescence, is homosexual, not transsexual. Sexuality at first is usually strong and may even range to hyperactivity. With time, however, in many cases, sexuality is gradually attenuated as security needs take precedence over sexual needs. Most subjects prefer the passive role in anal intercourse, but this is not an obligatory preference. Some report that sexual aim may take second place to effecting a sexual transaction with a desired partner. Under such circumstances they are quite capable of assuming the active role on request. A few effeminate homosexuals, particularly former drag queens, may even have a preference for it.

The transsexual impulse appears in effeminate homosexuals at times of disruption of the homosexual adaptation. In general, homosexuals suffer greatly from castration anxiety and under ordinary circumstances have no wish to part with their penises. Indeed, the homosexual adaptation allays castration anxiety, preserves maleness, and provides dependent gratification. Transsexual impulses develop only under conditions of stress, when the homosexual adaptation fails. At such times, effeminate homosexuals regressively consider sacrificing their penises to the overriding need for dependent security. The most common stress is rejection by a lover. The transsexual wish may also arise as a desperate effort to please and thus hold onto a current lover. In drag queens, and to a lesser extent in passive effeminate homosexuals, the stress may be a narcissistic blow, such as aging or the loss of a beauty contest at a drag queen ball.

Personality Inventory. Homosexual transsexuals vary in personality along a gradient, with passive hysterical personalities at one end and hyperaggressive narcissistic personalities at the other. These poles describe the typical personality styles of the cross-dressing passive effeminate homosexuals and the drag queens, respectively. Both groups are labile and theatrical, the latter more so than the former. Some subjects present an intermediate clinical picture, and any one subject may move back and forth on the gradient. Nevertheless, it is of some clinical usefulness to describe the polar extremes, since personality may be closely related to therapeutic outcome.

Passive effeminate homosexuals in many ways present a caricature of typical female norms. They are interested in such things as cooking and decorating, but most of all, they seek a love relationship with another man where they can assume the female role. They may perform well vocationally but the major thrust of their interests is in "love." On the surface, they are passive and dependent, but they often dominate their mates through oversolicitousness. In this respect, they tend to duplicate the close-binding behavior frequently ascribed to their mothers. Often a relationship is terminated because the lover feels suffocated. Despite their covert tendency to dominate, the members of this group perceive themselves as ultimately dependent on the magical resources of the love object.

Drag queens are usually involved in a community of other queens. They treat each other as "sisters," and sexual relations within the group are rare. The major thrust of their lives is split in two: most alternate between narcissistic pursuits and "love" interests. The narcissism is institutionalized in an endless series of drag balls and parties. For each event, the queen immerses himself in preoccupation with costume, hair style, and make-up. Love interests are complex and often contradictory. The queen claims he wants involvement with a hypermasculine man who will overpower him. Once involved, however, he may attempt to overpower his lover, particularly in bed, where he frequently prefers to be the active partner in anal intercourse. In addition, many queens hustle for a living. This practice affords them both narcissistic gratification and the expression of contempt for the men they fool. These queens are quick to violence, both verbal and physical. Some may be on hard drugs and live on the fringes of crime. Unlike the passive effeminate homosexuals, the members of this group have a distinct paranoid and grandiose coloring. In them, the wish for sex reassignment may go beyond any wish to be female per se. They may seek conversion primarily to enhance their standing as female impersonators or prostitutes.

Transvestitic Transsexualism

Case 3. E. is a fifty-six-year-old married transvestite. His appearance and demeanor, except when cross-dressed, is always appropriately masculine. He and his wife have two grown sons, age twenty-two and twenty-six, who no longer live at home. E. is very verbal, intellectual, tightly controlled, and emotionally distant. He is not capable of intimacy, either with his wife and sons or with anyone else. He is ambitious and competitive but masks his aggression behind a gentle façade. He views himself as a "helpful type" but is proud of his ability to "kick ass" when necessary. He is a highly skilled industrial designer and until recently was always extremely successful. He started taking hormones six months ago following a professional failure and is now contemplating sex reassignment.

E. is the oldest of three siblings. He has a sister one year younger and a brother three years younger. The parents had a tempestuous marriage and separated many times during E.'s early childhood. They ultimately divorced when E. was five. The first separation occurred before E. was one, when his mother was still pregnant with his sister. During each separation, he stayed with his maternal grandparents while his sister and brother remained with his mother. The grandparents' household consisted of the grandfather, the grandmother, a young aunt of about twenty, and two older uncles, who soon departed. Sometimes E. stayed with the grandparents even when his mother, father, sister, and brother all lived together. He does not know for certain why this occurred but believes his grandmother and aunt wanted him because he was such a "cute little kid." After the divorce, he lived with his grandparents as before, while his siblings were farmed out to other relatives. The mother lived her own life, seeing the children irregularly and then only for brief periods.

When E. was fourteen, she remarried, and all three children moved in with her and the stepfather, where they remained until adulthood.

E. has no memory of his father. His mother was a vivacious and friendly woman who "liked" men. It was reputed that she had numerous lovers in the period between her two marriages. She was never unkind to E. and he feels she loved him. With each separation, however, he feared he might never see her again and was repeatedly overwhelmed with sadness. In the grandparents' home, the significant figures were the grandmother and the young aunt. The grandfather, for the most part, ignored him. The grandmother was loving and permissive, while his aunt's ministrations were tender and at times seductive. Thus, as a young child, he recalls, "she treated me like a doll." She fondled him, combed his hair into curls, and rubbed him down with oil. He remembers an early attachment to her mohair blanket, but he denies that she ever cross-dressed him.

As he grew older, neither the grandmother or the aunt spent much time with him. In addition, they were permissive to a fault. They let him go his own way and do whatever he wanted. He could disappear and stay with friends for several days, and no one questioned his whereabouts. He presents this premature independence as a positive experience, but the fact is that he felt lonely and abandoned throughout his childhood. He believes that by and large he raised himself. He enjoyed boyish pursuits, participated actively in sports, and was a dedicated woodsman. He was never effeminate and did not play with girls. He was always a good student and after graduation from college achieved early monetary success in his chosen profession.

E. began to cross-dress in his aunt's clothes at age six. He wore her skirt and blouse, which he still remembers in vivid detail. The cross-dressing was always in secret and was never discovered. It was initially nonerotic and produced a state of relaxation—"like alcohol." The clothing was erotized in adolescence when he began to have spontaneous ejaculations while cross-dressed. Sometimes he ejaculated without an erection, an orgasm that he felt to be "female." Occasionally he masturbated, but usually he achieved climax without it. In his middle teens, he had sexual intercourse for the first time, with an older female neighbor. They had a brief relationship, and he was fully potent. After the affair ended, he had no further sexual contacts until he married his wife, when he was twenty-four.

The wife is described as a good, honest, religious woman with a bland personality. She is maternally warm, but not excessively so. E. feels she has always been very good to him. He told her about his cross-dressing when they married, and it was acceptable to her as long as she did not have to participate. E. never inflicted it on her and continued periodically to cross-dress at home in private. He still used only outer garments, either a dress or a skirt and blouse. He always responded fetishistically to the total ensemble rather than to any specific article of clothing.

After the birth of his second child, the impulse to dress became more pressing. Not only did he cross-dress more frequently, but now he began to dress more fully, adding shoes, hose, and undergarments. He bought himself a wig and began to use make-up. He began also to wear women's underpants when dressed as a man. The wife became alarmed because of the children and asked that he transfer his activities to his office, where he could insure privacy. E. thought this was a good idea and readily acquiesced. When he was thirty-six, he chanced upon a magazine for transvestites and for the first time learned that there were many men like himself. He promptly joined the network and became an active member of a transvestitic social club.

Concomitantly, as the cross-dressing escalated, sex with his wife began to diminish. For the past ten years, it has been virtually nonexistent. His wife was sexually reticent anyhow and has never protested. Since then, however, he has had several brief heterosexual affairs, but none of the women knew he was a transvestite. He has also met several times with a fellow transvestite to perform mutual fellatio while both were dressed as women. The meaning of this behavior is not clear. E. does not regard it as homosexual since he identifies himself as a woman and his partner as a man. To bolster this view, he makes the point that he has never been approached by a homosexual, nor has he ever sought one out. E. also fantasized that after sex conversion he would have a "lesbian" relationship with his wife. It would seem, therefore, that the mutual fellatio, though anatomically a homosexual act between two men, psychologically may represent either a heterosexual act in which he is the woman, or a homosexual act between two women, or both. It is also possible, of course, that at a deeper level the act is homosexual, but masked by the defense of denial. Such confusion about gender identity and the blurring of sexual roles are characteristic of transvestitic behavior in general.

E. has always had an increasing urge to cross-dress under stress. Two years ago, during a business recession, he lost his job. He responded with depression, bouts of drinking, and preoccupation with sex reassignment. This had occurred fleetingly to him before, but never as a real possibility. He eventually got a new job but had to settle for a lesser position and a lower salary. He remained despondent and felt he had "passed his peak." One year ago, in a supportive attempt, his wife suggested an emotional reconciliation, including sex. They went on a trip together, but he was totally unable to respond sexually. Shortly after their return, he began to take hormones. He no longer regards himself as a transvestite but as a "part-time" transsexual. He claims he may undergo sex conversion but is held back by the fear of losing his wife. He fantasizes that afterwards they might live together as friendly roommates, but in reality he is convinced she would abandon him.

Family History. Transvestitic transsexuals have the same family background as the transvestites from whom they originate. The mother is usually remembered as warm and affectionate; less often, as dominating and overbearing. In both instances, however, maternal care appears erratic, because of either ineptness or misfortunes that overwhelm the mother. In consequence, the child is not consistently deprived; rather, maternal gratification is repeatedly interrupted. In our opinion, this is the most prominent feature of the mother-son relationship in transvestism. As we have seen, Stoller states that the most prominent feature is the mother's need to feminize her little boy (Stoller, 1968a, 1970), expressed primarily through cross-dressing the boy as a girl. Stoller concludes that the transvestite is partly the creation of his mother's unconscious wish, not just the product of his own defenses.

Our clinical experience has been different from Stoller's. In an unselected sample of sixteen consecutive transvestitic patients, we elicited only two histories of maternal induction into cross-dressing, one punitive and one nonpunitive. In the predominant pattern, the child spontaneously cross-dressed, the activity most often remained surreptitious, and it was not reinforced by the mother or a mother-surrogate. We believe that the underlying problem in transvestism is not femininization by the mother but separation anxiety, engendered in a variety of childhood situations, and that the transvestitic defense is usually the patient's own invention. It is intimately related to the process of self-object differentiation and is sometimes "primed" by explicit parental directives but not created by them.

Another striking feature in the family histories is the high incidence of fathers perceived as either verbally abusive or physically violent. We do not know whether this is an accurate appraisal of the family situation, or a misperception born out of increased vulnerability in the oedipal period. In the minority of cases, the father was either absent altogether or perceived as aloof and self-contained. Psychodynamically, transvestism appears to us as more complicated than either primary transsexualism or effeminate homosexuality. This complexity is mirrored in the difficulty of defining the predominant family dynamics. We believe that there are several predominant trends, some of which we have described, but that the transvestitic defense may develop in a variety of family settings.

Developmental History and Clinical Course. In their early history, transvestitic transsexuals are indistinguishable from transvestites. They are never effeminate in boyhood, but are appropriately masculine, even hyperaggressive and hypercompetitive. They engage in boyish pursuits and neither play with girls nor become mother's helpers. They fantasize about being girls, particularly when cross-dressed, but invariably value their assertiveness and maleness. In this respect, they are unlike primary and homosexual transsexuals. Hence, their core gender identity is more firmly male and the least prone to ambiguity.

Cross-dressing begins in childhood or early adolescence in one of two ways. It can start nonsexually, to promote a sense of well-being, then secondarily be sexualized; or it can be sexual from the beginning, though accompanied by the same sense of well-being as before. Once fetishism is established, ejaculation occurs spontaneously or is induced by masturbation. Cross-dressing at first is intermittent, but in most transvestitic transsexuals, as compared with transvestites, it is escalatory, progressive, and eventually becomes continuous. The clothing is often dated and out of style, like the clothes "mother" used to wear. Transvestites in general have more difficulty mimicking feminine behavior than either primary transsexuals or effeminate homosexuals.

Transvestites are invariably preferential heterosexuals, although sometimes there is a history of occasional homosexual encounters. Frequently, they express a preference for the subordinate role in sexual intercourse—that is, with the woman on top. Fetishistic arousal can be intense, but interpersonal sexuality is almost always attenuated. It is unusual for a transvestite to report sexual experiences with more than three woman, and often experiences are limited to one or two.

Self-identification is more complicated than in the homosexual transsexual. Some of these patients regard themselves as "split personalities" and claim that their preferences, interests, and personalities are different depending on how they are dressed. They often express the feeling that the female personality is "fighting" with the male personality and crowding it out.[2] Still other patients regard the personality as continuous and more integrated. They initially view cross-dressing, therefore, as the expression of a female part of their personality, which is predominantly male. In both situations, these patients frequently express the belief that they are somehow "richer" than people restricted to an expression of one gender role only.

The transsexual wish in transvestites arises at times of intense stress. In this group, the stress consists of threats to both masculinity and dependent security—for example, vocational failure, competitive defeat, broken marriage, death of the mother, or the birth of a child. In a very few cases, the process of falling in love and living with a woman evokes immense jealousy of the

2. See, for example, the autobiography of Einar Wegener (Hoyer, ed., 1933).

woman. In such instances, the longing for the loved woman's clothes becomes almost intolerable. In these cases, there is a confusion between *loving* and *becoming*, a mechanism described by Greenson in his treatment of a cross-dressing effeminate boy (Greenson, 1968).

Personality Inventory. Transvestitic transsexuals have the typical personality structure of their parent group, transvestites. The personality is organized on an obsessive-paranoid axis with attenuation of both tender affectivity and sexuality. These patients are hypercompetitive, may be hypermasculine, and engage in endless struggles for power with other men. For this reason, transvestites preferentially seek self-employment in order to avoid conflicts with authority. There is a frequent history of job rotation, which on scrutiny reflects the pervasive power struggle. Tender affectivity, to the extent that it exists, is invested mainly in the marital partner. Relationships with children, while often dutiful or distantly loving, are seldom warm and affectionate. The relationship with the wife is essentially dependent. As such, its success is determined by the personality of the wife and her capacity to tolerate both cross-dressing and minimal sexuality. The tolerance apparently is not great, since there is a high incidence of divorce in the transvestitic population (Stoller, 1968a; Beigel, 1969).

A large part of the transvestite's life is spent in socializing with other transvestites and their wives. This, of course, also holds for the transvestitic transsexual before sex reassignment. The social life is mediated by "sororities" through meetings and correspondence. The competitiveness and aggressiveness of the typical transvestitic personality color the social relationships. Most often, the competition is expressed in terms of who makes the most credible woman. At such times, accusations of homosexuality are rampant. Nonetheless, transvestites are quick to recount the supermasculine exploits of other transvestites. They derive great pleasure from the bravado and danger that accompany successful forays into "straight" society while disguised as women. Thus, they may shop, ask a policeman for directions, or go to a restaurant. Stories of successful deceptions are endlessly recounted and passed along the transvestitic network. Despite the preoccupation with hypermasculinity, sexual encounters occasionally take place between transvestites, especially when dressed.

Mental life is characterized not only by irritability and preoccupation with power struggles but also by bouts of depression. These are either empty or angry and occur under stress whenever dependency or masculinity are threatened. They are countered most frequently by cross-dressing and in many instances by resort to alcohol. The latter is as prevalent among transvestites as is drug use among drag queens. Suicide attempts are common, as we would expect in a patient population so prone to depression.

Etiology of Male Transsexualism

We have derived male transsexualism from the unconscious wish to merge with the mother in order to alleviate early separation anxiety. We have emphasized the continuation of the fusion fantasy in the unconscious mental life of primary transsexuals and its reappearance regressively under stress in the unconscious mental life of secondary transsexuals. In the ultimate transsexual resolution, to negate the separation anxiety once and for all, the patient acts out his fantasy in a desperate attempt to become his own mother. This is a psychodynamic formulation, not an etiologic one. To explain transsexualism etiologically, one must explain why transsexuals, as distinct from other patients, deal with separation anxiety in a specific way—that is, through sex conversion. From our standpoint, the answer to this question must take into account four factors: the separation anxiety, the fusion fantasy, the ambiguity of core gender identity, and the evolution of the fusion fantasy into the insistent wish for hormonal and surgical sex reassignment.

Separation anxiety is the central psychologic problem not only in transsexuals but also in borderline patients. It is no surprise, therefore, that all the transsexuals in our sample, both primary and secondary, fell diagnostically in the borderline category. They uniformly displayed the clinical manifestations typically found in the borderline syndrome: chronic anxiety, empty depression, sense of void, oral dependency, defective self-identity, and impaired object relations with absence of trust and withdrawal from intimacy. These manifestations reflect not only unresolved separation anxiety but also the primitive defenses and defective ego functions developmentally associated with it.

In every one of our transsexual patients, there was ample evidence of the genesis of separation anxiety—either a history of actual separation or some serious aberration in the mother-child bond. Actual separation from the mother occurred in 50 percent of our sample (ten out of twenty). In eight cases (five primary transsexuals, two transvestitic transsexuals, one homosexual transsexual), the separation was due to illness of the child. In these patients, the trauma must be attributed not only to loss of the mother but also to physical incapacitation of the child. In two cases (one transvestitic transsexual, one homosexual transsexual), the separation was due to abandonment by the mother. Aberrations in the mother-child interaction have already been described for each type of transsexual in the *Family History* sections.

Thus, clinically and historically, separation anxiety and fusion fantasies are prominent findings in transsexual patients. Neither, however, is specific to transsexualism and hence cannot explain transsexualism in any etiologic sense. Separation anxiety and fusion fantasies occur intermittently as normal phenomena during the separation-individuation phase of infantile development, and they are widespread findings in many psychiatric disorders, particularly in the borderline range of psychopathology. Nevertheless, there are several significant differences between transsexuals and other borderline patients that may have a bearing on etiology. These have to do with gender disorientation and the integration of the fusion fantasy.

Core gender identity in transsexuals is ambiguous, and the fusion fantasy is intimately related to cross-gender identification. Thus, in developmental order, the major expressions of the fusion fantasy in transsexuals are first, the wish to be a girl, then cross-dressing, and finally sex reassignment. In other borderline patients, however, core gender identity is normal, and the fusion fantasy is not associated with a desire for sex change. It would seem, therefore, that the differential factor in transsexualism is the ambiguity of core gender identity. In the previous chapter, we derived the ambiguity from the fusion fantasy itself. However, it is still an open question whether the fusion fantasy in transsexuals in some way yet unknown disrupts core gender identity[3] or whether the ambiguity arises from some other source—psychologic, biologic, or both—and subsequently influences the evolution of the fusion fantasy. A further unanswered question is how the ambiguity promotes the pervasiveness of the fusion fantasy. Why isn't the fusion fantasy alone, or as enacted in the cross-dressing, enough to assuage the separation anxiety? Why must the fantasy evolve into the insistent wish for sex reassignment? Until questions such as these are unanswered, the etiology of transsexualism will remain unknown.

Treatment of Male Transsexualism

The rationale for hormonal and surgical sex reassignment rests on the assumption that there is no efficacious mode of psychologic intervention in the adult transsexual (Stoller, 1968a; Benjamin, 1966; Green, 1968a). The problem of treatment is compounded by the propensity of some of these patients to attempt suicide or self-mutilation of the genital when sex conversion is denied. Some psychiatrists, nonetheless, have raised the objection to conversion that the efficacy of psychologic intervention has not been adequately explored (Kubie and Mackie, 1968; Meerloo, 1967).

Limitations of Psychotherapy. The major limitation of psychotherapy is the unwillingness of the patient to participate. This unwillingness, whatever its psychodynamic motivation, is intensified by the ready availability of sex reas-

3. We are mindful here of Stoller's (1968a) "imprinting" hypothesis: that the reversal of core gender identity in transsexualism is caused by a symbiotic mother through a specific mother-son interaction. In our view, this would account for only a small subgroup of homosexual transsexuals.

signment. Although the major gender identity centers have established rigorous criteria for sex conversion, any patient with financial means can purchase both hormone therapy and surgery, with little or no psychiatric screening. Such treatment on demand has only recently become available in the United States, but it has been available abroad for many years.

A second limitation is created by the psychiatrists themselves. Nearly all our subjects had sought psychiatric opinion some time in adolescence or early childhood. Invariably, they described the encounter negatively. Their subjective experience ranged from useless to catastrophic. Many were initially loath to make contact with us because of our profession and did so only at the urging of the referring agency. Their intense negativism stemmed from the psychiatrist's propensity to judge the patient as psychotic and to dismiss the transsexual wish as delusional. In our opinion, the potential for viable psychotherapy, whatever its modality, rests on an open contract in which it is acknowledged that the patient may eventually choose sex reassignment. Any hint of coercion on the part of the therapist will inevitably cause the patient to withdraw from treatment.

Even a therapy conducted by an experienced psychiatrist who eschews a judgmental stance will still be severely limited by the transsexual's personality, particularly his poor aptitude for psychologic insight and his affective shallowness. Nevertheless, because of the radical nature of sex conversion, we strongly recommend that psychotherapy be attempted, often with the aim of stabilizing the patient somewhere short of surgical intervention rather than reversing the syndrome altogether.

Limitations of Sex Conversion. Sex conversion is both radical and irreversible. Except in the research-oriented gender identity centers, preoperative screening is often haphazard. Follow-up studies in general are inadequate. The operation is relatively new, and not enough time has passed for an accurate evaluation of the results. In addition, many patients fail to maintain contact with their physicians after surgery. It is undoubtedly true that a sizable number achieve some reversal of gender discomfort, depression, and other manifestations of psychopathology; others remain unimproved, attempt suicide, or enter prostitution. A few request a second reassignment, this time as men.

Recommendations for Treatment. We are in general agreement with Stoller's (1968a) comment that no matter what one does, including nothing, as far as the transsexual patient is concerned, one will probably be wrong. Because of the nature of the pathology, there is a risk of suicide with or without treatment, whether psychotherapy, sex conversion, or both. Nevertheless, one is forced to formulate a treatment plan for the individual patient. It is our contention that every patient should receive at minimum an extensive psychiatric evaluation and, if at all possible, a trial of psychotherapy. If this fails to stabilize the patient, sex conversion cannot be ruled out, but neither should it be recommended unless the patient meets certain criteria.

We favor the very rigorous procedures laid down by the Johns Hopkins University Gender Identity Clinic, the first such clinic established in this country in 1965 (and where the first sex-reassignment surgery took place in 1966) (Money and Schwartz, 1968; Knorr, Wolf, and Meyer, 1968). All applicants are first screened to make sure they are authentically motivated, not psychotic, and can overcome any social, economic, and physical obstacle to the change in sex. Selected candidates then receive female hormones, undergo epilation and cosmetic nongenital surgery, and live as women. The final judgment to operate on the genitals is made by evaluating the patient's adjustment to a preoperative period of about two years spent in the cross-gender role.

In terms of our classification, the primary transsexual theoretically should make the best candidate for sex reassignment. He is transsexual from the beginning. His core gender identity is very ambiguous. He suffers chronically from unrelieved gender discomfort. His major defense against separation anxiety is the unconscious fantasy of symbiotic fusion with his mother. He dislikes his penis and gets little or no erotic pleasure from it. It would seem, therefore, that in his case, surgery would be ego-syntonic and have the best chance for success.

The situation is different, however, with both homosexual and transvestitic transsexuals, who comprise the majority of applicants for sex reassignment. Their core gender identities are essentially male. They have less ambiguity and hence less gender discomfort. They have more than one defense against their separation anxiety. They value their penises and enjoy sex. These characteristics are not ego-syntonic with sex reassignment. Instead of being transformed into bona fide transsexuals, these patients could end up simply as castrated homosexuals and transvestites, with all their attendant problems unresolved and the means for coping with these problems surgically removed.

We would therefore be extremely cautious in recommending surgical sex reassignment in these two groups, especially for the transvestite, who is masculine and heterosexual and whose average age at application is about forty—rather old, it seems to us, for such a radical procedure. With both these types, one must first make every effort to rule out a transient impulse through a careful study of the precipitating stress. This would, of course, require psychotherapeutic intervention, which many of these patients might not be willing to undergo, particularly since bootleg treatment—both hormonal and surgical—is available. Their willingness or unwillingness, however, should not be the determining factor in laying down sound medical procedures. If, after a prolonged period of observation—say six to twelve months—the anxiety level remains high and the transsexual impulse persists, particularly if it intensifies, one could try hormones to see if they relieve the anxiety. Some of these patients may be satisfied just with breasts.[4] Also, as the hormonal level rises, some complain about loss of sexual drive and pleasurable sensations in their penises. This alone would rule out surgical intervention. If the motivation survives both the therapeutic exploration and the hormonal trial, we would require that the patient live as a woman for a year or two, and then recommend surgery only if he makes a satisfactory adjustment in the cross-gender role.

4. We believe breast augmentation in cross-dressing males relieves separation anxiety because the breasts symbolically represent the mother. A confirmation of this hypothesis, albeit in women, is reported by Druss (1973) in a psychiatric study of women who underwent augmentation breast surgery. Druss found that all the women unconsciously, through their newly enlarged breasts, sought to make up for early maternal deprivations through a narcissistic identification with their own mothers.

8

Transvestism: A Disorder of the Sense of Self

1976

LIONEL OVESEY AND ETHEL S. PERSON

TRANSVESTISM IS traditionally defined as heterosexual cross-dressing in which the clothing is used fetishistically for sexual arousal. It is usually classified by psychoanalysts as a sexual perversion, even though clinically the sexual component is far outweighed by nonsexual phenomena. We believe it may be more aptly described as primarily a disorder of the sense of self manifested by certain symptomatic distortions of both gender identity and sexuality rather than broadly as a sexual disorder (Ovesey and Person, 1973).

In most of the psychoanalytic literature on transvestism, the transvestite appears as a man who struggles with the wish to don female attire, or who may actually do so in the tortured privacy of his bedroom. This picture accurately reflects the presentation of those transvestites who seek psychoanalytic treatment, but the picture is skewed because there are many more transvestites, rarely seen by analysts, who manifest more widespread symptomatic behavior. Thus, transvestitic phenomena exist on a gradient from the simple, unenacted fantasy of wearing female clothes to the dramatization of floridly elaborated transvestitic fantasies, with extensive involvement in an actual transvestitic society. Some transvestites act out their fantasies to the extent of living full time as women, and a small number of these ultimately seek a transsexual resolution through sex reassignment (Person and Ovesey, 1974a,b). Transvestites intimately involved in the transvestitic network may occasionally seek psychiatric consultation for depression, but very few enter into psychoanalytic treatment.

This chapter presents an explication of our view that transvestism is best understood as a disorder of the sense of self. We will focus on patients rarely seen in the analyst's office—namely, the network transvestites, who not only have transvestitic fantasies but are compelled to act them out. These patients demonstrate an urgent need to objectify internal fantasies in the external world. Understanding both the fantasies and the urgency to action sharply illuminates the disturbed sense of self and is crucial to the conceptualization of transvestism.

The chapter is based on the psychiatric study of twenty network transvestites, ten of whom were seen for ten or more sessions, the other ten for one to five sessions; analytically oriented ongoing psychotherapy with two other transvestites; and observations made during visits to transvestitic sorority meetings and drag balls. It is supplemented by a study of a representative portion of the very extensive transvestitic literature, both pornographic and nonpornographic.

Developmental History and Clinical Course

Transvestites are never effeminate in boyhood but are appropriately masculine (Person and Ovesey, 1974a,b). Cross-dressing typically begins in childhood or early adolescence. It may start nonsexually, to promote a sense of well-being, in which case it may become secondarily sexualized, or it may be sexual from the beginning. The initial experience may involve partial or total cross-dressing; should it be the former, it often progresses to totality. When sexualized, the favored article of clothing becomes erotic in itself and may habitually be used as a fetish, first in masturbation, later in intercourse. Even when cross-dressing is sexualized there is a tendency in some transvestites for the sexuality to drop away, although cross-dressing continues as an antidote to anxiety. Cross-dressing, while intermittent in the beginning, in some transvestites is escalating, progressive, and may become continuous. Many transvestites at all times carry photographs of themselves as women; others may continually wear hidden female garments, such as underpants, when dressed outwardly as males.

Transvestites are invariably preferential heterosexuals, although sometimes there is a history of occasional homosexual encounterers. Frequently they express a preference for the subordinate role in sexual intercourse—that is, with the woman on top. Fetishistic arousal can be intense, but interpersonal sexuality is almost always attenuated. It is unusual for a transvestite to report sexual experiences with more than three women, and often the experiences are limited to one or two. (For a review of the transvestite's personality, see Chapter 7.)

Family History

The mother is usually remembered as warm and affectionate, less often as dominating and overbearing. In both instances, however, maternal care appears erratic, because of either ineptness or misfortunes that overwhelm the mother. In consequence, the child is not consistently deprived, but, maternal gratification is repeatedly interrupted. In our opinion, this is the most prominent feature of the mother-son relationship in transvestism.[1]

Another striking feature of the family histories is the high incidence of fathers perceived either as verbally abusive or physically violent. The majority of the fathers reported by our subjects fell into this category. In the minority of cases, the father was either absent altogether or perceived as aloof and self-contained.

Transvestitic Fantasies and Their Enactment

The key transvestitic fantasy is so simple and devoid of structure that one hesitates to call it a fantasy. For example, a patient reports that he goes to sleep thinking of himself in a blue dress. If he is asked what happened after he put on the dress, his reply is, "Nothing." In fact, the act of putting on the dress is the central action, the point of the fantasy, not a prelude to further action. Although the enactment of the fantasy—that is, actually dressing—may be accompanied by erection, masturbation, or sexual intercourse, this association is variable, and its frequency tends to diminish over the years as the transvestism itself continues. Nonetheless, it is this variable association between dressing and eroticism that has led to the classification of transvestism as a sexual disorder.

Some transvestites produce consciously elaborated fantasies. Others have a stereotypic or impoverished fantasy life and produce few dreams. With the latter, one can only surmise the underlying fantasies from their transvestitic

1. Stoller (1968a, 1970) states that the most prominent feature is the mother's need to feminize her little boy. According to Stoller, this need is expressed primarily through cross-dressing the boy as a girl. Stoller concludes that the transvestite is partly the creation of his mother's unconscious wish and not just the product of his own defenses.

Our clinical experience has been different from Stoller's. In our unselected sample of twenty-two consecutive transvestitic patients, we elicited only two histories of maternal induction into cross-dressing, one punitive and one nonpunitive. In the predominant pattern, the child spontaneously cross-dressed, the activity most often remained surreptitious, and it was not reinforced by the mother or a mother surrogate. We believe the underlying problem in transvestism is separation anxiety, not feminization by the mother. This anxiety is engendered in a variety of childhood situations and the transvestitic defense is usually the patient's own invention. It is intimately related to the process of self-object differentiation, and only sometimes "primed" by explicit parental directives, but not created by them. Even so, we recognize that we are dealing with retrospective data. The question is how widespread such practices are in the histories of transvestites and to what extent they lead to transvestitic behavior.

enactments or from their preoccupation with certain pornographic stories. Enactment assumes myriad forms.

THE "CLOSET" TRANSVESTITE

Certain transvestites, those pursuing transvestism in isolation from other people, spend a great deal of time reading pornography. By doing so, their interior fantasies are to some degree objectified in reality by sharing an intimate fantasy life with anonymous others.

TRANSVESTITIC PEN PALS

Some transvestites desire contact with other transvestites but not in the flesh. This aversion to meeting other transvestites is usually rationalized on the basis of reality fears—for example, fear of exposure with consequent damage to professional reputation or disclosure to family. We believe, however, that there is a more pertinent psychological reason. These transvestites have the need to objectify the reality of their fantasies but dread too complete a validation, which might threaten to engulf their everyday male identities. Such individuals happen upon the solution of exchanging tapes or letters with other transvestites.

There are numerous instances of such pen pal relationships, extended over years with a mutual sense of intimacy, in which the participants never meet. Some transvestites carry on multiple correspondences, sometimes in the hundreds. Frequently, they do not know one another's true identity but write to anonymous others known only by female pseudonyms at a post office box number. Contact is made through the classified section of transvestitic periodicals. These correspondences tend to persist insofar as the correspondents share certain fantasy preoccupations. Some pairs engage in collaborative writing of pornography, each composing alternate sections of a transvestite story or novel.

VICARIOUS TRANSVESTITES

Some transvestites who are no longer actively engaged in cross-dressing themselves achieve vicarious satisfaction by tutoring novices, serving as male escorts for dressed transvestites, or "rescuing" operated transsexual transvestites by finding jobs for them or offering them money. A few transvestites have formalized these activities into moneymaking propositions by setting up businesses that cater to the needs of the transvestite network, for example, clothing catalogues.

CROSS-DRESSING

Cross-dressing in solitude, usually in front of a mirror, is the simplest and most common enactment of the unadorned transvestitic fantasy. As already mentioned, many transvestites habitually wear some female undergarment or carry pictures of themselves dressed as women. These are mini-symbols for cross-dressing and enhance the illusion of being a woman even while dressed as a man.

PASSING

Not only does the transvestite wish to don female clothes; he also wishes to fool other people into thinking he is a woman. In consequence, transvestites derive great pleasure from the bravado and danger that accompany successful forays into "straight" society while disguised as women. Thus, they may browse the department stores, use the ladies' room, or go on holiday (the flights included). Stories of successful deceptions are endlessly recounted and passed along the transvestitic network.

INITIATION FANTASIES

Jucovy (1976) intuitively recognized the importance of initiation fantasies on the basis of his analytic experience with just one transvestitic patient. Initiation fantasies permeate the collective fantasy life of transvestites, as revealed through letters in the personal columns of sex magazines, transvestite pornography, and the social organization of transvestite sororities. In order to verify the widespread existence of such fantasies, one need only glance through the personal column of any sex magazine or newspaper. Many letters from transvestites invite the acquaintance of a woman or another transvestite for purposes of instruction in the art of dress. For example: "Novice wishes to meet T.V.s, T.S.s, interested females to dress me, make me up, sincere, go out together," or "Wish help of someone to turn me into complete woman." This theme of initiation may also be masochistically elaborated; for example: "Servant in silks: teach me, dress me, make me up, scold me, but don't hurt me. My wife has tried but no one person could satisfy this need to be totally FEMALE. Liberate me."

The central theme in transvestitic literature is female impersonation and its causes (Beigel and Feldman, 1963; Person, 1976). The comments on transvestite pornography that follow are based on an article by Beigel and Feldman (1963), which analyzes ninety-three transvestite publications, and our own studies that parallel those of Beigel and Feldman. As will become clear, the themes that appear in the pornography are often acted out in the lives of individual transvestites.

In the literature, initiation into cross-dressing is usually forced upon the hero either by a dominant, big-breasted, corseted, booted "phallic" woman, often glamorous as well as dominant, who "enslaves" him, or by a kindly, protective woman, who does so in order to save his life—for example, by disguising him and thereby concealing him from members of the Mafia who wish to kill him. In both instances he is taught about femininity by the initiator. In the stories, it is rare that the man had any desire to cross-dress prior to his initiation. Once he cross-dresses, the assumption is that he continues to live as a woman, or at least pursues a double life. The story often ends with the hero enjoying a sexual relationship with one or the other of the two women, either the dominant woman who enslaved him or the protective woman who saved him.

THE LESBIAN CONNECTION

Transvestites often use pornography featuring female homosexuality for genital arousal.[2] This preoccupation was first noted by Fenichel (1930). On the rare occasions in the pornography when the hero is castrated by a woman surgeon, he becomes a "lesbian" lover of that same woman. This pornographic theme also has its counterpart in reality; some operated transvestitic transsexuals remain on intimate sexual terms with their wives. In another realization of the lesbian fantasy, a transvestite who otherwise despises homosexuality (between males), will have sex with another transvestite while both are dressed as women.

THE COMMUNITY OF WOMEN

Sometimes, in the pornography, the conclusion of the story is not sexual at all; rather, the point of cross-dressing seems to be the permission it accords the transvestite to live in easy intimacy (nonsexual) with women—for example, in a dormitory or women's barracks—while his true sex remains unknown. This fantasy is reflected in reality through participation in organized transvestite social groups and activities.

TRANSVESTITE SORORITIES

The penultimate culmination of transvestitic acting out occurs at the sorority meetings and parties, drag balls, Mardi Gras festivals, and transvestitic vacation spas. Sororities of transvestites, some on a national scale with chapters in different cities, have existed in this country at least since the early 1960s. At such gatherings, the transvestite enters into his dreamworld made tangible, a world in which gender differences are blurred and only the female gender is in evidence. By and large, the parties and meetings are tame affairs despite the lurid appearance. Transvestites take the opportunity to dress, to exchange information on makeup and clothes. Many bring their wives. Talk varies from specifically transvestite concerns—wigs, magazines, future gatherings—to

2. Long after this paper was written, I understood that transvestitic fantasies (in the form of lesbian fantasies) had relevance to many heterosexual men, not just to transvestites. See Person (1986b). (Footnote added 1998.)

mundane exchanges about quite masculine topics—namely, fixing the roof, work problems, automobiles. Some groups founder over charges of homosexuality, but in the main overt behavior is clearly asexual.

COLLUSION WITH WIVES

Some transvestites avoid disclosing their transvestitic activities to their wives. Still others are determined to bring about full disclosure and to live at least part time with their wives as two women. Here again we see the transvestite's need to objectify his inner reality by insisting on its validation in the real external world. Many marriages break up over this issue; some few apparently thrive. (We would warn here that any global speculation about the wife's willingness or need to participate is unjustified; we have found the wives' motivation to be variable.) The need for wifely validation and support is sufficiently widespread so that the issue is treated extensively in the transvestitic press, which includes advice on disclosure to one's wife (above all, she must be reassured that the cross-dressing has no homosexual connotations), advice to wives on how to respond, and accounts of successful unions with full disclosure. One publication is edited by husband and wife.

FEMALE PHYSICALITY

Transvestites may develop transsexual impulses as a regressive phenomenon under stress (Person and Ovesey, 1974a,b). As previously stated, a few may become full-blown transsexuals and go on to surgical sex reassignment. A much larger number, however, who have no intention of becoming transsexuals, use female hormones and settle for the possession of breasts. An unhappy side effect of such medication, of course, is a decrease in sexual desire. The trick, therefore, is to take hormones to develop breasts, then to reduce the medication to a level that is sufficient to maintain them but that still permits potency. Such patients refer to themselves as "breast fetishists." Transvestites may also have pregnancy fantasies. These are rare on a conscious level but appear in dream images.

SEXUAL DISCHARGE

Transvestites use clothing fetishistically. Cross-dressing therefore may be accompanied by sexual discharge, either through masturbation or intercourse, and may be a prerequisite for discharge to take place.

SADOMASOCHISM

The fantasy or enactment of submission to a dominant woman while cross-dressed may be masochistically elaborated in the form of bondage, whipping, or discipline.

ENACTMENT WITH PROSTITUTES

Some transvestites attempt to enact elaborately scripted fantasies with the assistance of prostitutes.

There is a characteristic ebb and flow in transvestite fantasies in which periods of acting out alternate with periods of renunciation. For example: Mr. X. spends a year collecting a large assortment of female attire and dressing every lunch hour in his office. At the end of the year he throws out all his female clothes and resolves never to dress again. Some months later he is again irresistibly drawn to collecting female clothes.

Renunciation of the perverse activity while a patient is in treatment may lull some therapists into the mistaken belief that they have achieved a "cure." One of our patients was written up by his former therapist—a very famous psychoanalyst—as an example of a "cure" by psychoanalysis on grounds that the patient had given up perverse behavior—this despite the fact that he maintained his contacts with other transvestites. The patient's renunciation was attributed to a particular insight that emerged during therapy. Unfortunately, the renunciation was short-lived after the termination of treatment. In retrospect, it seems to us that insight had little if anything to do with the patient's renunciation of perverse activity; rather, the cycle of perverse behavior and renunciation has continued unabated.

In some patients, the cyclic nature of the acting out does not change with time; in others, although the transvestitic activity is punctuated by renunciation, the involvement is progressive.

The Sense of Self

In the full-blown syndrome, the transvestite often expresses the feeling that he has two personalities, male and female. The female personality may be perceived as "fighting" with the male personality and crowding it out. Even in less fully developed cases in which the transvestite subjectively feels his personality as more continuous, he experiences different ego states depending on whether or not he is cross-dressed. As a woman, the transvestite feels greater ease, but the differences are more comprehensive than differences in anxiety levels. For example, one transvestite described different appetites for food depending on how he was dressed; as a man he relished hamburgers for lunch, while as a woman he intensely disliked hamburgers. Differences in modes of assertiveness are paramount. Money (1974) highlights the split in personality or the dual identifications by entitling a paper "Two Names, Two Wardrobes, Two Personalities."

Transvestism has been viewed in several related yet subtly disparate ways by a number of observers. Dual or multiple identifications have been stressed by some (Arlow, 1954; Fenichel, 1930, Segal, 1965); alternatively, transvestism has been viewed by others as a defense in which the perversion represents a reparative condensation of self and object (maternal), either for purposes of security (Segal, 1965; Ovesey and Person, 1973; Person and Ovesey, 1974b) or to alleviate castration anxiety through identification with a phallic female (Bak, 1968). These explanations are not mutually incompatible, but the focus varies slightly. The variations are predicated on differences in psychodynamic interpretations of the same observations. In order to align these variant views, one must return to the Freudian concept of splitting the ego in the service of defense. Freud (1940 [1938]) formulated this concept to account for the simultaneous existence in the ego of two contradictory attitudes, one fitting in with the reality, the other with the wish to deny the reality. Freud found that such a rift or split occurred in many situations in which the infantile ego was faced with the necessity of constructing a defense against a trauma.

Thus, in transvestism, the dual self-representation reflects a split of the ego in which two mutually incompatible gender identities, male and female, coexist. In turn, the disorder of the sense of self, as experienced by the transvestite, reflects his dual self-representations. And here is the essential dilemma for the transvestite: he is trying to validate two realities that are ultimately incompatible, two realities that are predicated on a split in the ego and consequently in his sense of self. A considerable portion of the rhetoric in the transvestite press is designed to counter the tension the transvestite experiences from his double self-representations. As a result, many transvestites are militantly committed to the position that they have a richer personality because of their "femme" selves than "normal" people who are relegated to a one-gender role.[3]

Object Relations

Characteristically, transvestites relate relatively well to women and avoid intimacy with men except for other transvestites. Although many authors viewed transvestism as a defense against homosexuality, we see here both a similarity and a profound difference between homosexuals and transvestites. Both groups are uncomfortable in a world made up of two sexes, but each group eliminates a different sex. Some homosexuals live their lives as completely as possible in a world of gay men, whereas transvestites eliminate men, to some degree in reality and to an extensive degree in fantasy. The point of transves-

3. And here, ironically, is a curious foreshadowing of the contemporary cultural injunction endorsed by some literary critics and a few psychoanalysts: to expand psychically through embracing cross-gender identifications. (Footnote added, 1998.)

titic life is to live in a society of women. This is clear from fantasy, pornography, and in the social structure previously described. Explanations for this tendency vary. In our opinion, it derives developmentally from contrasting views of the pregenital mother: the homosexual sees her as engulfing and hence avoids her; the transvestite sees her as nurturing and hence holds onto her. We do not know whether this is an accurate rendition of reality or represents the child's distorted perceptions of the relationship with the mother.

There are certain relationships that provide clues to transvestites' characteristic modes of relating. The frequent pairing of transvestites and operated male transsexuals has been noted by Guze (1968) as well as by ourselves (Ovesey and Person, 1973). We know of three such instances that eventually led to marriage. Male transsexuals, of course, are men who "succeed" in becoming women, an actualization of the transvestite's key fantasy. These altered males are particularly attractive to the transvestite because he can so easily, through identification, put himself in their place and vicariously experience their femininity as his own. The following clinical vignette illustrates the complexities of such relationships.

> Mr. S., a transvestite, took hormones to grow breasts and was contemplating sex reassignment. In the meantime, he fell in love with Blanche, an operated transsexual. He immediately withdrew from hormones to regain his potency and become Blanche's lover. In this way, he affirmed and stabilized his male identity. Simultaneously, he projected his fantasied female identity onto Blanche and then reincorporated it by identifying with her—a mechanism we call *projective identification*. (We use this term in much the same way as Masud Khan, 1966.) Thus, in effect, Mr. S. seemingly achieved the impossible; he objectified his fantasy of being a woman but at the same time managed to remain a man. When Blanche ran off with a truck driver, Mr. S. therefore suffered a double blow. Momentarily, he was unable to sustain either aspect of his identity, male or female: the competitive defeat undermined the former, and Blanche's flight removed the latter. As a reparative measure, he reverted to hormones, assumed a predominant female identity, and, to reinforce it, became "mother" to two lesbian lovers.

Another mechanism used by transvestites in relating to objects is *introjective identification*, through which a person "takes in" a desirable aspect of another person and then experiences it as his own. The most desirable aspect for the transvestite, of course, is the feminine component of a woman. For this reason, the mechanism can be particularly troublesome for married transvestites, in whom the process of falling in love and living with a woman evokes immense jealousy of her femininity. In such instances, the longing for the loved woman's clothes becomes almost unbearable, and there is a confusion between *loving* and *becoming*—an observation made by Greenson in his treatment of a cross-dressing effeminate boy (Greenson, 1968). An illustrative example in a transvestite follows.

> T. fell in love and married early in life in the hope that he could stabilize his male personality. However, instead of forming a complementary relationship wherein he could enhance his masculinity through enjoying his wife's femininity, T. introjectively identified with her to such an extent that, instead of just loving her, he wanted to become her. His jealousy of his wife's clothing and of her biological right to be feminine greatly intensified his own interest in female impersonation. Thus, instead of becoming more masculine, as he had planned, he paradoxically became more feminine. The escalation in T.'s cross-dressing became intolerable to T.'s wife and eventually precipitated the demise of the marriage.[4]

These observations lead us to certain conclusions about object relations in transvestism that can be observed to varying degrees. Transvestites, in common with certain borderline personalities, do not always relate to people as people in their own right but tend to contaminate the relationships with components of their own self-representations via projective and introjective identifications. External objects are often denied a separate existence but are used as weights to maintain the balance of power between the male and female identities as each struggles for supremacy. That there is incomplete differentiation between self and object is clearly evident in pornographic cartoons of transvestitic masochism, in which dominant women and transvestites are identically depicted, both dressed in high heels and Merry Widow corsets. It is further evident in the name the transvestite assumes for his "femme" identity, frequently the name of an envied woman or lost love object.

Enactment of Fantasies and the Sense of Reality

Transvestites as a group are variably anhedonic and experience feelings of loneliness and emptiness. They find relief through preoccupation with and

4. I have seen in consultation several wives of transvestites who eventually left their husbands not because of their cross-dressing, but because they sensed their husbands' intractable envy. For one wife this was evident in the way her husband caressed her nightgown and not her body within it. (Footnote added 1998.)

enactment of transvestitic fantasies. As already suggested, it is characteristic that there are periods of activity interspersed with periods of renunciation. Although the fantasies have an obsessional cast in the sense of pervasiveness, they differ from true obsessions insofar as they are not experienced as ego-alien. In fact, the fantasies are a major source of pleasure and ease and sometimes are a prerequisite for orgastic release. As such, they present a constant temptation to withdraw from everyday life. As long as the transvestite is not under undue stress, both the preoccupation and the enactments occur in moderation and do not seriously interfere with everyday functions. At times of intense stress, however, the temptation to enact the fantasy expands to uncontrollable proportions, and the transvestite is beset by an urgent need to convert the primal fantasy into reality.

The fragility of both reality sense and object relations renders the transvestite unusually vulnerable to external stress. At best, therefore, the transvestitic defense system is unstable and easily overwhelmed by threats to masculinity and dependent security—for example, vocational failure, competitive defeat, broken marriage, death of the mother, or birth of a child. In such crises not only does the transvestite's own assertion fail him but he fails to derive security from real objects. He must rely more and more on fantasies and their enactment to alleviate his anxiety. As preoccupations with fantasy escalates, the transvestite's involvement with real objects diminishes even more. In addition, there is great resentment toward real objects, particularly wives, who interfere with his fantasy preoccupation. Such estrangement is experienced as a threat to the reality organization of the transvestite. Enactment becomes a way of lending objective validity to his fantasy and thus of reestablishing contact with substitutive real objects, albeit symbolic ones, to replace the objects that have been lost. The internal fantasy, thus objectified, becomes a substitute for the attenuated external reality.

These fantasied solutions cannot be sustained indefinitely but, for several reasons, are doomed to collapse. Failure of the transvestitic defense and consequent renunciation of acting out are often based on the relative inadequacy of the fantasy enactment compared to the fantasy itself.

> A masochistic transvestite, with a plethora of transvestitic fantasies, had a well-developed fantasy that a dominant woman forcibly cross-dressed him and then bound him with rope. He tried to enact the fantasy in a number of ways, with a prostitute, with a dominant woman who advertised in the sex periodicals, and with a transsexual who had been a drag queen. Much to his dismay, he discovered these enactments much less effective, both in sense of well-being and orgastic arousal, than the unenacted fantasy. This failure was due to his

awareness throughout the ritualized enactment that he was not in fact being forced to submit but rather that he himself was the author of the enacted events. Thus, there was a serious limitation to the illusion of reality.

However, there is a far more profound source of the pressure toward renunciation of perverse activity. Although acting out is predicated on the need to reestablish contact with substitute real objects and thereby preserve a sense of reality, there is another reality that is simultaneously threatened. Fear of immersion in the transvestitic reality is concretized by the transvestite's knowledge that some transvestites evolve into transsexuals. Several transvestites have described virtually the same experience: each felt painfully isolated until he discovered the transvestitic network, which revealed to him that he was not alone and, in addition, offered the framework for objectification of his fantasy life. The relief was all too brief, since he quickly became frightened of another contingency—namely, that he would sink so deep into the transvestitic world that he would lose his male identity. Thus, for most transvestites, there is a point of no return, a point beyond which they will not go.

Psychodynamic Considerations

What is the infantile trauma in transvestism that leads to the defense of splitting? Where does the wish to be a woman and the subsequent denial of male identity originate? Transvestism, as we have seen, is one of three interrelated gender disorders in men. We are in agreement with other workers (Stoller, 1968a; Segal, 1965; Socarides, 1968, 1970; Golosow and Weitzman, 1969; Weitzman, Shamoian, and Golosow, 1970; Gershman, 1970) that all of these disorders have their origin in the preoedipal period. We have proposed (1974a,b) that all three stem from unresolved separation anxiety during the separation-individuation phase of infantile development. To the transvestite, the female clothes represent the mother as a transitional object and hence confer maternal protection. Later, in the oedipal period, the basis is laid for their eventual use sexually as fetishistic defenses against incestual anxiety.

In transvestites there is evidence of an unusually intense and ultimately unresolved oedipal struggle in which the incestual object persists and oedipal rivalry is perpetuated. Thus, the female clothes simultaneously symbolize the mother as a transitional and incestual object. Not only is the first sexual object one of the mother's garments, but the clothes that transvestites favor when cross-dressing are often out of date, the clothes "that mother used to wear." In some transvestites, as we said earlier, the sexuality gradually drops away, although the cross-dressing continues unabated. In these cases, one might say there is a regression in which genital heterosexuality is sacrificed in order to preserve the earlier ties to the pregenital mother, both dependent and sexual. Here we have a clue to the meaning of the transvestite's initiation fantasies. The imposition of feminization through cross-dressing relieves him of responsibility for his incestual wishes and thus allays oedipal guilt.

Secondarily, the clothes represent a defensive posture in the oedipal constellation, originally against the father, later against other males. They magically protect the transvestite in two ways: (1) they symbolize an autocastration, a token of submission to his male competitors, which wards off their retaliation; and (2) they disguise his masculinity and serve to disarm his rivals. The clothes conceal his penis, the symbol of masculine power, and deny his hostile intent.[5] He therefore feels safe because his rivals do not know that secretly he is plotting their demise. He avoids detection by passing as a woman, which makes it possible for him to risk assertion and thus validate himself as a man.

We have already noted that the transvestite's personality is integrated on an obsessive-paranoid axis and that typically he is irritable, hyperaggressive, and hypercompetitive. We also noted that, in general, transvestites avoid the company of men except other transvestites. Relationships with men, when they exist at all, are characterized by covert, angry interactions. Passing—not being "read," "getting away with it"—represents an affront to the straight community, particularly the men, in which anger is discharged through contempt ("the straight didn't get it") and the risk is minimized through disguise. In the family histories, as we have said many fathers were perceived either as verbally abusive or physically violent. We do not know whether this is an early split in the representation of the family situation as it in fact occurred or whether it is a misperception borne out of an increased vulnerability in the oedipal period. We believe that there is an early split in the representation of the mother and that attributes of the bad mother are transferred to paternal images. Maternal shortcomings are often rationalized in terms of paternal demands.

We tend to view the transvestite's female identification as a reparative condensation of mother and child for purposes of security (Ovesey and Person, 1973) rather than as an identification with a phallic woman in order to allay castration anxiety and enhance masculine power (Bak, 1968). We believe, however, that both mechanisms exist and that the two are not mutually exclusive. The female identification is fostered not only by a defensive symbiotic bond with the mother but also to some degree by abhorrence of a masculine

5. A similar dynamic is also evident in many drag shows (predominantly gay). The culmination of the show is when the Drag Queen performer sings "I'll Do It My Way" and ends by dropping a G-string (or skirt) and exposes his penis, accompanied by major audience enthusiasm. (Footnote added, 1998.)

identification with a hated father. In this way, the transvestite avoids any actual acknowledgment of his wrath toward his mother and therefore toward women in general.

Most of the time, transvestitic defenses function reasonably well. At times of stress, however, the defenses may fail. In such circumstances, transvestites frantically step up the pace of acting out. Should such reparative measures fail, they regressively fall back on the more primitive fantasy of symbiotic fusion with the mother. It is at this point that transsexual impulses break out and may go on to a full-blown transsexual syndrome (secondary transsexualism).

Conclusion

We have conceptualized transvestism as a disorder of the sense of self characterized by a split in the ego into incompatible male and female gender identities. We have attributed the split to an early identification with the mother as a defense against unresolved separation anxiety during the separation-individuation phase of infantile development. We are well aware that we have not "explained" transvestism etiologically, nor was it our intention to do so. We cannot say why separation trauma results in the type of splitting that is the hallmark feature of transvestism. Splitting, as a Freudian concept (Freud, 1940 [1938]), can be applied to every neurotic defense. However, we have used splitting in a special sense, similar to Kohut's (1971) notion of a vertical split in the ego, in which there are two elaborated identities. It is this formal characteristic of transvestism that we believe links it to such disorders of the self as multiple personality, imposture, and certain types of psychopathy.

9

Transvestism: New Perspectives

1978

ETHEL S. PERSON AND LIONEL OVESEY

THE TERM "transvestism" literally means cross-dressing. In psychiatry, however, the term has been used not only phenomenologically but also diagnostically. Thus, the designation "transvestite" is traditionally reserved for the heterosexual cross-dresser who uses clothing fetishistically for sexual arousal. All reported cases, as far as we know, have been males.[1] The transvestite's heterosexuality differentiates him from the homosexual cross-dresser, and his desire to retain his penis differentiates him from the transsexual: his fetishism differentiates him from both. The definition is accurate as far as it goes, but in our opinion it is incomplete, since many transvestites also use female clothing nonfetishistically in order to relieve anxiety about gender identity and gender role.

The etiology of transvestism is unknown. Most investigators agree that the disorder occurs in the context of a disturbed parent child relationship, although there is no agreement as to its genesis. Different researchers emphasize

1. In her intriguing book *Female Perversions: The Temptations of Emma Bovary*, Louise Kaplan (1990) argues that there are in fact a multitude of previously unrecognized perversions in women. Yet many of the examples she gives are not perversions in the usual sense insofar as they do not accompany sexual acts. As regards transvestism, should it turn out that cross-dressing as a precondition to sexual arousal exists in heterosexual women, it still has not been demonstrated to my satisfaction. Even if it were to be demonstrated, the extreme differences in numbers would indicate a major difference between male and female. If one sticks to the definition of fetishistic cross-dressing, by which is meant that the individual is erotically excited by cross-gender garments, there are very few women. Stoller (1985a), in an extensive literature search, found a report of only one such person. (That case was reported by Gutheil [1930].) Stoller goes on to report on five cases, none of which completely corresponds to male transvestism (pp. 137–152). The principal difference, as he reports it, is that "the women are clear that they have homosexual desires powerfully present" (p. 151). (Footnote added, 1998.)

intrapsychic conflict, conditioning, or biologic predisposition. This dispute should not surprise us, because the same arguments are used to explain the development of normal masculinity and femininity. Thus, psychological conflict, learning, cognitive development, and biological differences have each been proposed as the leading cause of divergent gender development. But even if the etiology remains unknown, psychodynamic reconstruction through psychoanalytically oriented interviews and psychotherapies, as well as through the study of transvestite pornography and transvestite social organizations, can reveal both the conscious and the unconscious meaning of the cross-dressing.

Although there are no accurate figures on the incidence of transvestism or any other perversions in the general population, it is safe to say that perversions have received more attention in the psychological literature than incidence alone might warrant. Historically, the study of sex as a separate scientific endeavor began in the nineteenth century (Karlen, 1971; Kern, 1975). The biologists concentrated on reproduction while the psychiatrists and psychologists concentrated on sexual aberration, or so-called perversion.[2] Therefore, from the inception of sexology, perversions have occupied a central position both clinically and theoretically, and it was through the examination of aberrant sexuality that the nature of the sex impulse per se emerged as a major focus of study.

In psychoanalysis, Freud's first attempt to formulate a comprehensive theory of sexuality began with a conceptualization of the perversions. In his *Three Contributions to the Theory of Sex* (Freud, 1905b), he characterized infantile sexuality as polymorphous perverse in that much of the sexual excitement flowed from extragenital erotogenic sources, not the genitalia alone. The resemblances between perversions in adults, where extragenital erotogenic zones were so prominent, and the polymorphous perverse sexuality of children led Freud to view adult perversions as the direct expression of unrepressed partial sexual aims of childhood. Neuroses, on the other hand, were understood as the symptomatic (disguised) expressions of fixated partial sexual aims which had been repressed and defended against. Hence, the Freudian dictum: neuroses are the negative of perversions.

With the years, as clinical experience in psychoanalysis accumulated, it eventually became apparent that adult perversions differed in at least one respect from those expressions of polymorphous perverse infantile sexuality

2. In previous work we have avoided the term "perversion" because of its pejorative connotation. We have referred instead to sexual psychopathology, sexual aberration, or sexual deviation. The term perversion, however, is still in common usage in the psychoanalytic literature. We will therefore use it in this chapter because we wish to emphasize the historical continuity of psychoanalytic thought about perversions in general and about transvestism in particular.

in which gratification was nongenital. In adults, perversion is accompanied by orgasm; in fact, the purpose of the perversion is to facilitate orgastic discharge, and in many instances the perversion is a prerequisite for the discharge to take place. The conclusion became inescapable that the perversion in some way alleviated an anxiety that inhibited orgasm, thus allowing it to occur. In consequence, although the Freudian dictum that neuroses were the negative of perversions was retained as part of libido theory, its theoretical meaning was considerably modified. Both neuroses and perversions came to be viewed as the result of conflict inherent in libidinal development, especially in males, as the result of castration anxiety embedded in the oedipal struggle. In perversion, a partial aim was hypertrophied, so to speak, in order to counter enough castration anxiety to permit orgastic discharge, but the remaining castration anxiety and other pregenital sexual aims, excluding only the one explicit in the perversion, were repressed as in neuroses. There was recognition that the perverse symptom was not identical with a partial instinct but, like a neurotic symptom, had a defensive function: representing a compromise between instinctual forces and superego demands.

Thus, in the development of classical theory, castration anxiety was placed at the center of the perversions. Freud postulated that in fetishism, which he considered the prototypical perversion, the boy responded to the discovery of the woman's "castration" and the implicit danger to himself in that discovery by a split in the ego, one part of the ego affirming and one part denying his discovery (Freud, 1927). Such splitting has been viewed as the predominant defensive maneuver in the perversions, the predominance itself distinguishing perversion from neurosis. Freud left unanswered the question of why in some boys castration anxiety was surmounted whereas in others the outcome was fetishism or homosexuality (Freud, 1925) or, one might add, any other perversion or neurosis. Most classical theorists, prominent among them Bak (1968), emphasize belief in the phallic woman as the central mechanism in the perversions. Thus, for example, the fetish is seen as the equivalent of the female phallus. In sum, then, in classical theory, the study of perversions, which at the beginning was so important in the affirmation of the existence of childhood sexuality and its polymorphous perverse character, eventually served to highlight the structure of neuroses, and finally led to the description of splitting as a defensive maneuver of the ego. In our opinion, the concept of splitting is essential to the understanding of transvestism, as well as other perversions, as disorders of the sense of self (Ovesey and Person, 1976).

Gradually, there has been a shift in psychoanalytic theory. The early exclusive interest in the sexual instinct and later in its libidinal development has been supplemented, and at times challenged, by contemporary theories of ego psychology, object relations, the development of the self, separation-individuation, and gender identity. This shift is reflected in current psychoanalytic formulations of the perversions. On the one hand, preoedipal determinants have been increasingly emphasized, so that there has been less focus on the oedipal constellation and castration anxiety as the central dynamic factors. On the other hand, as theoretical issues have shifted to a study of the ego and its defenses, and more recently to object relations, the genesis of perversion has been viewed differently. Many analysts no longer believe that instinctual conflict is primary in the genesis of perversion; rather, they believe that disturbances in libidinal processes are secondary to disturbances in ego development. Thus, one may view the perversions as the end product of libidinal development which is filtered through distortions in ego development, and more particularly through distortions in the development of self and object representations. Certain features of transvestism seem to bear out the validity of both of these trends in the psychoanalytic theory of perversion.

Although perversions and neuroses alike symptomatically represent compromise solutions to unconscious conflict at both preoedipal and oedipal levels of development, we have argued elsewhere that perversions can be conceptualized as sexual neuroses (Ovesey and Person, 1973). The question therefore arises as to the contemporary usefulness of continuing to distinguish perversions from neuroses. In order to answer the question it is useful first to discuss perversions in the context of the sexual disorders.

Sexual disorders, or disorders with sexual symptomatology, fall into three groups. First, there are the *situational* sexual dysfunctions, in which there is little or no intrinsic intrapsychic sexual pathology. In such instances, sexual function becomes impaired in the context of an adverse interpersonal relationship or is inhibited by some overriding affect, such as anger. In the sexual disorders proper, whatever their genesis, some sexual anxiety per se plays a large role. In the male, sexual symptoms are understood primarily as ways of allaying castration anxiety. In the *neurotic sexual disorders,* such as erectile failure, premature ejaculation, retarded ejaculation, and sexual avoidance, the symptoms are pleasure inhibitors. In order to allay the anxiety, the symptom impairs the sexual capacity, either partially or totally. In the *perversions,* such as fetishism, sadism, masochism, exhibitionism, voyeurism, and transvestism, the symptoms are pleasure facilitators. They become the precondition—by allaying the castration anxiety—for erotic arousal and release of the impounded sexual impulse. Like Freud, we do not classify homosexuality as a perversion (Freud, 1905b). Instead, we view it as falling on a continuum in which the term "homosexualities" might best convey the notion that different disorders underlie homosexual symptoms (Ovesey and Person, 1973; Person, 1975; Person and Ovesey, 1984).[3] In our schema, only cross-dressing effeminate homosexuality or extreme effeminate homosexuality even without cross-dressing would be classified with the perversions.

So far, we have simply reiterated the observation that the difference between sexual neuroses and perversions resides in the inhibition or release of sexual discharge. However, in the perversions, one sees a prevalence of splits in the ego, object relations dominated by projective and introjective identification, and uncertainty about the boundaries of self image and body image. These differences between perversions and the sexual neuroses are not absolute but suggest that self and object differentiation and representation are more problematic in the perversions. In addition, in the three cross-dressing disorders (transvestism, cross-dressing homosexuality, and transsexualism) gender disturbance is paramount. Designating these disorders as sexual neuroses downgrades the gender disturbance, which has even greater weight in personality organization than in sexual psychopathology (Ovesey and Person, 1973).

The effect of this newer understanding of the perversions is to render the term "perversions" even more objectionable than before. It was bad enough to inflict a negative moral judgment on sexual disorders; it compounds the insult to extend the connotation to nonsexual disorders of the ego. We believe very strongly that the time is long past due for psychoanalysts once and for all to drop the term "perversions" from their vocabulary. The so-called perversions should either be incorporated within the conceptual framework of the neuroses or, better still, designated by another name, one that takes into account the prevalence of idiosyncratic disturbances of ego function derived from the early years of infantile development.

The purpose of this chapter is to reappraise transvestism in light of the new developments in psychoanalytic theory cited above. We will first provide essential background by describing some developmental and clinical features common to transvestites in general. Next, we will review the psychodynamics of transvestism as we have previously formulated them (Ovesey and Person, 1973, 1976; Person and Ovesey, 1974a,b). We will then discuss a number of theoretical issues, in particular the meaning of the transsexual-transvestite continuum, the role of aggression, the nature of self and object representation, the contrast with homosexuality, and the theoretical usefulness of separating gender from sex. Throughout our discussion we will make use of the new concepts of contemporary psychoanalysis to elucidate these issues, provide some answers to old questions, and open the door to some new ones.

3. If I were writing this chapter today, I would use the phrase "different dynamics" rather than "different disorders," and "homosexual practices" rather than "homosexual symptoms." I would make the parallel statement that different dynamics underlie different heterosexual behaviors. (Footnote added, 1998.)

Psychodynamic Formulations

[Clinical features are reported in the previous two chapters.]

The three interrelated gender disorders in men—transvestism, transsexualism, and cross-dressing effeminate homosexuality—all have their psychodynamic roots in the preoedipal period (Segal, 1965; Stoller, 1968b; Socarides, 1968, 1970; Golosow and Weitzman, 1969; Weitzman, Shamoian, and Golosow, 1970; Gershman, 1970). All three disorders are related to unresolved separation anxiety during the separation-individuation phase of infantile development (Person and Ovesey, 1974a, 1974b). In point of time, they appear to originate on a developmental gradient, transsexualism first, transvestism and effeminate homosexuality later. The symptomatic distortions of gender and sex reflect different ways of dealing with separation anxiety at progressive levels of maturation. Thus, transsexuals unconsciously resort to the fantasy of symbiotic fusion with the mother to allay separation anxiety. The final transsexual resolution is an attempt to get rid of this anxiety through sex reassignment; that is, the transsexual acts out his unconscious fantasy surgically and symbolically becomes his own mother. Effeminate homosexuals and transvestites resort to less drastic measures: the incorporation of part objects and transitional objects. The effeminate homosexual fears engulfment and annihilation by the mother. He therefore transfers his dependency and sexual needs to a male object. His partner's penis is equated with the mother's breast and is incorporated orally or anally as a part object. In transvestism, the female clothes represent the mother as a transitional object and hence confer maternal protection. Later, in the oedipal period, the basis is laid for their eventual use sexually as fetishistic defenses against incestual anxiety.

In transvestites there is evidence of an unusually intense and ultimately unresolved oedipal struggle in which the incestual object persists and oedipal rivalry is perpetuated. Thus, the female clothes simultaneously symbolize the mother as a transitional and an incestual object. Not only is the first sexual object the mother's garments, but the clothes transvestites favor when cross-dressing are often out of date, the clothes that "mother used to wear." In some transvestites, as we have said, the sexuality gradually drops away although the cross-dressing continues unabated. In these cases one might say that there is a regression in which genital heterosexuality is sacrificed in order to preserve the earlier ties to the pregenital mother, both dependent and sexual.

Secondarily, the clothes represent a defensive posture in the oedipal constellation, originally against the father, later against other males. They magically protect the transvestite in two ways: (1) They symbolize autocastration, a token submission to his male competitors, which wards off retaliation; and (2) they disguise his masculinity and serve to disarm his rivals. The clothes conceal his penis, the symbol of masculine power, and deny his hostile intent. He, therefore, feels safe because his rivals do not know that he is secretly plotting their demise. He avoids detection by passing as a woman, which makes it possible for him to risk assertion and thus validate himself as a man.

Most of the time, transvestic defenses function reasonably well. At times of stress, however, the defenses may fail. Under such circumstances, transvestites frantically step up the pace of acting out. Should such reparative measures fail, they regressively fall back on the more primitive fantasy of symbiotic fusion with the mother. It is at this point that transsexual impulses break out and may go on to a full-blown transsexual syndrome (secondary transsexualism).

Transvestic-Transsexual Continuum

Schafer (1976b) has argued, in a discussion of our previous paper on transvestism (Ovesey and Person, 1976), that if he wished, a "hard-bitten phallic oedipal analyst . . . could comfortably organize these data primarily in the familiar terms of incest, castration, phallic mother, the inverse oedipal position including its identification with the mother, and the like." Such an argument is possible only if one ignores the fact that transvestism, while it may be described as a totally distinct clinical entity, exists on a continuum with fetishism and transsexualism, and may occasionally be admixed with homosexuality as well. The transvestic-transsexual continuum is easy to document and has been pointed out by many investigators. A case reported by Bak (1968) in his classic paper on the phallic woman was diagnosed as a transvestite despite the patient's pervasive fantasy wish to be surgically transformed into a woman. Even so, Bak recognized the full range of dynamics; he states that the patient's masturbatory fantasies were "characterized chiefly by undoing the separation from the sister." This patient is well known to us; she has recently undergone sex-reassignment surgery and lives full time as a woman.[4]

The significance of the continuum of transvestism and transsexualism has not been fully grasped in the psychoanalytic community. Bemporad (1975) has argued convincingly that the male transsexual's insistence on ridding himself of his penis "is a strong blow to the classical theory, which postulated the penis

4. Bak has written elsewhere (Bak and Stewart, 1974) that after termination of treatment this patient made an abortive attempt to seek surgical alteration. Later, he contacted the therapist to notify him of his marriage and the birth of a son. The authors conclude: "One can speculate with some conviction of accuracy that the lengthy analysis in fact rescued him from his pathological feminine identification, but that the final resolution of the conflict could occur only after some separation from the analyst." We have pointed out elsewhere (Person and Ovesey, 1974b) the hazards in the assumption that one ever knows the end of the story in these patients. The patient just alluded to did eventually undergo surgery and consulted us for advice on how to handle his sex reassignment with his son. Some operated transsexuals have been known to "impersonate" men after their surgical transformation into women.

as the most highly prized possession and castration fear as the strongest motivating force" in the genesis of perversion. It would be incorrect to set up a strawman argument since, by and large, the significance of preoedipal determinants in the dynamics of perversion has been increasingly stressed by analysts (e.g., Sperling, 1947; Greenacre, 1953; Segal, 1965). However, some disagreement and confusion remain. Stoller (1968b, 1975a) has derived transsexualism from a specific mother-son interaction in which the mothers held their infant sons in close physical and emotional contact throughout infancy and for several years thereafter. According to Stoller, the transsexualism resulted from a nonconflictual process akin to imprinting, by which the mother's female gender identity was "imprinted" upon her infant son. The ease with which Stoller's hypothesis of imprinting has been accepted in the psychoanalytic community despite strong counterarguments (e.g., Ovesey and Person, 1973; Socarides, 1973; Mahler, 1973) is a case in point. If transsexualism is conflict-free and results from an imprinting mechanism, it must be viewed as a totally disparate phenomenon from transvestism and other perversions. In fact, Stoller states explicitly that transsexualism is a nonpathological conflict-free variant of sexual and gender behavior, whereas he classifies transvestism as a perversion. In our opinion, transsexualism, like transvestism, is the result of conflict and fits contemporary formulations of psychoanalytic theory.

By taking such a stand on transsexualism, Stoller introduces a strong component of conditioning and learning theory into the psychoanalytic theory of perversions, which have long been assumed to derive from conflict. He has extended similar arguments into his hypothesis regarding the genesis of other perversions. For example, Stoller views transvestism in part as the enactment of revenge for a literal childhood situation, one in which the mother or her surrogate cross-dressed the child (Stoller, 1970, 1975a). Stoller may or may not be correct, or perhaps he may be partially correct, but it is important to note that he increasingly emphasizes the effects of the mother's unconscious motives and behavior on the child. Therefore, perversion, in his view, represents learned and conditioned behavior as opposed to our position that it is the end product of a complicated intrapsychic process in which sexuality is filtered through distortions in ego development and object relations. In other words, the question becomes: To what extent is perversion the invention of the mother and to what extent the invention of the child? In our work on transvestism (Person and Ovesey, 1974a, 1974b; Ovesey and Person, 1976), we have found that cross-dressing is most often the intrapsychic solution of the child rather than one imposed by an outside agency. At first glance, the imprinting hypothesis, by eliminating transsexualism as a perversion, would seem to salvage early classical theory in the sense of permitting the phallic-oedipal explanation of perversions to remain intact. Paradoxically, however, the imprinting hypothesis, with its exclusive emphasis on conditioning and learned behavior, completely circumvents intrapsychic preoedipal determinants in the genesis of perversions. Therefore, in the end, it serves only to undermine the more recent concepts of contemporary psychoanalytic theory.[5]

Aggression and Transvestism

Although sado-masochistic interactions among homosexuals are well described, they have received scant attention in descriptions of transvestites, despite the acknowledged association of transvestism, bondage, auto-eroticism, and death by hanging (Litman and Swearingen, 1972). (The opening scene of the film "The Ruling Class" depicts such a death by hanging of an English gentleman in tutu.) This omission stems partly from psychoanalytic nomenclature; once the predominant perversion in a given individual has been established, other perverse or neurotic manifestations are relegated to the background, in order to preserve an orderly description of mutually exclusive categories. However, this practice gives short shrift to the actual situation in many of the sexual disorders—for example, the potency disorders, both erectile failure and retarded ejaculation, are to be found among homosexuals (Ovesey and Meyers, 1968; Person, 1975). Similarly, unless the psychiatrist is aware of how frequently sadomasochistic phenomena occur in transvestism, he may fail to elicit such information from a particular patient. To make the psychiatrist's task even more difficult, transvestites are often loathe to reveal their sado-masochistic practices. Thus, one transvestite interviewed in his home denied any such practices or preoccupations, despite the visible display of whips on his walls.

Masochistic behavior, which is more prominent than sadism, is more fraught with shame for the transvestite than are his cross-dressing practices. Masochism is much more extensive than acknowledged; this is easily observable, not so much in physical interactions involving the infliction of pain as in proclivities to humiliation and domination. One need only go to a drag ball, nowadays attended by all categories of cross-dressers, to observe the number of transvestites who appear dressed up as maids or occasionally as nurses,

5. While Stoller's formulation may appear to have continuity with today's emphasis on transgenerational transmission, there is still a substantial difference. Transgenerational transmission has to do with the contagion of affect or, alternately, of fantasy. I have argued that shared fantasy can take place only when there is some fit between the fantasy and the child's unconscious wishes, impulses, and conflicts. Therefore, I see such congruence as a more complicated phenomenon than the model of imprinting which Stoller proposes.

Perhaps it would be more accurate to say that transsexualism is the result of a fantasied magical repair in response to a sense of deprivation, whether internally or externally generated. (Footnote added, 1998.)

in contrast to the "Lady Days" and "Marilyn Monroes" among the homosexual drag queens. (The two groups favor different emblems of submissiveness and pain.)

Transvestites can be divided into two groups, masochistic and nonmasochistic (Ovesey and Person, 1973). Masochistic transvestites submit to service as maids or to bondage or whipping at the hands of a dominant woman, either in fantasy or in reality. Transvestic pornography divides sharply along masochistic and nonmasochistic lines. S-M (sado-masochistic) or B & D (bondage and domination) phenomena ought theoretically to serve as inroads for understanding the role aggression plays in masochistic transvestism. Even in nonmasochistic transvestism, the implicit power relationships, characterized by hyperaggressiveness and hypercompetitiveness, ought to serve the same function. In fact, although hostility, rage, and aggression are readily observable as manifest phenomena, the unconscious roots of these affects and their associated behavior are difficult to verify. One must rely on hypothetical constructs that "explain" the sequence of events, but they are second- and third-level abstractions in the sense that the unconscious interconnections are not easily elicited *as such* even in the analytic situation, presumably because analytic penetration is blocked by the rigidity of the transvestite's defense.

Stoller (1975a) has suggested that hostility lies at the center of perversion and that the rage is born out of the need to give up the mother and the identification with her. The boy fears that he may not succeed in this venture and, further, in the structure of his perversion, he wreaks vengeance on the mother for putting him into such a predicament in the first place. Thus, Stoller places revenge at the center of the perverse scenario. In contrast, we view anxiety as the central emotion, and although we agree with Stoller that hostility is an ever-present factor, we assign it a secondary role.

Here, we are in agreement with those analysts (for example, Greenacre, 1953) who see the perverse symptoms as the end-product of a two-stage process in which preoedipal events dictate the shape of the oedipal constellation. In transvestism, therefore, we view the compulsion to cross-dress primarily as an attempt to undo separation, thus allaying separation anxiety. At the same time, the explicit feminine identification in the transvestite results in a bisexual identification (Bak, 1968), which of necessity intensifies castration anxiety. For this reason, we have described the oedipal conflict with the father, together with the attendant hostility, as unusually intense in transvestism. There may in addition be rage at a mother who could not permit disidentification, as Stoller suggests, but insofar as this is true, this rage clinically seems most often to be transferred to the father in order to preserve the mother as a good object.

Although aggression is theoretically important in the genesis of transvestism, it is much more difficult to confirm its unconscious roots than the fully expressed emotions and thoughts surrounding symbiotic merger (Ovesey and Person, 1976). In fact, we have commented that the transvestite, unlike the homosexual, usually has a vested and persistent interest in perceiving his mother as good, though sometimes inept. It has been suggested that the periodic renunciation of cross-dressing and the concomitant throwing out of female clothes are safer outlets for hostility (Gillespie, 1956). There is, however, an alternate and more complicated explanation for this behavior, namely the need to patch over the split in the ego into male and female identities. This is achieved by renouncing the feminine identification at the same time that the clothes are renounced, thus enhancing the male identity at the expense of the female (Ovesey and Person, 1976).

In any case, the genesis of the aggression in transvestites is by no means as transparent as many theorists would have us believe. One patient, who was in psychoanalytically oriented psychotherapy, reveals the psychodynamic complexities that confront the therapist in determining the origin of rage. This patient's sexual fantasies depicted bondage and humiliation at the hands of a woman, but the fantasies were never acted out. His nonsexual masochism, however, flourished overtly in his interactions with men and eventually led to his voluntarily going to jail in the place of another man. Thus, in real life, his masochistic submission was to a man, not to a woman. While in jail, he sustained a rare period free of any fantasy preoccupation with either transvestism or its masochistic elaborations. The genesis of his rage, as it emerged in treatment, was clearly in response to an actual violent interaction with his father, and his identification with a phallic woman was defensive and reparative. This clinical example nicely demonstrates how the dynamics in transvestism may vary from patient to patient.

Gender Identity, the Sense of Self, and Object Relations

It is well known that sexual perversion is more widespread among men than among women and that, in fact, some perversions do not occur in women at all. Traditionally, female sexual development was believed to be more problematic than male sexual development (Deutsch, 1924; Freud, 1925, 1931, 1933b). The reverse now appears to be true in the development of gender identity. As the distinction between sex and gender has been clarified, there has been a growing assumption that consolidation of male gender identity may be more difficult than consolidation of female gender identity. In other words, the development of gender identity and the development of sexuality are separate though interrelated developmental processes. The difficulty for boys in the consolidation of gender identity stems from the boy's need to disidentify with his mother, a hypothesis first proposed by Greenson (1968). Any disruption in the separation-individuation phase of development, therefore, may compromise the consolidation of male gender identity. In girls, on the other hand, such disruptions will have significance for personality development, but not for gender. The fact that sexual dysfunction is widespread among women, but sexual perversion is not, has led to the inference that sexual perversion may be rooted in a disturbance of gender rather than a primary disturbance of sexuality (Stoller, 1974; Person and Ovesey, 1974c); hence, the preponderance of perversion in men.

There were prior explanations for this preponderance in males as compared with females. For example, the original classical explanation was that the boy defended against castration anxiety because he could be castrated whereas the female had already been castrated and hence had no penis to preserve. Another formulation posited that the sex drive in men was such that they would go to any lengths to preserve sexuality, whereas this was less true of women, in whom the sexual drive was not considered to be as strong. One cannot "prove" the intrinsic merits of any one of these theories over others. However, the study of transvestism tends to substantiate the explanation that favors problems in gender consolidation and self-object differentiation in the genesis of perversion.

Self-identification in transvestism is complicated. Some transvestites regard themselves as "split personalities" and claim that their preferences, interests, and personalities are different depending on how they are dressed. They often express the feeling that the female personality is "fighting" with the male personality and crowding it out. Other transvestites regard the personality as continuous and more integrated. They initially view cross-dressing, therefore, as the expression of a female part of their personality, which is predominantly male.

Self-identification in transvestism has been viewed in several related yet subtly disparate ways by a number of observers. Dual or multiple identifications have been stressed by some (Arlow, 1954; Fenichel, 1930; Segal, 1965). Alternatively, transvestism has been viewed as a defense in which the perversion represents a reparative condensation of self and maternal object, either for purposes of security (Segal, 1965; Ovesey and Person, 1973; Person and Ovesey, 1974b) or to alleviate castration anxiety through identification with a phallic female (Bak, 1968). These explanations are not mutually incompatible, but the focus varies slightly. The variations are predicated on differences in psychodynamic interpretations but attempt to explain the same observations.

It is probably more pertinent to refer to dual identities than to dual identifications. The dual self-representation in transvestites reflects a vertical split of the ego, as described by Kohut (1971), in which two mutually incompatible gender identities, male and female, coexist. This dual self-representation is frequently reflected in the subjective experience of the transvestite as a disorder in identity. In this sense, transvestism exists primarily as a disorder of the sense of self, manifested by certain symptomatic distortions of both gender identity and sexuality rather than simply as a sexual disorder. Vertical splitting is the primary characteristic of transvestism linking it to such disorders of the self as multiple personality, imposture, and certain types of psychopathy (Ovesey and Person, 1976).

There are certain relationships, prominent in transvestites, which provide clues to the characteristic modes of relating to objects. For example, transvestites frequently fall in love with transsexuals and are thus able to give up cross-dressing themselves. In such instances, the relationship is based on projective identification; that is, the transvestite projects his fantasied female identification onto the transsexual and then reincorporates it by identifying with "her." Another mechanism used by transvestites in relating to objects is that of introjective identification. This is a mechanism through which a person "takes in" a desirable aspect of another person and then experiences it as his own. The most desirable aspect for the transvestite, of course, is the feminine component of a woman.[6] In the transvestite's intimate relationships, he does not always relate to people as people in their own right but is prone to contaminate such relationships with components of his own self-representation via projective or introjective identifications. External objects are often denied a separate existence but are used as weights to maintain the balance of power between the male and female identities as each struggles for supremacy. There is incomplete differentiation between self and external objects; hence, relationships represent a symbiotic condensation of both. For example, lack of separation between self and object is clearly evident in pornographic cartoons of transvestic masochism in which dominant women and transvestites are identically depicted. It is further evidenced in the name the transvestite assumes for his "femme" identity, frequently the name of an envied woman or a lost love object.

Homosexuality and Transvestism

This discussion is restricted to a comparison of effeminate cross-dressing homosexuals and transvestites. The two groups are similar in that each participates to some degree in a female identification and in the urge to cross-dress, but they are different in terms of interests, mannerisms, sexual object choice,

6. See Ovesey and Person (1976) for clinical vignettes that illustrate both projective and introjective identifications.

the circumstances and erotic accompaniment of cross-dressing, and life styles. Some homosexual cross-dressers are in control over their urge to cross-dress in women's clothes; that is, they are able to cross-dress or not at will. In them, the motive for cross-dressing seems equally stoked by the desire to be outrageous and express anti-establishment sentiments as much as by the need to identify with or impersonate women. Some famous homosexual cross-dressers have been able to give up their cross-dressing in favor of an ultra-macho phase, when female impersonation and glitter became too common. The transvestite, on the other hand, is obsessed, plagued, and imprisoned in an involuntary world of cross-dressing and transvestic fantasies.

Although the attenuation of sexuality in transvestites has often been described, there are no comprehensive explanations for this phenomenon. One may offer a psychodynamic explanation for the transvestite's preference for the subordinate position in intercourse; namely, it simultaneously expresses submission and protection of one's rear from assault by competitive males. But it may also be true that the transvestite is better able to focus exclusively on genital sensations in this position, where the woman sits astride and there is little physical contact other than the genital. The exclusive genital contact may then compensate for a real attenuation of genital excitability. Effeminate homosexuals, on the other hand, are obsessively interested in sex, although in some, as in transvestites, actual genital discharge may be attenuated. Transvestites obsess about cross-dressing whereas homosexuals obsess more about sex or love. In essence, the transvestite is in love with his clothes and himself as "woman," whereas the effeminate homosexual is involved more externally with other people.

Most workers, including ourselves, believe that the basic sexual orientation of transvestites is heterosexual, but there are some who maintain that transvestism represents a defense against passive homosexual wishes. A few of our transvestic patients engaged in occasional homosexual practices, but only when dressed as women. Although such acts are anatomically homosexual, they are not regarded as such by the transvestite, to whom they appear to be heterosexual acts in which he is the "woman." In addition, there are those anatomically homosexual acts between transvestites in which both partners must be dressed as women. This act symbolizes the so-called lesbian relationship that so pervades transvestic fantasy life. Thus, although the sexual practices may occasionally be anatomically homosexual, neither the conscious nor the unconscious meaning appears to be homosexual. In some transvestites there is no doubt that unconscious homosexual wishes are a predominant feature; for example, in certain cases described by Segal (1965), he argues that homosexuality cannot be gratified because of shame. Even if one hypothetically concurs that homosexual psychodynamics predominate, one is left with the unanswered question: Why is homosexuality regarded with such shame by the transvestite whereas cross-dressing is not? To some degree, the answer resides in differences in total personality organization, transvestites presenting much more rigid superegos and constricted personalities. However, in our view, whatever the answer, the psychodynamics are different in the two groups.

Although many transvestites are gifted professionally and perform their duties with distinction, it is exceptional to find a full-blown transvestite who has much aptitude for the insight requisite to an analytic therapy. The one patient among our series of twenty-two who showed such a gift fell on a transvestic-homosexual continuum; that is, he had a mixture of transvestism and homosexuality. Although it would be difficult to compare transvestites with effeminate homosexuals on any scale of mental health or level of integration, the effeminate homosexual almost always has access to a wider range of affective responses. With effeminate homosexuals, the limitation of analysis is lack of motivation rather than incapacity for insight. In transvestism, it seems that the effect of the vertical split in the ego is an affective impoverishment; the unconscious fantasies may be enacted, but they serve as an antidote to anxiety or as a stimulus to sexual arousal, not as a stimulus to further verbal or emotional associations. Hence, one must attempt to treat the pornography, the events that occur at transvestite meetings, and the fantasies and their enactments as literary productions, so that, in studying transvestism, one has some of the same methodological problems inherent in the psychoanalytic study of a novel. Even in the few analytic patients in whom the transvestism was not as pervasive as in our nonpatient subjects, limitations in the same direction were noted. In many transvestites, dreams either are not remembered or are as repetitive and stereotypic as the waking fantasies.

Characteristically, transvestites relate relatively well to women and avoid intimacy with men except for transvestic men. Although, as we have already noted, some authors have viewed transvestism as a defense against homosexuality, in this respect transvestites are both similar to and profoundly different from homosexuals. Both groups are uncomfortable in a world made up of two sexes, but each group eliminates a different sex. Homosexuals live their lives as much as possible in a world of men, albeit gay, whereas transvestites eliminate men, to some degree in reality and to an extensive degree in fantasy. The point of transvestic life is to live in a society of women or pseudo-women. Explanations for this tendency may vary. It may derive developmentally from different views of the pregenital mother: The homosexual sees her as engulfing and avoids her whereas the transvestite sees her as nurturing and holds on to a blissful fantasy of a community of women. The difference may also be viewed as a differentiated response to the discovery of the sexual distinction and the attendant castration anxiety.

Whatever the difference in the genesis of the two groups, it occurs very early. The effeminate homosexual presents signs of effeminacy early in childhood, whereas the transvestite, despite the female identification (or identity), appears masculine or even hypermasculine in both childhood and adulthood. Overt signs of gender role behavior, either masculine or feminine, appear to be related to sexual preference rather than to self-identification. This finding is of some interest since the origin of those behaviorally masculine or feminine characteristics, while related to sexual object choice, precedes emerging sexuality (Person and Ovesey, 1974c). Gender role behavior in these two groups, effeminate homosexuals and transvestites, may well organize the direction of emerging sexuality, irrespective of self-identification, and then come to serve as a signaling device for sexual preference. Nonetheless, the ultimate source of the masculine and feminine behavioral manifestations remains obscure. In the end, it may turn out that the difference between these two groups is based upon the vertical split in the transvestite's ego, whereas the effeminate homosexual has an integrated self concept despite his female identification.

It is not generally known to psychiatrists that some boys have a transient transvestite episode in adolescence, which may or may not be accompanied by erotic arousal and masturbation. Subsequently, in adulthood they develop no transvestic fantasies or behavior whatsoever. The incidence of such transient phenomena has not been reported, but we know of three such cases, two in our own practices. Thus, there is a transvestic parallel to those transient homosexual episodes of adolescence that do not have any behavioral sequelae in adult life. This finding, if widespread, would suggest the hypothesis that transvestic symptomatology may appear in the course of development in response to conflicts in sexual (libidinal) development, but that such conflicts are resolvable; hence the symptoms are transient unless there is a more significant deficit in ego development that ultimately prevents resolution. We believe it is the disorder in self-representation and in the preponderance of introjective and projective identifications in transvestites that intensifies sexual conflict and impedes its resolution, although sometimes the transvestic symptoms serve temporarily to stabilize the sense of self.

Conclusion

We stated at the beginning that our purpose was to reappraise transvestism in the light of recent developments in psychoanalytic theory. We have therefore focused on transvestism, but at the same time we have tried to make it clear that the new concepts of psychoanalysis are equally applicable to the understanding of all the other perversions. It is true that the mechanisms of projective and introjective identifications and disorders in self-representations can be demonstrated not only in sexual disorders (aside from perversions) but in nonsexual disorders as well. However, it is the pervasiveness of these mechanisms in sexual perversion that warrants the study of the perversions as a diagnostic category separate from neurosis. Furthermore, perversions par excellence lend themselves to analysis in terms of self and object relations theory. In particular, the psychodynamic interrelationships between gender identity and sexual psychopathology in transsexualism, effeminate homosexuality, and transvestism dramatically illustrate the interconnections between gender development, sexual development, the development of self, and object relations.

10

Homosexual Cross-Dressers

1984

ETHEL S. PERSON AND LIONEL OVESEY

"DRAG," OBSERVES Edmund White, "was once a major gay pursuit throughout the country . . ." (White, 1980). He contrasts this with the increasing masculinization of gay life in the 1970s; some also would point to a growing preoccupation with leather, S-M, and the insignia of violence. (One must trace these changes to the Stonewall riot in New York City in 1969, precipitated by "queens" who taunted the police carrying out one of their periodic raids. After the police dispersed the original protesters, a vast protest march materialized.) This change in manifest mores from a caricature of femininity to identifiable and exaggerated masculinity is deserving of exploration because of what it reveals about some dynamics of gay life. But the phenomenon of cross-dressing, although it may no longer be a "major" element of gay life, still persists. This chapter is about "drag," but not about the drag that was—and in some places still is—completely elective or fashionable. Nor is it about professional drag. We propose here to address drag as practiced by homosexuals for whom cross-dressing has significant psychological meaning irrespective of the current gay trend toward a hypermasculine lifestyle.

We define homosexual cross-dressers as those for whom cross-dressing plays a central role in their psychological life. We are not including in this group homosexuals who dress in women's clothes on rare occasions for a "lark," such as attendance at a masquerade party or just to see how it feels. A lark of this type, whatever its motivation, undoubtedly has meaning, but that meaning, in terms of our definition, is neither central to nor decisive for the psychological life of the individual involved.

Homosexual cross-dressers can be distinguished from both other homosexuals and other cross-dressers. Homosexuals vary in gender role behavior along a gradient from hypereffeminate to hypermasculine (Ovesey and Person, 1973). Cross-dressing occurs almost exclusively among homosexuals at the extreme effeminate end of the gradient.[1] Although we do not know the percentage of cross-dressing homosexuals in the gay population, they comprise a small fraction of effeminate homosexuals, who, in turn, comprise a fraction of the total number of homosexuals.

Cross-dressing homosexuality is more difficult to define than either transsexualism or transvestism. This is because most men in this group are able to control their urge to cross-dress, except in periods of compulsive cross-dressing; that is, they are generally able to cross-dress or not at will. In contrast, the compulsion to cross-dress in transsexuals and transvestites is far more insistent and more ongoing. Furthermore, it is not very susceptible to willful control. This difference allows for much more variability in the cross-dressing behavior of homosexual cross-dressers. For example, some give up cross-dressing in favor of an ultra-macho phase when they judge that female impersonation and glitter have become too common. Others go through a period of many months or a few years during which they compulsively cross-dress, ultimately losing interest in female clothes. Still others fall on a homosexual-transsexual continuum and remain trapped in a world of cross-dressing. This group often develops transsexual impulses, and some even undergo sex reassignment.

It would be all too easy to limit our understanding of both effeminacy and cross-dressing to a cliché; that is, simply to ascribe these behaviors to identification with the mother. But cross-dressing is practiced differently and reflects different meanings in homosexuals, transsexuals, and transvestites. The major difference is that homosexuals act out fluctuating identifications with a variety of idealized women in contrast to the transsexual's and the transvestite's abiding identification with a lost object. This difference is related to dissimilarities in personality structure, particularly with regard to fantasy life, the self-system, object relations, and affectivity.

We have based this chapter on a psychiatric study of twenty-five homosexual cross-dressers, nineteen adults and six adolescents. The adults included five homosexual transsexuals. Ten adult homosexuals and all five homosexual

1. Many homosexuals cross-dress sporadically; for example, cross-dressing and bathing suit contests are a feature on gay cruises. What we were describing here is a situation in which cross-dressing is a pervasive concern. (Footnote added, 1998.)

transsexuals volunteered for research purposes and were seen for two to ten one-hour interviews, usually at weekly intervals. Two adults were seen in psychotherapy once a week, each for two years, and two adults were seen in psychoanalytically oriented psychotherapy three times a week for five years each. The six adolescents were seen in consultation for purposes of referral. In addition, some parents were selectively interviewed when they were available.

We will first examine some developmental and clinical features shared in common by homosexual cross-dressers. We will then discuss in more detail those aspects of cross-dressing homosexuality that particularly distinguish it from the other cross-dressing disorders: personality structure, fantasy life, self-identity, gender identity, object relations, and psychodynamics. In conclusion, we will comment briefly on some differences between cross-dressing homosexuals and the great majority who do not cross-dress.

Developmental History and Clinical Course

Homosexual cross-dressers are a disparate group, although two major personality types can be distinguished: passive-effeminate homosexuals with hysterical personalities, and hyperaggressive effeminate homosexuals with narcissistic personalities ("drag queens"). Their developmental histories and clinical course are essentially the same until adolescence, when the personality types begin to crystallize and the adult personalities gradually take form.

CHILDHOOD

When interacting with other children, preferences for girl playmates and girls' activities are pronounced.[2] In consequence, the boy keeps the mother company and shares in her feminine tasks and preoccupations. These need not be exclusively "dressing up" in her clothing but sometimes involve cooking, serving, and taking care of the house. The mother may be pleased by this simulation of intimacy. The children are frequently called "faggot," "fag," or "sissy" by other children and consistently elicit teasing. Effeminate mannerisms and a developed interest in female clothes may appear within the first two years of life (Green, 1974).

Cross-dressing begins in childhood, usually well before puberty. It is occasionally reported to cause relaxation, as it almost always does in transsexuals, but, more typically, the clothes are used as an accompaniment to fantasies of impersonating females. By the age of two, some of our patients were dressing in mother's, sister's or baby-sitter's clothes, often in front of a mirror, primp-

2. Our material is based on retrospective histories. The problem in interviewing effeminate children is that one is uncertain whether or not they will grow up to be homosexual.

ing and assuming female postures. All displayed an aesthetic interest in their mothers; they wanted to play beautician, pick out mother's clothes, make up her face, brush her hair. The child's good taste was frequently noted. Unlike other cross-dressers who are interested only in female clothing, these children were also experimenting with cosmetics and wigs. While mimicry of the mother may have predominated early, imitation was not restricted solely to the mother but involved other females as well.

The fantasies reflected in these behaviors contrast with the fantasy life of the transvestite in that the effeminate prehomosexual boy wishes to *do* to himself or to a woman what the transvestite wishes to have *done* to him. In other words, the transvestite fantasizes that a woman will initiate him into the art of femininity while the homosexual fantasizes and acts out beautifying not only himself but his mother and other women as well. The prehomosexual fantasizes himself in the roles of a series of girls and women. By latency, cross-gender fantasies are frequently tied to identifications with movie actresses. From the beginning, these effeminate children show an unusual aptitude for, and pleasure in, vicarious activities or identifications. They seem to have what may be termed a mimetic hunger.

These children appear not to like themselves or the realistic roles and adaptations that are open to them. They seem uncomfortable in their own identities. They spend time alone, pretending to be other people and acting out different roles through posing and verbalizing. Sometimes they appear solitary and withdrawn; more often, the theatrical flair is shared within the family and viewed as both charming and precocious. There is more evidence of familial reinforcement of theatrical behavior than of the dressing per se, but more acceptance of the dressing (though such acceptance is by no means universal) than is evident in the histories of transsexuals and transvestites.

For many, role-playing is the critical and all-consuming center of mental life. The various roles are predominantly, but not exclusively, female. The male roles are usually flamboyant and may be extremely macho, patterned after such folk figures as Joe Namath or Elvis Presley. Mannerisms, gestures, and speech vary with the role. Involvement with role-playing is energetic and skilled. Despite their early effeminacy, the children do not believe themselves to be female, though they may express a wish to be.

In addition to the fantasy identification with glamorous adult male and female roles, many of these children construct more complicated fantasies with ongoing plots involving a whole cast of characters—often a royal family. (Is there a connection between the preoccupation with royalty and the designation "queen"? We do not know the derivation of the term "queen" used in the gay community.) These are the precursors of the elaborate family romance fantasies that one sometimes sees fully developed in the adult "queen." There is frequently a preoccupation with pregnancy fantasies and doll-play, in which the identification fluctuates from mother to child. This preoccupation seems to be in the same line of development as insistence on mutual or alternating caretaking that one sees in a large part of the entire gay community (for example, as portrayed in the play *The Birthday Party*).

Closeness to the mother is predicated on sameness between mother and son and is not tinged with sexuality or seductiveness. The boy does not, for example, ask his mother to admire his muscles or athletic prowess. Nor does he disparage the mother, as so many boys typically do, or attempt to emulate the father and draw close to him. Unlike the usual oedipal situation, in which the boy resolves his attraction to his mother (and his dependence on her as well), these children perpetuate the dyadic situation, eschewing triangularity even when the father or a male figure attempts to intervene. The interests of these children remain the same, and the make-believe and role emulations continue unabated. In fact they are elaborated and do not give way to the typical organized games and interests usually associated with latency. Although these children may appear totally preoccupied with fantasy material, emotional lability is often noted.

ADOLESCENCE

From the subjective point of view, these patients experience more troubled lives with the onset of puberty. They are increasingly ostracized and taunted by peers and become less communicative with their families. At the same time, they respond to the physical changes of puberty in one of two opposing ways, and sometimes in both simultaneously. For some, their self-perception of sissiness is offensive and is viewed as masculine weakness. They feel inadequate as males and are envious of the "tough guys" in the schoolyard. Others feel stigmatized by the male insignia, which interfere with female impersonation. Depending on their predominant response, the clinical course may subsequently differ. Those who are predominantly envious of males usually engage in only periodic cross-dressing or may have only a single protracted period of cross-dressing. For them as adults, their favored sex partners are frequently chosen for their similarity to the admired "toughs" of adolescence. For those in whom envy of females predominates, cross-dressing is usually more pervasive and, in some, exists on a continuum with homosexual transsexualism.

It is during adolescence that one sees the emergence and development of certain mannerisms associated in the popular mind with "queens": archness, facetiousness, sarcastic wit, and bitchiness. These particular mannerisms are not, in fact, limited to "queens," but permeate a sizable part of the gay community. They comprise a cluster of defensive maneuvers, the object and purpose of which are sometimes difficult to intuit. Their real intent is not to be offputting, as is so frequently the effect in reality, but to be charming or to elicit admiration, or at least to be effectively manipulative. They express a false bravado, which discharges aggression but simultaneously pleads for recognition. The retrospective history of increasing troubles with the onset of puberty is suggested by interviews with adolescents. A typical case history follows.

> Patient M., eighteen years old, was referred because of family and school problems and severe depression. In the interviews, M. was charming even while being facetious and sarcastic. He was manifestly anxious. Despite some flirtation with a desire for sex change, his life was at a crossroads because his career choice seemed closed to him. He did not expect to be accepted at college because of his extreme effeminacy; at the same time, acting, his professed goal, was a dubious choice because he was unable to play anything but female parts. Homosexuality and frequent but periodic cross-dressing were well established. Extreme feminine identification was manifest in dress, mannerisms, and interests.
>
> M. had been a very beautiful baby. He was the middle child of three siblings. There was an older brother and a younger sister. From the beginning, his interests were different from those of his brother, a typical male. By the age of five, M. was already effeminate and cross-dressed regularly. He drew pictures of girls, played with dolls, and soon began to put on shows at home. He involved both his siblings in these productions, assigning them gender-appropriate parts while he played only female roles. At times, his brother chose to engage in other activities, and, although this made M. angry, the brother was too big to be intimidated. When M.'s sister refused to cooperate, he bullied her and beat her into compliance. Whenever he didn't get what he wanted, he kicked and pinched not only his sister but also other children and, on occasion, even his brother and his parents.
>
> By puberty, M. had become an overt homosexual. At the same time, his interest in writing and producing his own plays gave way to a preoccupation with movie mythology. As the parents gradually curbed his tyranny over his sister, he became increasingly coercive with them. The mode of coercion, however, switched from overt bullying to more subtle forms. He threatened self-harm—such as truancy, dropping out of school altogether, running away, and associating with undesirables—if he didn't get his way. His mother was particularly susceptible to such threats and usually gave in to his demands. Thus, he insisted on picking his schools and his camps, set his own allowance at increasingly high levels, and came and went as

he pleased. His demeanor became more and more sarcastic and condescending. By the time he was seen in consultation, he had completely assumed the arch mannerisms of the stereotypic "queen."

Our workup includes a battery of psychological tests whose results we could compare with tests taken at the age of nine. M. had been evaluated then at the suggestion of his school because he played only with girls. At that time, he gave the impression of having mild generalized apprehensiveness without clear-cut psychoneurotic symptoms. On psychologicals, there were phobic anxieties related to separation and abandonment, as well as confusion in sexual identification. Nonetheless, it was felt that "deep pathology" was absent and that he had excellent intellectual potential, imaginative gifts, and a capacity for emotional responsiveness.[3] His most serious disability seemed to be his propensity for dissociating unpleasant emotions from the events that elicited them. In contrast, current psychological reports revealed some impairment of reality-testing and tended toward a psychotic, or at least a borderline, diagnosis. Even so, our clinical impression was that suicide, not psychotic decompensation, was the major danger.

ADULTHOOD

Homosexual cross-dressers are children of fantasy grown to adulthood. They maintain an ease of mimicry and a propensity for shifting identities. Many were—and remain—movie "buffs" and love theater, music, and dance. Some place a premium on refinement and sensitivity. Their preoccupation with royalty and aversion to vulgarity reveal an overidentification with, and a romanticization of, female virtues (in addition to the obvious narcissistic implications); at the same time, in the opposite direction, they reflect an abhorrence of male crudeness and violence. Still others present more as "slut queens"; they are quick to anger, flamboyantly vulgar and aggressive, and intent on shocking their companions. Both groups have extraordinary access to the nuances of emotional life in others but very little control over their own emotional volatility. They are prone to narcissistic injury and depression, and, despite their emotional accessibility, their conscious sense of self may be so diffuse that subjectively they are often confused as to who they really are.

As already described, a consciously held female identification—single, multiple, or a changing series—is established early in childhood. The homo-

3. Clinically, there seems little doubt that this patient population looks more disturbed in adolescence than in childhood. However, preliminary data from the Gender Project (a study of effeminate boys) at Roosevelt Hospital reveal significant psychopathology in both clinical studies and in the psychologicals (S. Coates, personal communication).

sexual identification is made later, usually in puberty. Sexuality may range from attenuated to unusually strong. Some homosexual cross-dressers prefer the passive role in anal intercourse, but this is not an obligatory preference. Some report that the type of activity is secondary to preference for a particular partner. Under such circumstances, they are quite capable, on request, of assuming the active role, and some prefer it. Cuddling is often more important than orgasm. The desired partner is most often hypermasculine or "straight" and is someone the patient admires and envies and whose qualities he may overtly covet.

Some of our patients reported that they readily learned to project a more masculine façade after a traumatic event arising as a result of their effeminacy. This ability to control and transform behavior underlines the enormous power of mimicry that may be tapped by the homosexual cross-dresser, particularly the drag "queen."

> Patient O., when first seen at the age of twenty-five, did not appear markedly effeminate. As a child, however, he had been so effeminate that he was mercilessly teased for it. He dressed in his sister's clothes from the time he was four. He gave up cross-dressing in prep school for fear of exposure, although he wrapped himself in sheets and would dress for Halloween. At home, he wears caftans decorated in gold brocade and cross-dresses for drag balls and occasionally to go to straight places. He remained effeminate well into adulthood. His "limp wrist" and "light-on-the-carpet" stance hurt his chances as an actor. In the Navy, he was turned in by a hustler whom he refused to pay and was sent home in disgrace. "I came home much less swish." His tastes and interests remain the same, but in his new vocation (publicity), he appears relatively "masculinized."

Cross-dressing in the effeminate homosexual is not fetishistic and thus is not erotic.[4] As stated earlier, it is used mainly to enact certain fantasies of impersonation. At any drag ball, one can pick out the most familiar figures—the "Lady Days" with gardenias (Billie Holiday) or the platinum-haired Marilyns, for example. Sometimes cross-dressing seems propelled by the impulse to fool other people (and make fools of them), an impulse often admixed with the need to court danger. Both these latter motives are paramount among

4. One of our patients masturbated with a piece of male clothing—underpants that belonged to his roommate, a former sexual partner. He found the smell and touch exciting, particularly if the underpants were stained with semen or feces. The patient did not regard this as a fetish, but we do. We know of two other cases of fetishism in male homosexuals. To the best of our knowledge, this has not been reported elsewhere. However, the fetishistic cast of certain intense interests in the gay community—leather, buttocks, uniforms, etc.—is widely acknowledged.

some cross-dressing homosexual hustlers, who tape up the penis and cover it with a swatch of pubic hair, cut with a slit to simulate the vagina. This disguise enables the cross-dresser to perform "normal" intercourse with his customers, who are led to believe they have picked up a female hooker. Discovery, though, presents a serious potential for violence.

> Patient P. is a very tall, slender, elegant young man who makes a credible and sexy woman when cross-dressed. He is a typical "queen." He has an extremely tumultuous relationship with a hypermasculine homosexual, whom he supports by hustling. Fearful that a pick-up will discover his male sexuality, he always carries a switchblade, strapped to his ankle for "self-defense." P. is flamboyant, theatrical, and very labile emotionally, with rapid swings from anger to depression, usually focusing on the state of his love relationships. P. is also intimately involved in a network of queens, all hustlers and avid dressers at drag queen balls.

FANTASY LIFE: TRANSFORMATION FANTASIES

In homosexual cross-dressers, subjective mental life is permeated with fantasy and fantasy derivatives. The specific feature of this fantasy preoccupation is that the self that is fantasized is not an aspect of the "real" self. Instead, an entirely new self is created, one not visible to the external world. Homosexual cross-dressers rarely have extension fantasies of the "Walter Mitty" type, which simply extend and enlarge the abilities, talents, and powers of the objectively observable person. Neither do they have typical erotic daydreams. In their fantasies, characteristically, the self is transformed.

Such fantastical transformations of the self, of course, are not restricted to homosexual cross-dressers. In children, transformation fantasies are widespread and are exemplified by the child's almost apostolic identification with Batman, Superman, Wonder Woman, and all the superheroes. These fantasies reflect one aspect of the child's reality, the fact that he will someday be transformed into a powerful adult. Dracula and Dr. Jekyll/Mr. Hyde reflect another possibility, the expression of the evil self. (In deference to the current cultural preoccupation with sex transformation, there is even a 1980s film called *Dr. Jekyll and Sister Hyde*!) Transformation fantasies are regularly seen in psychotic delusions (*The Three Christs of Ypsilanti,* for example), but in psychotics reality-testing is lost, whereas it is preserved in homosexual cross-dressers.

In transformation fantasies, one imagines oneself to be a person whom one both admires and envies. But homosexual cross-dressers can achieve neither plausibility nor pleasure from visualizing themselves in the male gender role. No sports heroes or power brokers, but rather an array of female celebrities, most often stars of stage and screen, and sometimes royalty, constitute the imagined selves. The female roles assumed, almost always eroticized, can be divided into two groups—the manifestly dominant and the apparently helpless.

The first group is comprised of powerful glamour queens such as Joan Crawford, Marlene Dietrich, Mae West, Bette Davis, and Tallulah Bankhead. All are perceived as erotically dominant women who exert their power through their preeminent sexuality, physical attractiveness, and personal magnetism. In the homosexual cross-dresser's imagination, they are able at will to erotically ensnare and control any powerful man they desire. Thus, through identification, the homosexual cross-dresser vicariously achieves the same power. Occasionally the fantasy takes a masochistic turn in which the fantasized self suffers at the hands of a dominant and callous man.

Although these women are seen as "ballsy," in actuality they are a peculiar mixture of "masculine" and "feminine." They dominate men through their sexual seductiveness and therefore differ from the stereotypic "phallic woman" in psychoanalytic literature, who dominates men through the force of her "masculine" aggression. Because they are so successful as glamour queens or high-class harlots, they represent a put-on of the straight world, a joke on conventional sex roles—camp of the highest order. Among homosexual cross-dressers, drag queens in particular favor them as objects of identification. The "queens" are mistresses of the "camp-garbage aesthetic." In their impersonations, they strive to be simultaneously amusing and outrageous, to play to an audience by showing up someone else as square or pretentious.

The cross-dressing homosexual may also identify with glamorous child-women perceived as helpless waifs rather than as powerful and dominant. In this category, one sees such figures as Judy Garland, Billie Holiday, Marilyn Monroe, and Edith Piaf. They, too, control men through sexuality and personal magnetism, but their special appeal lies in their sensitivity, vulnerability, suffering, and the intensity of their passions. These identifications provide vicarious gratification for and glorification of dependent and masochistic needs, just as their more dominant counterparts vicariously satisfy frustrated needs for power.

Not only cross-dressing homosexuals but many other homosexuals are fascinated by the glamorous women we have described. In much of the gay community, they have been elevated to the status of cult figures. Fascination, however, is not the same as identification in the sense that we have been using the term. In homosexuals who do not cross-dress, any implied identification is neither extensive nor associated with transformation fantasies. Only in cross-dressing homosexuals do these identifications constitute a highly articulated imaginary self. For them the identifications serve a purpose that goes far beyond vicarious gratification of power and dependency: to consolidate the self through an intense excitement that counteracts the pervasive sense of deadness, depression, and identity-diffusion common to many homosexual cross-dressers. The transformation fantasy and corresponding impersonation energize and momentarily integrate the self. It is for this reason that drag, while not as insistent as cross-dressing in transvestism or primary transsexualism, does have qualities of addictive behavior.

Personality Structure

As stated earlier, homosexual cross-dressers vary in personality along a gradient with passive, hysterical personalities at one end and hyperaggressive, narcissistic personalities at the other end. These poles describe the predominant personality styles of cross-dressing, passive, effeminate homosexuals and drag queens, respectively. Both groups are labile and theatrical, the latter more so than the former. Some subjects present an intermediate clinical picture, and any one subject may move back and forth on the gradient.

In many ways, passive, effeminate homosexuals present a caricature of femininity, but most of all, they are preoccupied with romantic yearnings. They may perform well vocationally, but their major interest is in "love." They may be very competent and the financially successful may even support their lovers. They often dominate their mates by being oversolicitous. In this respect, they tend to duplicate the close-binding behavior of which they accuse their mothers. In fact, relationships are often terminated because the lover feels suffocated. The members of this group perceive themselves as ultimately dependent on the magical resources of the love object. Masochistic trends predominate over aggressive ones, though aggressive impulses may flare up, and passive aggressive traits are common.

Drag queens present different priorities and lifestyles. As described in an earlier paper (Person and Ovesey,1974b), we have found that they are often involved in a community or network of other queens. They treat each other as "sisters," and sexual relations within the group are rare. For some, the major thrust of their lives is institutionalized in an endless series of drag balls and parties. For each event, the "queen" immerses herself in a preoccupation with costumes, hair styles, and make-up. Love interests are complex and often contradictory, The "queen" claims that he wants involvement with a hypermasculine man who will overpower him, particularly in bed. Nevertheless, he frequently prefers the active role in anal intercourse. In addition, many "queens" hustle for a living. These queens are quick to violence, both verbal and physical, and psychopathic trends are common. Some are on hard drugs and often live on the fringes of crime. Unlike the passive, effeminate homosexuals, the members of this group often exhibit distinctly paranoid, grandiose, and narcissistic traits.

Gender Identity, Object Relations, and Developmental Dynamics in the Cross-Gender Disorders

Cross-dressing homosexuals are as closely related psychodynamically to transsexuals and transvestites as to homosexuals who do not cross-dress. This section will focus on the key differences among the three types of cross-dressers.

GENDER IDENTITY

Different mechanisms of identification decisively influence gender identity. Cross-dressing homosexuals, transvestites, and transsexuals are similar in that each participates to some degree in a female identification and the urge to cross-dress, but there the similarities end. They differ in interests, mannerisms, sexual object choice, and the circumstances and erotic accompaniment of cross-dressing. These differences occur very early and are related to gender identity.

In the transsexual, the merger fantasy is so pervasive that male core gender identity, as experienced, never fully develops, although, paradoxically, overt behavior in childhood is either neutral or masculine, not feminine. The effeminate homosexual presents signs of effeminacy early in childhood, whereas the transvestite, despite his female identification, appears masculine or even hypermasculine in both childhood and adulthood. Overt signs of gender role behavior, either masculine or feminine, appear to be related to sexual preference rather than to self-identification, although they precede the emergence of sexual identity (Person and Ovesey, 1974c).

In the transvestite, a major identification with a maternal object results in a so-called vertical split (the term is Kohut's, 1977) in self-representation. This split is manifest in simultaneously held male and female identities, which may be said to be stable. But this stability is at the cost of general impoverishment of both personality and affective availability. The female identity has a cardboard quality; femaleness or femininity has no complexity but it is construed strictly in terms of clothes or the physical attributes of femininity.

In homosexual cross-dressers, female identifications are shifting. Some may be of long duration while others come and go. But the behavioral concomitants of these identifications, compared to those of transvestites and transsexuals, have more texture and complexity and appear more authentically feminine. In other words, cross-dressing homosexuals may make credible-appearing females whereas this is hardly ever true of transvestites and initially not as true of the asexual transsexuals (primary transsexuals). In homosexual cross-dressers, the impermanent quality of their identifications seems to correlate with extreme emotional lability and the frequent eruption of massive anxiety, rage, or depression. Thus, one sees not only imaginative elaborations of their shifting identifications but also intense affective storms. At the same time, male identification is rudimentary and few of these patients can imagine much fulfillment in the male role. (Even so, some engage in heterosexual interludes on occasion.) Some find comfort in the "queen" identity per se—not just in the revolving female roles, but in the self who is able to assume and discard a variety of "roles." This is particularly true for "network queens," those who socialize predominantly with other queens.

In sum, cross-dressing in homosexuals represents the dramatization of a fluctuating series of identifications with idealized women, whereas in transsexuals and transvestites it represents an abiding identification with the maternal image. The latter two are obsessed, plagued, and imprisoned in an involuntary world of cross-dressing, while the homosexual has more control.

This difference in identification (and gender identity) between transsexuals and transvestites, on the one hand, and homosexuals, on the other, correlates with the difference in their dynamics. As already noted, in transsexuals and transvestites, the identification continues to represent the young child's perception of the preoedipal mother; the more textured female identifications in homosexual cross-dressers reflect constantly evolving imitations and incorporations of a series of envied women.

It is remarkable how many cross-dressing homosexuals appear "creative," whether or not that appearance is embedded in a concrete talent or achievement (and some are authentically gifted). This appearance of creativity is related to the lability of identification; it shares the quality of creativity that one sees in the fantasies and games of children who act out different roles. The cross-dresser's very diffuse sense of self predisposes to a kind of imaginative perception. Imagination is not checked in deference to the requirements of reality. However, the scope of imaginativeness is sometimes significantly limited, restricted by the urgency of the need for ego consolidation. This pseudocreativity is in marked contrast to the typical obsessive preoccupations of transvestites.

OBJECT RELATIONS

Object relations vary in accordance with underlying dynamics and obviously correlate with the sense of self. The transsexual is monomaniacally obsessed with enacting the merger fantasy and obtaining surgery. In the transvestite, mental life is permeated with derivatives of unconscious merger fantasies—female clothes, for example, or the semblance of breasts. Thus, mental life is drawn away from involvement with the external world, and attention is lavished almost exclusively on the closest clinical manifestations one will ever see of the theoretical self-object (Kohut, 1977). The transvestite's world is bounded by the literal limits of the physical self embellished by female clothes. If interest is redirected to the "external" world, it is to the transvestite world, where one may identify with other male-female self-objects. Although the transvestite may form stable attachments in the real world, the center of his emotional life is the symbiotic dyad of infantile life.

Transvestites obsess about cross-dressing; in contrast, cross-dressing homosexuals obsess about being in love or having magical sexual encounters. In essence, the transvestite is in love with his clothes and himself as "woman," whereas the effeminate homosexual is involved with seeking admiration, approval, and power.

The homosexual cross-dresser seeks two kinds of objects, though highly stylized ones, in the external world. First, he attempts to form relationships with admired women or other queens. Second, he looks for an erotic object, and his sense of self and self-esteem fluctuate markedly with the success or failure of his ability to elicit admiration. Just as the transvestite uses his reflection in an actual mirror to confirm his identity, the homosexual cross-dresser confirms his identity in the mirrored response of another's eyes.

The homosexual cross-dresser, in contrast to the transsexual and the transvestite, is, by the very nature of his psychodynamics, forced into more active searching encounters with the real world. Yet, these relationships, encumbered by the propensity to overidealize the object and subsequently devalue it, are highly unstable. Attempts to form stable relationships are frequently disrupted by feelings of disappointment and rage. Thus, the erotic encounters that serve the purpose of identity consolidation may be obsessively and endlessly reenacted. These encounters seldom achieve the permanence of the transvestite's relationships.

Relationships for both transvestites and cross-dressing homosexuals may be compromised by a psychological difficulty in acknowledging the partner's separateness. They may not be free to see objects as completely separate persons who exist in their own right, with their own individual stamp. For both, self-repudiated masculinity may be projected onto an object and then reincorporated through a merger enacted sexually either in fact or in fantasy. (We were surprised to meet the boyfriend of one queen, who had been described to us as hypermasculine; he was, in fact, somewhat effeminate in mannerism. The queen's distortion was motivated by his need to receive magical supplies from a masculine source and possibly, though less certainly, to reunite with his split-off, unconscious, and projected masculinity.) Relationships are saturated with components of introjective and projective identifications. In the cross-dressing homosexual, the encounter is further complicated by the simultaneous dread of loss of love (or abandonment) and of invasion of the self (loss of identity).

DEVELOPMENTAL DYNAMICS

Many investigators, ourselves among them (Ovesey and Person, 1973; Person and Ovesey, 1974a), have postulated that the central defect in cross-dressing homosexuals, transsexuals, and transvestites is the failure to form a coherent sense of self. The fragmentation-prone self appears to be the product of both separation anxiety and an intense primitive rage engendered in infantile life. In some patients, this appears to result from a deficiency in the mother-infant dyad during the separation-individuation period of infantile development. The sense of self does not consolidate, and the personality remains prone to an abandonment type of empty depression. The symptomatic distortions of gender and sex reflect different ways of dealing with separation anxiety and rage in consolidating the self at progressive levels of maturation. We have suggested that these disorders may be viewed as the end product of distortions in ego development, particularly of severe distortions in the development of self and object representations.

In order to stabilize the sense of self, all three groups resort to female identifications to counter separation anxiety, primitive rage, and empty depression. The nature of these identifications, however, depends on their motivation. We follow Jacobson (1954, 1964) and Schafer (1968) in differentiating between identifications aimed at achieving likeness, sameness or merger. We have postulated that the self-representation in transsexuals and transvestites is most likely the end product of unconscious merger fantasies between the self and the maternal object, originating in the infantile period. These two groups form an abiding identification with a lost object. In contrast, in homosexual cross-dressers, the shifting female identifications are not exclusively intended to preserve an affective tie to the object of identification; their purpose is to become the same as the object and to take its place.

Thus, transsexuals unconsciously resort to the fantasy of symbiotic fusion with the mother to allay separation anxiety. The final transsexual resolution is an attempt to get rid of this anxiety through sex reassignment; that is, the transsexual acts out his unconscious fantasy surgically and symbolically becomes his own mother. Transvestites resort to a less drastic measure, the incorporation of transitional objects. Female clothes represent the mother and hence confer maternal protection. Later, in the oedipal period, the basis is laid for their eventual use sexually as fetishistic defenses against incestual anxiety.

In contrast, homosexual cross-dressers do not have a fixed female identification. Their anxiety is not countered by an ongoing merger fantasy but is temporarily bound by a series of shifting identifications. If any merger is intended, it is the potential merger with a male made possible by assuming a female identity. In other words, the boy wants the mother's power, not the mother herself. He fears engulfment and annihilation by the mother, and, because he cherishes his separate identity, he transfers his dependency and sexual needs to a male object. His aim is to leave the dyadic relationship, though armed with the magical powers of the mother or her imaginative successors. His elusiveness and ability to form shifting identifications are acquired in the service of preserving his separate identity.

We infer that the homosexual cross-dresser has successfully navigated the early phases of separation-individuation and has established a sense of separate identity, though a truncated and fragile one. It is not the sense of self but the sense of a gendered self that is at jeopardy. This is in contrast to the transsexual and transvestite, in whom even the sense of a separate self is not fully achieved. Theoretically, one could argue that the infantile trauma is not in the separation phase but in the rapprochement phase. Why the gendered self is felt to be threatened is an open question. Most observers have postulated an intrusive mother who does not allow the child to declare his difference from her. In some instances, this seems to be the case and the adult may repudiate his mother, all the while displaying her very intrusiveness in his relationships with others. At the same time, we are impressed by the conscious and unconscious repudiation of masculinity, particularly when the paternal figure has been violent. We have speculated that this repudiation is in the service of repressing the child's own rage.

Cross-Dressing Homosexuality and the Other Homosexualities

Cross-dressing homosexuals differ from other homosexuals in important ways. Impersonation is under conscious control among cross-dressing homosexuals but not in transvestites. Yet, there is a fixed quality to the impersonation in cross-dressing homosexuals that is absent from other homosexuals. The wish to be female is obligatory; it is not a symbolic statement about role liberation, as it is sometimes romantically assumed to be. From the psychiatric point of view, cross-dressing homosexuals, at least those for whom female impersonation is the central emotional preoccupation, most often fall in the borderline range of psychopathology. In our opinion, this differentiates them from the vast majority of homosexuals, in whom there is no evidence whatsoever of borderline pathology. Although both groups are called "homosexual," this designation overemphasizes their similarity, which is simply one of erotic object choice; it underplays the extreme difference in underlying personality organization.

11

Extreme Boyhood Femininity: Isolated Finding or Pervasive Disorder?

1985

SUSAN COATES AND ETHEL S. PERSON

TWENTY-FIVE EXTREMELY feminine boys with DSM-III diagnosis of gender identity disorder of childhood were evaluated for the presence of behavioral disturbances, social competence, and separation anxiety. Using the Child Behavior Checklist created by Achenbach and Edelbrock in 1983, 84 percent of feminine boys were reported to display behavioral disturbances usually seen in clinic-referred children. Sixty-four percent of the sample had difficulties with peers that were comparable to those of psychiatric-referred boys. Sixty percent of the sample met the criteria for diagnosis of DSM-III separation anxiety disorder. Only one child in the sample fell within the normal range on all three of these parameters. Results suggest extreme boyhood femininity is not an isolated finding, but part of a more pervasive psychological disturbance. Additional clinical findings support this contention.
Journal of the American Academy of Child Psychiatry, 24, 6:702–709, 1985.

The following is the first of a series of reports on 25 extremely effeminate boys who met the DSM-III criteria for gender identity disorder (GID) of childhood and were referred for treatment and study by the Childhood Gender Identity Project of the Child and Adolescent Psychiatry Department at the St. Luke's-Roosevelt Hospital Center. The goals of this project are (1) to provide clinical care for severely gender confused children, (2) to investigate the natural history of boyhood femininity and its antecedents, and (3) to clarify psychodynamic issues as they emerge in in-depth psychotherapy.

To date, studies of boys referred to gender identity units have focused largely on establishing descriptions, exploring demographic variables and charting the natural history of extreme boyhood femininity. Few studies have focused either on the behavioral and emotional correlates of effeminacy or the early experiences of the child in his family matrix. In contrast, this project is designed to do both.

Most researchers agree that effeminate boys display the following characteristics: they express the wish to be a girl, claim that they will grow up to be a girl, or both; they show a marked interest in girls' activities such as playing with dolls and enjoy play-acting the role of girls; they like dressing up in girls' clothes and exhibit an intense interest in cosmetics, jewelry and high heeled shoes; and they prefer girls as friends (Bates et al., 1973, 1974; Green, 1974, 1976; Rosen et al., 1977; Zucker, 1982).

Significantly, research reveals that effeminate boys are not different from controls either in external genitalia or in karyotype (Green, 1976; Rekers et al., 1979).

In the most extensive demographic study reported in the literature (60 boys), Green (1976) found that femininity was unrelated to ethnic background, religion or educational level of either parent, the mother's age at the time she gave birth, or the number of years between the next oldest and next youngest child.

Long-term follow-up studies are few in number and difficult to interpret. The clearest of these was reported by Money and Russo (1979). Of 11 boys diagnosed with prepubertal gender-identity discordance, 5 were available for follow-up. At the time of the follow-up, all were in their twenties and all 5 considered themselves homosexual or predominantly so. Follow-up studies by Green (1979), Lebowitz (1972) and Zuger (1978) have been done at the time of adolescence, but this is too early an age to gauge outcome, since major shifts and consolidations in identity and sexuality occur during adolescence. Even so, these studies report from 37 to 75% atypical outcome in gender identity and sexual orientation.

It is clear from the data that boyhood femininity is correlated with an increased incidence of homosexual object choice in later life, atypical gender behavior, or both. However, we are presently unable to predict the development of heterosexuality, homosexuality, transvestism or transsexuality as these boys, treated or untreated, reach adulthood.

One of the critical issues in the study of these boys has been the question of whether extreme femininity is a behavioral pattern that is unrelated to other emotional difficulties in the child and in this sense is an isolated finding, or whether it is etiologically associated with other pervasive personality difficulties.

Stoller (1975a), with regard to his sample of effeminate boys, explicitly states, "These mothers do not cripple the development of ego functions in general or even body ego, except in regard to this sense of femaleness. . . . None of these boys has shown the slightest evidence of psychosis or precursors of psychosis" (p. 54). Stoller thus appears to view extreme boyhood femininity as an isolated finding that is not inextricably connected to more pervasive psychopathology. (Note: Stoller does not distinguish extreme boyhood femininity from childhood transsexualism. He believes that the sample of boys he studied were a special sample of very young transsexuals. We do not share his assumption since there is no way to make this diagnosis in childhood.) Most systematic studies, however, have failed to confirm Stoller's contention. Three studies from the UCLA Gender Identity Unit suggest gender-referred boys have more concomitant behavioral disturbances than a control group and are pervasively behaviorally disturbed. ("Gender-referred" boys, in the UCLA studies, refers to all boys referred to their gender unit. Their sample was not limited to DSM-III diagnosed GID boys.) The samples from these three studies are overlapping and do not represent separate groups of children. In one study based on parental reports, 15 gender-referred boys scored significantly higher on a behavior disturbance factor than controls. Items in this factor included "acts defiant when given orders," "has temper tantrums," "restless and overactive," and "cries easily" (Bates et al., 1973).

In a second study of 29 gender-referred boys, clinical evaluation material was rated by staff clinicians on 88 items derived from clinical literature, theory and experience with the families. One of the four-factor analytically derived item scales combined items descriptive of an inhibited, fearful child, and items descriptive of an inhibiting, protective family environment. Effeminate boys scored higher on this factor than controls (Bates et al., 1974).

In a third study, 13 gender-referred boys were compared to both normal and clinical controls. The clinical controls were mainly diagnosed as conduct and personality disorders. Mothers rated the boys on the Gender Behavior Inventory for Boys (Bates et al., 1973). Both the gender-problem and clinical boys were rated by their mothers as marginally higher on the behavioral disturbance factor than normal controls. Behavior disturbance did not differ in the two clinical groups. The authors conclude: " . . . gender-problem boys evidence a general personality or behavioral disorder rather than simply a narrow set of deviant gender-attitudes or gender behavior tendencies" (Bates et al., 1979).

The Clarke group in Toronto (Bradley et al., 1980) compared a combined group of effeminate boys and masculine girls to psychiatric controls and found no differences in the Child Behavior Checklist (Achenbach, 1978; Achenbach and Edelbrock, 1979). Thus, gender-referred children in their sample were as behaviorally disturbed as their psychiatric controls. Results from both the

UCLA and Clarke groups provide growing evidence that boyhood femininity occurs in the context of behavioral disturbance.

Rosen et al. (1977) claim that the majority of gender-confused boys suffer from an "abnormal amount of depression and social conflict resulting from peer rejection, isolation, and ridicule of their feminine behavior" (p. 96).

Other clinical reports suggest that feminine boys have difficulty with their peers. They are often scapegoated, ridiculed and treated with verbal abuse by their cohorts (Green, 1974; Rekers et al., 1977). Research studies have found feminine boys to have a minimal interest in competitive athletic activities (Green, 1976) and to have less athletic competence than their peers (Bates et al., 1979). Systematic studies of general social competence have not yet been reported in the literature.

There are several limitations of the previous studies of behavior disturbances and peer relationships in cross-gender boys. First, all of these studies have used subjects with varying degrees of femininity, including both those who would and would not qualify for a DSM-III diagnosis of GID, making it difficult to compare one study to the other. In the studies by Bates et al. (1973,1979), only a narrow range of behavior disturbances was investigated, while Bates et al. (1974) based their ratings on case reports rather than on direct standardized assessments. Although the Clarke group used a comprehensive and standardized behavior disturbance scale, they included gender cases of varying degrees of severity (children who both qualified and did not qualify for the DSM-III diagnosis of GID). Furthermore, both sexes were combined in their data analyses, which may have obscured some important differences between the sexes.

The present study attempts to rectify these difficulties first by limiting the study to boys who were diagnosed as DSM-III GID. This both restricts and defines the sample more clearly. Secondly, a comprehensive and standardized behavioral scale was used. Third, a standardized social competence scale was used to assess a broader spectrum of social competence than has been studied previously.

Another goal of this study has been to assess separation anxiety in GID boys. This rationale is based on clinical studies of adults with extreme gender problems who reveal a high incidence of separation anxiety (Ovesey and Person, 1973, 1976; Person and Ovesey, 1974a, 1974b).

The study predicted that GID boys would exceed normal children and be comparable to other clinic-referred children in behavioral disturbance and that they would show less social competence than normal boys and be comparable to clinic-referred children. It also predicted an increased incidence of separation anxiety compared with that anticipated in a normal population.

Method

Boys were referred to the Childhood Gender Identity Project if they showed behavioral signs of femininity. The sources of referral were psychiatrists, psychologists, social workers, pediatricians and teachers. Referrals came primarily from local public and Catholic schools that knew of the Childhood Gender Identity unit. Children were initially referred for evaluation and treatment. Five children were first seen in the Child and Adolescent Psychiatry department for presenting problems other than gender identity disorder and were only subsequently referred to the gender unit when a gender disorder came to light as a major issue. Initial diagnoses of these five children included overanxious, dysthymic, adjustment and conduct disorders. Six children were referred privately to Dr. Coates for gender problems and these children were referred to the gender unit for evaluation. One was referred from the Roosevelt Pediatric department and one from another outpatient child psychiatry unit. Out of a total number of approximately 40 referrals, 25 boys were accepted for study. All those excluded failed to meet the criteria for DSM-III diagnosis of GID. All of the 25 boys accepted did meet the criteria. All who were accepted for study participated in the study. All of these boys persistently expressed the wish to be a girl; all displayed female stereotypical behavior, while 40% repudiated their male anatomy. There were no intersexed children in this sample. External genitalia were normal in all boys except one who had unilateral cryptorchidism.

At the time of referral, as Table 11.1 shows, the boys in this study ranged in age from 4 to 14 years, the average being 7.4; 48% of the sample was white, 40% Spanish and 12% black. The high percentage of Spanish families reflects the racial patterns of the catchment area of the hospital.

On the Four-Factor Index of Social Status (Hollingshead, 1975) assessed by education and occupation, this sample ranged from 11 to 66 on the socioeconomic scale. The average was 34. Five children were only children. Of the remainder, 8 were first born and 11 were last born.

The range of Full Scale Wechsler IQ in this sample was 60–137, the average being 103. Only one child scored in the retarded range.

PROCEDURES

Each child was seen for 5 or 6 sessions which included a psychiatric evaluation, extensive psychological testing and an observation of free play.

Mothers were seen for 2 or 3 sessions to obtain information on the history of the gender problem, to gather an extensive developmental history, and to rate the presence of behavioral problems in the child. At the end of this clinic evaluation, families were invited to participate in an extensive research study of the mothers and fathers that focused on their lives during the first 3 years of

TABLE 11.1
Sample Characteristic of Gender Identity Disorder (GID) Boys (N = 25)

Ethnic groups (*N*):	
White	12 (48%)
Hispanic	10 (40%)
Black	3 (12%)
Age (yr):	
Mean	7.4
Range	4–14
Social status (Hollingshead):	
Mean	34
Range	11–66

their sons' lives. These data are not dealt with in this report, but will be reported subsequently.

ASSESSMENT METHODS

Each child was administered psychological testing that included the WPPSI or WISC-R, Draw-a-Person, Rorschach, Thematic Apperception Test and Sex-typed Animal Preference Test. School achievement and learning disability tests were administered when it was deemed clinically appropriate.

Developmental history was explored with the mothers through a structured interview that is rated for presence, absence and frequency of behaviors. These interviews focused on the child's perinatal experience, medical history, temperament, separation experience, behavior problems and gender development during the first 5 years of life.

The Child Behavior Checklist (CBCL) (Achenbach and Edelbrock, 1983) was administered to the mothers (and jointly to the fathers when present) during the initial evaluation, usually at the end of the first session or in the second.

The CBCL includes 118 behavior problems rated by the child's parents on a three-point response scale. A total score reflects the degree of overall behavioral disturbance. Behavior problem scales were derived by factor analysis of the item intercorrelations based on a clinic referred population, for ages 4–5, 6–11 and 12–16 (Achenbach and Edelbrock, 1983). Norms for these factor-based scales were derived from nonclinical standardization samples. The CBCL also includes three social competence scales encompassing the parent's reports of their child's participation and performance in areas designated as (1) Activities, (2) Social, and (3) School. The Activities subcluster assesses participation in sports and jobs; the Social subcluster, involvement with friends and organizations; the School subcluster, overall performance in school. A total score reflects the degree of the child's social competence in all three areas.

The presence of separation anxiety was evaluated using the DSM-III criteria for separation anxiety. This evaluation was based on the evaluation interview with the child and the interview with the mother.

Mothers were assessed using the Rorschach, Beck Depression Inventory, and the Gunderson Diagnostic Interview for Borderlines. In addition they received a structured interview that focused on their relationships with their own parents, on their relationship to their child during the first 3 years of life and on their own psychological status during the child's first 3 years of life. The results of the mothers' psychological assessment have been reported by Marantz (1984).

The results of the CBCL and of the interviews concerning separation anxiety will be reported in this paper. Since funding for a control group was not available, the analysis of the CBCL scales involved comparison with normative data. This required partitioning of the total sample into the age groups 4–5 (N = 11), 6–11 (N = 10) and 12–14 (N = 4). In addition, pertinent clinical findings will be reported.

Results

CBCL SCORES

On the CBCL, 21 of the 25 boys had a total behavior problem score in the clinical range (90th percentile or above: Table 11.2). Only 4 children scored in the normal range. Thus, 84% of the GID boys were as behaviorally disturbed as the majority of boys referred to psychiatric clinics in general. The behavior problem scales on which at least 50% of the boys scored in the clinical range (defined as scores above the 98th percentile) were: for ages 4–5, social withdrawal, depressed, immature and sex problems; for ages 6–11, schizoid, depressed, uncommunicative, obsessive-compulsive and social withdrawal; for ages 12–16, all nine factors (somatic complaints, schizoid, uncommunicative, immature, obsessive-compulsive, hostile-withdrawal, delinquent, aggressive and hyperactive). (The items with the highest loadings on the sex problems factor are: (1) wishes to be the opposite sex and (2) acts like opposite sex. Thus the name "sex problems" is misleading and fails to reflect the cross-gender nature of the behaviors that are rated.) With regard to Social Competence, 64% of the boys had a total score in the clinical range (10th percentile or lower). On the Activities scale, 24% scored in the clinical range (below the 2nd percentile); on the Social scale, 48%, and on the School scale, 43%.

The overall results of the School scale may be misleading. The finding of 43% of the boys falling in the clinical range is based on a restricted sample.

TABLE 11.2
Child Behavior Checklist (CBCL) Results

Total Behavior Problem Score	Normal Range ≤90th Percentile	Clinical Range >90th Percentile	Comparison with GID sample
CBCL standard samples:			
Nonclinical	90%	10%	0.001[a]
Clinical	26%	74%	NS[b]
Boys with GID ($N = 25$)	16%	84%	
Total Social Competence Score	**>10th Percentile**	**≤ 10th Percentile**	
CBCL standard samples:			
Nonclinical	90%	10%	0.01[a]
Clinical	43%	57%	NS[b]
Boys with GID ($N = 25$)	36%	64%	

[a] Binomial test using the CBCL standards as population values; 1-tailed.
[b] One-sample χ^2 using the CBLC standards for the calculations of expected values; 2-tailed.

This scale does not apply to children under age 6. Thus, the scale was not rated for 11 boys. In our older boys, ages 12 and above, 3 out of 4 cases were in the clinical range in the School scale. If one calculates the rate of school problems for the two samples separately, only 22% of the 6–11-year-olds scored in the clinical range and 80% of the older boys scored in the clinical range. We believe that the older boys are a more extreme sample. First, their continued wish to be a girl and intense female stereotypical interests have continued unabated since early childhood. This is not the usual pattern reported in the literature. In particular, the expressed wish to be a girl usually stops in middle childhood (Zucker, 1982). We believe that this subsample is a more extreme subgroup not only in terms of gender disturbance but also in terms of behavioral disturbance and, therefore, is not representative of the GID population as a whole.

CLINICAL FINDINGS

Separation Anxiety. A major clinical goal of our work has been to document the frequent coexistence of separation anxiety and effeminate behavior. Separation anxiety was evident in a large number of our cases. Out of 25 children, 15 (60%) met the DSM-III criteria for separation anxiety disorder at the time of the examination. Six children had no indications of separation anxiety and 4 showed fewer criteria than required to meet a DSM-III diagnosis. Of the separation anxious group, 8 of the 15 were currently or had been school reluctant, school avoidant or both.

Behavioral manifestations of separation anxiety were observed in the initial evaluations of the child and in ongoing psychotherapy and were elicited by history in interviews with the mothers. Many of the boys had difficulty leaving their mothers in the waiting room and several of the younger children could not be separated from their mothers without becoming severely agitated.

Mothers reported that their boys ceaselessly shadowed them around the house, refused to sleep in a bedroom by themselves and had major difficulties when left alone even for short periods of time. Several boys worried that their mother would be killed in a catastrophe while she was away from them. One mother reported that her child had tantrums whenever she spoke on the phone to another person.

Early in their psychotherapy, these boys displayed profound anxiety and rage when issues of being left by their mothers arose. In addition, rage often emerged dramatically in psychotherapy at the end of therapy sessions. Some children would bite, kick and scream at the end of sessions; one child regularly threatened to jump out the window as soon as his therapist told him his session would soon be over. Others would attempt to cope with the separation by "flipping" into a female role. This solution seemed to ward off the anxiety generated by the separation from the therapist. For some children, the prospect of separation from the mother created such severe anxiety that they had to be treated with the mother present in the room.

According to parental report and our own observation, three children showed no evidence of even age appropriate separation anxiety. One child was brought by his mother for a research appointment for herself that she knew would take 6 hours and would not include her son. She was clearly accustomed to leaving him for hours alone and proceeded to leave him in a room alone nearby. He remained by himself for hours making no protest whatsoever. Two of the children with no manifestation of separation anxiety developed severe manifestations after they were in psychotherapy and had begun to become affectively involved.

Of the six children who displayed no separation anxiety at all, three had histories of chronic asthma. This surprising finding raised the question of whether asthma served to bind their separation anxiety or whether asthma itself was a predisposing factor to boyhood femininity. In addition, two children who were separation anxious also had a history of asthma. Thus, in this small sample of children, 5 out of 25 (20%) had histories of chronic asthma.

Peer Relations. Both the parents and the boys themselves report that they are isolated from their peers. They rarely have male friends and rarely engage in athletic pursuits or in rough-and-tumble play. Most often they have friendships with girls, but these relationships are not described as close and most often do not last long. School-aged effeminate boys usually befriend girls who will allow them to participate in traditional girls' activities. Several of the boys in our study described themselves as being lonely, noting that no one liked them and that they did not like themselves either.

During adolescence, they suffer even further disruption in their peer relations. They are frequently treated abusively by being taunted, called "sissy" or "faggot." Many boys refuse to go to gym class because they are humiliated by their incompetence at athletics and by exposing their bodies to other males while changing in the locker room.

These findings (taken in conjunction with Social Competence data) suggest greater peer problems in adolescence, as would be anticipated with the increasing social disapprobation as well as the problem of emerging sexuality. But because age trends reported here are based on cross-sectional data we are unable to determine whether this represents a true developmental trend or sampling fluctuation. Longitudinal follow-up of the sample would help to clarify this.

Depression. None of the children in our study met the criteria for a DSM-III major depressive episode at the time of referral to our unit. One child had been hospitalized for suicidal gestures some years earlier. At least one other boy had a history of suicidal gestures. Seven children had histories of suicidal ideation.

As we have already noted, however, on the Child Behavior Profile, at both age levels that have a depressive factor (age 4–5 and 6–11), over 50% of our sample fell within the clinical range.

Several mothers reported that their sons repeatedly expressed the feeling of hating themselves. One boy said to his mother "I hate myself. I don't want to be me. I want to be someone else. I want to be a girl." Other self-deprecatory ideation was reported by mothers and by their sons as well. Many boys expressed a sense of being inadequate and unable to do things competently. Others referred to themselves as stupid, dumb, and ugly.

Although this study has not focused on depression as a central issue, we believe that enough evidence for depression emerged in our sample to warrant further systematic evaluation.

Personality Integration. Despite their gender confusion, peer isolation and other behavior problems, separation anxiety and depression, the boys seldom displayed either gross impairment in reality testing or psychotic functioning. In two cases, however, the children had transitory delusional episodes. One child feared for a short period that he would be taken over by the devil and would start attacking others as a result of this transformation. During these episodes, he would not sleep with the window open for fear that the devil would enter through the window and invade his body. This anxiety increased whenever his mother left him at home alone. Despite his severe emotional upset during these episodes, he continued to function adequately in school and other structured situations. The second boy had a delusion that the spirit of a particular woman had entered and taken over his body. His family took him to a spiritualist who attempted to exorcise the spirit of the woman. When this failed he began psychotherapy and his delusion disappeared some months later.

These boys functioned relatively well (adaptively) on psychological tests, if the tests were structured (Coates and Tuber, 1985; Tuber and Coates, 1985). On unstructured tests they displayed major ego impairments. On the Rorschach test, content indicating primitive object relations and boundary disturbances characteristic of impaired personality integration were commonly seen.

Thus, while there is evidence for personality disorder, these boys do not fall within the psychotic range.

Summary of Findings. If one compares individual children across three parameters (the total behavior problem score of the CBCL, the total Social Competence score of the CBCL and the absence or presence of DSM-III diagnosis of separation anxiety), all but one child scored in the clinical range on at least one of them: 51% scored in the clinical range in all three parameters, 24% on two and 24% on one.

Conclusions and Discussion

The question must be raised as to whether our sample is representative of GID boys in general. While we have no absolute way of ascertaining its representativeness, we are impressed by the fact that 20 of the 25 referrals were made because of effeminacy, not because of social or behavioral disturbances which emerged in the course of our research. Even so, we are not in a position to know how frequently extreme boyhood femininity occurs without accompanying behavioral disturbance and as a result does not come to the attention of mental health workers.

The large number of Spanish referrals to our unit is a reflection of the ethnic balance in the Roosevelt Hospital catchment area. The proportion of upper-middle-class children is atypically large for the Roosevelt Child and Adolescent Psychiatry department and reflects the fact that several of the cases were private referrals to Dr. Coates who were in turn referred to the childhood gender unit for evaluations. Inspection of scatter plots revealed no ethnic patterns for any of the subgroups. In terms of demographic proportions, the sample is not representative of New York City or even the hospital population. For this reason the study must be considered exploratory.

The fact that the CBCL was given after the families were initially interviewed may have resulted in a warm-up effect, the result of which may have been that families reported more problems than they would have to total strangers. Although this may have elevated scores to some degree, we doubt that it has produced a major distortion in our results. Clinical interviews and ongoing psychotherapy provided a more elaborate picture of these children's behavioral difficulties supporting the questionnaire data.

We believe that our findings confirm our major hypotheses. GID boys appear to exceed normal children in behavioral disturbance and separation anxiety and they are less socially competent. Our data suggests that extreme boyhood femininity occurs in the context of a more pervasive psychological disorder, and that it is not a single or isolated finding. We believe the data speaks for itself regarding this contention and supports a growing body of research indicating that extreme boyhood femininity is typically associated with significant behavioral disturbance. (It can be argued that the results on behavioral disturbance, social competence and separation anxiety have been artificially inflated by the inclusion of 5 children who were originally referred to a child psychiatry unit for behavioral problems other than extreme femininity. If one reanalyzes the data omitting these 5 boys [one of which was the retarded boy] the following results emerged. On the behavior problem checklist 75% of the boys were in the clinical range. On the Social Competence scale 65% were in the clinical range and 60% met the criteria for a DSM-III diagnosis of separation anxiety. Thus our hypotheses remain corroborated.)

A significant finding has been to correlate a high incidence of separation anxiety with GID. A higher percentage of GID boys had a diagnosable separation anxiety disorder than we can estimate to be the upper limits for normal boys. Orvaschel and Weissman (1985) report that "no epidemiologic data are available regarding anxiety disorders in children." However, they report the classical epidemiologic study of Lapouse and Monk (1978) who found that 41% of the children between the ages of 6–12 had a fear of "anyone in the family getting sick, having an accident or dying," which may be viewed as an item related to separation anxiety. In a cross-sectioned survey of preschool children from two Danish municipalities, Kastrup (1976) found fear of separation in 12% of boys. We can estimate that these are upper limits for indicators of separation anxiety. In all likelihood DSM-III-defined separation anxiety must be considerably lower than these upper limit estimates. Even so, our sample had a higher percentage of separation anxiety disorder than those reported in these epidemiological studies.

Several of the children in our study began cross-dressing for the first time on the heels of a precipitous actual separation from their mother. In psychotherapy with these children, clues as to the meaning of the relationship of their cross-gender behavior to separation anxiety symptoms have emerged. A number of children appear to use cross-gender behavior and dressing as an attempt to restore a fantasy tie to the physically or emotionally absent mother. In imitating "Mommy" they confuse "being Mommy" with "having Mommy." This symptom appears to allay, in part, the anxiety generated by the loss of the mother.

Because Stoller (1975a) predicated mother-son symbiosis as the etiologic agent in extreme boyhood femininity, one might say that our research findings of separation anxiety could be predicted by his theoretical formulations. But nothing could be further from the case. Although Stoller believes that if the mother extends a blissful symbiosis with her infant son for too long, the result is femininity in the little boy, he regards this femininity as a product of imprinting. In his formulation, imprinting produces a conflict-free feminine core gender identity, so that these little boys feel themselves to be females in the face of demonstrable male anatomy.

Thus, although his formulation might intuitively seem to suggest that one would see evidence of separation anxiety in effeminate boys, Stoller himself posits that imprinting is nonconflictual. He does not believe that imprinting of a feminine identity affects other aspects of personality development. His contention has been criticized on theoretical grounds by Mahler (1975), and on clinical grounds by Person and Ovesey (1974a, 1974b), Socarides (1975), and Weitzmann et al. (1970).

Moreover, our research on the family matrix (to be reported subsequently) indicates that separation anxiety more often results from actual separation trauma or a distant, a disturbed mother-child interaction rather than from any blissful symbiosis.

Insofar as this sample shows correspondence to retrospective histories gleaned in the studies of adult groups of cross-gender disorders, they most closely resemble those derived in studies of cross-dressing homosexuals (Ovesey and Person, 1973; Person and Ovesey, 1984) or those elicited in a group of extremely effeminate adolescent homosexuals (Bieber et al., 1962). (In particular, Ovesey and Person posited separation anxiety as a necessary but not sufficient condition for the development of severe cross-gender pathology as seen in adults.) However, it would be a mistake to assume the congruence of these groups, as erroneous as it is to assume that one can study the childhood of transsexuals by studying effeminate boys. The correspondence between these groups remains unknown and indicates one of the lines of longitudinal investigation that should be undertaken.

We also believe that the finding that 40% of our sample did *not* evidence separation anxiety is extremely important. It suggests that the pathways leading to boyhood femininity are disparate. This particular finding may suggest an important subdivision in antecedents to feminine behavior.

While there is some agreement in the literature that effeminate boys suffer depression and peer problems, there are two opposing explanations to account for these findings: either they are secondary to the pain of social ostracism and being labeled deviant, or they are more intrinsically associated with the gender confusion and may even be prerequisite to the development of effeminacy.

As for the argument that the associated behavioral difficulties, depressions and separation-anxiety should be exclusively attributed to social ostracism, we find this position far from convincing. In the younger age ranges, the child is primarily at home, where social disapproval is not even an issue. In fact, Green (1974) points to family *reinforcement,* not disapproval, and yet we see that many very young effeminate boys suffer from severe separation anxiety and constantly shadow their mothers. It seems clear that although social ostracism and labeling as deviant almost certainly compound the psychological problems for this group of children as they grow older, the time sequence demonstrates the integral coexistence of psychopathology with extreme boyhood femininity.

In sum, we agree with investigations from the UCLA and Clarke gender units that have found extreme childhood effeminacy to be a part of a pervasive disorder rather than an isolated finding. However, it is still far from clear what the implications are for adult personality organization. Furthermore, these conclusions apply only to those instances of boyhood femininity of such magnitude that they fall within the DSM-III criteria for diagnosing childhood gender-identity disorder.

In terms of future research, our findings point to a need for more systematic studies of a wide spectrum of diagnostic disorders in GID boys to determine whether separation anxiety is a major predisposing factor in its development and/or whether other disorders may play a significant role as well. Our findings suggest that while separation anxiety is important in one large subgroup, the sample may consist of different subtypes with different underlying structures.

PART III

Sex and Fantasy

12

From Sexual Desire to Excitement: The Role of Sexual Fantasy

1998

ETHEL S. PERSON

DESIRE, THE subjective sense of longing, is hardly ever discussed as such in the psychoanalytic literature, even though it is central to our experience, particularly in the realm of sex.[1] The word desire does not rate a listing in the general subject index of *The Standard Edition of the Complete Psychological Works of Freud*. It's not an entry in Moore and Fine's *Psychoanalytic Terms and Concepts* (1990) or in *The Language of Psychoanalysis* (1973) by Laplanche and Pontalis. No doubt this is because sex was first conceptualized as libido, an endogenous energy with a preordained developmental unfolding. While the sense of desire—or its absence—has always had clinical relevance, it has become more theoretically relevant with the shift in psychoanalytic theory to a focus on subjectivity and intersubjectivity.

As is so often the case, a mental disposition such as sexual desire is first theorized when an abnormality is noted in the way it is experienced or enacted. So, for example, the concept of erotic desire appears in Freud's paper "On the Universal Tendency to Debasement in the Sphere of Love" (1912), an early but brilliant account of psychogenic impotence.[2] Freud observes that "if the practicing psycho-analyst asks himself on account of what disorder people most often come to him for help, he is bound to reply—disregarding the many

This chapter has not been published previously. An earlier version was presented at a conference "From Erotic Desire to Sexual Excitement" sponsored by the Association for Psychoanalytic Medicine, New York City, 1996. A somewhat different version was presented at the 18th Annual Spring Meeting, Division of Psychoanalysis (39) "Psychoanalysis and Sexuality: Reflections on an Old Love Affair" in April, 1998.

1. While desire refers to realms other than sex, when I use the word *desire* unmodified in this chapter, I am referring to sexual desire.

2. Freud was one of the first physicians to theorize the causes of what we now call inhibitions of sexual desire. Stekel and Ferenczi also wrote on the subject.

forms of anxiety—that it is psychical impotence. This singular disturbance affects men of strong libidinous natures, and manifests itself in a refusal by the executive organs of sexuality to carry out the sexual act, although before and after they may show themselves to be intact and capable of performing the act, and although a strong psychical inclination to carry it out is present" (p. 179). The sexual dysfunction of impotence is aptly named since the man or woman so afflicted experiences the sexual disability as the loss of power, as powerlessness. In essence, the impotent man is rendered powerless to carry out his intent, his will. But why?

Freud's explanation for this incapacity is encoded in his phrase "where they love they do not desire and where they desire they cannot love" (1912, p. 183). His insight hinged on his understanding of the development of sexuality. To the degree that a wife is a stand-in for the original incestual object, her husband's sexual desire for her is compromised, and he transfers his sexual longings to a debased object. Today a loss of spousal desire is more often understood in terms of sexual boredom. As I will discuss later, understanding the replacement of pre-existing desire by sexual boredom is essential to theorizing the psychology of desire.

Two anecdotes reveal different ways in which psychogenic impotence may be engendered. The first is recounted by Abram Kardiner in his memoir, *My Analysis with Freud* (1977, pp. 73–75). One of Kardiner's American colleagues, also in Vienna to be analyzed by Freud, became impotent with his wife. As Kardiner tells the story, his friend had been seeing a young girl who was a violinist. The friend's wife, who was in New York, heard that her husband was involved with a "younger and more attractive woman" and promptly returned to Vienna, where she confronted him. Although he had always boasted to Kardiner about his sexual prowess, when his wife arrived—and this was after he had completed his analysis with Freud—he discovered that he was impotent with her. He quickly panicked: "What? Impotent *after* analysis?" He felt there was no choice but to write to Freud for an appointment. In his letter he told Freud about the situation in which he found himself. He was convinced that Freud would tell him he needed more analysis. But Freud surprised him. He did not interject a single word during their interview, but when the hour was up, Freud seized his former analysand's hand and said, "Well, now I see that you are a really decent fellow!" and showed him out (p. 74).

A group of Kardiner's friends in Vienna met to discuss the meaning of Freud's "laconic utterance." Finally, they came to what they believed was a plausible conclusion. "What Freud meant was this: Up to now—that is, before you were in analysis—you were a bit of a scoundrel, but since your analysis you have at least the decency to be impotent with the woman you betrayed. So this impotence is witness to the fact that you have undergone a change of character—for the better" (Kardiner, 1977, pp. 74–75).

Kardiner reports that his friend regained his potency when he gave up the violinist (who then became psychotic). Kardiner views this story as an illustration of how Freud "could condense a whole sermon into a single sentence" (p. 75). Yet this story, by implicating guilt as the source of impotence, posits an etiology for loss of desire different from the one Freud had proposed more explicitly in his paper of 1912 and suggests that Freud was aware of several different root causes of such a loss of desire. (Parenthetically, this vignette also illustrates how the cultural *zeitgeist* invariably influences how we judge sexual acts. Today, few if any psychoanalysts would say as Freud did, "Well, now I see that you are a really decent fellow" in response to a failure of potency following infidelity.)

The second anecdote involves an elderly man whom I knew many years ago. He told me that his wife had complained about his impotence. Deeply distressed, he went from psychiatrist to psychiatrist, all of them offering him one or another interpretation, but to no avail. Eventually, in despair, he went to his family physician, who asked him a simple question: "Impotent with whom?" My friend realized it was only his wife he could not function with, and since it was not his passion to do so, he declared his "potency disorder" cured. His inhibition toward sleeping with his wife stemmed not from his love for her but rather from loathing her. His problem was that he confused duty with desire. His body spoke the truth of his feelings, of his lack of desire.

For sexologists, the exploration of different kinds of impotence led to a fuller explication of desire, while for psychoanalysts, the study of perversions led to an emphasis on the central role of erotic fantasies in desire. The key texts that launched the exploration of sexual desire as such are Helen Kaplan's *Disorders of Sexual Desire* and Robert Stoller's *Sexual Excitement: Dynamics of Erotic Life*, both published in 1979. While far from identical in their theses, these two books taken together provide a framework within which to begin to theorize desire. As will become clear, the terms *sexual desire* and *sexual excitement* do not have the same meaning for sexologists and psychoanalysts, nor have these terms been defined with any consistency within the psychoanalytic community.[3]

3. There are studies on desire in other disciplines. So, for example, Roger Scruton (1986) writes of the longtime philosophical distinction between sexual desire and erotic love. He points out that "according to Plato's view, our animal nature is the principal vehicle of sexual desire, and provides its overriding motive. In desire we act and feel as animals; indeed, desire is a motive which all sexual beings—including the majority of animals—share. In erotic love, however, it is our nature as rational beings that is primarily engaged, and, in the exercise of this passion, altogether finer and more durable impulses seek recognition and fulfilment" (p. 1). I believe Scruton's conflation of sexual excitement and sexual desire in humans is an error, as is his conflation of the expression of sexual desire in humans and in other animals.

Sex Therapy and Disorders of Desire

Masters and Johnson (1966) identified three stages in the sexual cycle: arousal, excitement, and orgasm. They observed that any one of these stages could be the locus of sexual dysfunction, hence the clinical usefulness of their classification. Later on, sex therapist and psychoanalyst Helen Singer Kaplan (1979, 1995) called attention to disorders of desire (some of which were cases of complete sexual aversion) and came to identify desire as a stage antecedent to arousal. She arrived at this diagnosis in the course of reviewing the charts of her patients who had failed to respond to sex therapy. What she discovered was that they had little or no desire for sex or for sex with a particular partner. Their inhibition was the product of trying to make love "without feeling lust or desire" (1979, p. 2).

In defining desire, Kaplan emphasized an important but frequently overlooked distinction between desire and excitement: "Sexual desire is an appetite or drive which is produced by the activation of a specific neural system in the brain, while the excitement and orgasm phases involve the genital organs" (1979, p. 9). She emphasized that sexual arousal and excitation are most often first mediated through a mental act, the invocation of sexual fantasies. In contrast, the sexual act itself is dependent on the friction of particular dermal surfaces. Hence, for Kaplan, sexuality is compounded of fantasy and friction.

In her schema, which is largely compatible with Freud's view of libido, sexual desire is experienced as specific sensations that motivate the individual to "seek out or become receptive to sexual experience" (1979, p. 10).[4] She regards the sex drive as basically similar to other drives in that it depends on the activation of a specific anatomical brain structure (not yet clearly identified), which includes centers of drive enhancement and drive inhibition, is served by both inhibitory and excitatory neurotransmitters, and, most important for therapists, is connected to other parts of the brain in such a way that it is affected by the individual's entire life experience, past and present.

Inhibited sexual desire (ISD), in Kaplan's schema, is analogized to anorexia nervosa. In both, fear takes precedence over pleasure. The magnitude of the fear distinguishes ISD from the more commonly encountered and more easily treatable potency disorders and sexual dysfunctions, in which the accompanying emotion (conscious or unconscious) may be guilt, fear, shame, or

4. Similarly, Kernberg (1995, p. 13) quotes Bancroft (1989) to the effect that "human sexual arousal is a global response that includes specific sexual fantasies, memories, and desires, and an increased awareness of and search for reinforcing external stimuli that are relatively specific to the individual's sexual orientation and sexual object. Sexual arousal . . . includes the activation of the limbic system under the influence of this cognitive-affective state, which stimulates the central spinal and peripheral neural control centers that determine engorgement, lubrication, and heightened local sensitivity of the genital organs, providing a central feedback of awareness of this genital activation."

sometimes anger. These inhibiting emotions become attached to the act of intercourse or to some other aspect of sexuality; sometimes they are attached to a specific partner, sometimes they are more generalized. They are elicited not only by specific sexual conflicts but by a host of cognitive and experiential factors, some of them nonsexual. These include misinformation, negatively valenced past experience, learning, cultural or religious inhibitions, and aspects of the relationship (both sexual and nonsexual). Some therapists consider the relational component to be of such magnitude that they regard any sexual dysfunction as the couple's problem rather than the individual's. While the causes of functional or psychogenic sexual dysfunctions are numerous and varied, most of them are not the product of deep unconscious conflict and are readily treatable.

Kaplan observed that ISD, in contrast, stemmed from deep conflict and that the therapeutic outcome was more problematic. The leading cause of ISD does not center on the madonna-whore dynamic that Freud proposed. Often it involves a fear of engulfment, hence the not-uncommon situation of a man who has enjoyed sexual relations with his fiancée but becomes impotent after the marriage vows have been exchanged. ISD is frequently the byproduct of conflicts around intimacy and fears of bodily harm. It may also occur when rage is symbolically attached to the act of ejaculation. One of my patients was unable to have sex his wife because he unconsciously feared that his ejaculate was destructive; he became potent with her only after he had decided to get a divorce, so that it no longer mattered to him whether he destroyed her.

Given that Kaplan was an analyst as well as a sex therapist, it is of some note that she makes no reference in her work to Freud's ever having touched on the subject of disorders of desire (and she is one of the relatively few sexologists who references Freud at all). In fact, Kaplan became well known for introducing the diagnosis of disorders of desire into the literature as her independent observation, based on the presenting complaints of her many patients. We can only assume that whatever the impact of Freud's insight into disorders of desire, it does not appear to have traveled in any straight line into the field of sexology.[5]

Of the many kinds of therapists, sexologists are probably the most attuned to the erotic fantasies mobilized to initiate arousal. They frequently prescribe that the patient invoke fantasies or view pornography to overcome sexual inhibitions. But because sex therapists only infrequently see perverse patients or patients with potentially dangerous fantasies (for example, pedophiliac fantasies), they essentially consider most fantasies innocuous and their origins

5. While Freud's 1912 paper changed the way we think about impotence, assigning to it a psychogenic cause, it is not widely referred to today in the context of discussing impotence per se. Its importance is in the role it, along with other key texts, played in opening up a dialogue about the nature of sexuality.

inconsequential (with the important exception of fantasies deriving from childhood sexual abuse). Their focus is ultimately not on the nature of fantasy but on its usefulness as an ancillary tool to promote arousal. In contrast, psychoanalytic discourse emphasizes not only the uses to which sexual fantasies may be put but also their deep connection to the individual's life history, intrapsychic conflicts, and core issues. This may be because psychoanalytic theories of desire stem in large part from the study of perversions, as was certainly the case with Robert Stoller.

Psychoanalysis and Theories of Desire

In the contemporary psychoanalytic discourse, the work that first theorized sexual desire as such is Stoller's *Sexual Excitement* (1979). His contribution is twofold. First, in focusing on what he called sexual excitement, he introduced the issue of desire and emphasized its connection to key erotic fantasies. Second, in theorizing the role of hostility in sexual excitement, he made explicit that what is subjectively felt as sexual is never purely sexual but is an amalgam of different wishes, fantasies, and feelings.

For Stoller, sexual excitement is one kind of excitement, and excitement, while not quite an affect, may color an affect (1979, p. 4). Stoller posits that excitement arises in a very specific way: it "implies anticipation in which one alternates with extreme rapidity between expectation of danger and just about equal expectation of avoidance of danger, and in some cases, such as in eroticism, of replacing danger with pleasure." Sexual excitement, as one subtype of psychic excitement, refers to the period of anticipation before the sex act, to the sensual build-up, to genital and nongenital sensations, and to a total-body erotic involvement. It is a mental state associated with "a perceived complex sensation that one senses is the product of fantasy (past experience remembered and reinvented to serve a need)." For Stoller, sexual excitement is a package that includes fantasy, desire, arousal, and excitement. This definition encompasses desire but also includes sexual excitement. By using the broader category, Stoller inadvertently blurs what the sexologists divided into the separate stages of desire, arousal, excitement, and orgasm.

My definition of sexual *desire* is congruent with one aspect of Stoller's definition of sexual *excitement;* that is, desire is a "perceived complex sensation that one senses is the product of fantasy (past experiences remembered and reworked to serve a need)," except that I would add "directed toward action." That specific fantasies are connected to desire is well illustrated by the fact that chance encounters with erotica or pornography that strike a chord with one's key sexual fantasies often lead to sexual desire and arousal. (In fact, this is precisely why sex therapists invoke fantasies as a tool to stimulate desire in their patients.) Sometimes, an individual is surprised by some of the fantasies that stoke his or her sexual desire, thus demonstrating how some of our key fantasies are just below consciousness—a point I will return to later. The subjective sense of sexual desire is infused with many different affects. (Here Stoller makes an important contribution by naming these affects—fear, rage, etc.) In contrast to desire, sexual *excitement* is the subjective experience of physical sexual arousal, which is often accompanied by conscious fantasy and is probably always linked to unconscious fantasy.

However, while conscious sexual fantasy frequently initiates sexual desire, it is not a prerequisite to sexual arousal and excitement. There are other ways to achieve sexual excitement that may bypass conscious fantasy—for example, direct genital stimulation by one's partner, anxiety of one or another kind, or sudden spurts in androgen, as happens with adolescent boys. (As an aside, let me add that hormones generally exert their effect through their absence.) Some people experience sexual arousal and excitement with no conscious fantasy whatsoever but seem to be preoccupied in the moment with the image of sexual congress with the real partner.

In my view, which parallels that of the sexologists, desire is generally the precursor to sexual arousal and excitement. But we still need to hypothesize what triggers desire. In working out a sexual theory, the question is what lights the fire and why. In essence, there needs to be a distinction between desire per se, often encompassed in the narrative of a sexual scenario, and the trigger that sets desire into motion, unless we are content to rely solely on instinct as the motor force.

"The trigger that sets desire into motion" refers to the motivation and to the reasons desire arises at a particular moment. The practical advantage in keeping the trigger to desire, desire, arousal, excitation, and orgasm as distinct terms referring to distinct stages is (as the sexologists have demonstrated) that these distinctions are important in isolating the specific mechanism of a sexual disorder, formulating its etiology, and recommending the appropriate therapy.

What Triggers Sexual Desire—The Role of Hostility, Anxiety, Attachment, and Narcissism

Even in infancy, stroking the genital organs appears to give pleasure. Therefore children, adolescents, and adults know full well the pleasure quotient that can derive from genital stimulation. However, it would be disruptive to other areas of life to be preoccupied with sexual stimulation too much of the time, as is sometimes the case with people afflicted with compulsive cruising or what is sometimes referred to as sexual addiction. It would be dysfunctional if too many different scenarios stoked sexual desire. Over time sexual desire gets connected to particular situations and fantasies, that is, the fantasies that tend to arouse us are limited in number. In essence, there is an adaptive advantage in the intermittent nature of sexual desire.

While sexual fantasies are of necessity connected to a sexual wish and the pleasure it promises, they almost always incorporate nonsexual fantasies on the preconscious level and sometimes on the conscious level as well. Many of these precursor fantasies may have originated even before the individual experienced genital arousal or excitation as such. Such early fantasies are recruited to genital excitement so that the conglomerate (or composite) of the fantasies gratified during sex are not restricted to genital ones but comprise other longings, desires, wishes, and compensations as well.

Stoller privileges hostility as the motor force in desire and excitement. He proposes that "in the absence of special physiological factors . . . it is hostility—the desire, overt or hidden, to harm another person—that generates and enhances sexual excitement. The absence of hostility leads to sexual indifference and boredom. The hostility of eroticism is an attempt, repeated over and over, to undo childhood traumas and frustrations that threaten the development of one's masculinity or femininity. The same dynamics, though in different mixes and degrees, are found in almost everyone, those labeled perverse and those not so labeled" (1979, p. 6). Stoller grants that what is usually called sexual excitement has at least one erotic element—that is, a sexual impulse—but that this must be conjoined with triumph, rage, revenge, fear, anxiety, and risk, "all condensed into one complex buzz" (p. 26).

Thus, for Stoller, sexual excitement is almost always predicated on hostility and the triumph of revenge, on fantasies that embody the reversal of humiliation. Note, though, that one could broaden his formulation by suggesting that it is the reparation of trauma and the management of dysphoric affects along with narcissistic restitution that trigger desire. Otto Kernberg's ideas are in line with Stoller's insofar as he too implicates sadomasochism as an essential part of sexual excitement; for Kernberg (1991b) sadomasochism is an ingredient of infantile sexuality and an essential part of normal sexual functioning and love relations.[6] Perhaps the question ought to be seen as one of degree. *How* important are sadomasochistic impulses?

6. But Kernberg's definition of sexual excitement is different from Stoller's: Kernberg suggests that sexual excitement is one of the basic affects. Maybe, but then one would have to enlarge the definition of affect, which more often refers to a primary feeling state distinct from cognitive or fantasy content.

For Kernberg (1991b), erotic desire is not what sets sexual excitement into motion. On the contrary, erotic desire is the expression of a "concrete direction of that affect [sexual excitation] toward a particular object" (p. 333). Further, he differentiates erotic desire from love, which he defines as "the integration of erotic desire with the complex affects implied in a tender, loving relationship" (p. 344). Thus, he sees erotic

While most analysts agree that hostility plays a major role in perversion and in perverse sexual scripts, there is less agreement that hostility is the *central* motivation in ordinary sexuality. In the paraphilias sexual fantasies are generally restricted to a very narrow range, and it is here that one most often observes major derivatives of hostile impulses, often portrayed in images of power and powerlessness, dominance and submissiveness, sadism and masochism. Paradoxically, the very fantasies that promote sexual desire may impede sexual expression in the case of some individuals with extreme sadomasochistic fantasies, who are fearful that in the throes of passion they will be tempted to enact their fantasies.

Moreover, in individuals who harbor few perverse strains, hostility often leads not to desire but to its suppression. What of the husbands who hate their wives, or at least dislike them, and whose mode of revenge is a refusal or an inability to have sex with them? Then hostility takes the form of sexual withholding or denial, not of sexual excitement. In fact, hostility is often a root cause of sexual dysfunction, rather than the source of sexual desire. In such cases, sexual desire may well be directed toward someone else, with some other fantasy stoking the fire.

More importantly, if conflicts are resolved and hostility is reduced, let us say in analysis, in Stoller's theory sexual excitement should wither, diminish, or disappear. If successful analysis meant the death of desire, psychoanalysis would never have flourished. The theory that it is primarily hostility that generates sexual excitement is clearly too narrow to account for all the motives that comprise sexual desire.

Stanley Coen (1992) uses the term "sexualization . . . to designate phenomenologically that aspect of sexual behavior and fantasy whose goals and functions are not sexual arousal and sexual pleasure but defense. . . . Since defense is always one possible perspective on behavior/fantasy, sexualization is always one possible way of viewing sexuality. . . . However, it should refer to the extensively elaborated, defensive use of sexual behavior and fantasy" (pp. 128–129). He emphasizes that "sexual fantasy and behavior, like all fantasy and behavior, subserve multiple functions and can be examined from many sides" (p. 128).[7]

The triggers of sexual desire *are* multiple, including the desire to merge with the loved object. In fact, sex may be the primary vehicle for the expression of intimacy in a culture in which so many other expressions of physicality are

---

desire as a more mature form of sexual excitement rather than as the precursor to sexual excitement. (Here he is close to Scruton, 1986.) There is nothing wrong with his definition per se. Our problem is the lack of consistency among the various definitions offered by analysts.

7. Coen gives a very interesting analysis of how sexualization is used in masturbation, with the proviso that he is not discussing adult masturbation per se but masturbation in the service of defense (pp. 134–135).

proscribed. Fairbairn (1952) proposed that the primary aim of the sex "drive" is object seeking rather than pleasure seeking. Maybe he goes too far, but many psychoanalysts agree that at the very least internalized object relations are encoded in sexual fantasies as desire.

Because sexual fantasies serve many diverse purposes, sexual desire is stoked by different kinds of psychic disequilibrium—for example, the need to overcome isolation, to assuage gender discomfort or competitive defeat, to distract oneself from psychic pain, including anxiety and depression, to reassure oneself that one is liked and admired. To experience one's self as the desired object of someone else may stoke desire. One woman's primary mode of becoming sexually desirous and aroused was to see her lover admiring her breasts. Desire and the fantasies it encompasses can be the vehicle of the expression of love, dependency, hostility, and many other impulses and affects as well. Many different kinds of sexual fantasies can neutralize dysphoric affects or undo trauma. But dysphoric affects are not the only—and not even the primary—triggers to desire. And sexual fantasies and enactments are not the only way to counter dysphoric affects. Many nonsexual highs are predicated on a buzz compounded of triumph, rage, revenge, fear, and anxiety—for example, when one undertakes to humiliate an employee or outshine a colleague.

Stoller made an important contribution to understanding sexual excitement, but his is far from a general theory. I do, however, want to emphasize how much ahead of his time he was. By 1979, he already understood the role of the fantasied reparation of an underlying trauma, and he knew that this reparation was often sexual. His insight has fully entered the mainstream of theory only in the context of current studies on the sequelae of trauma—for example, the by-now-frequent observation that childhood beatings may become eroticized and enter into adult sexuality in the form of sadomasochistic fantasies. He surely demonstrated the key role of hatred and aggression in many of the perversions (Stoller, 1975a, 1979, 1985a). More importantly, Stoller began to change our thinking about the formation of fantasy. Whereas psychoanalysts had viewed the text of fantasy as largely deriving from instinct, Stoller emphasized how fantasy drew its narrative content from experience.

However, in his emphasis on hostility as the major force in sexual excitement, Stoller left out the important motives of attachment of symbolic merger, and of assuaging anxiety, as well as other motives already mentioned. Because Stoller came to the study of sexual excitement through a study of the so-called perversions, he may have weighted hostility too heavily, based on his patient population. But even in the paraphilias, attachment, castration anxiety, fear of abandonment, and survival anxiety clearly figure just as much as hostility in the genesis of the core erotic fantasy. Nevertheless, Stoller's main point is well taken; sexual fantasies do double or triple duty insofar as they encompass more than one wish or aim. The fire in erotic desire does not come from libidinal drives alone.

The Ability of Sex to Recruit Nonsexual Fantasies

Any given fantasy or act serves multiple functions. What makes sexual fantasy, desire, and arousal a prime site for the recruitment of nonsexual wishes and impulses? I argued in 1980, as did Stephen Mitchell in 1988, that sex par excellence lends itself to the symbolic enactment of many different kinds of object relationships. Internalized object relations get encoded in fantasy scripts. Whereas Mitchell focuses on "the meaning of sexual desires as a powerful, physiologically mediated response within a particular interplay of self and other, within a larger, subjectively structured, inevitably conflictual relational design" (p. 104), I emphasize that self-other configurations connected to sexual feelings generally are encoded in fantasy (Person, 1995). Sexual fantasies condense genital feelings and other body sensations, memories, internalized scripts, reaction formations, emotions, and the hope for gratification into the subjective sense of desire.

In general, sex and sexual fantasy become a primary "arena in which relational struggles and issues are played out" (Mitchell, 1988, p. 102). That is, sex becomes the setting, the hospitable stage, on which fantasies are readily enacted. But how are the pleasures of sex so constituted as to absorb into themselves the possibility of expressing solutions to a variety of conflicts, dysphoric affects, and memories of past trauma through the simultaneous gratification of fantasies, wishes, and needs? Mitchell proposes at least four major reasons that this should be so:

(1) Because "bodily sensations, processes, and events dominate the child's early experience," these early bodily experiences become "basic organizational signifiers for later experiences" (Mitchell, pp. 102–103). Mitchell quotes Schafer (1978) to the effect that early body experiences become paradigms for all subsequent psychological events, and, of course, many of these experiences either take place in the context of the relationship between the infant and its caregiver or are interpreted by the infant to do so. As Chasseguet-Smirgel puts it, "*a number of unconscious fantasies are initially connected with bodily sensations and not attached to words and visual representations*" (1995, p. 111; her italics). As she sees it, interpersonal fantasies may be mobilized as a defense against the infant's powerlessness when he or she is overcome by painful sensations. Thus it may be "more comforting to fantasize an internal enemy" that can be

expelled than to acknowledge the pain as one's own. Or it may be more comforting to fantasize an external enemy. The origin of fantasy, its structure and content, remains somewhat obscure, but fantasy draws not only on object relations but on bodily sensations and on those internalizations and projections that "distort" any mirror-image perception of the "real" mother-child relationship.

(2) Because the act of sex involves contact between and penetration or interpenetration of bodies, it presents a stage for the enactment of fantasies related to longing, hostility, merging, and a host of other wishes.

(3) Very importantly, as Mitchell points out, "the powerful biological surges in the phenomenology of sexual excitement, the sense of being 'driven,' provide a natural vocabulary for dramatic expressions of dynamics involving conflict, anxiety, compulsion, escape, passion, and rapture" (p. 103).

(4) Because life is divided into the public sphere and the private sphere, in which sexuality is enacted, and also because the child feels excluded vis à vis the parents' sexuality, sexuality will frequently have the quality either of struggling to overcome exclusion or of transgressing social norms. Both Mitchell and Kernberg (1991a, 1995) emphasize this point.

There are still more reasons that sex serves as the premiere stage for the expression of diverse fantasies and impulses. Kernberg (1995) extends our understanding of the role of transgression. He sees transgression not only as "overcoming the prohibition implied in all sexual encounters, a prohibition derived from the oedipal structuring of sexual life" (p. 23) but also as "transgression against the sexual object itself, experienced as seductive teasing and withholding. Erotic desire includes a sense the object is both offering and withholding itself, and sexual penetration or engulfing of the object is a violation of the other's boundaries." It is in this sense that Kernberg sees the incorporation of aggression into love as inevitable, insofar as the lover himself reverberates "with the capacity to experience pleasure and pain, and [projects] that capacity onto the object" (p. 24).

Narcissistic gratification is also always intimately intertwined with the text of sexual desire. Narcissism may be invested in the act of capturing the object of one's desire or, alternatively, in the gratification of being chosen, of being the object of desire (Person, 1985). Achieving reciprocity from the object of one's desire or being the object of someone else's desire confers both narcissistic gratification and a sense of power. The need for narcissistic restitution often acts as the trigger to sexual desire. Consider, for example, the blow to narcissism when a man is fired and the common restitution of initiating a new sexual conquest or affair.

Although Chasseguet-Smirgel (1985) sees idealization as a major defense against any acknowledgment of anal regression and castration anxiety in perversion, she also recognizes that idealization in romantic love redounds both to the object and the self. I have made the point that idealization in romantic love exalts rather than depletes the lover (Person, 1988). Similarly, in a sexual connection with an idealized other, one experiences not only sexual pleasure but an increase in one's own self-esteem.

There is still another factor that leads to the choice of sexuality as the medium for the expression of so many diverse wishes, fantasies, and desires. We know well that some important fantasies based on early "bodily sensations, processes and events that dominate the child's early experience" find expression in *non*sexual narratives, such as the fantasies that infuse the variety of eating disorders. However, the realm of sexuality presents certain adaptive advantages that make it the preferred site for the gratification or illusory gratification of fantasy. Because sexual acts can so easily be enacted, either autoerotically or interpersonally, sexuality gives easy access to the actualization of fantasy, conferring on it almost a kind of virtual reality. Orgasm validates the fantasy and the various wishes, needs, and desires embedded in it (Person, 1980).

If, as I believe, the purpose of fantasy is seldom restricted to a substitute gratification but, rather, that fantasy is generally pressing for actualization or enactment of some kind, what better locus than the arena of sexuality? (Person et al., 1992; Person, 1996). Sexual activity is always possible: one can always masturbate. The individual's pressure to enact one or another sexual fantasy has a great deal to do with the durability of prostitution as a cultural institution; sex with prostitutes provides the site for the enactment of fantasies.

Moreover, sexuality as the vehicle for expressing diverse preoedipal fantasies has the additional advantage of having the cultural connotation of being mature; that is, it appears to be separated from too much smell of mother's milk. One can conceal a good many infantile fantasies by clothing them with sexuality, thereby passing them off to one's self as expressions of mature rather than "immature" interests.

Sexual Boredom

If a theory of sexual motivation is to be considered valid it has to be useful in explaining the widespread phenomenon of sexual boredom. Beginning with Freud's cogent observations (1912), it has been widely noted that for many, if not most, long-term bonded sexual partners, sexual interest declines. In Helen Kaplan's view, fantasy can be recruited to stave off boredom. For this reason, many sex therapists prescribe sexual fantasy as a goad to flagging sexual interests: Kaplan's prescription of fantasy and friction.[8]

Many different explanations have been invoked to account for the paradoxical fact that a fantasy may have more aphrodisiac power than a beautiful or handsome sexual partner of one's own choosing available and lying next to one in bed. But none of these explanations, including Freud's, is fully satisfactory.

If we review some of the factors that go into making sexuality the principal locus of the expression of fantasy, one component gives us some clue about why sexual desire frequently declines in long-married people. Exclusion from the parental bedroom, the primal scene fantasy, and the project of overcoming exclusion are major components of many fantasies that get encoded in sexual desire, particularly oedipal fantasies. To the degree that the original exclusion was more than usually painful, a reversal of exclusion may become part of one's central sexual fantasy, and then the fact of automatic acceptance vitiates desire. (So, for example, "buddy fuckers" go after the girlfriends of their close friends, or a wife desires not her own husband but the husband of her best friend.)

To the degree that the sense of transgression is part of one's central sexual fantasy, this, too, may account for the onset of boredom in some marriages because sex is sanctioned in marriage. If so, ardor sometimes may be resurrected by jealousy, by triangulation, and this often seems to be the motive for flirtations at parties or the impulse by one partner to stoke jealousy in the other. As Alexandre Dumas put it: "The bonds of wedlock are so heavy that it takes two to carry them—sometimes three."

Explaining why overcoming exclusion and transgression are major components in many people's sexual fantasies is difficult without invoking the power of oedipal fantasies; hence the general agreement with Freud that oedipal fantasies are central organizing sexual fantasies.

However, there is another important factor that vitiates against sexual excitement in close relationships. The enormous pleasure of sexual fulfillment and the dependence on one object only may lead to a fear of loss of the separate self. Kernberg (1991a, p. 28) writes of "the oscillation between the wish for secrecy, intimacy, and exclusiveness, on one hand, and the wish to shift away from sexual intimacy, for a radical discontinuity" (he attributes this insight to a personal communication from André Green). This dynamic is analogous to the fear of the loss of the separate self that often occurs in romantic love

8. Couples often act out joint fantasies to try to keep passion alive. An English novelist, who knew I had written a book about fantasy, told me (and not in confidence) about a well-known writer who left home every morning, briefcase in hand, only to return an hour later, dressed as a traveling salesman or as a sailor on shore leave, "force" an entry and make passionate love with his wife. Even so, he eventually ran off with another woman.

(Person, 1988). In this situation, the fear of engulfment may be defended against by a loss of sexual interest. It is at such a juncture that an interpersonal crisis may be precipitated in order to reestablish one's separateness and independence and thereby rekindle the fires of sex or love or both. Consequently, many couples feel much closer after a major fight "that clears the air." But it is important to note that although boredom is a problem for many individuals, it is by no means universal.

On a more practical level, if we find ourselves in a sexual situation not conducive to arousal for any of a variety of reasons, we may invoke fantasy to achieve arousal. If we cannot change our lives to make them consonant with our fantasies or change our fantasies to make them consonant with our lives, we can at least mobilize our fantasies to disguise our situation; that is, we fantasize in order to create a virtual reality and thereby to achieve arousal.

Fantasy and Desire

Desire is encoded in fantasy.[9] Most of us have key erotic fantasies that may waft into consciousness unbidden or be invoked at will to achieve sexual arousal. These fantasies generally evolve in sequential editions to form several concomitant series over a lifetime. Sometimes, as in the paraphilias, our fantasies are restricted to a very narrow range.[10]

While fantasy is impacted upon by the child's earliest experience, desire is not generally coded in fantasies that are simple mirror images of the child's earliest experience but are intertwined with projections and introjections. The real experience of the mother-child relationship should not, as it sometimes threatens to, become a substitute for instinct, to be used as the successor ideology to "explain" the origin of those fantasies that are formed and recruited to sexuality.

As already suggested, erotic history precedes genital activity. Sexual fantasies incorporate elements of our entire erotic life, beginning with the earliest sensual pleasures (and pains) of the skin, the oral and anal mucosa, the internal organs, and the genitals themselves; they draw on the feelings we experience in our body parts—not just the genitals and mouth and anus but also buttocks and belly, arms and legs—and our comparisons of our body parts with those of others.

9. There may well be a genetic component to desire insofar as object choice is concerned. For example, some studies are beginning to suggest a genetic component in sexual orientation. See, e.g., Hamer et al., 1993.

10. Joyce MacDougal has made the point that the sexual fantasies of "perverts" are rigid and impoverished compared with others' (1980). This is a point that Ovesey and I also reported (1973). MacDougal ascribes this "disability" as a relative incapacity to symbolize and create an inner fantasy world in the face of an intolerable reality.

Leaving aside the degree to which unconscious fantasy consists of repressed conscious fantasy or is wired in and coexistent with drive, as some Kleinians suggest, many precursors of fantasies, if not fantasies themselves, are intimately connected with body sensations and are formed prior to visual representations or the development of language.

Because sexuality encompasses body surfaces that have nonsexual as well as sexual functions, sexual experience is symbolically interlocked with other sensual activities or aims. Consequently these activities may become sexualized and sometimes inhibited. For example, a person may sexualize and then defend against eating, as some anorexia nervosa patients do.

Sexual fantasies have received more attention than other conscious fantasies, in part because of their sheer abundance. The fact that more sexual fantasies are generated than other kinds and that more are repeating fantasies (that is, they have durability over the life span) is at least partly due to the enormous pleasure of the orgasm accompanying the fantasy, which serves a powerful reinforcing agent. Sexual fantasies are particularly durable in those people for whom they are a prerequisite to sexual arousal. Within the category of sexual fantasy, "perverse" fantasies may be the most persistent because they, more than others, are often obligatory for achieving sexual arousal and orgasm.

But sexual fantasies are also important, profuse, and persistent because they are organizing fantasies that condense and incorporate in their scripts our early identifications, childhood sexual theories and fantasies, experiences, and solutions to important childhood conflicts. Erotic fantasies constitute part and parcel of the uniqueness of each individual.

As adults we each have a specific erotic pattern—what I have elsewhere called a sex print (see Chapter 2)—that includes a range of specific sexual fantasies we preferentially invoke as a means of arousal in masturbation and often as an ancillary or obligatory aid to intercourse and other kinds of interpersonal sex.[11] And most of us have a fairly large repertoire of sexual fantasies. Consequently, although the sex print involves some narrowing of sexual possibilities, it is not experienced that way by the individual. This does not mean that "new"sexual fantasies may not emerge, but by and large they have been present as a potential in the preconscious, sometimes previously gleaned only in dream images or in our surprised response to a sequence of erotic images in a film or novel.

The fact that some individuals make a switch in their object choice late in life is used as an argument for the fluidity of sexual object choice and against the stability of sex prints or lovemaps. The argument often articulated in

11. The term sex print, which I coined in 1980, is similar to the term *lovemaps*, coined by John Money in 1980. Perper (1985, p. 9) uses the term *templates* to refer to the individual's sexual object.

support of fluidity invokes the case of the numerous heterosexual women who convert to lesbian sex in mid-life (a state of affairs not synonymous with bisexuality; there is indeed a small cadre of life-long bisexuals). I have been privileged to see a number of such women in consultation. In all but two there was a history of lesbian fantasies and attractions in early life though these were never previously acted on. In one of the two patients who constituted the exceptions, the image of a female-female tender embrace, though not explicitly sexual, had constituted a major part of her dream life, though not of her conscious fantasy life.[12] The switch is often precipitated by a traumatic rupture of a heterosexual relationship, and sometimes by its gradual erosion.

People's attitudes about their own fantasies vary widely. For some, sexual fantasies seem to be natural extensions of what they experience themselves as being and feel quite comfortable. Their sexual fantasies and everyday personalities are more or less of a piece. The unity of our sexual fantasies with our everyday personalities—or their divergence—is not itself a predictor of mental health. An angry, hostile individual whose sadistic fantasy life is consonant with his character may nonetheless have a neurotic problem that he himself recognizes as problematic.

Sometimes, however, sexual fantasies entail scenarios that appear to be completely at odds with who the person is in everyday life. As a typical example consider the masochistic scenario of being tied hand and foot, which may be the preferred or even obligatory sexual fantasy of a successful and assertive businessman. The apparent anomaly of the fantasy does not necessarily dictate that the fantasizer will be uncomfortable with it, however. Such a man may be completely at peace with his masochistic fantasies, viewing them as a welcome respite from his daily experience of always having to be in charge.

For other people, however, the discrepancies between who they are or wish to be and how they appear in their erotic fantasies may be deeply troubling. Because of her political beliefs, a feminist may disapprove of her own almost involuntary masochistic fantasies but be unable to concoct a pleasurable substitute. The problem is that even when masochism is deplored as a socially constructed box into which some women feel they have been herded, they may still feel its lure. Despite our conscious wish to change our fantasies, this is a freedom that most often eludes us.

To understand and forgive ourselves for erotic fantasies of which we disapprove we must remember that the self is not always—or ideally—unitary, though in the more conscious regions of personality it often appears to be. A repeating sexual fantasy sometimes carries a part of the personality that has

12. Interestingly, some gays and lesbians are worried about the postmodernist claim of "fluidity" of object choice, fearing that this will be grounds for the religious right to proclaim that what can be chosen (and is not "by nature") constitutes a sin and not a variation.

been disavowed in all other areas. Occasionally enacting it may be pivotal in reclaiming, and subsequently rechanneling, a disavowed part of the self.

Conclusion

It is nearly impossible to shift our preference for certain sexual fantasies to others. We do not seem to elect our sexual fantasies; rather, they have elected us. Why sexual fantasy operates in a relatively fixed range—sometimes narrow, sometimes broad—is one of the questions that must be addressed in any comprehensive theory of sexual motivation and desire, but it is perhaps the least theorized aspect of sexuality.[13] Certainly, as I have suggested, it would not be conducive to a balanced life if *every* situation was potentially sexual.

It is of course true that, within limits, one can add to one's effective repertoire of fantasies and that fantasies can evolve; for example, an S in an S&M relationship may become an M, and vice versa. Here, the key is that one is in the same fantasy, merely playing another role. In other individuals, more deeply buried fantasies may emerge. Even so, the sense of one's sexuality as bedrock derives not only from the experience of pleasure but also from the fact that the same erotic stimuli generally remain effective. While we may theoretically envy someone else's fantasies, we may not so easily own them. Someone else's pornography (the concentration of their fantasies) is our bore.

To reiterate: From a subjective point of view, the sex print is experienced as sexual "preference." Desire carries the subjective impression of being part of the private self, impervious to external demands, autonomous. In this sense, sexual desire appears to be part of the private realm, distinct from the public one. But the role of cultural norms plays a role in its genesis.[14]

Sexual desire, encoded in fantasy, leads to sexual excitement; sexual desire is triggered by a number of internal and external stimuli. I have found it most useful to invoke an object relations theory, which posits as the motor force of sexuality certain schemata in the form of fantasies, provided that we understand these internalized objects relations not as mirror images of any real relationship but as shaped, to some degree, by projections and internalizations. Moreover, early body experiences play a major role along with object relations. Sexual fantasies are designed to stoke sexual desire while at the same time gratifying fundamental wishes and mediating intrapsychic conflicts, as-

13. I have discussed this previously in "Sexuality as the Mainstay of Identity," here reprinted as Chapter 2.
14. For example, we know that in some other cultures, as in classical Greece, people did not so clearly self-identify as heterosexual or homosexual but appeared to be able to function quite well with either sex. My belief is that these differences in cultural response to sexual practices are integral to the core dynamics of a particular culture and therefore difficult to change. I concur with those gay and lesbian theorists who argue that understanding the function of homophobia in our culture may be essential to countering it.

suaging dysphoric affects, and undoing early trauma. The reasons that sexuality recruits nonsexual fantasies to sexual scripts are multiple. The undertheorized aspect of sexual desire is how preferential "families" of fantasies come to carry sexual desire. In essence, the question is how the individual comes to rely primarily on only certain fantasies. This process appears to relate to the way in which gender and sexuality are implicated in the formation of identity; thus the coherence of identity and gender identity are intertwined with the ongoing effectiveness of erotic fantasies.

13

Gender Differences in Sexual Behaviors and Fantasies in a College Population

1989

ETHEL S. PERSON, NETTIE TERESTMAN, WAYNE A. MYERS, EUGENE L. GOLDBERG, and CAROL SALVADORI

THIS STUDY presents male and female responses of 193 university students to questions about sexual experiences and fantasies. There are few significant gender differences in experiences, but many in fantasies. Males fantasized about sex more and exhibited greater interest in partner variation and in the spectrum from domination to sadism. While male sexuality is often described as aggressive/sadistic and female sexuality as passive/masochistic, most men and women in our population do not *report fantasies supporting such stereotypes.*

This chapter analyzes data derived from the questionnaire responses of 193 university students in the years 1982 to 1983. We compare male and female responses to individual questions about sexual experiences and fantasies to examine the validity of widespread beliefs about gender differences in sexual behavior and fantasies. Our findings suggest specific gender similarities and differences that in part contradict the cultural stereotypes.

This research has been supported by two grants from the Foundation for Psychoanalytic Research, the American Psychoanalytic Association, and No. 903-E556 from the Biomedical Research Support Grant, Research Foundation for Mental Hygiene Inc. We appreciate the help of Michael Borenstein in our statistical analysis.

The research in the "Fantasy Project" was centered at the Center for Psychoanalytic Training and Research, Department of Psychiatry, College of Physicians and Surgeons, Columbia University.

Method

SUBJECTS

Subjects were 193 students in four classes (one undergraduate, three graduate) at an urban university. Eighty percent of the subjects were between the ages of 20 and 26. Approximately 40 percent were female. Eighty percent were single, 90 percent heterosexual; 14 percent foreign born. Seventy-five percent listed their fathers' occupation as professional. Religious backgrounds were 27 percent Catholic, 27 percent Jewish, 20 percent Protestant, several Moslems, and 22 percent unaffiliated. Sixty-eight percent reported a current sexual relationship; of these, almost 70 percent reported the relationship as satisfying. Twenty percent reported a stable sexual relationship with a live-in partner. In general, this was a young, single, advantaged group, most of whom were engaged in satisfying heterosexual sexual behavior.

THE SEXUAL INVENTORY

The Sexual Inventory solicits information about sexual experience and fantasy. There are 67 experience items and 55 fantasy items. Subjects rate each for frequency in the recent and distant past on a four-point scale (never; not in the last three months; fewer than five times in the last three months; more than five times in the last three months). The inventory also examines the association between each individual experience/fantasy and reported orgasm. Many items were taken from an existing instrument (Derogatis, 1978); numerous items were added with the aim of eliciting more material of relevance to gender difference.

We analyzed responses to each item and listed them by quarters, in descending order of frequency. We labeled Quarter 1 "popular" because these items were reported by the largest percentages of women and men; Quarter 4 was labeled "rare" because these were reported by the fewest subjects. The second and third quarters were considered the "middle" group.

The Z-test (Ott, 1984; Fleiss, 1981) was used to compare the differences in the proportions reported for men and women, item by item. Each test was evaluated with alpha (2-tailed) set at .05, which means that the probability of a type-1 error (a false positive finding) is five percent for any particular item. The probability of a type-1 error is higher for the study as a whole, which includes many such comparisons. Therefore, the discussion emphasizes patterns of significance of several related items.

We classified each item as "recent" if it occurred within the last three months (whether more or less than five times) or "cumulative" if it was part of the subject's total life experience (whether or not it was also current). Clinically, it is important to know if a behavior is part of a subject's recent experience and whether it has ever occurred at all. For some subjects, it might be easier to acknowledge a past, rather than a current, event.

PROCEDURE

Subjects were administered the Sexual Inventory during regular class time while the professors were absent. Participation was voluntary. More than 90 percent of class members participated. Using numbers rather than names assured confidentiality.

Results

EXPERIENCE

There was little gender difference in the content or variety of sexual experience (the mean $\pm$ SD of different recent experiences reported by women = 29.7 $\pm$ 11.9 and 33.2 $\pm$ 11.6 by men). Most subjects reported more diverse experiences than fantasies, even taking account of the questionnaire bias of including more experience items.

Among "recent sexual experiences" (see Table 13.1) the most frequently endorsed behaviors (Quarter 1) are mainly conventional, romantic, and non-genital, dealing with kissing, fondling, or sex play. There is no essential gender difference.

In Quarters 2 and 3, gender frequencies are essentially the same with few exceptions. Men reported "reading/watching pornographic material" significantly more often ($p < .01$). "Sex that lasts for hours" and "watching sex partner masturbate" were also reported more by men ($p < .05$). Women reported no items more frequently than men.

The rarer practices (Quarter 4), including voyeurism, exhibitionism, sadomasochism, and the use of force, are reported infrequently (less than 10 percent) by both sexes. Only one experience, "sex with a virgin," is at a significantly higher level for men ($p < .05$).

Table 13.2 indicates the incidence of these behaviors on a cumulative basis. As was true of recent experiences, men were more likely to report "reading/watching pornography" and "sex with a virgin" ($p < .01$). In addition, they were more likely to report "masturbation alone," "having partner masturbate you," "mutual petting of genitals," "sex with a stranger," "sex in unusual locations," and "exhibiting body in public" ($p < .05$). Women were more likely to report "intercourse, vaginal entry from rear" and "being forced to submit" ($p < .05$).

FANTASIES

In contrast to experiences, in which the reports of men and women were comparable, many significant gender differences appear in fantasies. Men

TABLE 13.1
Recent Sexual Experiences

Experience	% Females	% Males	Z	Significance
Quarter 1				
Kissing on the lips	85	87	0.3922	n.s.
Breast petting (nude)	81	82	0.1752	n.s.
Kissing of sensitive areas (nongenital)	81	81	0.0000	n.s.
Stroking/petting partner's genitals	79	80	0.1685	n.s.
Walking hand-in-hand	79	78	0.1656	n.s.
Erotic embrace (clothed)	79	80	0.1685	n.s.
Genitals caressed by partner	78	77	0.1629	n.s.
Naked caressing and embracing	78	75	0.4814	n.s.
Deep kissing	78	85	1.2266	n.s.
Male kissing female's nude breasts	76	82	1.0023	n.s.
Watching partner undress	73	75	0.3102	n.s.
Masturbating alone	71	83	1.9402	$p<0.10$
Having one's genitals orally stimulated	71	64	1.0169	n.s.
Male lying prone on female (clothed)	70	72	0.2999	n.s.
Male petting female breasts (clothed)	69	78	1.3876	n.s.
Masturbating sexual partner	69	70	0.1478	n.s.
Quarter 2				
Sexual intercourse	68	68	0.0000	n.s.
Oral stimulation of partner's genitals	68	60	1.1340	n.s.
Intercourse/female superior	67	60	0.9893	n.s.
Intercourse/male superior	66	68	0.2894	n.s.
Mutual undressing	60	71	1.5745	n.s.
Having partner masturbate you	54	58	0.5483	n.s.
Mutual petting of genitals to orgasm	51	48	0.4083	n.s.
Intercourse—vaginal entry from rear	51	43	1.0906	n.s.
Mutual oral stimulation of genitals	50	56	0.8180	n.s.
Having anal area caressed	50	36	1.9241	$p<0.10$
Intercourse side-by-side	50	38	1.6449	n.s.
Intercourse—sitting position	41	32	1.2720	n.s.
Intercourse—unusual positions	41	34	0.9838	n.s.
Being seduced	40	31	1.2797	n.s.
Reading/watching pornographic material	37	58	2.8613	$p<0.01$
Caressing partner's anal area	35	45	1.3889	n.s.

TABLE 13.1
Continued

Experience	% Females	% Males	Z	Significance
Quarter 3				
Using dirty language	32	31	0.1465	n.s.
Seducing a sexual partner	31	39	1.1412	n.s.
Watching sexual partner masturbate	23	38	2.2168	$p<0.05$
Having sex that lasts for hours	23	38	2.2168	$p<0.05$
Being discovered making love	18	13	0.9400	n.s.
Dressing with erotic garments	16	7	1.9195	$p<0.10$
Having partner watch you masturbate	14	16	0.3811	n.s.
Using artificial devices	14	6	1.8144	$p<0.10$
Intercourse—different/unusual locations	13	17	0.7622	n.s.
Performing sexual acts before a mirror	11	18	1.3527	n.s.
Anal intercourse	10	6	1.0032	n.s.
Being forced to submit to sexual acts	6	1	1.8512	$p<0.10$
Watching others make love	5	4	0.3282	n.s.
Sex with a stranger	5	6	0.2985	n.s.
Being tied/bound during sex activities	4	3	0.3702	n.s.
Dressing in clothes of the opposite sex	4	1	1.3074	n.s.
Being sexually degraded	4	1	1.3074	n.s.
Homosexual experience if heterosexual/heterosexual experience if homosexual	2	1	0.5598	n.s.
Quarter 4				
Sex with a virgin	1	7	2.0833	$p<0.05$
Being tortured by a sexual partner	1	0	0.9647	n.s.
Forcing partner to submit	1	3	0.9720	n.s.
Sex with two or more people	1	4	1.3074	n.s.
Mate swapping	1	0	0.9647	n.s.
Degrading sex partner	1	1	0.0000	n.s.
Being whipped/beaten by partner	1	1	0.0000	n.s.
Torturing sexual partner	1	1	0.0000	n.s.
Exhibiting body in public	0	4	1.9440	$p<0.10$

TABLE 13.1
Continued

Experience	% Females	% Males	Z	Significance
Being involved in sexual orgy	0	0	0.0000	n.s.
Watching someone make love to partner	0	0	0.0000	n.s.
Sex with close relative	0	1	0.9647	n.s.
Sexual relations with animals	0	0	0.0000	n.s.
Whipping/beating partner	0	2	1.3677	n.s.
Seeing pictures/film of self making love	0	0	0.0000	n.s.
Being a prostitute	0	0	0.0000	n.s.
Performing sexual acts for audience	0	3	1.6793	$p<0.10$

TABLE 13.2
Cumulative Sexual Experiences
(Includes only items that are statistically significant for gender difference)

	Females (%)	Males (%)	Z	Significance
Quarter 1				
Masturbating alone	85	95	2.2680	$p<0.05$
Quarter 2				
Intercourse—vaginal entry from rear	81	68	2.0294	$p<0.05$
Having partner masturbate you	73	85	2.0046	$p<0.05$
Mutual petting of genitals to orgasm	70	83	2.0862	$p<0.05$
Reading/watching pornography	65	88	3.6909	$p<0.01$
Quarter 3				
Intercourse—unusual locations	37	53	2.1883	$p<0.05$
Sex with stranger	18	33	2.3416	$p<0.05$
Sex with virgin	17	55	5.3866	$p<0.01$
Being forced to submit	13	4	2.1958	$p<0.05$
Quarter 4				
Exhibiting body in public	8	21	2.5122	$p<0.05$

TABLE 13.3
Recent Sexual Fantasies

	% Females	% Males	Z	Significance
Quarter 1				
Being sensuously touched	86	90	0.8375	n.s.
Naked caressing	84	93	1.9195	$p<0.10$
Touching/kissing sensuously	81	94	2.6746	$p<0.01$
Walking hand-in-hand	62	58	0.5556	n.s.
Oral-genital sex	61	89	4.3998	$p<0.01$
Being seduced	59	71	1.7118	$p<0.10$
Getting married	54	55	0.1366	n.s.
Sex in unusual locations	51	68	2.3563	$p<0.05$
Seducing partner	49	75	3.6447	$p<0.01$
Intercourse in unusual positions	49	71	3.0556	$p<0.01$
Sex that lasts for hours	43	67	3.2824	$p<0.01$
Gaining love of previously rejecting lover	42	49	0.9565	n.s.
Having partner masturbate you	42	57	2.0413	$p<0.05$
Watching partner undress	40	76	4.9629	$p<0.01$
Quarter 2				
Sex with mysterious stranger	40	46	0.8246	n.s.
Masturbating your partner	40	70	4.1030	$p<0.01$
Melting heart of cold partner	35	34	0.1431	n.s.
Being rescued from danger by one who will become my lover	34	11	3.7476	$p<0.01$
Forbidden lover in sex adventures	34	45	1.5311	n.s.
Homosexual fantasies if hetero-sexual/heterosexual if homosexual	29	16	2.1182	$p<0.05$
Two or more lovers	27	52	3.4797	$p<0.01$
Making love with possibility of being discovered	25	33	1.1996	n.s.
Watching others make love	21	29	1.2571	n.s.
Being involved in an orgy	20	40	2.9696	$p<0.01$
Being forced to submit	20	15	0.8954	n.s.
Being tied up or bound during sex activity	20	15	0.8954	n.s.
Dressing in special costumes	20	4	3.3501	$p<0.01$
Sex with a much older person	19	33	2.1717	$p<0.05$

TABLE 13.3
Continued

	% Females	% Males	Z	Significance
Quarter 3				
Sex with famous persons	17	36	2.9293	$p<0.01$
Watching partner masturbate	16	42	3.8987	$p<0.01$
Having partner watch you masturbate	16	21	0.8761	n.s.
Anal intercourse	14	38	3.7229	$p<0.01$
Using dirty language	13	19	1.1136	n.s.
Being brought into a room against my will	13	9	0.8698	n.s.
Watching someone else make love to your partner	13	9	0.8698	n.s.
Mate swapping	12	21	1.6498	$p<0.10$
Sex with a virgin	12	39	4.2149	$p<0.01$
Performing sex acts before a mirror	12	19	1.3161	n.s.
Performing before an audience	12	7	1.1603	n.s.
Being sexually degraded	12	5	1.7079	$p<0.10$
Sexual relations with animals	11	1	2.8651	$p<0.01$
Quarter 4				
Fantasizing that you are of opposite sex	10	13	0.6398	n.s.
Exhibiting body in public	10	10	0.0000	n.s.
Being a prostitute	10	5	1.2916	n.s.
Being tortured by sex partner	9	5	1.0667	n.s.
Being whipped/beaten by partner	8	5	0.8280	n.s.
Seeing pictures of yourself having sex	7	10	0.7319	n.s.
Sex with a close relative	7	11	0.9510	n.s.
Sex experiences with a much younger partner	5	29	4.3473	$p<0.01$
Forcing partner to submit	5	31	4.6047	$p<0.01$
Dressing in clothes of opposite sex	2	3	0.4358	n.s.
Whipping/beating partner	1	7	2.0833	$p<0.05$
Being attracted to someone with physical abnormality	1	9	2.4976	$p<0.05$
Degrading sex partner	1	7	2.0833	$p<0.05$
Torturing sex partner	0	6	2.3932	$p<0.05$

reported more fantasies both recently and on a cumulative basis ($p < .01$). For men, the mean ± SD of recent fantasies = 26.2 ± 8.9; range 9–55 (of a possible total of 55). For women, the comparable mean ± SD = 14.2 ± 10.1; range 0–49. While 10 percent of both sexes reported as many as 35 different fantasies, twice as many women (37 percent vs 18 percent) reported 15 or fewer fantasies.

Table 13.3 lists the proportion of respondents who report having fantasized about each of the 55 discrete fantasy items within the last three months. Quarter 1 contains the most frequently cited items, which again are romantic and conventional. Four fantasy items are mentioned with equal frequency by men and women, but 8 of the 14 are mentioned more frequently by men: "touching/kissing sensuously," "oral-genital sex," "seducing partner," "intercourse in unusual positions," "sex that lasts for hours," and "watching partner undress" ($p < .01$): "sex in unusual locations" and "having partner masturbate you" ($p < .05$).

Quarters 2 and 3 include fantasies related to partner variation, exhibitionism, voyeurism, and homosexuality. Approximately half of these were mentioned with equal frequency by men and women. Reported more by women ($p < .01$) are "being rescued from danger by one who will become my lover," "dressing in special costumes," and "sexual relations with animals" ($p < .01$); "homosexual fantasies if heterosexual, or heterosexual fantasies if homosexual" ($p < .05$). Reported more by men are "two or more lovers," "being involved in an orgy," "sex with famous persons," "sex with a virgin," "masturbating your partner" ($p < .01$); and "watching partner masturbate," "anal intercourse," and "sex with a much older person" ($p < .05$). Among current rare fantasies (Quarter 4), most are endorsed by 10 percent or less of both sexes. Six items were reported significantly more often by males: "forcing partner to submit" and "sex experiences with a much younger partner" ($p < .01$); "whipping/beating a partner," "degrading sex partner," "torturing sex partner," and "being attracted to someone with a physical abnormality" ($p < .05$).

Table 13.4 reports the male/female comparison on a cumulative lifetime basis. The most commonly reported fantasies remain romantic and traditional, with 10 of 14 endorsed more by men ($p < .01$ or $p < .05$). In Quarters 2 and 3, differences ("homosexual fantasies if heterosexual/heterosexual fantasies if homosexual" and "sex with animals") disappeared. In this group and in Quarter 4, the male preference for variation in partners was even more striking, as were "sex with a virgin," "masturbating partner," "watching partner masturbate," and "anal intercourse." More women endorsed "being rescued from danger by one who will become my lover," "dressing in special costumes" ($p < .01$), and performing "sex acts before an audience" ($p < .05$).

In Quarter 4, the following differences, reported more frequently by men

TABLE 13.4

Cumulative Sexual Fantasies

(Includes only items statistically significant for gender difference)

Fantasy	% Females	% Males	Z	Significance
Quarter 1				
Being sensuously touched	87	96	2.1958	$p<0.05$
Naked caressing	87	97	2.5080	$p<0.05$
Touching/kissing sensuously	84	99	3.6597	$p<0.01$
Being seduced	69	84	2.4071	$p<0.05$
Oral-genital sex	68	96	4.9589	$p<0.01$
Sex in unusual locations	67	84	2.6895	$p<0.01$
Intercourse in unusual positions	65	88	3.6909	$p<0.01$
Seducing partner	62	83	3.2001	$p<0.01$
Sex that lasts for hours	57	78	3.0507	$p<0.01$
Watching partner undress	57	86	4.3711	$p<0.01$
Quarter 2				
Having partner masturbate you	52	70	2.5110	$p<0.05$
Two or more lovers	52	78	3.7090	$p<0.01$
Being rescued from danger by one who will become my lover	51	23	3.9460	$p<0.01$
Sex with mysterious stranger	48	63	2.3416	$p<0.05$
Masturbating your partner	46	80	4.7916	$p<0.01$
Sex with famous persons	38	62	3.2660	$p<0.01$
Watching partner masturbate	35	60	3.4063	$p<0.01$
Being involved in an orgy	31	67	4.9000	$p<0.01$
Watching others make love	30	50	2.7778	$p<0.01$
Sex with much older person	30	57	3.7057	$p<0.01$
Quarter 3				
Dressing in special costumes	27	12	2.5760	$p<0.01$
Performing sexual acts before an audience	23	11	2.1732	$p<0.05$
Sex with a virgin	22	71	6.6845	$p<0.01$
Sex with a much younger partner	21	53	4.5097	$p<0.01$
Anal intercourse	20	52	4.5361	$p<0.01$
Mate swapping	19	37	2.7277	$p<0.01$
Quarter 4				
Sex with a close relative	13	25	2.0813	$p<0.05$
Forcing partner to submit	9	24	5.3960	$p<0.01$
Being attracted to someone with physical abnormality	5	19	2.9314	$p<0.01$
Dressing in clothes of opposite sex	2	14	3.0096	$p<0.01$
Whipping/beating partner	1	20	4.2132	$p<0.01$
Degrading sex partner	1	15	3.5113	$p<0.01$
Torturing sex partner	0	12	3.4381	$p<0.01$

for recent fantasies, were reported more frequently on a cumulative basis as well: "sex with a close relative" and "sex with someone with a physical abnormality" ($p < .01$).

Most striking is the continued pattern around domination and sadism. Endorsed more frequently by men ($p < .01$) were "forcing a partner," "degrading a partner," "whipping and beating," and "torturing." "Dressing in the clothes of the opposite sex" was also more frequently endorsed by men ($p < .01$).

Discussion

EXPERIENCE

Sexual behaviors show only a modest degree of gender influence, not a surprising result. Most behavioral items refer to interpersonal, consensual acts. Since our population is predominantly heterosexual, we would anticipate a close correlation between male and female behaviors. Most frequently enacted are romantic, traditional, nongenital sexual encounters, closely followed by sexual intercourse and its variations (changes in position, etc.).

For men, masturbation by self or partner, watching pornography, mutual genital petting, and intercourse in unusual locations emerge with greater frequency. The male predilection for masturbation may imply a greater propensity for initiatory behavior (different from sex drive, which we define as including both initiatory *and* consummatory behavior [Person, 1993]). The greater male involvement in pornography has been well known since Kinsey's 1948 study (Kinsey, Pomeroy, and Martin, 1948). "Exhibiting the body in public" by males may represent a cultural machismo (phallic narcissism) or a counterphobic reaction to underlying castration anxiety. "Sex with a virgin," reported more often by men, may represent male power interests, as "being forced to submit" may be an index of women's physical and cultural vulnerability. Both differences are consistent with current studies, which report a tendency toward aggression and violence among men and vulnerability among women (Malamuth, 1988; Mosher and Anderson, 1986; Koss, Gidyez, and Wisniewsky, 1987).

FANTASY

More differences between men and women emerge in reports of fantasies, a not unanticipated finding since fantasies, which are independent of partner consensus, reveal individual desires.

Confirming other studies (Giambra, 1979; Hunt, 1974; Hasselund, 1975), we found that men fantasize more. They fantasized as much about romantic, tender themes as women did; as much about being women as women fantasized about being men; and as much about being seduced as seducing. The overall greater male preoccupation with sexual fantasy may be evidence of greater initiatory behavior in men or of greater initiatory inhibition in women.

Whereas only one behavior on the three-month basis and two behaviors cumulatively were experienced differently ($p < .01$), 18 fantasies (three-month period) and 26 fantasies (cumulatively) evoked a different gender response ($p < .01$).

In the three-month frame, 15 of 18 fantasies were endorsed more by men, 3 by women. The 15 fantasies preferentially endorsed by men fall into a small number of categories, including partner variation ("involvement in orgies," "sex with famous persons," "sex with a virgin," "sex with a much younger partner," "sex with an older partner," "sex with two or more lovers"); domination ("forcing partners to submit" and "anal intercourse"), and active, initiatory fantasies ("watching the partner undress," "masturbating your partner," "seducing partner," and "touching, kissing sensuously").

Men show more interest in "oral-genital sex" and "sex in unusual positions," which may be understood as a desire to stretch the boundaries of conventional sexual conduct, with heightened danger as a source of sexual arousal. "Sex that lasts for hours" might be related to a greater sex interest or a greater need to control the object or to assert sexual potency.

The three fantasies preferentially endorsed by women are: "being rescued from danger by one who will become my lover," "dressing in special costumes," and "sexual relations with animals." "Being rescued" is a romantic fantasy but may be a derivative of an unconscious masochistic fantasy. "Sex with an animal" can be interpreted as female-dominant, self-degrading, or a defense against intimacy. "Special costumes" may be the female counterpart of the males' "public exhibition of body"—that is, narcissistic exhibitionism (Singer, 1975).

Our data support the notion that men fantasize as well as enact more initiatory events, with a much greater interest in partner variation. The extent to which the differences are biological or psychological is unknown (Symonds, 1979; Johnson, 1980). Men may wish to defy societal norms, at least in fantasy, whereas women are selectively subjected to more conformist pressures.

Our most significant finding refutes the belief that male sexuality is innately aggressive/sadistic and female sexuality innately passive/masochistic. Some individuals do conform to the stereotypes but most do not. The fantasy of "forcing sexual partner to submit" was reported by almost one third of our male subjects over the three-month period, but two thirds of the sample did not endorse it. Unlike some earlier studies (Hariton and Singer, 1974; Barclay, 1973), we found no equivalent wishes for submission or masochism in women.

Among cumulative fantasies, 26 of the 55 items show a significant gender difference ($p < .01$). Our data offer little support for the contention that women are masochistic but reveal fantasies of domination and sadism in a significant minority of men. The fantasy of "forcing sexual partner to submit" is now reported by 44 percent of the men. A smaller number reported sadistic fantasies: whipping, 20 percent; degrading, 15 percent; torturing, 12 percent.

Both sexes report the same level of masochistic fantasies: "being tortured by sex partner" (10 percent women, 11 percent men); "being whipped" (15 percent women, 14 percent men); "being brought into a room against one's will" (20 percent women, 16 percent men); "being tied up or bound during sex activities" (30 percent women, 31 percent men), and "being forced to submit" (31 percent women, 27 percent men). The one item that may suggest a female tendency to passivity or masochism is the fantasy of "being rescued from danger by one who will become my lover."

It is less apt to describe female sexuality as submissive/masochistic than to describe male sexuality as aggressive/sadistic, though we are reluctant to make even this statement. While 44 percent of men reported a fantasy of wishing to dominate, 56 percent did not. Fourteen percent of men now report fantasies of "dressing in clothes of the opposite sex," revealing some feminine identification for a sizable minority. "Attraction to someone with a physical abnormality," reported by 19 percent of men, appears to confirm the psychoanalytic hypothesis that some men are counterphobically attracted to a "castrate."

Our sample is restricted to a college age population. In older groups, we anticipate a greater variety of behaviors as individuals gain experience in converting wishful fantasy to reality. We would also anticipate some diminution in the range of fantasy because of the achievement of a more satisfactory sexual life. Men's fantasies of domination might decline with age as a result of the consolidation of strong masculine identities. Hence, it is important to collect data on fantasy differences over the life cycle.

Our data may prove valuable for unanticipated reasons, as we administered our questionnaire just prior to the widespread consciousness and fear about AIDS. It will be instructive to repeat this study as one index of the effect of fear on sexual behaviors and fantasies.

14

Associations Between Sexual Experiences and Fantasies in a Nonpatient Population: A Preliminary Study

1992

ETHEL S. PERSON, NETTIE TERESTMAN, WAYNE A. MYERS, EUGENE L. GOLDBERG, and MICHAEL BORENSTEIN

WE HAVE been interested in devising some methodology short of psychoanalytic therapy to study the relationship of conscious fantasy to personality trends and behavior. Presented here is a pilot study, utilizing the questionnaire technique, the sample consisting of 193 students enrolled at one prestigious urban university, that reports on the prevalence and content of conscious sexual fantasies in a normal (nonpatient) population and their relationship to sexual behaviors.

Factor analysis suggested four experience and four fantasy clusters. Those individuals who score high on one experience factor are apt to score high on all other experience factors as well. The same is true of the fantasy factors.

Our findings indicate that low sexual activity and low levels of sexual fantasy go together, whereas more sexual experience is connected to a greater range of sexual fantasy. Consequently, erotic fantasies cannot be viewed as compensation for lack of sexual outlet. Instead, there is a positive correlation between the two domains of sexual fantasies and sexual behaviors. Our overall results lead us to conclude that, by and large, people are sexual generalists not specialists.

This chapter reports the findings of a pilot study from the Fantasy Project of the Columbia Psychoanalytic Center. The long-term purpose of the Fantasy

This research has been supported by two grants from the Foundation for Psychoanalytic Research and the American Psychoanalytic Association and grant No. 903-E556 from the Biomedical Research Support Grant, Research Foundation for Mental Hygiene Inc.

Project is to study the occurrence and distribution of conscious fantasy in a normal (nonpatient) population and gauge its function, its adaptive value, and its relationship to personality trends. One salient question about the significance of conscious fantasy concerns its relationship to actual behavior; the answer to this question has obvious clinical significance, for example, in the case of suicidal, aggressive, or masochistic fantasies.

In one of the earliest psychological formulations of fantasy, Freud (1908b) asserted that "the motive for the phantasies are unsatisfied wishes, and every single phantasy is the fulfillment of the wish, a correlation of unsatisfied reality." Interpreted literally, this suggests that the *sole* purpose of conscious fantasy is wish fulfillment in the absence of actual fulfillment and, therefore, that conscious fantasy would occur only when a wish failed to find expression either for some external (realistic) or internal (psychological) cause. If this were the only motive for fantasy, one would expect fantasy and behavior to be inversely related. However, subsequent generations of analysts have broadened our understanding of the sources and structure of fantasy. Fantasy is shaped by contributions from instinctual wishes, the ego, and the superego, and it serves many diverse functions, including, for example, self-soothing or the assuagement of a narcissistic wound.

There still is a tendency for many analysts (with certain notable exceptions, such as Jacob Arlow [1969]) to stress the difference between unconscious and conscious fantasy, except insofar as the latter "are dynamically linked to unconscious fantasies, particularly those persisting from childhood" (Inderbitzin and Levy, 1990). Because of this distinction, there has been relatively little emphasis within psychoanalysis on the systematic study of conscious fantasy, which has been largely the province of psychologists.

Among psychologists, Jerome Singer and his collaborators (especially Singer, 1966; Singer and Antrobus, 1963) have most extensively studied fantasy from an empirical perspective. They suggest that conscious fantasy is used in the service of substitutive wish-fulfillment (wishes being broadly defined) but also in role-rehearsal, problem solving, and other areas.

In agreement with Singer and Antrobus (1963), we hypothesize that the function of fantasy is more diverse than wish fulfillment alone. We take the position that while many fleeting fantasies may be incidental in response to transient external events (as implied in the passage quoted from Inderbitzin and Levy), recurrent fantasies are importantly related to unconscious fantasies, on the one hand, and to values, affective bents, personality trends, and behaviors, on the other.

One goal of our project was to devise a methodology to trace the connections between conscious fantasy and behavior. As a preliminary approach to studying this relationship we focused on one subset of fantasies—sexual fantasies—because it offers an important strategy for conceptualizing the relationship between fantasy and behavior. First, sexuality refers to a category of impulses or wishes considered ubiquitous. With few other categories—achievement, aggression, dependence, and so on—is there agreement as to their universality. Secondly, the behavioral correlates of sexual fantasies are relatively easy to effect, compared, for example, with ambitious fantasies, such as writing the great American novel, winning a Nobel Prize, or marrying a prince. Thirdly, in the domain of sexuality it is easy and economical to elicit information on both fantasy and behavior using a questionnaire format. And, finally, we chose this domain because of the centrality traditionally accorded sexuality in psychoanalytic theory.

This report concerns the overall associations between sexual fantasy and sexual experience. A previous paper (see Chapter 13) addressed the question of gender difference in sexual behaviors and fantasies (Person et al., 1989).

Method

In order to minimize the bias inherent in utilizing volunteer subjects particularly in research involving sex, we chose to contact groups in which we could aim for 100 percent participation rather than to recruit subjects through advertisements. Gaining the participation of such groups was more difficult than we had anticipated. The nature of the refusals leaves no doubt that sex is still a more highly charged area than the media would lead us to believe. Two national magazines with which we had personal contact refused to participate on the ground that they would not want sexual profiles of staff made public. They declined even when assured of institutional anonymity.

Consequently, we chose to interview students in several classes of a local university because of the greater possibility of achieving close to total participation of each group (class) contacted. Our initial sample, analyzed here, consists of 193 students enrolled in one undergraduate and three graduate classes. The participation from each class was at least 90 percent. When the questionnaire was distributed during a regular class session the professor briefly introduced the investigator as a member of a university research team and then left the room. A brief introduction was given by one of the investigators, outlining the purpose of the study, its totally voluntary nature, and its confidentiality. Identification of subjects was coded anonymously. The students filled out the questionnaire during class time.

Eighty percent of the subjects were between the ages of 20 and 26. Approximately 40 percent were female. Eighty percent were single; 90 percent were heterosexual. Only 14 percent were foreign-born. Seventy-five percent listed the occupations of their fathers as "professional." The subjects reported a variety of religious backgrounds: 27 percent were Catholic, 27 percent Jewish, 20 percent Protestant, and 22 percent unaffiliated. Sixty-eight percent reported a current sexual relationship; of these, almost 70 percent reported these as satisfying.

In general, then, this was a young, single, advantaged group of individuals, most of whom were regularly engaged in satisfying sexual behavior with members of the opposite sex. Yet there was a sizable minority either lacking an interpersonal sexual history or engaged in an unsatisfying one. Almost 10 percent had never had a sexual relationship, and 30 percent found their existing relationships inadequate; 6 percent had never experienced orgasm.

For the analyses discussed here the responses to a list of 67 items detailing specific sexual experiences were collapsed into two categories: The respondents either had participated in the activity within the past three months (positive) or had not (negative). Similarly, responses to a list of 57 items detailing specific sexual fantasies were collapsed into yes/no categories.

The statistical procedure of factor analysis was employed to identify groups of items that tended to cluster together. For technical reasons, experiences and fantasies reported by less than 10 percent of the sample were excluded from the factor analyses. However, for clinical reasons we wished to retain them. They were therefore grouped together, found to cohere with one another, and assigned to a factor labeled "rare/kinky."

Results

RESULTS OF FACTOR ANALYSIS

The factor analyses were conducted separately for experiences and for fantasies. In both cases a series of analyses were run, generating three factors, four factors, and so on. In each case the three-factor solution was selected as the one that generated "meaningful" factors—that is, factors whose items form an intuitively meaningful composite as well as being related to one another empirically. In addition, the rare items were seen to cohere and were labeled Factor IV.

As regards experience, factor analysis yielded the following four factors: (I) Foreplay/Romantic, (II) Variations on Intercourse, (III) Exhibitionistic/Voyeuristic, and (IV) Rare/Kinky experiences. Table 14.1 shows the items included in each factor, the proportion of persons reporting each item included in the scale, and the reliability of the scale.

As regards fantasies, factor analysis yielded the following four factors: (I) Exhibitionistic/Voyeuristic, (II) Partner Variations, (III) Foreplay/Romantic, and (IV) Rare/Kinky fantasies. Details are provided in Table 14.2.

OVERALL RELATIONSHIP BETWEEN EXPERIENCE AND FANTASY SCORES

The first issue to be considered involves the relationship between overall scores on the Experience section and on the Fantasy section of the questionnaire. For this purpose we used global measures, the total summary scores for both Experience and Fantasy. There is a moderately high positive association between Experience and Fantasy summary scores ($r=.42$, $p < .001$); in other words, individuals reporting more sexual experience also report more sexual fantasy.

In addition, to provide a clearer picture of this association, each respondent was classified as belonging either to the lowest 10–15 percent of the sample, to the middle (approximately 75 percent), or to the upper 10–15 percent of the sample with regard to the overall number of different fantasies reported and different experiences reported (see Table 14.3). Of interest is the fact that no one identified as reporting many fantasies reported few experiences, and only one individual identified as reporting few fantasies reported a great variety of experiences. In general, then, a greater range of experiences is associated with a greater range of fantasies and a narrow range of sexual experiences with a narrow range of sexual fantasies.

Twelve individuals reported no orgasmic experiences whatsoever. Of these, two were men who reported no sexual activity other than kissing and touching. Of the 10 women who reported no orgasm, one woman had a live-in partner and was sexually active but had never experienced orgasm, while nine had had scant experience. Two of the nonorgasmic women reported no sexual fantasies, and two were among the group we labeled active fantasizers (their fantasies included Rare/Kinky, particularly the sadomasochistic). The other eight respondents had fantasies limited to the romantic.

These data also confirm the overall proposition that the domain of experience and fantasy are connected. But the two women who are active fantasizers may represent a population described by therapists—those who compensate for lack of experience through fantasy. They, however, are the rare group in our sample.

RELATIONSHIPS AMONG THE VARIOUS FANTASY SCALES

The most commonly reported fantasies were those associated with Factor III (Foreplay/Romantic). On average, each item associated with this factor was endorsed by 65 percent of the respondents. This is followed by Factor II (Partner Variations), with a 34 percent rate of endorsement for each item; Factor I (Exhibitionism/Voyeurism), with a 15 percent rate; and Factor IV (Rare/Kinky), with the typical item being endorsed by only six percent of the respondents.

Table 14.4 shows the correlation among the four fantasy scales. The mean correlation between pairs of scales is .45, indicating that there is a tendency for

TABLE 14.1
Experience Factors

Item #	Item	Proportion reporting
	Factor I. Foreplay/Romantic[a]	
12	Male kissing female nude breasts	.79
09	Kissing sensitive nongenital areas	.81
24	Breast petting nude	.80
20	Deep kissing	.82
02	Stroking-petting partner genitals	.78
23	Kissing on lips	.84
14	Male petting female breasts clothed	.74
05	Genitals caressed by partner	.78
67	Walking hand-in-hand	.77
49	Naked caressing and embracing	.76
03	Erotic embrace clothed	.79
54	Watching partner undress	.73
01	Male lying prone on female	.70
52	Masturbating sexual partner	.68
19	Mutual undressing each other	.66
21	Intercourse—male superior	.67
18	Having genitals orally stimulated	.66
47	Having partner masturbate you	.57
11	Masturbating alone	.78
06	Mutual oral stimulation of genitals	.54
	Factor II. Variations on Intercourse[b]	
10	Intercourse sitting position	.37
08	Intercourse side by side	.43
16	Intercourse female superior	.64
27	Having intercourse in unusual position	.38
04	Intercourse vaginal entry from rear	.46
07	Oral stimulation of partner's genital	.64
55	Being seduced	.36
44	Intercourse in unusual locations	.15
17	Mutual petting of genitals to orgasm	.50
65	Seducing a sexual partner	.34
21	Intercourse—male superior	.67
50	Sexual intercourse	.68
	Factor III. Exhibitionistic/Voyeuristic[c]	
62	Having partner watch you masturbate	.16
58	Watching partner masturbate	.15
61	Performing sexual acts in front of mirror	.15

TABLE 14.1
Continued

Item #	*Item*	*Proportion reporting*
13	Having anal area caressed	.43
15	Caressing partner's anal area	.41
25	Reading or watching pornographic material	.52
57	Having sex that lasts for hours	.30
63	Using dirty language	.30
48	Dressing in erotic garments	.11
	Factor IV. Rare/Kinky[d]	
26	Having sex with two or more people	.04
41	Being tied up during sexual activity	.04
53	Being forced to submit to sex acts	.04
60	Watching other people make love	.04
66	Having sex with a virgin	.04
28	Exhibiting your body in public	.03
30	Whipping or beating sexual partner	.03
31	Being whipped or beaten by sexual partner	.02
33	Dressing in clothes of opposite sex	.02
38	Homosexual experience	.02
43	Being sexually degraded	.02
32	Forcing partner to submit to sexual acts	.01
35	Being a prostitute	.01
36	Being tortured by sexual partner	.01
37	Torturing sexual partner	.01
39	Involved in sexual orgy	.01
40	Mateswapping	.01
42	Degrading sex partner	.01
46	Seeing pictures of self having sex	.01
59	Sex with a close relative	.01
29	Having sexual relations with animal	.00
45	Watching someone make love to your partner	.00
22	Anal intercourse	.09
34	Using artificial devices for stimulation	.09
51	Performing sex acts for an audience	.05
64	Sex with a stranger	.08

[a] $r_{xx} = .96$, Mean = 14.52, $SD = 6.57$
[b] $r_{xx} = .89$, Mean = 5.32, $SD = 3.80$
[c] $r_{xx} = .74$, Mean = 2.54, $SD = 2.20$
[d] $r_{xx} = .76$, Mean = .72, $SD = 1.60$

TABLE 14.2
Fantasy Factors

Item #	Item	Proportion reporting
	Factor I. Exhibitionistic/Voyeuristic[a]	
48	Having a partner watch you masturbate	.15
23	Seeing pictures of self having sex	.09
49	Using dirty language	.17
32	Performing sex acts for an audience	.10
36	Being forced to submit to sexual acts	.16
47	Performing sex acts front of mirror	.16
13	Dressing in special costumes	.10
57	Being brought into room against will	.11
03	Exhibiting your body in public	.10
44	Watching partner masturbate	.32
17	Being tied up during sexual fantasies	.16
29	Fantasizing that you are of opposite sex	.10
54	Having partner watch you masturbate	.19
14	Homosexual fantasies	.20
25	Being rescued from danger by future lover	.20
	Factor II. Partner Variation[b]	
15	Being involved in sexual orgy	.32
41	Sex with much younger partner	.22
01	Having sex with two or more people	.40
50	Sex with mysterious stranger	.42
16	Mateswapping fantasies	.16
02	Having intercourse in unusual position	.61
46	Watching other people make love	.24
42	Making love with possibility of discovery	.28
37	Having sex with a famous person	.30
51	Seducing sexual partner	.64
20	Anal intercourse	.27
07	Forcing partner to submit to sex acts	.22
35	Gaining love of someone who had formerly rejected you	.45
40	Sex with much older partner	.28
21	Intercourse in unusual locations	.60
53	Having sex with virgin	.29
10	Forbidden mistress or lover in sex acts	.39
22	Watching someone else make love to partner	.10

Table 14.2
Continued

Item #	Item	Proportion reporting
	Factor III. Foreplay/Romantic[c]	
28	Touching/kissing sensuous areas of partner	.88
27	Naked caressing and embracing	.89
33	Masturbating sexual partner	.58
31	Having sensuous areas of body touched	.86
55	Walking hand in hand	.57
38	Watching your partner undress	.62
34	Oral-genital sex	.78
39	Being seduced	.63
26	Having partner masturbate you	.51
43	Having sex that lasts for hours	.57
52	Getting married	.53
30	Melting the heart of a cold partner	.35
	Factor IV. Rare/Kinky[d]	
45	Sex with close relative	.08
06	Being whipped or beaten by sexual partner	.07
09	Being a prostitute	.07
11	Being tortured by sexual partner	.07
19	Being sexually degraded	.07
05	Whipping or beating partner	.05
18	Degrading a sexual partner	.05
04	Having sex with animals	.04
12	Torturing sexual partner	.04
56	Attracted to someone with physical abnormalities	.04
08	Dressing in clothes of opposite sex	.03

[a] $r_{xx} = .86$, Mean $= 2.28$, $SD = 3.07$
[b] $r_{xx} = .86$, Mean $= 6.20$, $SD = 4.40$
[c] $r_{xx} = .82$, Mean $= 7.74$, $SD = 3.11$
[d] $r_{xx} = .62$, Mean $= .62$, $SD = 1.15$

TABLE 14.3
Relationship between Range of Experiences and Range of Fantasies

Range of Experience		
Low (00–01)	=	22 cases (12%)
Middle (02–33)	=	135 cases (73.4%)
High (34–45)	=	27 cases (14.7%)
Range of Fantasy		
Low (00–06)	=	22 cases (12%)
Middle (07–29)	=	142 cases (77.2%)
High (30–47)	=	20 cases (10.9%)

Associations among Experiences and Fantasy by Groups

Fantasy level	*Low experience*	*Middle experience*	*High experience*
Low	4 (18.2%)	17 (77.3%)	1 (4.5%)
Middle	18 (12.7%)	108 (76.1%)	16 (11.3%)
High	0 (00.0%)	10 (50.0%)	10 (50.0%)
Experience level	*Low experience*	*Middle experience*	*High experience*
Low	4 (18.2%)	18 (81.8%)	0 (0.0%)
Middle	17 (12.6%)	108 (80.0%)	10 (7.4%)
High	1 (3.7%)	16 (59.3%)	10 (37.0%)

persons who report higher frequencies for one factor to report higher frequencies for other factors as well, but this tendency is of only moderate strength and varies, as one would expect, depending on the factor. The strongest correlation is .59, with persons who endorsed items in Fantasy Factor I (Exhibitionism/Voyeurism) also more likely to endorse items in Fantasy Factor II (Partner Variations). Factors I, II, and III are all significantly correlated ($p < .001$) with each other. The single lowest and nonsignificant correlation (.17) is between Factor III (Foreplay/Romantic) and Factor IV (Rare/Kinky).

RELATIONSHIP AMONG THE VARIOUS EXPERIENCE FACTORS

The most commonly endorsed experience items were those associated with Factor I (Foreplay/Romantic). On average, each item associated with this

Table 14.4

Correlations among Fantasy and Experience Factors

	Experience				*Fantasy*			
	Foreplay/ Romantic (I)	Variations on Intercourse (II)	Exhibitionistic/ Voyeuristic (III)	Rare/ Kinky (IV)	Exhibitionistic/ Voyeuristic (I)	Partner Variations (II)	Foreplay/ Romantic (III)	Rare/ Kinky (IV)
Experience								
Foreplay/Romantic (I)		.75**	.55**	.20*	.26**	.32**	.15	.13
Variations on Intercourse (II)			.61**	.21**	.37**	.39**	.21**	.17
Exhibitionistic/Voyeuristic (III)				.29**	.52**	.46**	.26**	.30**
Rare/Kinky (IV)					.24*	.20*	.03	.25**
Fantasy								
Exhibitionistic/Voyeuristic (I)						.59**	.40**	.54**
Partner Variations (II)							.57**	.43**
Foreplay/Romantic (III)								.17
Rare/Kinky (IV)								

*p <.01; **p <.001

factor was endorsed by 73 percent of the respondents. This was followed by Factor II (Variations on Intercourse), with a 44 percent rate of endorsement for each item; Factor III (Exhibitionistic/Voyeuristic), with a 28 percent rate; and Factor IV (Rare/Kinky), with the typical item being endorsed by only three percent of the respondents.

The mean correlation between all factors is .43. The single highest correlation (.75) was found between experience Factor I (Foreplay/Romantic) and Factor II (Variations on Intercourse). Factor III (Exhibitionistic/Voyeuristic) is significantly correlated with all other experiences ($p < .001$). The lowest correlation (.20) is between Factor I (Foreplay/Romantic) and Factor IV (Rare/Kinky).

RELATIONSHIPS BETWEEN FANTASY FACTORS AND EXPERIENCE FACTORS

We next examined the relationships between Experience and Fantasy Factors. The highest overall correlation (.52) is between Experience Factor III (Exhibitionistic/Voyeuristic) and Fantasy Factor I (Exhibitionistic/Voyeuristic).

Experience Factor III (Exhibitionistic/Voyeuristic) is strongly related to all Fantasy Factors. Experience Factors I through III (all factors other than IV, Rare/Kinky) are highly correlated with Fantasy Factors I (Exhibitionistic/Voyeuristic) and II (Partner Variations). In other words, individuals who report a good deal of sexual experience (other than kinky) are likely to fantasize about more exotic sexual encounters (Fantasy Factors I and II) than about those which are more restrained or conventional situations (Fantasy Factor III, Romantic). Fantasy Factor IV (Rare/Kinky) is significantly related to Experience Factor IV (Rare/Kinky).

Discussion

Individuals who report participation in a wide variety of sexual experiences are most likely to acknowledge the widest spectrum of sexual fantasies as well. In general, there is a positive correlation between the two domains of sexual fantasies and sexual behaviors.

If we turn to an analysis of the factor scores, we find that individuals who score high on one experience factor are likely to score high on all factors ($p < .01$). In addition, individuals who score high on one fantasy factor tend to score high on all fantasy factors (with the single exception between romantic and kinky fantasies). This leads us to conclude that most people, except at the extremes ("repressed" or "kinky"), are sexual generalists, not specialists. This finding may prove to have great clinical value. We predict that persons with perversions will display specialization, while homosexuals (like heterosexuals) will report more generalized fantasies and behaviors.

Conventional sexual fantasies are the most common among people in general. But subjects with less sexual experience are more likely to restrict their fantasies to conventional sexual encounters than to entertain more exotic fantasies. Individuals who score high on experiences of an exhibitionistic-voyeuristic nature are seen to score high on fantasies of all kinds. Correlations between any reported experience and exhibitionistic-voyeuristic and partner-variations fantasies are higher than with other fantasies. In other words, the greater the range of sexual experience, the more exotic the fantasies reported, except, as has been noted, for the Rare/Kinky fantasies that correlate with Rare/Kinky behaviors. Again, wide experience seems to be associated with a greater degree of variety (creativity?) of sexual fantasy. Conversely, individuals who fantasize most about exotic sexual encounters are apt to be the most sexually active.

As observed in young adults, then, low sexual activity and restriction of the range of sexual fantasy go together, whereas experience is connected to greater range of fantasy in the sexual sphere. While we may occasionally observe a lonely schizoid masturbator who dwells upon wild and exotic sexual encounters, this probability is rare, at least within the purview of our data.

In essence, erotic fantasies cannot be viewed as compensation for lack of sexual experience. Thus the earliest psychoanalytic model of wish fulfillment, that fantasies provide gratification for individuals suffering from a state of deprivation, does not appear to be applicable to the sexuality of young adult subjects. One interpretation of the data is that sexually uninhibited individuals engage in more activities and produce a greater range of fantasies, whereas sexually inhibited individuals suppress both behavior and fantasy. Another possible interpretation is that reality experiences may serve as a stimulant (or source) of the material for fantasy.

Nevertheless, there may be some support for the compensatory model insofar as the content of the fantasies is not highly specifically correlated with behaviors. The finding that exhibitionistic and voyeuristic experiences are most strongly related to all fantasy clusters may suggest that utilization of visualization in sexuality is related to the utilization of visual imagery in general and therefore associated with a high level of fantasy.

Overall, the finding that fantasies in general are associated with experiences in general (the correlations are not restricted to fantasies and experiences that are related to specific content) suggests two separate possibilities. One hypothesis gives some credence to Freud's contention that fantasy represents the forbidden (such as oedipal wishes). The more sexually active have more "exotic" fantasies—fantasies of behaviors that may still be internally (psychologically) or externally (culturally) prohibited. Put another way, as the individual achieves more sexual freedom in behavior, there may be a shift in the direction of more radical or unusual fantasies to encompass that which is still "forbidden" behaviorally. The fact that sexual behaviors do not countervail the impulse toward fantasy could then be understood in the following way: sexual fantasies incorporate not just an impulse to sexuality but an impulse toward the forbidden, which might be aggressive or incestual. This would relate theoretically to our knowledge that sexuality unfolds in the context of forbidden fantasies, particularly the incestuous fantasies of childhood. It may well be that the wish for the forbidden finds an outlet in sexual fantasy rather than simply in sexual activity alone. This hypothesis would support Freud's dictum that fantasy provides gratification for the individual in a state of deprivation, despite the fact that the individual has a sexual outlet. Nonetheless, in our sample, rare, kinky fantasies are significantly associated with rare, kinky behaviors.

The second hypothesis is that the controlling factors for content in fantasies and behaviors arise from different sources. We suggest that social expectation governs sexual behavior and dictates that behavior (at least in this age group) is more conventional than sexual fantasies, which are to a greater extent under the reign of unconscious factors. It would, of course, be of great interest to administer the questionnaire to a more mature population. It may well be that with greater experience and ease in sexual matters, behavior changes in the direction of fantasies. A longitudinal study would be indicated to decide this question.

PART IV

Sex and Gender: Female Sexuality and Femininity and Male Sexuality and Masculinity

15

The Erotic Transference in Women and in Men: Differences and Consequences

1985

ETHEL S. PERSON

THE TALKING cure, as is well known, was developed in the course of Josef Breuer's therapy with Anna O, but it was the disruptions of that same therapy that circuitously led to the concept of transference and provided an insight into the nature of the erotic transference.

Breuer's preoccupation with Anna O's treatment evoked his wife's jealousy. Belatedly recognizing this problem he terminated Anna O's treatment. Shortly afterward, he was called back to find his patient in the throes of hysterical childbirth. He calmed her down and, the next day, took his wife on a second honeymoon. Freud recounted the story in a letter to Martha. According to Jones (1953, p. 225), Martha "identified herself with Breuer's wife, and hoped the same thing would not ever happen to her, whereupon Freud reproved her vanity in supposing that other women would fall in love with her husband; 'for that to happen one has to be a Breuer.'" Freud, then, even denied the possibility that such an event might happen to him, while Martha seemed to understand intuitively the universal nature of the problem. Only later did Freud come to see Anna O's reaction as the rule rather than the exception.

An earlier version of this chapter was given as the plenary address at the 1983 winter meetings of The American Academy of Psychoanalysis. I consider this chapter an extension of questions raised by both Karme (1979) and Lester (1983) in their thought-provoking papers. It represents an elaboration of my discussion of Eva Lester's "The Female Analyst and the Eroticized Transference," presented at the 1982 winter meetings of the American Psychoanalytic Association.

The author would like to thank Dr. Eleanor Schuker and Ms. Ilene Lefcourt, who read an earlier version of this chapter and offered many valuable suggestions and insights.

Szasz (1963) believes that Freud first understood transference in the context of Breuer's experience with Anna O. It was perhaps inevitable, he feels, that the theoretical observations of the phenomenon were first made by someone other than the therapist involved. In other words, the transference and countertransference experiences belonged to Anna O and Breuer, the theoretical explanations to Freud. As Szasz put it, "Because Anna O was not Freud's patient it was easier for him to assume an observing role toward her sexual communication than if they had been directed towards himself."

The erotic transference may well be the most famous of all transference reactions, providing the earliest paradigm for understanding the concept of transference. Yet the erotic transference does not develop to the same degree in all analyses. Although it "should" be universal, it is variable in its expression. It is traditionally assumed that in every analysis, maternal and paternal transferences referable to both the positive and negative Oedipus complexes will emerge, and that the transference unfolds in similar ways in nearly all analyses (Fenichel, 1945, p. 328). Yet we know that the traditional formulation is oversimplified.

The erotic transference is apparently seen more frequently in women in treatment with men than in the reverse situation (Lester, 1983), and, in fact, the classic description was based on the feelings of female patients toward male doctors (Freud, 1915). The question naturally arises as to the reasons for this sex difference and its consequences, if any.

Drawing on Gill's elaboration of the distinction between transference resistance and resistance to awareness of the transference,[1] I propose that, in general, the erotic transference utilized as resistance is more common among women in analysis—particularly among women in treatment with men—while resistance to the awareness of the erotic transference is more common among male patients. In other words, I am suggesting that the erotic transference is not inevitably experienced and expressed in identical form in every analysis; its overt manifestations vary not only as a function of the patient's unconscious conflicts and personality structure but also, in part, as a function of the sex of the patient and as a function of the sex of the patient vis-à-vis that of the analyst. These differences appear to be related to different analytic problems, both technical and substantive.

Definitions

The term *erotic transference* is used interchangeably with the term *transference love.* It refers to some mixture of tender, erotic, and sexual feelings that a

1. As Gill suggests, "in resistance to the awareness of transference, the transference is what is resisted, whereas in resistance to the resolution of transference, the transference is what does the resisting" (1979,

patient experiences toward his or her analyst and, as such, forms part of a positive transference. Sexual transference components alone represent a truncated erotic transference, one that has not been fully developed or is not fully experienced.

There is a fundamental confusion in the way we think about transference because the word "transference" is used to describe two different levels of the transference phenomenon—its manifest content and its motivational source. In general, any given transference (for example, positive, negative, erotic, paranoid, or idealizing) is named in terms of its manifest content. Thus, according to Blum (1973b), "a paranoid transference is not called homosexual, although the homosexuality is present in latent form." While the usefulness of designating a transference in terms of its manifest content is self-evident (after all, in treatment it is an ongoing or current phenomenon), transferences are also designated in terms of their source or motivational structure. Thus, we see references to paternal and maternal transferences, as well as oedipal and preoedipal transferences.

When we think about the erotic transference, these two different levels are confused. The term is used at one and the same time to designate the manifest content (affectionate, tender, and sexual) and the motivational source (oedipal). The erotic transference is frequently confused with the eroticized transference. According to Blum (1973a, p. 63),

> There are countless ways, more or less disguised, in which patients may be seductive—e.g., with gifts, financial advice, etc. These reactions and those of affectionate transference and the usual erotic transference manifestations are related phenomena. The eroticized transference is a particular species of erotic transference, an extreme sector of a spectrum. It is an intense, vivid, irrational, erotic preoccupation with the analyst, characterized by overt, seemingly ego-syntonic demands for love and sexual fulfillment from the analyst.

Thus, while the erotic transference and the eroticized transference have certain surface similarities—the same manifest content—they are generally stoked by different motivational bases. I would argue that the simple erotic transference is largely oedipal but is only one subset of a group of related oedipal transferences. As such, it plays an important role in the analytic process. It may also subsume preoedipal components without being regarded as an erotized transference.

---

p. 264). This distinction can be inferred in Freud (1917) and was extended by Greenson (1967) and Stone (1967).

The Therapeutic Potential and the Therapeutic Liabilities of Transference Love

By 1905, Freud had formulated fairly explicit concepts about transference. He described transference reactions as "new editions or facsimiles of the impulses and phantasies which are aroused and made conscious during the progress of the analysis; but they have this peculiarity, which is characteristic for their species, that they replace some earlier person by the person of the physician" (p. 116). In this formulation, emphasis is placed on the repetition inherent in transference and not on its subjective reality for the patient.

Schafer, citing a personal communication from Charles Rycroft, says, "It has been suggested . . . that Freud's stress on repetition was in part a response to real and threatened public disapproval of the erotic transferences that female analysands developed in relation to their male analysts" (1977, p. 340). In contrast, Szasz (1963) has emphasized that the patient experiences "transference" as a reality; it is the doctor who regards it as mere repetition. The psychiatrist evokes the theoretical construct not only as an aid in understanding the patient but also as a defense against a situation that threatens him or her.

Freud himself was not unaware of the different perceptions of transference held by the patient and the doctor. By 1915, he had begun to formulate a theory about the relationship between the erotic transference and the nature of love (Bergmann, 1982).[2] At that time, though, he maintained his belief that an erotic transference was solely an impediment to the therapy and advised the therapist to demonstrate to the patient that she fell in love with him only in the service of resistance to the analysis. Even so, Freud acknowledged the shared qualities of transference love and love.

But how one regards transference and transference love has implications for both theory and technique. Schafer neatly captures the double, and perhaps contradictory, sense in Freud's conceptualizations of transference love and the ramifications that bifurcation has for current therapeutic ideas:

> On the one hand. transference love is sheerly repetitive, merely a new edition of the old, artificial, and regressive (in its ego aspects particularly) and to be dealt with chiefly by translating it back into its infantile terms. (From this side flows the continuing emphasis in the psychoanalytic literature on reliving, reexperiencing, and re-creating the past.) On the other hand, transference is a piece of real life that is adapted to the analytic purpose, a transitional state of a provisional character that is a

2. Bergmann (1971, 1980, 1982) has chronicled the changes in Freud's thinking about transference, transference love, and love in three very rich papers on love. My abbreviated account of Freud's changes in conceptualizing transference love largely follows Bergmann's account.

> means to a rational end and as genuine as normal love. (From this side flows the emphasis in our literature on the healing powers inherent in the therapeutic relationship itself, especially with respect to early privations and deprivations.) We are not in a position to disagree entirely with either conception of transference, transference neurosis, and transference laden therapeutic effects. The problem is how to integrate the two (1977, p. 340).

Bergmann, unlike Schafer, denies any contradiction in Freud's dual conceptualizations of transference love. He believes that transference love "is not by itself adaptive. It is only the sublimation of this love with the aid of the analyst that makes it adaptive for the purposes of cure, when inquiry is substituted for gratification" (1982, pp. 106–107). He also argues that it offers a new opportunity for the reworking of oedipal material and the opportunity to make new and better choices.

At the same time that the erotic transference has a significant therapeutic potential, problems referable to it continue to confound present-day analysis. Despite the ascendency of the belief that transference is the most effective vehicle for psychoanalytic intervention, the erotic transference maintains its problematic connotations. Compared with other types of transference, it has always been tainted by unsavory associations and continues to be thought of as slightly disreputable. It remains both goldmine and minefield.

The erotic transference, heterosexual or homosexual, may be unmanageably intense, leading to a stalled treatment or a reactively hostile one. It may also be so frightening to some patients that they break off the treatment.

It may be complicated by sexual acting out, either in or out of the analytic situation. The potential for a sexual encounter between patient and therapist has existed from the beginning and has occurred in many instances, some of them quite well known.

Moreover, there appears to be a preponderance of manifest erotic transferences among women. Thus, despite generalizations about the universality of the erotic transference, it was originally described as a reaction women developed to their male psychoanalysts and, in part, continues to be viewed as a complication. Such an assumption distorts our conceptualization of the erotic transference and incorrectly suggests that the phenomenon is a problem of female psychology, and not one of general psychological interest.

To assume that the erotic transference is a problem of female psychology also diverts attention from consideration of the absence of erotic transference manifestations as a problem. Yet the failure to develop a well-articulated erotic transference does pose problems of its own. While no one has explicitly described the limitations of an analysis when the erotic transference fails to develop, they may be inferred. But we have yet to systematically address the consequences of these differences.

Analytic problems related to the erotic transference can occur depending on whether it develops fully within the analytic situation, is enacted extra-therapeutically, or remains undeveloped and is neither fully experienced nor expressed. The particular form the erotic transference takes corresponds in part to the sex of the patient vis-à-vis the analyst, but also to the patient's sex, irrespective of the sex of the analyst.

To illustrate differences in presentations of the erotic transference and the potential problems to which its expression or suppression may predispose, it will be useful to outline some common variants as they appear in the four therapy dyads (female patient-male analyst; male patient-female analyst; and the two so-called "homosexual" couplets) and some consequences of those variants.

Transference Love in the Four Treatment Dyads

Analysts have increasingly been exploring the influence of the analyst as a real object. As far back as 1971, Blum raised the question of the effect of the analyst's attributes on the transference. Addressing the influence of the analyst's sex, he remarked: "With a female analyst a maternal transference will usually appear first, before the succession of other transferences. The paternal transference may appear in fantasies about her husband, or be displaced onto paternal figures outside the analysis" (Blum, 1971, pp. 50–51).

The most significant recent contribution emphasizing the importance of the patient's sex in relationship to the therapist's sex in the unfolding of the transference is that of Karme (1979). While she concurs with the conventional wisdom that there are paternal and maternal transferences to analysts of both sexes, she cautions against equating them with transferences that arise during the development of the transference neurosis.[3] Karme posits that, in the oedipal situation, the positive Oedipus complex leads to a specific transference depending on the sex of patient and analyst:

> With a male analyst the patient develops a maternal transference in the pregenital phase, but whenever oedipal strivings or longings erupt they are directed towards the rival or the loved father-analyst depending on whether the patient is male or female (the reverse occurs in the negative oedipal situation). With a female analyst it is not different, i.e. pregenitally there is a maternal transference, and oedipally she is either the loved

3. By transference neurosis, Karme means transference reactions derivative from the oedipal period.

> or the rival mother-analyst. In other words, during the oedipal phase the patient's transference is maternal or paternal according to the analyst's sex" (1979, p. 259).

While it is frequently the case that the dominant manifest oedipal transference is in line with the analyst's real sex, this is not invariably so. In some analyses, the transference to the analyst is both maternal and paternal in both the positive and negative oedipal configurations and may oscillate between them. Even when the dominant manifest oedipal transference reflects the analyst's real sex, one often sees fragmentary maternal and paternal transference material relating to both oedipal constellations.

However, in many instances, it is my impression that there is one dominant oedipal motif. For example, a heterosexual woman who might have a strong erotic transference in treatment with a male analyst may have a similar experience in treatment with a woman analyst, with this very significant difference: the manifest, predominant oedipal role "assigned" the woman analyst is usually that of the rival mother, not the erotic object, while the manifest, predominant erotic feelings and longings are more often directed to a real or fantasied male figure outside the analysis (Person, 1983).

Although the overt, consciously experienced manifestations of the oedipal transference most frequently (but not invariably) depend on the sex of both patient and analyst, we know that an analyst of either sex can successfully treat a patient of either sex. This can occur only because the predominant oedipal transference role assigned the analyst, paternal or maternal according to the sex of the analyst, does not ultimately constrict the field of the analysis.

How is this possible? As Greenacre pointed out, "The degree to which the transference attitudes are played out in current relationships [other than the analytic relationship] . . . varies considerably" (1959, p. 485). Despite arguments about the primacy of transference interpretations in fostering structural change, there is no evidence that the analysis of direct experience of transference material within the analytic relationship leads to better or more complete results than the analysis of those same manifestations experienced outside the analytic situation. If this were not the case, the sex of the analyst might sometimes limit the possibility of a complete analysis of oedipal material, which is triadic by its nature. The same issues are dealt with in treatment irrespective of the sex of the analyst, but the analyst may not be assigned both roles, or at least not with the same intensity, in the triangular drama.

Even so, the nature of the predominant affective manifestations of the transference may present special opportunities for analytic growth and special vulnerabilities to analytic failure. Whether or not the erotic transference is a central, consciously experienced part of the transference appears to be a case in point. This seems to be somewhat influenced by the sex of the therapist vis-à-vis the patient (same sex or cross-sex), but women in general appear to experience more intense and fully developed erotic transferences.

In comparing differences in the four treatment dyads, I necessarily give short shrift to differences that exist among pairs belonging to the same generic dyad. Obviously, it is folly to think that all women patients with male analysts follow the same patterns in analysis, and so on with all the dyads. However, some abstractions are useful insofar as they allude to common, if not universal, trends. What follows are my impressions, to be confirmed, modified, or negated depending on other analysts' observations. My material is drawn from my own case material, from supervision, from the literature, from case conferences and conversations with colleagues. Even so, it is to be noted that the one dyad I have no firsthand information about is male-male.

FEMALE PATIENT-MALE ANALYST

While the erotic transference has been best and most often described as it occurs with female patients in treatment with men, the overt expression of erotic manifestations in the treatment situation is not invariable. Some women develop a marked erotic transference, while others do not. Some of the latter group act out erotic preoccupations outside the analytic situation, sometimes initiating love affairs at crucial points in the analysis. There is no systematic inquiry or research that reveals whether the difference lies in the woman patient or the male analyst.

Gill's point is probably pertinent here: the analyst can foster the experience of the erotic transference within the analytic situation insofar as he interprets the resistance to awareness of the transference. Sometimes, the tendency for the male analyst is to elicit but not analyze an erotic transference. I was told by several male analysts that following difficult therapies in which the erotic transference was unruly and unmanageable or evoked an erotic countertransference, they noticed that their subsequent female patients had less tendency to develop such intense erotic transferences. This would suggest that some subtle change in the analyst's behavior constitutes the controlling factor. Even so, fundamental differences among women in personality configurations, dynamics, and superego composition may be the decisive factors. (The nature of these differences will become clearer after the discussion of male patients.)

While we generally focus on the complications of the erotic transference, we should not lose sight of the fact that it may confer on the patient a new appreciation of the possibilities inherent in relationships. I was asked by a male psychiatrist to see one of his women patients who was experiencing an erotic transference that had become too intense and was impeding her therapy.

The woman, in her thirties, had arrived at a marital arrangement that had appeared to be satisfactory for many years. The daughter of an extremely successful and forceful entrepreneur, favored by her father and rejected by her mother, she had eschewed any choice similar to her beloved father. Instead, she had married a man whom she regarded as a good lover and who ultimately became a good father to their children, but one with whom she quickly became dissatisfied. She had little respect for him, because of his passivity and his failure to achieve much in business. She balanced her life by sexualizing work relationships and was thus able to make an adaptation that seemed good enough. Her "compromise" marriage no doubt reflected some flight from her childhood oedipal victory. This precarious arrangement was shattered at the onset of a family crisis, during which her husband was unable to give her what she thought was adequate support. It was at the height of that disappointment that she entered into analysis.

In the acute phases of her difficulties, her doctor was extremely helpful and mobilized expectations in her that had long since been buried, if they had ever consciously existed. She began to long for a serious communication with a man and for a relationship with a man more nearly like her father. When I saw her, she was extremely confused as to whether the relationship with the doctor was a portent of what she wanted or whether it was actually the doctor she desired. While it is unclear what the outcome of her therapy will be, it is clear that she had awakened to the possibility of an intimate communication and a richer life as a result of her transferential experience. Whether the patient will benefit by that experience and attempt to improve her life situation or will stay bogged down in transference hopes and demands is still an open question. The outcome will depend on the interaction of her observing ego and the analyst's skills.

At the same time, there are certain problems that typically complicate the therapeutic process when an erotic transference is prominent. First, one may see perpetuation of an ongoing sexually toned transference-countertransference interaction. Though not usually acted upon, it is not usually fully analyzed either. In such a case, the patient maintains an overidealization (which may or may not be overtly sexual) of the therapist, one that is often accepted at face value by the therapist. Insofar as it is accepted without question and not analyzed, it reflects a countertransference problem in the male analyst (Person, 1983).

When the erotic transference is experienced but not fully analyzed, it becomes the resistance to the analysis. The limitation of such therapies is a tendency for the strength of the erotic transference to obscure other important dynamics and conflicts. The perpetuation of the erotic transference takes two forms—longing to be the recipient of the analyst's love (or insisting on it), or experiencing love and longing for him. Both, if unanalyzed, interfere with the emergence of the negative oedipal transference and the preoedipal phase that, in women, may be continuous with the negative Oedipus complex. Freud believed that stage almost impossible to revive, at least in analysis with him, because the patient clung to the "very attachment to the father in which they had taken refuge from the early phase that was in question" (1931, p. 226).

There are several negative ramifications of the perpetuation of the erotic transference. In one of the worst outcomes, the patient drifts along in analysis, using the erotic transference as a substitute for gratifications in life. One sees many instances of female analysands unable to mobilize effectively to form intimate relationships with men outside the analytic situation. In essence, the patient uses the analyst as a phantom lover and mate, although she may prosper in other areas of her life. One is reminded of the almost erotic fervor with which some nuns give themselves to Christ. Some women, already coupled, use the idealized transference to the analyst to denigrate their partner and find him less than adequate. One might regard this as a split transference with all negative perceptions and feelings attached to the partner. This dynamic, unanalyzed, leads some part of the lay public to regard the beginning of an analysis as the end of a marriage.

In other instances, women may feel that they have recovered the capacity for affectionate relationships with appropriate partners as well as more affectionate relationships with their fathers and family members, but these relationships may be overidealized and somewhat infantile (dependent or worshipful). At the same time their relationships with women remain somewhat problematic. Essentially, they recover the capacity for a loving relationship with a man without working through their self-identity as women, their loving or competitive feelings toward women, or their inhibitions against self-expression. The price may be the perpetuation of a low-grade depression or a subjective sense of inauthenticity. To some degree, the experience of the self is distorted by the persisting negative identification with the "bad" mother. Moreover, the shape of the attachment to the male partner is frequently colored by unanalyzed material pertaining to the negative oedipal relationship and the preoedipal mother-daughter relationship. Feelings and attitudes toward the mother have been transferred to the husband or male friend.

In short, the very strength of the erotic transference in these dyads, while it has significant therapeutic potential, often acts as a strong transference resistance. It is often fused with preoedipal components, masks dependency gratification, competitive strivings, and hostile feelings, and disguises self-loathing. As such, it may act as an insuperable impediment to thorough analysis and to the initiation of extra-analytic change.

FEMALE PATIENT-FEMALE ANALYST

In these analyses, when the patient is heterosexual, erotic transferences are most often not explicitly sexual but expressive of tender, affectionate feelings and the wish for intimacy, to be understood and cared about. They can be dramatically sexual, however, and these homosexual transferences might be either manifestations of a negative oedipal complex or eroticized components of preoedipal material. Although it might be argued that these are paternal transferences, I have not observed any analytic data in my own practice to substantiate this conjecture. The erotic manifestations often appear in the context of an idealizing transference, which may be a reaction against a competitive transference, and they also appear in the context of problems in the patient's erotic life with men as a regressive maneuver. In homosexual women, erotic transferences may be extremely intense and occur with some regularity.[4]

However, the most intense maternal transferences one generally sees are not erotic but reflect the emergence of fury, envy, rivalry, and fear as part of the oedipal constellation. These fears are often expressed in oral, sometimes cannibalistic, terms. The woman's fear is of loss of love, of starvation, and of annihilation. Most likely, competitive fears take these forms because the object of competition is also the source of nurturant and dependent gratification (Person, 1982).

MALE PATIENT-FEMALE ANALYST

As Lester (1983) points out, there are almost no references in the literature in which male patients are reported to experience strong erotic transferences to their female analysts. Bibring (1936) reported an eroticized transference, infused with primitive elements, that cannot be properly considered an erotic transference. Lester (1983) reported that she had encountered strong erotic and eroticized transferences in her female patients, but only mild, transient, muted, and unstable ones in her male patients. Karme (1979), in her case report, discusses a male patient's erotic transference to her, but it consists mostly of allusions to triangular situations in associations and dreams, with only a few explicitly erotic dreams and fantasies about her.

There does seem to be a difference in the expression of the erotic transference in the female patient-male therapist dyad and the male patient-female therapist dyad. In the former case, the erotic transference is more often overt, consciously experienced, intense, long-lived, and directed toward the analyst, and focuses more on love than sex; in the latter, it is muted, relatively short-lived, appears indirectly in dreams and triangular preoccupations, is seldom

4. In recent years, I have seen in consultation several homosexual women in treatment with homosexual women, in whom the erotic transference is unusually intense and sometimes enacted, just as it sometimes is in heterosexual women in treatment with heterosexual men. (Footnote added, 1998.)

consciously experienced as a dominant affective motif, is frequently transposed to a woman outside the analytic situation, and most often appears as sexual rather than as a longing for love.

Sexual fantasies, however, may be quite prominent. They are most often devoid of erotic longing. A sexual thought, such as "sucking her cunt," may appear ego-alien and be accompanied by embarrassment. Some sexual fantasies betray preoedipal components, sometimes aggressive in nature, as a defense against affectionate longings. Frequently, one witnesses defenses against the erotic transference rather than the transference itself.

Even so, male patients can be extremely sensitive to imagined slights and may demand attention, or special accommodations even while denying any personal involvement or desire whatsoever. Like women, they may idealize the analyst, but the idealization is not merged with erotic longing.

However, there are some exceptions, and one occasionally sees well-developed and sustained erotic transferences in male patients to their female doctors. One sometimes sees them in older men in relation to younger women, most often in the training situation, frequently in low-cost clinics. For a variety of reasons, including the youth and inexperience of the analyst, this has not been reported in the literature. This also appears to occur more frequently in men with either a strong bisexual identification or homosexual conflict, but *not* in homosexual men.[5] In these cases the erotic transference to the female analyst may serve as a defense against the more threatening homosexual longing; that is, the positive oedipal constellation serves as a defense against the negative one.

With male patients there is frequently a pronounced tendency to reenact the whole oedipal drama outside the transference and maintain the female analyst either as a nurturing, maternal ally against competitors or as a threatening and potentially castrating predator mother. It is difficult, and sometimes impossible, for the analyst to successfully interpret the resistance to experiencing the transference and to ask the patient to confront the displacement outside the transference. An experience from my own practice illustrates this point.

5. I am grateful to many of my women colleagues and students for sharing their observations with me. Any number reported specific exceptions to the generalization I had made about the paucity of well-developed erotic transferences in men. However, most of the exceptions fell within the two categories cited. A few women had witnessed strong erotic transferences in borderline patients. Bibring's patient, mentioned above, may fit within this group diagnostically.

One woman made the interesting suggestion that, among private patients, men who choose woman analysts and are thus self-selected may form a subgroup with special psychodynamics. I find this suggestion intriguing because I think many men *do* select women when they are too competitive to see other men. This focus on dominance as a dynamic fits in well with my understanding of the male resistance to the erotic transference. (See the following sections.)

Mr. M., a successful entrepreneur down on his luck, incurred the wrath of his wife, who apparently depended on his strength. He entered treatment in a depression. He worked well, using insight so long as this occurred at a distance from the transference. During his treatment I appeared on television. He watched my appearance while he was in bed with a woman (not his wife). He came in the next day and gave me an insightful critique of my performance, although he was unable to watch the complete show because of his sexual activities with his new woman friend. He remained unconvinced that the whole episode reflected any sexual fantasies about me whatsoever. In fact, Mr. M. considered the suggestion preposterous. Although he regarded my analytic skills as superior, he insisted that I was definitely "not his type." As Gill would put it, he had a resistance to the experience of the erotic transference.

The dangers of successfully suppressing or repressing the experience of the erotic transference are less clear and less dramatic than the dangers attendant to the erotic transference used as resistance, but they are nonetheless substantial. The inability to merge sexual and dependency yearnings perpetuates instability in the male's capacity to form enduring love relationships. Many men experience emotional attachment only as sexual and doubt their fundamental capacity to love. Some even question the desirability of falling in love or loving.

What is the motive for this avoidance of the erotic transference in men, which is in marked contrast to the tendency of so many women to rush to embrace it? For the male patient, to feel erotic urges toward the female analyst would be to emphasize his overall need for her, a need that apparently undermines his sense of autonomy. To the degree that he can, the man preserves or juggles his autonomy and independence by separating sex from dependency (and intimacy) and controlling his sex object. He fears dependency connected to sexuality insofar as it represents weakness and loss of control, feelings that must be avoided if he is to successfully transcend those feelings of inferiority relative to both mother and father invoked during his childhood.

Some male patients even have a paucity of sexual fantasies about the female analyst. Because of their own overestimation of sex as power, to de-sex a woman is to castrate her, to rob her of her power. By desexualizing his woman analyst, the male patient also dehumanizes her, and she becomes an object of somewhat contemptuous affection for him. Desexualization sometimes allows the emergence of more affectionate material. The common turn-of-the-century belief that women lacked sexuality reflected a sentiment (or wish) regarding their powerlessness. To desexualize the female analyst is to castrate and demean her. This point is exactly opposite to the traditional contention that the man is simply protecting the sainted woman from his sordid oedipal desires. Taking away sexuality takes away power; it does not confer sainthood. But it does permit the male patient to enjoy the analyst's nurturance of him with no threat to his manhood.

Because power considerations vis-à-vis the analyst are kept out of the analysis, power motivations may not be adequately analyzed. Furthermore, the unconscious contempt and the prevalence of pregenital aggressive components in relation to the female analyst, if not brought into the analysis, continue to corrupt his capacity for relationships with women.

Similar dynamics are seen in those women who never develop an erotic transference to their male analysts. Their protest that the analyst is "unattractive" masks a fear of dependency if it is linked to sexuality and reveals the need for compensatory dominance.

In addition to the male patient's dynamics, the female analyst's countertransference serves as a source of counterresistance to the expression and development of an erotic transference. The relative subordination of the patient and authority of the analyst are not congruent with the predominant female erotic fantasy. If a woman therapist does have sexual or erotic fantasies about male patients, she is less likely to dwell on or openly acknowledge them because of cultural prohibitions. Her own inhibitions about such fantasies subtly inhibit inquiries into the patient's defenses against his erotic feelings toward her. Her embarrassment at presuming to be found "sexual" and erotically desirable, despite the patient's disclaimers, also serves as an impediment to interpreting the resistance to the erotic transference.

MALE PATIENT-MALE ANALYST

Here, too, the erotic transference is muted. This is true of both heterosexual and homosexual patients. When an erotic thought, dream, association, or trend occurs, it is the occasion for dissociation. The sudden overt sexual thought is devoid of desire and often regarded as ego-alien. Yearnings for attachment and dependent gratification do appear as significant trends and may be experienced as homosexual. The homosexual transference is often transmuted into envy of women, their role, prerogatives, and so forth. If the erotic transference is too strong and erupts into consciousness it leads to massive anxiety and well-known homosexual panic.

It is the relative paucity of homosexual erotic transferences, even among homosexual patients, that confirms the underlying male resistance to the experience of the erotic transference.[6]

6. This chapter was written before I has much knowledge of male homosexual patient/male homosexual therapist dyads. In such dyads an overt erotic transference will be seen more frequently. (Footnote added, 1998.)

Discussion

In general, erotic manifestations are greater in cross-sex dyads (at least in heterosexual patients), while rivalrous constituents are more prominent in same-sex dyads. But women patients have a greater propensity than men to exhibit overt and sustained expressions of the erotic transference toward the analyst, whether male or female, and to experience the erotic transference as such.

The difference between the two cross-gender dyads in their treatment behavior parallels a difference in life. The reaction of a younger dependent female to an older authoritarian male is traditionally conducive to an erotic relationship, not just in the therapy situation, but outside it as well. In contrast, it is traditionally taboo for an older, experienced woman and a younger, inexperienced man to be together in an erotic situation, though this prohibition appears to be weakening. This dichotomy parallels the family experience, in which father-daughter incest, while not sanctioned, is more easily tolerated than mother-son incest.

This difference between the sexes cannot be reduced to a difference between hysterical and obsessive personality types. It transcends any simple difference in personality organization. One must look at male and female development separately to discern why in female development a prolonged erotic attachment becomes the pseudosolution to so many problems whereas in male psychology the problem is to achieve a love relationship integrated with sex.

The antecedent factors are multiple and so densely intertwined—a mix of cultural, contextual, and developmental factors—that they are hard to tease apart in any definitive fashion. They certainly include the way femininity and masculinity are constructed in our culture but also reflect early object relations and the asymmetric structures of the oedipal complex.

In general, women achieve their self-identity as women by virtue of certain defining relationships (Chodorow, 1974; Gilligan, 1982), whereas men achieve their self-identity as men through achievement and autonomy. Girls define themselves more in terms of their relationships or affiliations than do boys. In women, the preoccupation with pair-bonding, both establishing and preserving it, has social determinants that are self-evident. Men may have the same magnitude of dependency needs and affiliative yearnings but are less fearful that they will go unfulfilled. While both sexes may fear engulfment and potential annihilation of the self, men feel their masculinity threatened by self-acknowledged dependency on the love object. In essence, men are taught to despise their overt dependency needs. Women do not feel their femininity to be similarly threatened by that same dependency. Therefore, forming love relationships is generally more problematic for men than women. In part, it is the self-preservation of one's identity as feminine or masculine that leads to different experiences and presentations of the erotic transference.

However, this external reality appears to be supported by an inner reality. In other words, cultural factors alone do not seem adequate to account for the difference in the manifestations of the erotic transference or in the way love is valued. There are experiences in the early development of both sexes that seem to provide underlying psychic support for compliance with contemporary cultural dictates.

As it emerges in analyses, the major underlying dynamic in women is fear of loss of love. Self-preservation frequently becomes symbolically linked to pair-bonding, which emerges as the dominant motif in mental life. This tendency reflects an adaptation based on gender socialization, role expectations, and external prohibitions but is also implicit in the developmental sequence of female object relations. However, the female preoccupation with pair-bonding may be best understood in the context of the female oedipal constellation. Whatever the reasons, most girls do ultimately turn to the father as their primary libidinal object. But the girl's erotic rival, her mother, is also the source of dependent gratification, a situation that intensifies the girl's fear of retaliation. Fear of loss of her dependency object leads the girl to experience dread of loss of love, a fear that is displaced from mother onto all subsequent love objects. Erotic longing is compensatory against the fear of loss of love, and securing love becomes the girl's lifelong problematic.

Fear of loss of love is further reinforced by another aspect of the girl's oedipal configuration: the renunciation of her mother implicit in her turn to her father. In some women, the fear of loss of love is activated not by any slight on the part of husband or lover but by an adulterous impulse. This occurs so regularly that it seems to recapitulate some earlier confusion: did the girl renounce her mother, or was she rejected by her? The girl's renunciation of her mother may be experienced not just as a loss but as a betrayal. The preoccupation with loving may here be seen as a defense against hostile and aggressive impulses.

Preoccupation with love relates to the oedipal configuration in still a third way. While the boy has an ongoing relationship with his mother, the little girl must forge a more intense relationship with her father. Though, to some degree, he is already part of her psychic world, the relationship seldom has the ongoing intensity of the preoedipal mother-daughter dyad. The female appetite for Gothic novels, in which the central theme (fantasy) is winning the heart of a remote, cold, man, appears derivative of that period of time when the girl had to engage the distant father (distant compared with her mother) in a close, affectionate bond.

This formulation emphasizes the effects of the female monopoly of child care, with its attendant asymmetry during the oedipal situation, and not just the sexual difference. It is consonant with Freud's discovery of the girl's preoedipal tie to her mother (Freud, 1931, 1933b). It is the girl's ambivalent tie to her mother that appears to be at the root of the girl's pervasive dread of loss of love and her preoccupation with longing for love and finding self-definition through relationships. It is only the continuation of those relationships that can reassure the girl that her dependency needs will continue to be gratified despite her sexuality, self-assertion, and aggression.

The erotic transference in women, like the oedipal tie to the father, may not be easily renounced. In perpetuating the erotic transference and failing to analyze the many dynamics that may contribute to it from different levels, a limited analytic outcome is inevitable.

In the male, too, certain developmental factors mold the configuration and experience of the erotic transference. Lester (1983) suggests that the muting of the erotic transference in the male patient in treatment with a woman represents a particular vicissitude in the transference. By this she means that the transference to the powerful preoedipal mother inhibits the expression of erotic fantasies toward the oedipal mother. In other words, the patient fears being engulfed by the preoedipal mother. Her argument is almost certainly correct, at least in part, but it is difficult to credit this as the sole inhibition to experiencing the erotic transference within the analysis when fear of that same preoedipal mother does nothing to dampen the erotic transference of a female patient in treatment with a female analyst. This latter transference takes place frequently, despite the fact that such a love relationship is equally threatening to the integrity of the self and, in addition, is not culturally sanctioned. It is not the self that is more threatened in males but the sense of a gendered self. Erotic dependency is not consonant with masculinity as culturally defined.

There are additional factors in the boy's oedipal and postoedipal development that predispose him to split the object of nurturance from the erotic object. The boy, like the girl, must renounce his libidinal tie to his mother. Freud (1920a) has suggested that he abandons it not just out of fear of his father's retaliation but out of his narcissistic mortification that he is inadequate to replace his father. The boy's narcissistic wound persists; it may be revealed in his continuing fears about the size and adequacy of his penis. For many men, these fears do not abate despite years of adequate sexual performance. Performance, not love, is the male's central problematic, a preoccupation that permeates many aspects of a male's life, as clinically revealed.

Control of the sexual object serves as a compensatory device that defends against his childhood inadequacy and his sense of inferiority to both parents. Out of revenge, the man reverses his infantile experience: he stands ready to demand sexual fidelity while disavowing it himself.

Women sustain their integrity and femininity through the establishment and continuation of relationships, men preserve their separateness and masculinity through the use of action and power modalities. The cultural prescription that women achieve identity through coupling and men through achievement and autonomy is reinforced by the consequences of the asymmetry in female and male oedipal constellations. These differences are clearly expressed in the strikingly different forms the erotic transference takes in women and men.

Summary

Although the erotic transference is believed to be universal, it is variable in its expression. Drawing on the distinction between transference resistance and resistance to the awareness of the transference, I have proposed that, in general, the erotic transference utilized as resistance is more common among women, while resistance to the awareness of the erotic transference is more common among male patients. Erotic transference as resistance poses different analytic problems than resistance to its awareness.

Among women in treatment with men, the erotic transference is more often overt, consciously experienced, intense, long-lived, directed toward the analyst, and focused more on love than sex; among men in treatment with women, the erotic transference is muted, relatively short-lived, appears indirectly in dreams and triangular preoccupations, is seldom consciously experienced as a dominant affective motif, is frequently transposed to a woman outside the analytic situation, and most often appears as sexual rather than as a longing for love.

In women, the strength of the erotic transference may obscure other important dynamics and conflicts. While it has significant therapeutic potential, it often acts as a strong transference resistance to working out underlying conflicts. In contrast, in male patients in treatment with women, there is a resistance to the experience of the transference, and one frequently witnesses defenses against the erotic transference rather than the transference itself. Yet, the dangers are substantial when the erotic transference fails to develop or is suppressed.

This difference in the manifestation of the erotic transference parallels an extratherapeutic difference. In general, women achieve their self-identity as women by virtue of certain defining relationships, whereas men achieve their self-identity as men through achievement and autonomy. The reasons for these differences have been explored in terms of cultural dictates, but more particularly in terms of an asymmetry in psychological development.

16

Female Sexual Identity: The Impact of the Adolescent Experience

1985

ETHEL S. PERSON

IT IS generally believed that men suffer more from gender identity problems and that women suffer more from sexual problems.[1] While it is true that men experience more gender identity problems, the extent and nature of sexual problems in women (frigidity and anorgasmia) are not well documented. They are believed to result most frequently from cultural inhibitions. The corollary belief is that such problems, particularly among young women, have now vanished because of the beneficial and sweeping influence of "sexual liberation."

Yet these popular beliefs are too optimistic. In discussing consciousness-raising groups during the 1960s, the noted feminist and novelist Alix Kates Shulman says, "I was surprised to hear so many women who had come of age in the sixties talk resentfully about their sexual experience, for I had believed the media version of the great sexual revolution among the young. But far from having felt freed by the so-called sexual revolution of the sixties, those young, dedicated women—many of whom had been politicized in the New Left—actually felt victimized by it" (1980, p. 23). Her observation remains true of young women today.[2]

The author wishes to thank Dr. Eleanor Schuker and Ms. Ilene Lefcourt for reading an earlier version and making many valuable suggestions.

1. The run on Viagra as soon as it was released suggests that the high incidence of male potency problems may have been one of the best-kept secrets of the past few decades. It is now an open question whether women do in fact have more sexual problems. (Footnote added, 1998.)

2. In the 1990s, the problem seems to be receding but is still the same in some pockets of society and in some still inhibited individuals. (Footnote added, 1998.)

Orgasmic sex continues to be difficult to achieve for adolescent and young adult women in heterosexual relationships because of sexual and social differences between the sexes that blight heterosexual encounters and because of persisting social conventions that act to inhibit female sexuality. The resulting sexual problems should be attributed not to female hyposexuality or to disordered individual development but more to the failure of both sexes to translate the findings of sex researchers into new behaviors that might promote more sexual pleasure in women. Some psychological barrier still exists that precludes the utilization of new information. It appears that the sexual revolution has promoted sexual activity without addressing those differences between women and men that create problems in realizing sexual pleasure for women, with obvious consequences for sexual self-esteem and sexual identity.

If one assumes that the achievement of orgasmic sexual pleasure is requisite for consolidation of a well-integrated sexual identity, the corollary is that problems in achieving orgasmic sex result in a problematic sexual identity. (This is true of either a heterosexual or a homosexual identity, though the focus in this chapter is on heterosexual identity.) As an example of the necessity of confirming sexual identity by actual sexual experience, consider the fact that college men who have not yet had heterosexual intercourse frequently express the fear that they may be homosexual—this despite the absence of any homosexual behavior or fantasies on their part (Coons, 1971). Similarly, lack of experience or sexual problems on the part of young women impedes consolidation of their mature sexual identities.

Insofar as sexual problems derive from common contextual causes (e.g., socialization) and not from intrapsychic conflicts, the corresponding problems in sexual identity may be considered normative, not neurotic. Most often such problems *are* normative, not the result of disordered psychosexual development. They frequently surface during the period of the adolescent's induction into sex—an experience that is different for females and males. The impact of one's induction into sexuality continues to exert a profound effect on its subsequent course.

I propose here to define sexual identity, describe the path of its normal consolidation in late adolescence, elaborate on the *normative* problems that interfere with sexual gratification in many young women during adolescence and young adulthood and thereby interfere with the consolidation of sexual identity, and finally to outline the *conflictual* (or neurotic) problems that plague a minority of young women.

Sexual and Gender Identity

Although its experiential roots go back to infancy and early childhood, sexual identity first becomes patterned during the oedipal phase and fully established following puberty, when fantasy and desire can be expressed in physical sexuality. However, the establishment of sexual identity does not occur automatically on a predetermined timetable and may not be fully consolidated until much later, if ever. The ultimate consolidation of sexual identity rests on the achievement of an actualized sexual life, characterized both by the development of a sociosexual role and by the experience of sexual gratification.

Sexual identity is difficult to define precisely, first, because identity itself is such a poorly defined concept. Moreover, the fact that in sex one is both the desiring subject and someone else's desired object makes the definition of sexual identity necessarily complicated and elusive. Whereas self-identifications as both sexual subject and sexual object play a role in sexual identity, one or the other facet is often exaggerated to the impoverishment of the other—the male more often overidentifying as the desiring subject, the female as the object. In either instance, extreme self-typing as subject or object leads to a marred or incomplete sexual identity. Moreover, although sexual identity refers to one's self-definition as a sexual being, it is not a unitary construct. Its two major components are sexual role and what I have called the "sex print" (Person, 1980).

Sexual role refers to the sociosexual role assumed by the individual to indicate that she or he is following sexual expectations within a societal or cultural context. Sexual role, as culturally defined, is not insignificant. It may take priority over subjective desire when the two are not congruent. The "sex print" refers to the experience of desire, sexual arousal, and discharge as well as to the behaviors and fantasies that stimulate them. An individual's sexual horizons are progressively narrowed from infancy and childhood (the stage of polymorphous perverse sexuality) to adulthood, at which time sexuality has most often crystallized into a preferential pattern. The sex print is the mature individual's erotic signature. It conveys more than preference for a particular sexual object and a particular sexual activity; it also reflects the individualized scripts that elicit erotic desire. It often includes an individual's strong preference for specific erotic techniques. From the subjective point of view, the sex print is experienced as sexual "preference." (For most people, it is a generalized script or a "family" of individual scripts; only in the perversions is the script singular and rigid.)

Yet gender identity seems to be more basic to personality development than sexual identity. It begins to develop intertwined with the development of a self-identity and is integral to any well-articulated concept of self. Gender identity, the feminine-masculine polarity, reflects a psychological self-image and can be loosely defined as an individual's self-evaluation of psychological femaleness or maleness—-the belief that "I am feminine" or "I am masculine" as measured against the prevailing standards of feminine or masculine behavior.

Because sex and gender are developmentally intertwined, any sexual problem causes anxiety about the adequacy of gender identity, and reciprocally, any gender problem will impact on sexual identity. More important, the content of femininity and masculinity, as culturally dictated, will shape the expression of sexuality or even inhibit it.

Late Adolescent Years in Developmental Perspective

A major task of the late adolescent years is the achievement of both a degree of autonomy and social success. However, as pointed out by May (1980) and Douvan and Adelson (1960), these tasks are emphasized differently by females and males. Females are more committed to achieving interpersonal competence, males to achieving autonomy. According to Douvan and Adelson: "For the girl development of interpersonal ties—the sensitivities, skills, ethics, and values of object ties—forms the core of identity, and it gives expression to much of developing feminine eroticism. Feminine sexuality, consciously inhibited from active and direct expression, seeks more subtle, limited, and covert expression" (p. 347). Though the differences between the sexes noted by Douvan and Adelson were based on interviews conducted with adolescents in the mid-1950s, their observations still appear to be true. The difference now is that many young women are also committed to achieving autonomy in terms of work, but their dedication to interpersonal competence continues undiminished. The size of their burden is thus doubled.

When Douvan and Adelson's insight is applied to the realm of sexuality, it becomes clear why females overemphasize their role as the desired object rather than the role of desiring subject. "Being chosen" is central not just to the female's sexual identity but to her total gender identity as well.

A second task is the consolidation of a sexual identity and the integration of sex into an intimate relationship. Blos (1979) has described the difficulties of achieving a coherent sexual identity and suggests that a somewhat ambiguous sexual identity is the rule rather than the exception prior to adolescence. He postulates the existence of both homosexual conflict in adolescent sexual identity formation as part of normal development and a specific adolescent response to it—the oedipal defense. Blos makes the important point that "sexual activity per se is no indication of normal adolescent closure and offers no assurance that gender-specific sexual identity has been attained" (p. 419). He points out that the expression of preoedipal attachments by the adolescent are most often denied or silenced both in life and in treatment by diversionary heterosexual activity. Consequently, the achievement of an authentically articulated sexual identity may be impeded by too abrupt an assumption of a sexual role.

The older adolescent, by virtue of separating from the family either symbolically or concretely (e.g., going to college), may experience a revival of separation anxiety as well as dependency yearnings generated by the knowledge that she or he will soon be independent. Late adolescence, then, is often a time of generalized anxiety during which longings for the restitution of security and certainty are paramount. Establishing a sexual relationship is sometimes felt as extremely urgent, not primarily for sexual reasons or simply as a reaction-formation against homosexual or incestual impulses, but for reasons of security, dependent gratification, self-esteem, or vicarious strength in countering assorted insecurities, anxieties, and loneliness.

The enactment of a sociosexual role is often used to confer adult status on the self or to form a dependent relationship and thus may serve to override or defer underlying psychological problems, but it certainly does not ensure that a mature sexual identity has been achieved. On the contrary, the achievement of a secure sexual identity is complicated by sexual activity that is laden with many nonsexual purposes on top of those sexual conflicts normally encountered.

For the young woman, the temptation to use sexuality for nonsexual purposes may be even greater because of the common cultural demand that she achieve autonomy by coupling. Young women, in order to confirm gender identity, are so dependent on maintaining relationships that they may enter into sexual relationships prematurely and may be tempted to sacrifice erotic gratification to intimacy. Paradoxically, then, the demand of establishing a coherent feminine gender identity through being chosen and through coupling creates problems in the expression of sexuality for its own sake.

While a number of authors warn against premature sexuality (Klebanow, 1975; Kestenbaum, 1975), they focus almost exclusively on the dangers of perpetuating unconscious fixations or conflicts, stressing either preoedipal object fixations or an unresolved oedipal conflict as the limiting factor. For many women, such problems are compounded by a low pleasure yield in their early sexual encounters. Inadequate sexual gratification itself then becomes the starting point for a new set of problems that may disrupt sexuality for the remainder of the life cycle.

Normative Problems in the Consolidation of Sexual Identity

For most young women, consolidation of sexual identity is not problematic in any serious sense—that is, in the sense of intrapsychic conflict or individually disordered psychosexual development. Even so, sexual identity may be negatively impacted because of the difficulty young women encounter in achieving a gratifying interpersonal sexual life (qua sex) and integrating it into the context of a relationship.

The best contemporary evidence shows that adolescent girls today, although they engage in more sexual activities, have problems of the same nature and scope (relative to pleasure, not behavior) as those of their peers prior to "sexual liberation." They still have considerable difficulty in realizing gratifying sexual lives. The immediate cause can be attributed to problems in achieving orgasms in heterosexual intercourse, still the "prescribed" way of achieving sexual gratification.

Sexual difficulties in young women are easily overlooked because most studies of adolescent sexuality focus more on sexual behavior than on the subjective experiences accompanying it, especially whether there is pleasure or not. Although sexual behavior has certainly changed, the same cannot be said of the subjective experience. The few studies on adolescent sexuality clearly indicate changed behaviors in response to the sexual revolution. Sorensen (1973) documents that among his population of adolescents ranging in age from 13 to 19 years, 59 percent of the boys and 45 percent of the girls had experienced intercourse. This is in contrast to Kinsey's study (1953), in which the incidence of premarital intercourse among girls was only 3 percent until the age of 15 and 20 percent for ages 16 to 20.[3]

In Sorenson's data, 46 percent of the boys and 26 percent of the girls reported that they were excited in response to first intercourse. But only 17 percent of the boys, contrasted with an astounding 63 percent of the girls, reported that they were afraid. In general, a much higher percentage of adolescent boys than of girls report happy, affirmative, self-confident feelings. Conversely, the percentage of girls reporting negative, pessimistic, anxious, and self-doubting feelings about first intercourse is much higher. Significantly, however, Sorensen's data on the differential response of females and males to first intercourse, while extremely revealing, are cited less frequently than his statistics on changes in behavior (for an exception, see Kalogerakis, 1975). It would seem that psychologists and scientists share the underlying assumptions of the sexual revolution that what counts is behavior, not subjective experience.

Clinical Examples of Sexual Problems in Young Women

The following descriptions of sexual life by young women patients may serve to illustrate the ongoing problem of low pleasure yield for many women,

3. In my own study, Person et al. (1989) 68 percent of women and men, all between the ages 20 to 26, have reported intercourse within the past three months. I have no doubt that the figures for intercourse in the late teens and early twenties have continued to increase. (Footnote added, 1998.)

particularly those who are sexually inexperienced, despite their participation in sex and the absence of any serious intrapsychic conflict about sex.

> S.R., 24 years old when first seen, gave the following account of her sexual life. Never orgasmic prior to treatment by any route whatsoever, she had nevertheless enthusiastically entered into a series of heterosexual relationships and had extensive experience with intercourse in her late high school and college years. Her aim in life, as she saw it at that time, was to have an affair with a man and ultimately get married. The excitement of new relationships was enough to sexually stimulate her. She invariably romanticized a series of sexual relationships though she had no actual orgasmic release in any of these. It was only later that she came to focus on the fact that she did not have orgasms and began to feel that something was wrong with her. Romance had taken priority over sexuality. Therefore, while S.R. readily adopted an "appropriate" sociocultural role, her sexuality remained undeveloped and undefined.

That anorgasmia is a common experience is reported by Toolan (1975, p. 261): "There has been a definite pressure on the female not only to be involved sexually, but also to achieve orgasm. Not infrequently the therapist is consulted by young women who are very concerned about their sexual adequacy because they are unable to achieve orgasm with any regularity."

In addition, although many young women can achieve orgasm regularly through masturbation or through manual or oral stimulation in an interpersonal situation, many are nonetheless unable to reach orgasm during coitus. A 20-year-old college junior illustrates this not infrequent pattern:

> A.D. had a long masturbatory history and was able to reach climax quite easily. In ongoing sexual relationships she could achieve orgasm either through manual or oral manipulation but was not orgasmic during coitus. She was initially excited by initial sexual encounters. Despite her intense arousal, she experienced no physical release because those encounters did not focus on foreplay. Gradually, she began to restrict her sexual life to ongoing relationships in which she would educate her partner to her orgasmic requirements.

Among the contemporary generation of young women, sexual behavior, sexual responsiveness, and orgasmic competence are all extremely variable. Some young women have difficulty achieving orgasm and may not even have a history of masturbating (let alone masturbating to orgasm), while some others are readily orgasmic on manual or oral stimulation, and a significant minority experience orgasm during coitus. For those who do achieve orgasm during intercourse, orgasm is often facilitated by specific fantasies, by direct clitoral stimulation simultaneous with intercourse, or by assuming the female-superior position.

> L.H. is a 20-year-old gifted art student now involved in a long-term relationship with another artist. She experiences a readiness to feel rejected by him over minor slights. On the surface they have a "good" sexual relationship. However, she feels compelled to have an orgasm first, because if he has one first she assumes that the sexual encounter is terminated. She generally achieves orgasms when stimulated orally but may be orgasmic during intercourse if in the superior position. She is puzzled by her automatic assumption that the sexual encounter lasts as long as her partner's excitement, but has always felt that way. It is striking that she never masturbates.
>
> L.H. began having sexual intercourse at the age of 13. In retrospect, it appears "all fucked up" because there was no pleasure for her. The point of sex, in early adolescence, was to appear grown up and to be in a relationship.

Some Reasons

How are we to account for these continuing difficulties in young women (and older women) once we observe that the lifting of some cultural inhibitions has not resolved them? Must we revert to traditional psychoanalytic explanations of female "hyposexuality"? These would have us believe that female sexuality is inherently debilitated because of two prerequisites to normal female psychosexual development: the necessity of switching the organ from clitoris to vagina, and the necessity of switching the object from mother to father.

The first hypothesis was nullified by the work of Masters and Johnson (1966), which demonstrated the central role of the clitoris in female sexuality. Very few "experts" now believe that the shift in organ can or should take place. The second hypothesis, the necessity of switching the object, would better explain a tendency for homosexual potential among many women than any tendency toward hyposexuality, particularly since homosexual women (those who theoretically did not make the shift from mother to father) are neither more nor less sexual than other women. Both popular and psychoanalytic assumptions have proved inadequate to explain female sexual problems and so-called female hyposexuality. Sexual problems in women do not seem to result primarily either from strictures implicit in female psychosexual behavior or from cultural inhibition alone.

It seems, instead, that the nature and habit of heterosexual practice, particularly in adolescence, are not geared to ensure orgasm for women. Yet difficulties in realizing sexual pleasure must of necessity diminish sexual self-esteem in women.

Women's sexual problems appear to originate in pronounced sexual and social differences between the sexes, particularly pronounced in the induction into sex during adolescence. They are further exaggerated by the different priorities incumbent in establishing culturally appropriate "femininity" or "masculinity." The ongoing power of these differences is reflected in the inability of the two sexes to incorporate what they "know" about sex into their actual sexual behavior. Moreover, the revision of cultural attitudes toward sexuality is not as extensive as some assume; the ongoing strictures still act selectively against the expression of sexuality in women.

Divergent Sexualities

The relative lack of female enthusiasm for initial intercourse and for coital experience in general has been misunderstood. Instead of being perceived, correctly, as stemming from a discrepancy between the typical heterosexual practice (intercourse) and the preferential route of satisfaction of many women (manual or oral), it is commonly ascribed to individual frigidity. Many women defer to what they and their female and male peers regard as sexual "normality" and therefore inadvertently preclude the possibility of sexual pleasure and orgasm. As Campbell (1980) puts it, "Women's nostalgia for pre-fucking sex, rather than the unmemorable first fuck, seems to be for the rampant sensuality of those adolescent fumblings and gropings. When the agonized decision about whether to go the 'whole way' or not was resolved into 'doing it' the fun seemed to stop." Sexuality that concentrated on foreplay was more pleasurable than normal "grown-up" sex.

While the majority of women most easily have orgasms with manual or oral stimulation, the minority (reported as up to 30 to 40 percent in different studies) achieve orgasm either sporadically or regularly during heterosexual intercourse, but this often depends on the assumption of a special position (most often female superior), an obligatory fantasy, or concomitant clitoral stimulation. Therefore, although intercourse is still considered to be the normative sexual encounter for heterosexuals, it is more reliably sexually gratifying for men than for women. This is not to say that women who do not have orgasms during coitus do not like penetration or intercourse; it is to say that intercourse does not seem to provide the surest route to orgasm for the majority of women. These differences in mode of orgasmic discharge are not indications of any differences in maturity and do not reflect the presence or absence of psychological conflict.

Sorensen's tentative interpretation of the different responses to intercourse his data revealed was that "boys responded more positively than girls because they clearly felt less anxiety-ridden at the time of first intercourse" (1973, p. 206). But the difference is not solely attitudinal or conditioned by negative affect. It also derives from the fact that the pleasure component in these early experiences is far less developed in the female than in the male. Anxiety is pervasive in both sexes, for reasons of continuing cultural restraints as well as problems inherent in intrapsychic development. But the pleasure component in sexual encounters may be great enough in boys to override feelings of anxiety or guilt. Girls do not necessarily have more anxiety or guilt, but they may not have the same pleasure component in casual encounters that would counteract any accompanying negative affect.

Thus, one might justly reverse Sorensen's hypothesis that boys experience more excitement because they are less anxious. On the contrary, they are less aware of anxiety because erection, ejaculation, and pleasure come so easily in the "prescribed" form of heterosexual encounter.

Divergent Masturbatory Histories

I have emphasized the finding that heterosexual males, whatever their preferential route of orgasmic discharge, can generally come to orgasm through intercourse, whereas this is not true of many heterosexual females. This discrepancy, not generally confronted in either the popular or the scientific literature, is compounded by the fact that the two sexes meet sexually in adolescence and young adulthood with different masturbatory histories. The difference in masturbatory practices (almost always more extensive in males) ensure that males generally have greater sexual experience than females prior to first intercourse. (I discussed the implications of this different route of induction into masturbation in a somewhat different context in an earlier paper [Person, 1980, reprinted here as Chapter 2].)

In males, adolescence almost invariably marks the beginning of overt sexual activity. The hormonal activity causes body changes that focus attention on emerging sexuality and frequently result in spontaneous arousal and orgasm. Many young adolescent males are troubled by their seemingly perpetual erections. In contrast, spontaneous orgasm is relatively rare in adolescent girls, and although they may be caught up in romantic yearnings, relatively few young girls are perpetually sexually aroused. For most females, menstruation is the key event of adolescence, compared with ejaculation in males. Menstruation may tend to inhibit sexual exploration both for symbolic reasons and because it carries not just the promise but also the threat of pregnancy. It is not surprising, then, that sex is organized differently by the two sexes.

There may be some small shift toward greater female masturbation, but most studies reflect an ongoing predominance of masturbation in males. Males typically achieve arousal and orgasm earlier. In Kinsey's studies, over 80 percent of males had masturbated to orgasm by age 15, whereas only 20 percent of females had done so (1953, 1948). This discrepancy was still apparent in data collected 20 years later, which found that masturbation in females is more erratic than it is in males. In females only about two-thirds ever masturbate to orgasm, and of those, half discover masturbation after being introduced to orgasm in an interpersonal context.

Sorensen (1973) found that 58 percent of boys and 39 percent of girls of all ages had masturbated at least once and that boys masturbated more frequently. Arafat and Cotton (1979) conclude, "The percentages of both males and females who masturbate appear to approximate the figures given by Kinsey et al." Hunt (1979) suggests that his figures approximate Kinsey's but that there may be a small overall increase. In contrast to coital behavior (age and incidence), in which the sexual difference has tended to disappear, the difference in masturbatory behavior has persisted. Females may eventually demonstrate as much or more sexual interest or drive as males, but for many this is consolidated later and remains tied to relational preoccupations. Thus, while interpersonal sexual patterns have changed, adolescent masturbatory patterns have not.

Because of their relative lack of sexual experience and lack of knowledge about how to achieve orgasm (even through self-stimulation), adolescent girls are often unable to specify to themselves or to their partners what is required sexually. The differences in masturbatory histories make this problem almost inevitable and exaggerate the difficulties in achieving orgasm. Consequently, girls often feel diminished during the sexual encounter because they know less about sex than the male does and because they do not achieve orgasm as readily. They worry about making themselves appear adequately sexual, internalize responsibility for their failure to achieve orgasm, and fail to insist on sexual pleasure, sometimes out of ignorance, sometimes out of a sense of inadequacy, sometimes out of interpersonal intimidation. One girl said she felt as though she ought to be able to exhibit prowess she did not have. Many young women worry about having an orgasm and about how long it takes. Many believe the male will be insulted if his partner does not have an orgasm.

Female Deference in Sexual Interaction

Given two major sexual realities—that females generally have less sexual experience than their partners and that the normative heterosexual practice is often less gratifying for women than for men—it is not surprising that many young women experience difficulties in incorporating sexual gratification into their sexual relationships. This is intensified by the socialization of women to preserve relationships even by deferential behavior when necessary. Whereas boys are free to seek sexual pleasure per se as a confirmation of gender identity, the girl seeks approbation of her femininity more through being the object of desire and through the formation and perpetuation of a relationship.

It should come as no surprise, then, that adolescent girls caught in the struggle to ensure their autonomy and personal identity may of necessity put sexual gratification at a relatively low level of priority. Confirmation of their gender identity through behaving as a social-sexual person frequently takes priority over the achievement of sexual gratification. Insofar as the adolescent girl experiences sexual anxiety, it is often more a fear of rejection than a fear of sex per se.

Because young women often recognize (or fear) that their need to form relational bonds is greater than that of males, they are sometimes tempted to be submissive in order to secure more permanent relationships. This tendency reveals itself both in the feeling adolescent girls have that they must have sex before they really want to in order to preserve a relationship and, once in bed, in the tendency to subordinate their needs and pleasure to those of the male. Even among young women who achieve orgasmic competence relatively early, priority is still given to the male's sexuality. This is evident in the persisting assumption that male ejaculation terminates the sexual encounter.

Although intercourse may be used to consolidate sociosexual role and guarantee adult status even when unaccompanied by orgasm, the very lack of orgasmic gratification eventually exacts a price. That price does not stem from the "ravages of repression" but reflects a loss of sexual self-esteem. The feeling that one must be deferential, even to the extent of sacrificing one's own pleasure, subverts subjective feelings of self-esteem, perhaps irrevocably.

A sexual encounter in a relationship can be experienced as an interpersonal defeat vis-à-vis the partner while it simultaneously confers the feeling of social confidence and social success, fulfillment in the larger social sphere. Sexual identity is sacrificed to gender identity. Thus, there may be ambivalence at the heart of relationships that are formed in order to negotiate gender-role identity and social-sexual role. This is particularly poignant for young women because the conflict takes place at the time of life when another important developmental task—at odds with so much deference—is to seek a sense of autonomy vocationally and personally.

Inasmuch as the male achieves gratification and the female does not, the young woman inevitably begins to resent her subordination to the sexual needs of the male. Any pervasive sense of inadequacy, particularly in comparison with the male, conflicts with the phase-specific adolescent need to feel important, independent, and autonomous.

Adolescent girls have devised a number of strategies to preserve their self-esteem despite the felt need for sexual and relational deference. Some girls overcome the ambivalence in relationships, seeking to normalize deference by initiating relationships with older men in which deference appears to have more to do with age than with gender. Some girls turn the dilemma around, playing the role of little girl as a covert method of manipulation. Others develop a compensatory contempt for the purported social immaturity of boys just as many women maintain a contempt for the purported male insensitivity to emotional nuance.

Toward a Resolution

There are potential solutions to these female-male differences with their inherent problems, particularly prominent during adolescence. Fortunately, there is more dissemination of accurate sexual information among the current generation of young people, more sexual experimentation, and more knowledge among both sexes about the requirements for female orgasm.

Portrayal of noncoital sex, particularly oral sex, has become common in films and television, yet this is still a recent development. One of the early commercial or general-release film portrayal of sex other than coital sex in the missionary position was the erotic relationship depicted in the movie *Coming Home* between a young woman (Jane Fonda) and a paraplegic (Jon Voight). The film was transitional in the sense that oral sex was requisite to the plot because coital sex was physically impossible. Since that film, paraplegia has not remained a prerequisite for portraying noncoital sex. When intercourse is suggested in films, it is now frequently with the female in the superior position.

If I stress film, it is because this medium is uniquely suited to the wide transmission of information about sexuality and undoubtedly plays a major role in the evolution of new normative practices. In part, the importance of film rests on its intrinsic and immediate emotional and sensual impact. By and large, silence prevails regarding the specifics of sexual encounters in other media and even in personal life. The individual feels freer discussing partners and encounters than orifices, lubrication, strokes, and so forth. It appears that sexual liberation is extremely selective. Scientifically and personally, we are still under the constraints of prudery to a much greater degree than the rhetoric of sexual liberation would lead us to believe.

Yet greater dissemination of information will not totally resolve the sexual difficulties between women and men because the problems do not derive simply from lack of information. Cultural inhibition of female sexuality still persists, though in less obvious forms. The lower rate of masturbation in women relative to men may in part be a product of different biologies, but it also appears to be a product of strictures still engendered in socialization. That this may well be the case is suggested by the presence of masturbatory freedom in a significant minority of girls, a freedom that seems to be linked to later ease in sexuality. Nonlabeling of female genitals, different conventions for the excretory functions, and other subtle discriminations against acknowledgment of the female body and sexuality may inhibit the female freedom for erotic self-exploration.

In addition, the perpetuation of gender-role stereotypes also serves to limit sexual pleasure and competence. The persistence of women's sexual deference reveals that sexual liberation is not the same thing as gender-role liberation and that the latter, still unrealized, may have to be achieved first. Both sexes still seem to agree that the nature of male sexuality determines the conduct of heterosexual encounters. This is the assumption that underlies the belief that the sexual encounter is terminated when the male reaches orgasm. Here one must look not just at female deference but also at male complicity. The male reluctance to understand the requirements of female sexuality reflects the desire many men have to believe that when a woman gives pleasure she automatically experiences pleasure. Even so, the inability of both sexes to use what they "know" is a complex and crucial question that remains to be explored.

Intrapsychic Impediments to the Consolidation of Sexual Identity

Thus far I have focused on normative problems in the consolidation of sexual identity. In addition to those factors already discussed, other experiential factors unrelated to deep psychological conflicts may contribute to sexual dysfunction and thereby interfere with consolidation of sexual identity. These include misinformation, painful past experiences, cultural and religious strictures, and aspects of the relationship to the partner (some already alluded to). For young women, fear of pregnancy, anxiety about birth control, and fear of venereal disease (particularly herpes and, most of all, fear of AIDS) play a central role. But problems in consolidating sexual identity sometimes have their roots in intrapsychic conflict rather than in late adolescent sexual life. It is only because in the psychic conflict is more widely discussed in the mental health literature that I have chosen to emphasize contextual problems first.

Establishing a sexual identity means incorporating the sense of oneself as a fully sexual person into one's identity, and it depends on the successful resolution of the Oedipus complex. The Oedipus complex is normally resolved to some degree during the years before puberty and its resolution has an impact on the child's future character, relationships to others, sexual identity, and sexual patterns favored in later life.

The inability to resolve the Oedipus complex may derive from either preoedipal or oedipal conflict. Preoedipal problems may distort sexual expression and sexual identity as well. For example, sexual promiscuity or excessive masturbation, while they appear to be of a sexual nature, often derive from preoedipal conflicts. Inhibitions of future sexual development may begin following parental intimidation of a preoedipal child's early assertiveness, which triggers greater fearfulness in the child during the oedipal phase of development. If childhood intimidation is severe and persistent, normal resolution of the Oedipus complex may be seriously impaired, insofar as rivalry and competitiveness may be experienced as capital offenses. The fearful fantasies of childhood can remain intrusive and may not recede; sexual impulses may then be experienced as dangerous enough to demand either total renunciation or at least a severe degree of inhibition or distortion of sexual expression.

In general, however, the inability to consolidate a sexual identity in young women is usually based on one of three major dynamics referable to the oedipal period: the avoidance of identification with a despised mother, competition with the mother and fear of her retaliation, or fear of the paternal or male figure.[4] If, in development, her view of her mother is too demeaned, the girl will form a compensatory identification with her father. Many such women can function extremely well in most feminine activities and may even be completely orgasmic. Yet some of these women seek to avoid sex even though they are orgasmic, not because it is unpleasurable but because it reminds them of their femininity and their underlying identification with a demeaned female. Some women, able to negotiate an active sexual life, nonetheless find themselves threatened if pregnancy and childbirth confirm the dreaded female identification.

More typically, oedipal conflicts arise when the aims of sexual union are opposed by fears of retaliatory punishment from the rival parent. Conflicts of passivity and activity then develop, as well as a confusion about masculine and feminine identifications. Women have a special problem resolving the Oedi-

4. And nowadays we know that some form of childhood sexual abuse may well be the culprit. (Footnote added, 1998.)

pus complex. Because the oedipal rival of the girl is also the chief supplier of early love and dependency gratification, rivalry with the mother sets up a double jeopardy. The girl is threatened not only with the equivalent of the castration anxiety seen in boys and men but also with the broader fear of losing the rival mother's love and subsequently suffering alienation and separation from her, a depressing and oppressing danger. In my experience, when penis envy emerges as a major inhibitory factor, it is usually in conjunction with one of the dynamics already alluded to.

If the Oedipus complex is incompletely resolved, one sees either fear of injury from the male or fear of loss of love from the female. Most often, fear of loss of love (of the mother) is then transmuted into a fear of loss of the male partner. The underlying fear of loss of the mother has been transposed to the male figure during development.

In analyses and psychotherapies, these various conflicts are not manifested separately but appear intricately interwoven, as shown by the case below.

Case Example

With most young adult women, problems involving sexual dysfunction and sexual identity emerge in the course of treatment initiated for other reasons. The following case illustrates the complexity of untangling the different conflicts impeding consolidation of a mature sexual identity.

> A.W. is an attractive 19-year-old woman who was referred to treatment because of poor school performance that eventually resulted in her dropping out. She is the second child, first daughter, in a professional family. Even though during A.W.'s adolescence her mother was revealed to have a major depressive illness requiring hospitalization and shock therapy, A.W. first recalled her childhood as uneventfully happy. She initially reported she received great love and support from her mother while growing up but had a violent relationship with her father, particularly in early adolescence.
>
> As with so many adolescents, the treatment focused for many months on her current situation with peers, not on the family or on her earlier years. Her most immediate problem involved an adjustment to starting school in a new location while most of her friends were elsewhere. She talked about her feelings of loneliness and subjective isolation. She desperately longed to have a boyfriend. Those contacts she did have with young men did not result in any enduring relationships. Occasionally, she would engage in sexual activity but

was unwilling to say much about it. Her self-confidence gradually increased as her performance in school got better and she began to establish a social life, first with girls, then with an extended group of both sexes.

About a year and a half into treatment, she formed a relationship with a young man. It was only in this context, after the relationship had lasted for some three months, that her sexual fears emerged. She became frightened of having intercourse. The simplest explanation for her reluctance to have intercourse seemed to be to ascribe it to the negative association of an earlier abortion and the trauma about the abortion, emotionally and with her family. By this time, however, she had developed the capacity for considerable insight and began to recall that the abortion merely served as a convenient rationalization for a long-standing sexual inhibition.

Although she had extensive sexual experience, it was usually accompanied by great anxiety, and she preferred men of a lower social status than her own. Her choices, rationalized in terms of rebellion from the family background, concealed an attempted restitution to what she regarded as an unequal power relation between the sexes. This feeling was unconscious and unconnected to any feminist ideology, which she abhorred; rather, it derived from a defensive masculine identification with her father. Sex clearly disrupted that identification.

While unconsciously disliking and fearing her father, she had formed a compensatory identification with him. Underneath her near worship of her mother was a heavily disguised contempt of her mother's submissiveness to her father and inability to protect A.W. from her father's whims. This was accompanied by a growing awareness of her mother's serious psychological disability. Her identification with her father in part represented her flight from an identification with her mother.

A.W.'s many arguments with her father reflected the similarity in their personalities. While identifying with him defensively, she also feared him. Her fear of men was evident in her fears of injury during the sex act and her fears of an erect penis.

Alongside her identification with her father, she had an underlying identification with her mother, whom she perceived to be inadequate and submissive. The low regard in which she held her mother first surfaced in the therapy in her low regard of other women. She began to see how she avoided "stereotypic" female behaviors in order to avoid the dreaded identification with her mother. In her behavior

> she was one of the boys, quite proficient athletically, liking to socialize and drink with them.
>
> Gradually, she began to remember that she had felt rejected by her mother. She feared that females might abandon her. Not only were they too weak to help her, but she believed that they all preferred men. Her unconscious male identification was in part derived from penis envy and the hope of reconciliation with her mother. Ambivalent relationships with women were based on her fear of them. This attitude first emerged in a fantasy she had whenever she first went out with a boy: she pictured that when she met his parents the father would accept her but the mother would be extremely disapproving. She became conscious of the fact that she did not trust girls and expected them to betray her. She became aware of her own oedipal rivalries only after being struck by the overt competition between her aunt and her female cousin.

This case illustrates four major dynamics: the experience of maternal rejection with resulting penis envy, fear of identification with a demeaned female image, fear of the rivalrous mother, and fear of a threatening male imago.

Summary

Achievement of sexual gratification in an interpersonal relationship is a precondition for realizing a fully consolidated sexual identity. While sexual identity may be disrupted in young women for reasons stemming from disordered psychosexual development, more often any disruption stems from normative, contextual problems. Too often, the need to be desired (the desired object) takes priority over competence in the role of the desiring subject. Orgasmic sex is difficult for women to achieve because of sexual and social differences between the sexes. This is particularly true in adolescence, but the adolescent experience has profound effects on subsequent sexuality. Differences in socialization, in sexual preferences, and in masturbatory histories and female sexual deference pertain to the problems of low pleasure yield for women in "normative" sexual encounters. In addition, neurotic conflicts may impede the consolidation of sexual identity.

17

Some Mysteries of Gender: Rethinking Masculine Identifications in Heterosexual Women

1998

ETHEL S. PERSON

FOR A long time, psychoanalytic as well as general opinion held that sexual object choice and gender identity automatically went together. As Judith Lorber put it, the consensus was that "each person [has] one sex, one sexuality, and one gender, congruent with each other and fixed for life, and . . . [that] these categories [comprise] only two sexes, two sexualities, and two genders" (1994, p. 96). But the consensus was wrong.

The idea of a congruency among sex, sexuality, and gender should have been suspect from the time it was first proposed. Homosexuality presents a challenge to any such formulation inasmuch as not all gay men are feminine, not all lesbians masculine. Nor, of course, are all heterosexual men masculine or all heterosexual women feminine. However, these exceptions to the dominant mind-set were not noted; instead it was reasoned that a gay man's object choice demonstrated his femininity, a lesbian's object choice her masculinity, and so on—a bit of circular thinking that gave priority to sexual object choice in defining gender role identity.

In recent years, this thinking has been effectively challenged. Observations on the relationships among biological sex, sexual orientation, and gender identity in a group of intersexed patients demonstrated that sex and gender

An earlier version of this chapter was given as the H. Lee Hall Memorial Lecture at the Emory Psychoanalytic Institute in Atlanta, Georgia, April 26, 1997. My thanks go to Drs. Gail Berry and Eleanor Schuker for reading this chapter and making valuable suggestions and to Morris Eagle, Ph.D., for his discussion of a shortened version of the paper presented in Boston, April 25, 1998, at the 18th Annual Spring Meeting, Division of Psychoanalysis (39) "Psychoanalysis and Sexuality: Reflections on an Old Love Affair."

have separate though sometimes intersecting developmental pathways, more subject to change over time than was previously thought. In addition, gays and feminists have pointed out how previous formulations of sex and gender were contaminated by sexist and heterosexist biases. And some contemporary psychoanalytic writers, influenced by the postmodernist theoretical emphasis on social construction, now posit a degree of fluidity of desires, sexual identities, and gender patterns of such magnitude that the persistence of *any* stable patterns of sexuality and gender is brought into question. While the complexity of the interrelationships between sex and gender has been established, the argument for essentially limitless fluidity over the life cycle seems to be exaggerated, as I will argue in the course of the chapter.

It is true, of course, that changing cultural attitudes—the product of the insights of the liberationist movements in conjunction with medical advances (for example, the birth control pill) and social and economic changes—have permitted new social realities to emerge. To take one of the most commonly cited examples of a large-scale change, consider the huge numbers of women who have entered the work force over the past twenty-five years. Many of them have achieved positions of considerable power and prestige, made possible once professional aspirations were liberated from the stigma of being essentially masculine in nature. If we could now retrospectively interview turn-of-the-century women who had such aspirations, we would no doubt discover that their ambitions had many different sources. For a few, such ambitions may have been based on an identification with the intellectual or professional aspirations of their mothers, for others on an identification with their fathers that did not impact on their sense of femininity, while some would have been acting out a paternal identification experienced as masculine. And these possibilities barely hint at the range of motivations and identifications that may have led to professional ambition in women in that bygone era. But, whatever their motivations, there's no doubt that such trail-blazing women were at the time considered to be in conflict with their own femininity and that a variety of social sanctions punished them severely for their "deficient" femininity.

Many, if not most, of those women were at war not with their own femininity but with their culture's concept of femininity. Nonetheless, however beneficial the cultural analysis of today's feminists is, psychoanalysts cannot fail to observe that not all gender conflicts are the result of a clash between the individual and the culture. While identifications with both typical feminine and masculine aspects of gender roles may be integrated and blended in a particular individual, significant cross-gender identifications sometimes have their roots in unconscious intrapsychic conflict. These may be all too easily overlooked in the analysis of women in whom gender conflict is often automatically assumed to originate in cultural prejudices. Alternatively, rigid gender role polarization and specificity may be utilized as a mode of resolving conflicts. Eleanor Schuker gives the example of how an exaggeration of concordant role-taking can be used for conflict resolution, as when a little girl utilizes hyperfemininity to counter separation problems (personal communication). Once formed, cross-gender identifications, whether the product of the imperfect resolution of unconscious conflict or of the formation of pathological self-objects, can themselves become the locus of ongoing preconscious or conscious conflict.

As part of an ongoing attempt to understand the different ways in which a divided gender identity can be expressed in women, I will explore in this chapter different kinds of cross-gender identifications in heterosexual women, their diverse origins, and their impact on everyday adaptations. Before I turn to the exploration of masculine identifications in women, I will summarize some current thinking about sex and gender, with an emphasis on how our scientific ideas about gender role identity have changed and are still in the process of changing.

Sex, Gender, and Sexuality

Given the degree to which the concept of gender now permeates psychology, psychoanalysis, women's studies, and gay and lesbian studies, it's hard to believe that gender is a term first introduced into the medical literature in the 1950s. Through their studies on intersexed children, Money, Hampson, and Hampson (1955a,b) developed the concept of gender and then demonstrated that the initial and indispensable step in gender differentiation is the child's self-designation as male or female. This self-designation (core gender identity) evolves according to the sex of assignment. Core gender is the child's resulting sense, unconscious as well as conscious, of belonging to one or the other sex. Consequently, core gender identity does not necessarily correspond to biological sex. For example, a genetic male—perhaps a male child with a severe hypospadia, a deformity of the penis that makes it look like a vulva—mistakenly assessed at birth as female and labeled as such, will self-identify as female and develop along feminine lines. It is this kind of work which is the basis for the constructionist theory of core gender identity.

We know, however, that biology impacts on gender role identity. In boys, a high level of assertive/aggressive play is seen cross culturally, and this is true for other mammalian species. The current consensus of scientific opinion has it that this assertion/aggression is most likely due to prenatal exposure to the male hormones known as androgens (Friedman and Downey, 1995).

Now, however, the role of biology in core gender identity—and not just in gender role identity—is being reassessed, in part because of the unexpected outcome of one of John Money's cases. In 1967, at the age of seven months, one of a pair of identical male twins, whose penis was accidentally ablated during circumcision performed by means of electrocautery, was reassigned as female. The parents, described as young and confused, did not implement their decision to raise the child as a girl until he was seventeen months old, at which time they changed his name from John to Joan and changed his clothing and hairstyle (Money, 1975). When the baby was twenty-one months old, "the surgical first step of genital reconstruction as a female was undertaken" (Money, p. 67), by which I understand that an orchiectomy was performed. S(he) later had construction of a vagina and at age twelve was put on estrogens.

But by 1980, "Joan" asserted his maleness, contending that throughout his development his interests had always been masculine (Colapinto, 1997). He underwent the removal of her (his) breasts and at a later date had his penis reconstructed. The case of John (Joan) challenges the theory that core gender is almost totally socially "constructed."[1] As a result of this case, there is underway a reevaluation of the relative roles of sex of assignment and biology (particularly of prenatal horomones) in establishing core gender identity. (For a critique of the constructionist approach, see M. Diamond and K. Sigmundson [1997].)

Meyer-Bahlburg presents a good overview of the complex problems underlying the way we understand (and treat) intersexed patients. He reports that there are basically three philosophies governing gender assignment and reassignment (1998, p. 2). The traditional approach is determining the "true sex" which is usually understood as the true *biological* sex, in which case gender is assigned accordingly. But as Meyer-Bahlburg points out, when sex is made up of determining genes, sex chromosomes, gonads, sex-hormone levels, sex-hormone receptors, external genitalia, internal genitalia, sex-dimorphic brain structures, and perhaps still other factors, there's no way to identify "true" sex. The second policy, which for some years has been the one most accepted is called "optimal gender" and it attemps "to assign the gender that for a given child carries the best combined prognosis for good reproductive function (if attainable at all), good sexual function, minimal medical procedures, and overall gender-appropriate appearance, a stable gender identity, and a reasonably happy life" (p. 2). It is this latter policy which has dominated sex reassignment for intersexes. The third philosophy rests on the notion of acknowledging a

1. For an already well-known exception to the model of social construction, see a study by Imperato-McGinley and associates (1979).

"third gender," and it is the position of a small, but militant transgender movement in the United States made up of people with a variety of intersex manifestations (Bolan, 1994; see also *FTM International Newsletter*).

The preponderance of opinion still holds that in most intersexed children, sex reassignment has proved successful (Meyer-Bahlburg, 1998). Thus, sex of assignment is still believed to be the major determinant in core gender identity in most intersexed patients.

Whatever its genesis, core gender identity by and large establishes the same-sex object—male or female—as the primary model for imitation and identification (Ovesey and Person, 1973; Person and Ovesey, 1983). But the exceptions are clearly important to any comprehensive theory of the formation of core gender identity. These exceptions include not only those intersex patients in whom biological factors of one or another kind are sufficiently strong to overcome the power of the sex assignment, but also transsexuals, for whom some psychogenic constellation is presumed to play a role since most studies have failed to establish any biological factors (this in contradistinction to the case of intersex patients).

Sexuality, like gender, has its own complex developmental history. Sexuality, too, transcends any strictly dichotomous categorization and is composed of diverse elements: sexual object choice, sexual fantasy, eroticization, desire, and conscious sexual identity. Not only are there sexualities encompassing different objects (for example, opposite-sex objects, same-sex objects, opposite- *and* same-sex objects for bisexuals, part-object or inanimate objects for fetishists, and so on), but sexualities encompassing different aims (for example, orgasms through masturbation, genital union, oral-genital union, etc., or sexual pleasure through masochistic suffering or sadistic practices, and so on). Some patterns are difficult to categorize. Consider, for example, a woman who is exclusively homosexual in behavior but exclusively heterosexual in sexual fantasy. How would we classify her? And how are we to classify individuals whose sexual orientation changes abruptly in mid-life?

Just as our ideas about core gender gender are in flux, so, too are we reevaluating our ideas about sexual object choice, and placing more emphasis on the possible role of a hormonal influence. For example, Money and colleagues (1984) report that girls with the adrenogenital syndrome (who were exposed to androgen-like hormones prenatally) have a higher incidence of homosexual object choice than their peers.

We now conceptualize biological sex, gender, and sexuality as separate but mutually interacting entities, each of which has its own constituent parts. Not just the influence of prenatal hormones but the subjective experience throughout development of one's body may set limits to the social "construction" of gender and sex.

From the intrapsychic point of view, what usually—but not invariably—happens is that different basic fantasies develop depending on gender attribution. Thus, one's sense of oneself as female or male becomes the scaffolding around which personality develops and behavior takes shape. What is generally set into motion are self (or core) fantasies that are distinctive for males and females (Person, 1993). Not only does the young child form a mental image (representation) of herself (or himself) as gendered and of the people most important to her (or him) as gendered, but s(he) also forms gender specific representations of the interactions between them, their relationships, and even their dialogues. These representations of role relationships are a major component in the basic fantasies that are eventually formed.[2]

The gendered story line that is most fully articulated takes shape during the oedipal phase, its key components dependent on how the child identifies with, competes with, and loves and hates each parent, issues that are in turn dependent on the sex and in some way, not altogether clear, on precursors of the future sexual preference of the child.[3] During this phase, no matter what the outcome of the Oedipus complex, there is ample psychic room for both nonconflictual and conflictual cross-gender identifications. The result is a dizzying mosaic of individual patterns, all impacted on not just by the ongoing experiences of the oedipal phase but also by what has gone before.

Although our social conventions and our conscious self-appraisals make a sharp divide between masculinity and femininity, there exist in the preconscious and unconscious ranges of the mind a plethora of wishes, impulses, and fantasies that derive from each individual's specific developmental history and multiple identifications (Chodorow, 1994; Person, 1996). Against what appears to be a "dichotomous, categorical expression of gender," there exists in each person a complicated, multilayered interplay of fantasies and identifications, some "feminine," some "masculine" (Dahl, 1993, p. 117).

For most of us, the social pressure to conform acts to suppress any significant expression of cross-gender characteristics. The psychoanalysts Joseph and Anne-Marie Sandler have described in general how conformity is mediated, and their explanation has great relevance to gender conformity: "As the child develops the increasing capacity to anticipate the shaming and humiliating reactions of others . . . so he will become *his own* disapproving audience and

2. As Joseph and Anne-Marie Sandler put it, "Not only do the concepts of object choice and object relationship come together if we think in terms of the individual seeking particular role relationships (in the transference or outside in his everyday life) but the traditional distinction between the search for objects on the one hand and the search for wish-fulfillment or need-satisfaction on the other fades into insignificance. *The two can be regarded as being essentially the same.*" (Sandler and Sandler, 1978).

3. For example, most boys whose passionate interests resemble those of the effeminate boy in the film *Ma Vie en Rose* (*My Life in Pink*, 1977, a film by Alain Berliner) would be destined to be homosexual and to develop a different configuration of the Oedipus complex than those destined to be heterosexual.

will continually internalize the social situation in the form of . . . censorship. Only content that is acceptable will be permitted through to consciousness. It must be *plausible* and not ridiculous or 'silly.' In a way [this censorship] is . . . a narcissistic censorship. . . . The narcissism involved often tends to center around fears about being laughed at, being thought to be silly, crazy, ridiculous, or childish—essentially fears of being humiliated" (Sandler and Sandler, 1987, p. 337). Thus, as the growing child or adolescent discovers that his or her behavior and desires are at odds with the gender prescriptions of family culture, he or she suppresses or transforms them (Person, 1996).

While conformity leads to the suppression of many cross-gender identifications, desires, and fantasies, it does not necessarily lead to their eradication. Thus, each of us harbors a multiplicity of self-identifications that are suppressed under the aegis of conformity to cultural norms. In essence, conscious unity and unconscious diversity co-exist. The diversity, the lack of unity, in the unconscious and preconscious—in contrast to the conformity at the surface—may serve as a potential locus of shifts, of fluidity, in the expression of gender role identity, in response either to individual experiences or, on a larger scale, to shifting cultural mores (Person, 1996).

Generally speaking, our mosaic of identifications gives our specific gender role identity its uniqueness. In most individuals, surface behavior is generally consonant with what the culture prescribes as feminine or masculine gender role identity. Consequently, we come to identify ourselves as *either* and *only* masculine or feminine (though not always adequately so, as revealed, for example, in the statement, "I think I'm not really feminine enough").

In some individuals, different gender tendencies are not contained within an overall conscious sense of masculinity or femininity but emerge into consciousness as conflictual. For example, the study of transvestites—by definition, heterosexual—is a dramatic example of a divided and conflicted gender role identity. Transvestites alternate between their everyday public lives, most frequently lived as real "he-men," often in possession of hypermasculine jobs (for example, Green Beret, heart surgeon), and their private lives, in which they secretly, or sometimes openly, act out their desires to dress in women's clothes and even to impersonate women. The transvestite frequently alternates between an impulse to rid himself of his female identity—to throw out his female wardrobe and live totally as a man—and the reverse impulse, to rid himself of his male identity and live predominantly as a woman. Here we see a conflict between female and male identifications that has emerged into consciousness. The separate identifications appear to be the best solution the transvestite can manage to resolve (or contain) an underlying conflict, but the split itself has profound consequences for adaptation and is itself the source of new conflict (Ovesey and Person, 1976; Person and Ovesey, 1978). Less extreme split-gender identifications, even when they do not reach consciousness, may also be the source of further conflicts and symptoms.

Much less has been written about the consequences of masculine identifications in women than about feminine identifications in men. This may be because there are fewer reports of cross-gender disorders—particularly transsexualism and transvestism—in women. It may also be because femininity in men is more socially stigmatized than masculinity in women. But cross-gender identifications in women, and the problems that go with them, are surprisingly common as well as interestingly diverse in expression and underlying causes.

Cross-gender Identifications in Heterosexual Women

Because discussions of cross-gender problems often get bogged down in the confusion between unconscious, intra-psychic conflicts and the quite conscious feeling of being in conflict with one's culture, I find it useful to begin with Joan Rivière's concept of the feminine masquerade (1929). Rivière sees exaggerated femininity as a masquerade that some women consciously use to protect themselves against cultural prejudice at the same time that it can be understood as stemming from deep unconscious conflict.[4] Her concept of the feminine masquerade thus straddles two domains of discourse. As one commentator puts it, "[Her] paper gives us the psychical and the social together and simultaneously keeps them apart, returning to the former over the latter" (Heath, 1986, p. 57).

"Womanliness as Masquerade:" In her influential paper published in 1929, Rivière discusses a group of women "who wish for masculinity" and who, in order to avert the retribution consequently feared from men, put on "a mask of womanliness" (p. 303) as a defense. She presents the case of a successful woman who, each time she spoke in public, sought immediate reassurance from men in the form of sexual attentions: "To speak broadly, an analysis of her behavior after her performances showed that she was attempting to obtain sexual advances from . . . men by means of flirting and coquetting with them in a more or less veiled manner. The extraordinary incongruity of this attitude with her highly impersonal and objective attitude during her intellectual performance . . . was a problem." Her flirtatious behavior was understood by Rivière to be "an unconscious attempt to ward off the anxiety which would ensue on account of the reprisals she anticipated from the father-figures after

4. Louise Kaplan in her book *Female Perversions* (1990) suggests that some masquerades can serve as the equivalent of perversions in men.

her intellectual performance" (p. 305). Here Rivière touches on the woman's need to fend off the cultural prejudices against women as thinkers.

But Rivière also proposed an explanation for the woman's behavior that had to do with unconscious conflict. Using a Kleinian perspective, she described both her patient's parents as her rivals and, consequently, objects of her sadistic fury. The patient's original trauma was a "disappointment or frustration during sucking or weaning, coupled with experiences during the primal scene which is interpreted in oral terms, [in consequence of which] extremely intense sadism develops towards both parents" (p. 309). Thus she wishes to disembowel the mother and devour her and castrate her father by biting off his penis. Through her professional success she becomes her father—that is, she acquires his penis—but through her masquerade of womanliness, she dominates and conciliates her nice husband. The masquerade is, as Rivière puts it, a "reaction-formation and concealment of her hostility," which allowed her to gratify her id-impulses, her narcissistic ego and her super-ego at one and the same time" (p. 311). It is a disguise in which she presents herself as castrated, and thus it serves as an antidote to having successfully performed in what she perceives as a masculine role.

Although women are more comfortable with their ambitions today, some still invoke the masquerade not so much to disguise so-called masculine ambitions as to disguise aggression. Some of the world's great femme fatales are unconsciously utilizing stereotypic and exaggerated feminine wiles to disguise the aggression embedded in their manipulations and ambitions. For these women, no less than for Rivière's subjects, the fact that the masquerade is consciously invoked does not detract from the fact that it may also be rooted in preconscious or unconscious conflict. We miss out on the complexities when we look at this phenomenon from a strictly social perspective.

Masculine Identifications in Heterosexual Women: In the two vignettes that I will present, there is evidence that marked unconscious masculine identifications give rise to interpersonal conflicts and neurotic enactments. Both patients were unremarkably feminine in appearance and had no conscious awareness of any conflict around the issue of gender. Neither can be adequately understood within the terms of the cultural debate about gender. That is, their problems have little or nothing to do with what the culture defines as feminine or masculine. Their problems were not connected to latent homosexuality. Nor could they be explained in terms of penis envy understood literally as organ envy. Both women suffered conflictual cross-gender identifications that stemmed from different sources and were manifest in different symptomatic complexes.

Case 1: A recent transplant to New York from San Francisco, Ms. Eastlake, a woman in her mid-twenties, entered treatment for work-related problems.[5] Eventually she confided that she could have an orgasm during intercourse only if she fantasized walking through the door of a yellow-painted, wooden Victorian house, a fantasy that first appeared in her early adolescence as a masturbatory accompaniment.

The image of the yellow house turned out to carry a heavy freight of symbolic meaning that unfolded only gradually during the course of the analysis. The color yellow referred symbolically to her almost obligatory preference for Asian men as sexual partners: in essence, she could not be easily aroused by men other than Asians. Over time we traced this strong preference to the historical circumstance that from the time she was three until she was six her father had been stationed in Vietnam; on an unconscious level she associated Asian men with her father. In treatment she discovered that her preference for Asians concealed an underlying oedipal fixation. (On the surface, a Caucasian girl's almost exclusive preference for Asian men might look like father rejection.)

However, oedipal resolutions invariably draw on what has gone before. When Ms. Eastlake was finally able to talk about her fantasy and begin to analyze it, it was key to her tackling a much deeper and more painful problem than a simple oedipal fixation. She revealed that, to her distress, while she was sexually drawn to Asian men, she was at the same time deeply ashamed of them. She viewed her partners' smooth, relatively hairless bodies as a sign of their effeminacy. Nonetheless, seeing her partner as feminine (castrated), turned out to be key to her ability to reach a climax. On the preconscious level, it allowed her to maintain the underlying fantasy that she was the phallic partner, her lover feminine. Hence her orgasm was tied to the moment that she, as a kind of body phallus traversing the doorway of the yellow house, established her phallic prowess.

The underlying wish in the yellow house fantasy was to posit herself as the active, penetrating participant during sex and to deny any sense of being passive and penetrated; it is she who crosses the threshold, not a man who enters her. The fantasy image disguises the patient's underlying repudiation of what she deems the passive feminine role while still allowing her to enjoy sex, so long as it is with Asian men viewed as feminine. The yellow color of the house is associated to the skin color of the Asian man.

But in addition to its oedipal components (her father longing), what was being expressed in her fantasy was compliance with her mother's wish that she be a penis-girl, a kind of substitute husband during her father's absence, and also her own need to differentiate herself from an older and very feminine

5. I first reported this case in *By Force of Fantasy: How We Make Our Lives*, 1995.

sister, with whom she felt inadequate to compete. Adding to the complexities of the Victorian house symbol was the fact that her mother had grown up in just such a house; thus the yellow house symbolized both her mother and her father.

For Ms. Eastlake, her masculine identification was fostered by a longing for her mother, from whom she felt she lacked adequate attention. Therefore she took on the role of substitute husband that her mother prescribed, and in her fantasy life she symbolically became a kind of body phallus. Thus in fantasy she could provide a fleshly link to her mother. At the same time, she preserved enough identification with her mother so that she could fantasize an oedipal romance with her absent father.

As it turned out, her shame concerning the "effeminacy" of her Asian partners was a projection of her own sense of impaired gender adequacy. She had not been either "man" or "woman" enough to please her mother. The yellow-house fantasy, then, encompasses a minor cross-gender identification, though a largely circumscribed one; that is, she never consciously wanted to be male, never consciously hated being female, as would a woman with a more pronounced cross-gender identification. Nor was she ever drawn to women sexually.

Analysis of the yellow-house fantasy was pivotal in her treatment, leading her to recognize her repudiation of femininity in many areas of her life, not just the sexual one, and to deal with its causes in her early life. The process ultimately freed her to interact with men from different backgrounds (not excluding her own), to more completely accept her own sexual identity as female, to connect with a man as both a sexual partner and an equal, and to regard Asian men as *men*.[6]

Case 2: In her mid-thirties when first seen, Ms. Blondell was a powerful, tough-talking woman in the entertainment industry. She was married to a substantial figure in the same industry, though she was clearly the dominant force in their union.[7]

Ms. Blondell suffered periodic bouts of hypochondriasis, centered around any minor complaints she had—for example, a slight temperature, a cough, or any irregularity in her menstrual cycle—and these symptoms, along with an emergent conflict at work, were the proximate cause of her entering treatment.

6. However, the fantasy itself was never entirely eliminated, nor was that ever the goal. The point of analyzing a fantasy is hardly ever to eradicate it (except in those few instances when enactment would prove devastating to oneself, the object of the fantasy, or both—as, for example, when pedophile fantasies are on the verge of being enacted). Rather, the goal is to use the fantasy to delineate and resolve core conflicts that continue to impede the patient's life. Sometimes the fantasy fades under the spotlight of analysis, sometimes not.

7. I was reminded of this patient in the course of editing the IPA Monograph *On Freud's "A Child Is Being Beaten"* (1997).

In the course of treatment it emerged that she had "fits" of beating her six-year-old son when she found him slow to respond to her wishes. (This was a completely ego-alien symptom, which did not manifest itself in her relationship with her daughters.) She remembered that as a child, beginning at about the age of eight or ten, she had had a, pleasurable and self-soothing fantasy of beating a male infant—a fantasy that was not, however, a prelude to sexual arousal.

Ms. Blondell was the older and more gifted of two daughters born to a successful and bon vivant father and a somewhat depressed and inhibited mother. She was extravagantly devoted to her father though he was not overly attentive to her. In part, her intense father attachment originated in her flight from her mother's suffocating devotion and her sense of her mother as a failed person. Her mother had selected her, as the first born, to fulfill her own unrealized ambitions.

Not only was Ms. Blondell closer to her father than to her mother but she despised her mother, whom she saw as weak and inadequate. Her major conscious identification was with her father. Because she devalued her mother and was ashamed of her, she had formed a counteridentification with her father, a kind of reaction formation against a deeply disturbing identification with a demeaned maternal figure.

As she grew toward womanhood, Ms. Blondell had an apparently good adaptation; she did well academically and was socially active and capable of close friendship. She entered into a robust heterosexual sex life. Already established in her field, she married in her late twenties and promptly had three children, the oldest of whom was the son, her favorite, and the one toward whom she would periodically erupt in rage.

Ms. Blondell's dynamics are perhaps best understood within the frame of Freud's description of the sequences of the "a-child-is-being beaten" fantasy. Freud described this fantasy as occurring in a three-stage sequence in girls: (1) the fantasizer sees her father beating another child, her rival; (2) she is beaten by her father; (3) a father substitute, such as a teacher, is beating children, usually boys, and the fantasizer is again present, as in the first stage, as a spectator rather than as a participant. Ultimately, Freud suggested that the beating fantasy condenses a girl's debased genital love for her father and punishment for her incestuous wishes.

In Ms. Blondell's beating fantasy, she is the dominant figure towering over the small boy whom she is beating. Her fantasy can be interpreted as a variant of what Freud described as the third stage of the girl's beating fantasy (that stage which Freud believed signaled the fantasizer's assumption of a masculine role as a resolution of oedipal love). In Ms. Blondell's fantasy, the action is not projected onto some nameless (male) authority figure beating nameless boys, a fantasy in which the fantasizer identifies with the victim: *she* is the aggressor beating a helpless boy. This fantasy embodies her wish to be masculine or, more accurately her wish not to be feminine, largely the result of her need to disidentify from her mother.

Paradoxically, though, she may have been identifying with what appears to have been her mother's own masculine identification. Late into treatment Ms. Blondell told of an event in her early adolescence about which she was particularly embarrassed. Looking out her bedroom window, she saw her mother in the backyard, her eyes glazed, staring into the middle distance, standing with her legs apart and urinating like a man, apparently not wearing any underwear. Ms. Blondell was so frightened and humiliated by what she saw—and thought of as a mental disturbance on her mother's part—that she had never previously told anyone what she had witnessed. She had always seen her mother as unkempt and had long sensed that her mother had repudiated her own femaleness. But since the episode in the backyard, she had intuited that her mother was impersonating a man, and she was horrified.

Ms. Blondell maintained a feminine identification through a *complementary* relationship with her father, not through an *identificatory* relationship with her mother. (In essence, heterosexuals get two chances to work out their primary gender role identity, through an identificatory relationship with the same-sex parent or a complementary relationship with the opposite-sex parent. If they have grown up in a one-parent family they may enlist surrogates to fill in the gap.) Her oedipal tie to her father was too strong for her to renounce her erotic desire for him in the service of any masculine identification, however engendered. That is, her feminine identification was maintained through—and in large part originated in—her idyllic infatuation with her father. Throughout her life, she maintained femininity through her sexual attraction to men and her attractiveness to them. Her core identity was that of a heterosexual woman, but she had strong masculine identifications in some other areas of her life, particularly in her professional life. This hybrid gender identity preserved her heterosexuality and her desire for pregnancy.

Ms. Blondell's adaptation worked fairly well except for the beating "fits" she inflicted on her son, which thoroughly disturbed her. The invocation of a beating fantasy with her in the active role protected her against an underlying sense of vulnerability. But because her son represented her childhood alter ego, beating him was beating herself; therefore it also represented a kind of self-punishment or masochistic activity. Moreover, her hypochondriacal symptoms represented punishment for her angry rejection of her mother, her father love, and her incestuous longings. It was her guilt that stoked self-punishment in the form of hypochondriacal anxiety.

Why did her masochism take the form of hypochondriasis rather than either characterological masochism or sexual masochism? The choice of symptom is always overdetermined. In Ms. Blondell's case the symptom may have been structured in part by an appendectomy when she was seven. Her illness, hospitalization, and surgery appear to have been interpreted as punishments for her father longing and served as a precursor to structure her guilt along hypochondriacal lines. The result was that her fear led to a preoccupying hypervigilance. From the dynamic point of view, Ms. Blondell's hypochondriasis was the equivalent of a beating fantasy with herself as the victim.

What of the role of penis envy? In the course of discussing her beating fantasy, Ms. Blondell recovered a memory of poking a boy in the neck with a broomstick when she was about five, a transgression for which she was severely punished. This is a kind of screen memory that embodies some early penis envy. However, this penis envy appeared to be not so much the result of envy of another male as it was a desire for a bodily signifier that she was unlike her mother.

Paradoxically, what may well have set a limit to her invocation of the penis as such a signifier was her unconscious recognition that her mother had either a fantasy penis or an imaginary one—that was how she understood her urinating in a standing position. Thus the intensity of her penis envy was limited by her need to *disidentify* with her mother, as both demeaned female and phallic woman.

Ms. Blondell formed her femininity not out of any identification with her mother but in complementarity with her father; in contrast, Ms. Eastlake achieved femininity in part through identification with her mother, in part in complementarity with her father. Ms. Eastlake would be more likely than Ms. Blondell to at some point develop a homosexual inclination insofar as her psyche was organized in part around mother longing. It seems unlikely that Ms. Blondell would ever express any homosexual inclination, simply because she had such an aversion to her mother's female flesh.

The most significant element in Ms. Blondell's analysis was her need to disidentify from her mother, not penis envy. Ms. Blondell resembles to some degree those women who in analysis exhibit strong masculine identifications, but who consciously self-identify not as masculine or feminine but as neuter.

Neuter Women: I have treated two high functioning professional women and seen in consultation two others whose appearances and demeanors were unremarkably feminine despite their repudiation of any self-identification as feminine. Interestingly, each referred to herself as neuter. (I have been told by several colleagues that they, too, have seen women who independently self-identify as neuter.) Unlike those women described by Rivière who invoke extreme femininity as a masquerade to disguise their "masculine" aspirations, these women mobilized feminine "disguises" or masquerades to maintain a necessary connection *to* men. Their romance with men persevered even though they had renounced their identifications as female. Although they appeared feminine to outside observers, underneath they felt they were neuter. (Thus, they went further in their cross-gender identification than Ms. Eastlake and Ms. Blondell, both of whom maintained a conscious sense of themselves as female and feminine.)

Women who self-identify as neuter generally want to maintain a romantic relationship with a male, but their need to disidentify with femaleness is sometimes intense enough to dampen any wish for pregnancy (not necessarily for motherhood) and to impact negatively on their enjoyment of their own female bodies. They often have an aversion to the changes of puberty, to the growth of breasts and to menstruation, and often to the act of intercourse, despite the urgency for some kind of physical connection to a man.

One such "neuter" patient was Ms. Dorman, an ad executive whose therapy I supervised. She sought treatment in order to improve her sexual performance so that her boyfriend would marry her. She is a beautiful woman who believes she looks masculine, though few would agree with her. She covers over a major masculine identification with a feminine veneer, specifically to maintain an attachment to men, with whom she desires sex of a specific kind: she is primarily interested in performing fellatio. It is this kind of attachment to the penis that ultimately gives her pleasure. In essence she is a "suckling." She uses the penis as a breast-penis with the semen (milk) serving as a substitute for parental solicitude. Although she responds sexually, lubricates, and has vaginal contractions, she feels no sexual pleasure; her vagina is virtually anaesthetized.

Ms. Dorman is the elder of two daughters of significantly impaired parents, both of whom appear to have borderline features. She remembered that throughout her life she had consciously tried to be different from her mother. Her father brutalized her mother, and Ms. Dorman appears to have identified with the aggressor rather than with the victim.

From earliest childhood she repudiated her femaleness. As a young child she remembers asking her mother how one would know if she were a girl or boy if she wasn't wearing clothes. Essentially, she denied any anatomic sexual distinction and thought the sexual difference pertained only to what she wore. She was unhappy and ashamed when she first got her menstrual period and tried to hide her stained undergarments in her closet. She was humiliated when her mother discovered them and confronted her. Until very recently she hated her breasts, which she saw only as organs of sustenance for others and as potential cancer sites. But in the context of her relationship with her boyfriend she had begun to have pleasurable sensations in her breasts even before she entered therapy. She sees pregnancy as a disease and loathes the idea of nurturing children. At the same time she is a rescuer and a nurturer in more impersonal kinds of situations. Here, perhaps, is to be seen the remnant of some long forgotten affection for one or the other parent.

In a sense, Ms. Dorman is an extreme case of the neuter woman, but her unconscious masculine identification comes much closer to consciousness. She almost always identifies with the male characters in movies and books and tends to see most women as victims. She hopes in therapy to resolve her conflicts so that she can marry her boyfriend, who she feels loves her. It is for this reason—to be attached to him and to his penis—that she wants to change. This patient presents more difficult therapeutic problems than the two patients previously presented, though the recovery of feelings in her breasts even prior to therapy bodes well.

I have distinguished between masculine identifications that do not affect femininity and others that involve some degree of feminine self-doubt. Masculine identifications may take the form of pleasurable nonconflictual identifications with one's father's interests, ideals, or modes of being. These identifications are readily observable in many high achieving women who are justifiably irritated by cultural prejudices about achievement such as theirs and by being labeled as too masculine. In contrast are the more conflicted cross-gender identifications I have described in this chapter.

Among the many diverse dynamics that account for conflictual masculine identifications in women, I've emphasized four: (1) the need to serve as a masculine figure (sometimes in fantasy, a woman with a penis) in order to connect with the mother or mother surrogate, but accompanied by enough oedipal romance so that heterosexuality is maintained; (2) the need to repudiate any female identification because of a strong negative response to the maternal figure (one of disgust or revulsion) or a fundamental disruption in the mother-daughter interaction; (3) a specific counteridentification with a mother perceived as a victim and an identification with the aggressor; and (4) identification with the mother's masculinity. In some instances, masculinity may be the product of the parents' subliminal communication that they wanted a son, not a daughter.

Masculine identifications in women are now seen more as the product of vicissitudes in separation-individuation and in early object relations than as the result of penis envy (as originally formulated in psychoanalytic theory) and its impact on oedipal dynamics. In fact, persistent and intractable penis envy, like all other symptoms, is a multidetermined compromise formation.

My focus here has been on the dynamics of masculinity in women, which only sometimes relate to penis envy. Even when penis envy is prominent it has more to do with early object relations, particularly the mother-child relationship and the oedipal situation, than with penis envy per se. In particular I have emphasized that the wish for a penis or the fantasy of a penis may serve to reconnect to the mother. (For a more general view of the penis-as-link, see Birksted-Breen, 1966.) It may also serve as the insignia of disidentification from a maternal figure.[8]

More Extreme Cross-Gender Identification

Cross-gender identifications may be of such magnitude as to constitute cross-gender disorders. As cases of major cross-gender disorders, I include women who invoke imaginary (not just fantasy) penises to provide stability, extremely masculine lesbians, and female transsexuals. In these women, masculinity is evident in behavior, mannerisms, and desires. (I take cognizance of lesbian writing that views the caricature of masculinity as theater, as a gender critique; I credit this as a brilliant explanation of intermittent impersonation but as a contributory element—insufficient motivation in and of itself—to the *ongoing* assumption of masculinity so often observed.) Here one is addressing not just the multi-layering of feminine and masculine identifications or even conflicted cross-gender identifications but an almost wholesale repudiation of those characteristics that are consonant with femininity. (But not always. What is sometimes preserved is the desire to be pregnant or to have children. However, the desire for procreation should probably not be viewed as exclusively feminine.) In these cases, the primary source of cross-gender identifications almost invariably occurs in the preoedipal period, though one must also take account of the possibility that constitution and temperament have predisposed to the creation of intrapsychic conflicts or their resolution through cross-gender identifications (Lothstein, 1983).

For most women who harbor masculine identifications of such degree that they constitute cross-gender disorders, the preferential sexual object choice is female. But not always.

Even though one might assume that a female transsexual would by definition want to live as a man and that this would generally include the wish to have sexual relationships with a woman, this is not always the case. Consider the following story. During the course of my research on transsexualism, I met a male transsexual and a female transsexual who had formed an intense romantic and sexual liaison. One of the ties that bound them was their shared

8. George Awad suggests that three distinct interrelated states have been identified that fall under the general rubric of penis envy: "*envy* of the other's superiority or success in the context of the discovery of genital differences, a *wish* to have a penis as a result of that envy, and the *fantasy* of having one" (Awad, 1992).

fantasy during sex that it was the unoperated female transsexual who possessed the one penis in play—that is, the male transsexual's penis. When I met them, they were in a major relational crisis because the male transsexual's desire to have transsexual surgery and rid himself of his penis threatened the female transsexual with the loss of her virtual (partially actualized) penis—that is, his penis, which she experienced as her own. When I was last in touch with them, they still maintained their tenuous balance.

Perhaps even more compelling evidence for the complexity of the relationship between sex and gender in to be seen in the emergence of a new group of female-to-male transsexuals (FMT) who describe themselves as TransFags, whose preferential sexual object choices are homosexual men and who view themselves as male homosexuals engaged in homosexual relationships with other men. (See, for example, *FTM International Newsletter* and *TransFag Rag: Information and Networking for Gay/Bi Transmen.*)[9]

Conclusion

Although there is a new openness within psychoanalytic theory to more complex and pluralistic theories of gender,[10] variations remain difficult to conceptualize and categorize, particularly as they pertain to women. It is perhaps telling that while we generally refer to cross-gender identifications in men, we more often speak of penis envy and masculine aspirations in women.

I have presented a clinical account of several kinds of masculine identifications in women. My aim has been to show that significant masculine identifications occur in heterosexual women, not just in homosexual women.

Viewing cross-gender identifications as the result of unconscious conflict may go against the grain of those who herald "the reconciliation of masculinity and femininity in the post-oedipal female mind." This position holds, as psychoanalyst Donna Bassin puts it in a thoughtful article, "that symbols, with their transitional bridging functions, can reunite such early, now-polarized

9. The meetings of FTMs are organized in or around San Francisco as are the meetings of TransFags. Thus far I have seen only one research patient who self-identifies as male (though she has no wish to undergo sex transformation surgery) and whose strong sexual preference is heterosexual men. In contrast, TransFags self-identify as male homosexuals and their preferential object choice is *homosexual* men. While one would have thought that they would have trouble integrating into a homosexual community, in which so much focus is placed on the penis per se, their reports seem to indicate that they have overcome this hurdle. Here we may be witnessing the female counterpart to transvestitic transsexuals. After all, transvestitic transsexuals want to become women *and* to relate sexually to women. There is a major difference, however. While transvestic transsexuals view themselves as women having sex with women, they do not pick female sexual partners who are lesbians.

10. In part this change derives from an internal dynamic within psychoanalysis (object relations theory, self psychology), in part from major insights emerging from gay studies and women's studies.

component instincts as active and passive, and dichotomous images of genitals" (1996, p. 157). What Bassin proposes is possible up to a point. A broadening of what the culture deems permissible will allow more nonconflictual cross-gender characteristics to be expressed and integrated. And this is an extremely important project. However, the creative use of symbols will not easily transcend the distress attached to cross-sex identifications that are born in conflict or later on embroiled in conflict.[11] Moreover, it is never a therapeutic goal that each and every separate unconscious tendency should find expression in either behavior or consciousness (Morris Eagle, personal communication).

The practical problem is that many cross-gender identifications are extremely difficult to resolve, as clinical work with the more extreme cross-gender problems makes clear. Perhaps the most interesting question of all is why identifications with one or another person, father or mother, is represented in the unconscious in terms of masculinity or femininity. In other words, why do such identifications carry a gender valence? This is, at one and the same time, both a pragmatic and a metaphysical question. Sigmund Freud, Melanie Klein, and Jacques Lacan have all tried to answer this question in the terms of their particular theoretical perspectives. The point on which they all agree is that our unconscious representations of masculinity and femininity are in no way covalent with biology and social reality but correspond to an internal reality that is shaped from the beginning in terms of fantasy.

Given that gender is profoundly related to, if not determined by, one's sex, perhaps the question should be not why there are only two genders, but why we are so insistent on sharply dichotomizing them. It is the *rigidity* of the gender division that is most disquieting, the degree to which we are invested in making black-and-white distinctions as to gender. Muriel Dimen observes that referring to the masculinities and the femininities rather than to masculinity and femininity does not alter their basic duality (personal communication). I would add that the same is true for the current practice of speaking of the heterosexualities and the homosexualities.

The problem of gender, then, is a question not only of twoness but of either/or-ness. Given what we know about the diversity and fluidity of gender, why are we so absolutely rigid—and by "we" I mean both the culture we live in and the profession we practice—in our concept of the duality of gender? Of course it is just not *our* culture that does this. There is a profound insistence in

11. An extreme intellectual "perversion" in the current cultural *zeitgeist* can be seen in the case of transsexualism, where transsexuals are often romantically viewed as portraying the ultimate freedom—the ability to jump over the strictures of biology. Yet most analysts who have worked with transsexuals observe the pervasive internal conflicts and unhappiness that transsexuals—operated or unoperated—generally suffer. The important and necessary cultural support for tolerance of variations in gender role should not confuse us as to the psychological reality of those who suffer from cross-gender disorders.

most cultures we know about on maintaining this distinction—even though the actual *content* of gender role identity varies greatly from culture to culture.[12] The insistence on duality speaks to something apparently deep within us, no matter how transient, fluid, and variable the manifestations of that duality are.

12. Meyer-Bahlburg (1998) reminds us that some cultures employ the designation of a "third gender" to describe individuals who adopt cross-gender behavioral characteristics. The concept may also be applied to particular local groups (clusters) of intersexed individuals. In the first case one sees the so-called "berdache" categories in some Native-American societies. In the second category (intersexes) one sees, for example, the guevedoces in the Dominican Republic where there is a disorder in which a group of boys develop penises only at puberty (Imperato-McGinley et al., 1979).

18

Male Sexuality and Power

1986

ETHEL S. PERSON

MALE PSYCHOLOGY is beginning to attract the kind of attention paid to its female counterpart since the early 1970s. However, while the assumption that female sexual masochism is primary, universal, and defining has been challenged, the popular belief that male sexuality is innately aggressive and sadistic has persisted with minimal questioning.

The cultural stereotype of male sexuality is of a kind of phallic omnipotence and supremacy, a phallus invested with the power of mastery. At the very least, this view depicts a large, powerful, untiring phallus attached to a very cool male, long on self-control, experienced, competent, and knowledgeable enough to make women crazy with desire. As Zilbergeld has said, "It's two feet long, hard as steel, and can go all night" (1978, p. 23). In the shared cultural fantasy, even the normally reticent female is perceived to be utterly powerless and receptive when confronted by pure macho sexuality.

But phallic power is also viewed as easily corrupted into sexual domination and violence. This is clear in the common depiction of male sexuality in pornography, movies, and TV, in sexual humor, and in much of the major fiction of our time.

Although Kate Millet's *Sexual Politics* (1970) is certainly one of the seminal books in the feminist movement, it is essentially a study of male psychology and a condemnation of the power motive perceived in male sexuality. She analyzes the work of four distinguished male authors whose descriptions of male sexuality centered on ideas of ascendancy and power: Henry Miller, D. H.

Lawrence, Norman Mailer, and Jean Genet. According to Millett, "As one recalls both the euphemism and the idealism of descriptions of coitus in the Romantic poets (Keats's "Eve of Saint Agnes") or the Victorian novelists (Hardy, for example) and contrasts it with Miller or William Burroughs, one has an idea of how contemporary literature has absorbed not only the truthful explicitness of pornography, but its antisocial character as well. Since this tendency to hurt or insult has been given free expression, it has become far easier to assess sexual antagonism in the male" (1970, p. 46). Zilbergeld quotes Harold Robbins, Mickey Spillane, James Baldwin, and others, as well as Henry Miller and Norman Mailer to make the same point about our culture's view of male sexuality as domineering and even violent.

There is a genre of popular fiction in which the common thread is heroic, macho, adventurous, and virile. Men's preoccupation with this type of literature is comparable to women's with the romance novel. The female novels are so popular that the word "harlequin," after the publishing house of the same name, has become a descriptive term. The equivalent term for the male novel might be "herotica." A passage from Eric van Lustbader's *The Miko* (1984) captures the way male sexuality is portrayed in this body of writing. The plot hinges on the idea that Akiko, a woman trained in the arcane mystic and martial arts, is sworn to avenge a loved one by killing the hero, Nicholas. She is portrayed as a master assassin in perfect control of all her feelings, but her response to Nicholas compels her to have a sexual encounter with him:

> For the first time in her life Akiko was open to the universe. Nothing in all her long arduous training had caused this ignition inside of her.
>
> She was so dizzy that she was doubly grateful for his strong arms about her. All breath had left her as he had uttered her name, how she ached for him! Her thighs were like water, unable to support her. She felt a kind of ecstasy at his touch she thought only possible in orgasm.
>
> What was happening to her? Swept away, still a dark part of her mind yammered to be heard. What strange force had invaded her mind? What turned her plans of vengeance inside out? What made her feel this way about a hated enemy? [p. 277].

In one remarkable example of "herotica," the hero is so well schooled in the erotic arts that if he hates a woman and wishes to destroy her forever, he makes love to her so skillfully that she knows that she will never be satisfied by any other man.

Observers from diverse disciplines have suggested that macho sexuality either is sanctioned as the cultural ideal or is an accurate portrayal of male sexuality. May claims that, in addition to the general cultural directive for males to be assertive, "the popular prescription for male sexuality is also heavily invested with assertion and activity. The man is supposed to be constantly on the move and on the make. The image of the tireless seducer differs only in style and degree from that of the rapist" (1980, p. 131). The only question is whether the male attracts and seduces the female or overpowers and forces her. May's view echoes that of Susan Brownmiller. In *Against Our Will: Men, Women and Rape* (1976), she declares: "Throughout history no theme grips the masculine imagination with greater constancy and less honor than the myth of the heroic rapist. As man conquered the world, so too he conquers the female. Down through the ages, imperial conquest, exploits of valor and expressions of love have gone hand in hand with violence to women in thought and in deed" (p. 320).

As already noted, there is an assumption, particularly in some of the feminist literature, that the pervasive macho image accurately reflects the male's preoccupation with sexual domination and violence. Sexual violence, including wife abuse, marital rape, and rape, is regarded as the tip of the iceberg, an indicator of the innate male propensity to sexual sadism. This position postulates a continuum between male sexual violence and normal male sexuality. Yet there has been no systematic attempt to assess the pervasiveness of the macho stereotype as an ego ideal in individual men or to gauge the relationship of the cultural stereotype of macho sexuality to the interior fantasy life of men. The larger question is whether the domination and sadism fantasies and impulses one does see are primary. Is male sexuality inherently aggressive, or are the aggressive fantasies a reaction to life experiences or compensation for feelings of inadequacy?

In this chapter, I challenge the popular cultural notion that male sexuality is by its nature aggressive. To some degree, conscious male sexual fantasies, as revealed in both clinical work and non-clinical survey studies, do resemble the cultural stereotype. But there are significant differences. First of all, sexual violence and aggression are not primary fantasy themes for many males. Some men do not have fantasies of sexual domination. Control both of the sexual apparatus and of the partner takes precedence in the fantasies of a significant portion of the population.

Furthermore, it would be naive to restrict one's conclusions about male sexuality to conscious wishful fantasies alone. Fearful fantasies must also be taken into account in assessing the overall nature of male sexuality. Taken together, they present a more balanced picture. Wishful fantasies often are about domination and aggression, but they are also about size, hardness, endurance, skill, and willing females. Fears are partly the negative reflections of the wishful fantasies; as such, they focus on inadequate penis size, impotence, lack of skill, fear of female rejection, female damage to the male (vagina dentata fantasies), and homosexual dread. (While unconscious fears do not appear to be fantasies, at least not to those who experience them, they are clearly fantasies or fantasy derivatives.) Most important, data from analyses reveal the unconscious fantasies of patients that underlie conscious wishful and fearful fantasies and suggest the correspondence of unconscious fantasies to developmental events.

The pervasiveness of the dominant and aggressive theme of male sexual fantasies—and the macho image in general—may represent a shared cultural ideal to some degree, but it is ego-syntonic or an actual personal ego ideal for only a minority of men. Those men for whom sexual domination is a primary concern generally reveal particular conflicts in their sexual development. However, the nature and origin of their unconscious conflicts as revealed in psychoanalyses point to the universal "fault lines" in more typical (or "normal") male development.

Drawing on conscious male wishful and fearful fantasies and some clinical material that reveals the interplay of macho sexuality and sexual fears, I am here attempting to place power and domination concerns in perspective by proposing that control over the penis and the sexual object is a central concern in male sexuality, more fundamental than aggression, and intimately intertwined with the genesis of castration anxiety. The emphasis on the power of the phallus and power remedies vis-à-vis the female (or male) partner are, at least in part, compensatory responses to anxieties engendered in the male developmental experience. These anxieties must be understood as an amalgam of castration anxiety, fear and envy of both sexes, and the fear (or experience) of loss of the object and loss of love.

My focus is on some of the sources of the central anxieties concerning control that have been less extensively explored than castration anxiety. The case material I present suggests one set of developmental factors that predisposes men, on the one hand, to unusually intense sexual anxiety and fear of loss of the object and, on the other hand, to sexual dominance and macho sexuality as compensatory mechanisms. Male sexual aggression may be almost universal, but it is a transitory and generally inconsequential stage in childhood unless it is reinvoked and consolidated in a series of power strategies as a defense against sexual anxieties. In this respect, male sexual aggression may be viewed as analogous to primary and secondary female sexual masochism.

Conscious Fantasies

Fantasy life is extremely varied, and sexual fantasies are no exception. Among men, the wide range (even within our one culture) is well documented in popular books and professional journals. But despite this variability, there are fundamental differences between male and female fantasy life.[1]

Female sexual fantasies may be diffusively romantic; male fantasies are usually explicitly sexual and often impersonal. Autonomy, mastery, and physical prowess are central concerns (May, 1980). Male fantasies frequently portray domination, as the widespread rape, control, and transgression themes would indicate. But although domination is unquestionably a major motif, male fantasies may also be passive, submissive, or masochistic in content. In fact, Freud first described "feminine" masochism as it occurred in men (1924b).

There are other male fantasies that are at least as common, possibly more so. Two of the most common are fantasies of the "omni-available woman" and "lesbian" sex (see Person, 1986b, reprinted here as Chapter 19). The omni-available woman is totally accessible. She is often fantasized as lying on a couch awaiting the arrival of her lover, forever lubricated, forever ready, forever desiring. Both from my own patients' reports and from reading the popular and scientific reports of fantasies, it seems evident that for men the woman's availability, ready sexuality, and unqualified approval constitute a major common thread. It is her availability and enthusiasm that bolster his virility.

Barclay (1973), in a study on the sexual fantasies of college men and women, noted that "male fantasies sounded like features of *Playboy* Magazine or pornographic books, and included elaborate descriptions of the imagined sexual partner. . . . They were stereotyped . . . without personal involvement. Women are always seductive and straightforward, ready to have intercourse at any given moment . . . [with a] major emphasis on visual imagery" (p. 205).

In men's fantasies, women are viewed as desirable but dispensable. In contrast, as Thorne (1971) points out, women see themselves as both desirable and indispensable.

Young boys, prepubescent and pubescent, commonly have fantasies about naked girls available to them in such powerless positions as being bound to a bed (Thorne, 1971). These often contain elements of sadism (Lukianowicz, 1960). A young boy's sexual fantasies are mainly involved with the exploration and discovery of female anatomy. They are colored by a literal preoccupation with girls. Boys seem generally to fantasize about the sexual compliance of girls or about sexual advances from them. In these fantasies, girls don't complain about the bad treatment they may be getting but gratefully accept the status of sexual toys.

1. The only major statistical analysis of fantasies remains that of Kinsey et al. (1948, 1953). They discovered that not only the content but also the formal attributes of sexual fantasies vary with gender. For example, most males fantasize during masturbation and have nocturnal sex dreams. Fantasy among females is much more variable. Females tend to fantasize about what has actually occurred; males more frequently about unfulfilled desires. (Kinsey's group also noted some social-class differences that alert us to the fact that fantasies from any one sample are not easily generalized.)

The same themes continue to be found in the fantasies of young men, although some of the overt force may be reduced. The developmental significance of the change in male fantasies as boys grow older—the partial replacement of physical dominance as a theme by the presence of a bevy of willing females—suggests that these fantasies are on a continuum. The common feature is the assurance of the sexual availability of the female. The wish is that girls are panting for sex; in extreme cases, this accounts for the common defense in rape trials—"she was really asking for it."

Forcing a partner is one way of insuring her presence. Nancy Friday, in her study of write-in fantasies (1980), found that the largest single fantasy category for men was of sadomasochistic sex. But she noted that the wish was not usually to hurt the woman, only that she enjoy the encounter. This fantasy, in its intent, seems to be on a continuum with the fantasied presence of a woman in a perpetual state of sexual readiness, with no other purpose than to receive the man's sexual advances. Control of the woman, even in domination fantasies, is most often in the service of phallic narcissism. It may also protect against the potential threat of castration from the woman. Only rarely is the point to harm the woman for the sake of sadism and violence per se.

The results of the Fantasy Project at the Columbia Psychoanalytic Center for Training and Research (Person et al., 1989; reprinted here as Chapter 13) suggest a greater predilection for dominance in males as compared to women, but this group of fantasies is among the least frequently reported for both sexes. Only 11 percent of the men reported fantasies of torturing a sexual partner and 20 percent of whipping or beating a sexual partner, but 44 percent fantasied forcing a partner to submit to sexual acts. The comparable figures for women are 0 percent, 1 percent, and 10 percent.

Just as striking as the sex difference is the percentage of men who do *not* report any conscious fantasies of domination (56 percent). Furthermore, far fewer men report fantasies of actual violence or torture than report domination fantasies. We have not tested the results of an older population, but I would guess there would be progressively fewer fantasies of overt force with increasing age.

Another prominent feature of the erotic fantasy life of heterosexual men is a preoccupation with lesbian themes. In part, the fantasy of two women making love suggests an abundance of women whose primary interest and sole function are sexual, insuring that the man will never be humiliated by the absence of a sexual object.[2] At this level, the fantasy is a variant of the fantasy of the omni-available woman. Like fantasies of women happily making love with

2. The meaning of the male preoccupation (in fantasy and in practice) with lesbian sex is more complex but is beyond the scope of the primary concern of this paper. In part, I think it reflects an unconscious feminine identification, which is personified in the image of one or the other of the women (see Chapter 18.)

animals having gigantic penises or of women masturbating with dildoes, fantasies of lesbian sex portray lusty women. They cannot accuse the man of being an animal or dirty; they are female versions of the man's own sexual self-image.

Conscious Fears: Their Interplay with Cultural "Macho" Sexuality

Sexual fears are almost mirror images of wishes. A very large number of men feel that their penises are inadequate in either length or girth. This concern appears more widespread than female self-doubts about breast size, perhaps more closely approximating female concerns about fat. Both heterosexuals and homosexuals agonize not just about physical endowment but about performance as well. There is one significant difference: heterosexuals feel much more threatened by the appearance of another man's erect penis.

As to performance, men worry about getting it up, keeping it up, and satisfying their partners. That they frequently ask the partner "Did you come?" is testimony to this. It also betrays a basic imbalance in sex—men are stuck with the fact that their sexual excitement is visible. There is no hiding the failure to achieve an erection and no certain way to gauge the woman's sexual arousal or orgasm. It is difficult for a man to know whether he is really a good lover, and men are often unable to accept reassurance. The fear surfaces in some men's obsessions about their partners' past lovers: "Was he better?" "Did she have more orgasms? Better orgasms?" Of those men who are confident in their performance, some are so intent on controlling the female that their own participation lacks spontaneity. Some men feel comfortable pursuing their own pleasure only after they have brought the woman to orgasm; some attain full erection only when the woman is sated.

The most striking feature of the male's sense of inadequacy is his belief that other men are truly in possession of macho sexuality. He feels that macho sexuality is unattainable for him personally, but not that it is a myth. In light of this belief, his own endowment and skills appear even more meager. Many men suffer because of their idealization of the male adolescent experience, the only time perpetual readiness appears to be the rule. But the overestimation of other males' sexuality appears to have its deepest roots in the oedipal boy's awe of his father's superior sexual endowment.

In order to compensate for the sense of genital inferiority, performance anxiety, and the fears of female rejection or infidelity, men resort to power remedies in fantasy. Through denial and reversal, the penis emerges as all-powerful, performance as extraordinary, and sexual partners as plentiful. Dominance and aggression are reparative themes that betray another state of affairs—a fear of sexual powerlessness, female unavailability, and rejection. When I say that the male resorts to power remedies, I use the term "power" not in the sense of a set of impulses to defeat competitors but in the sense of imbuing the penis with potency and insuring the source of gratification by supplying a fantasized plethora of lusty women over whom the man is lord.

On one level, "macho" sexual fantasies are adaptive and counteract underlying fears, but at the same time they aggravate an already pervasive sexual anxiety, because the man literally believes that other men are doing better. Thus uncertainty about his sexual prowess appears to be much more basic to male sexuality than its reputed aggressive content. This is not to deny the aggressive element but to suggest that it is neither universal nor primary.

Living the Life: Clinical Examples of Macho Sexuality

The following four clinical vignettes are of patients who lived and idealized some version of macho sexuality entailing multiple partners, lesbian sex, and phallic narcissism. These patients all shared certain conflicts that lie hidden behind the macho defense. While these conflicts are not synonymous with Everyman's erotic sensibility, they are suggestive of "fault lines" in male development. All these patients were periodically beset with overt outbursts of fears about sexual adequacy. The first two vignettes are extremely brief, simply examples of the different forms macho fantasies may take. The second two are rendered somewhat more fully. All these patients were "lovers" of women, though their need to dominate and their hostility toward women were not far from the surface. None of these patients showed extreme hostility or violence to women. However, I have never had in analysis any man who fell at the violent end of the sexual spectrum. I don't think this is accidental. Such individuals are not likely to present themselves voluntarily for analytic treatment, particularly to a female therapist.

> R.M. fantasied about sex with two women simultaneously and about lesbian sex, but he did not enact either fantasy. What he did instead was to set up his wife, his primary mistress, and an ancillary mistress in apartments within walking distance of each other. He essentially established a harem, though the women were unaware of each other. He was particularly proud of the fact that he could see his own apartment from his mistresses' flats. Despite his sexual bravado, he was not infrequently impotent, an occurrence he generally attributed either to a wish to be elsewhere or to guilt. When either the

wife or the primary mistress threatened to leave him, he fell completely to pieces, even going so far as to threaten suicide.

B.D. always maintained at least two sexual relationships, both of which he considered significant. He never asked the women to have a simultaneous sexual encounter, but he did apprise each of his sexual activities with the other. He was apparently an extremely proficient lover, utterly devoted to the sexual fulfillment of his partner during any sexual encounter. His sexual withholding was enacted by his ostentatious alternation of weekends between the women and his refusal to see them during the week.

M.D. is a middle-aged writer of considerable reputation and affluence. He sought treatment at the insistence of his wife of fifteen years. She felt it was a sign of his emotional liability or disability that he insisted on an open marriage, which she refused. Their relationship had gradually deteriorated, and their time together was frittered away in petty power struggles with mutual withholding of sex.

In adolescence and early manhood, M.D. had a retarded sexual life, having come out of a repressive religious background, and he was monogamous in his first marriage. It was only when his first wife left him that he embarked on a totally different kind of sexual career. At this point he moved out of a sheltered conservative suburb into a more artistic and bohemian milieu. He never again pursued a monogamous path and always had at least two female friends nearby. It was with some trepidation that he married for the second time, now with the conviction that he wouldn't be faithful. He saw his passion for multiple sexual relationships not as neurotic but as an interest in variety, a sincere appreciation of many different women. He had begun to lie to his wife to avoid conflict but very much resented the need for concealment and ultimately felt that this was a bourgeois compromise.

During the treatment he became emotionally involved with another woman. However, despite his many dissatisfactions with his marriage and his new friend's willingness to share him with other women, he maintained that he could not "make it" with either woman. When his wife was out of town he became frightened at being alone with his mistress and arranged to see other women as well. One of his worst fears was that he might suddenly lose all the women with whom he was involved. Being with no one seemed to him the worst fate of all.

He periodically experienced sharp pain in his penis and lived in fear of the time when his sexual powers might fail. He had a dim awareness that his inability to leave his wife or attempt to ameliorate the situation betrayed a conflictual attachment.

S.M., a successful professional, came into treatment because of recurrent depressions. He was extremely proud of his beautiful, well-preserved wife and obviously pleased by her voracious sexual appetite. Although he was morbidly jealous of the lovers she had had prior to their marriage, he had initiated threesome sex, mostly with one other woman, but occasionally with another man. He enjoyed talking about how much his wife liked these sexual encounters. He was proud of her rapture but also pleased because she was so clearly at his disposal. Despite her willingness to oblige, he had a number of ancillary women friends, though he in no way regarded this as being unfaithful.

During his depressions, usually triggered by business reversals, he became impotent. This was invariably followed by an obsessive preoccupation with his wife's former relationships, pathological jealousy, and the suspicion that she was currently unfaithful. He would then reject her and accuse her of being a dog in heat.

He had a series of paired dreams with slight variations. In one of the pair, his wife was all-powerful and drove a chariot while he clung to her feet and she fertilized the land with great streams of water. In the paired dream, he controlled two giant stallions and dragged his wife along behind him. These oscillations in his perception became very rapid and revealed the way in which he perceived his wife and himself as locked in a bitter struggle for power and yet yoked together.

To varying degrees, the men I have described perceived themselves as living the macho life. They played out different facets of two prominent macho fantasies: the omni-sexual woman and the fascination with lesbian sex.

All four men had certain characteristics in common. None viewed himself as having ongoing sexual fears or concerns. In fact their sexual behavior was not only egosyntonic but idealized as well, viewed as the emblem of true manhood. However, each was subject to intermittent fears about the health and intactness of his penis, impotence, and the loss of a sexual partner. All described themselves and were described by their partners as being unusually proficient lovers. This proficiency, particularly in the case of B.D., was seen as an important instrument in maintaining control over their women, despite the women's objection to some of the arrangements. All had experienced what they bitterly regarded as rejections by women in adolescence or young adulthood. These experiences had not dampened their enthusiasm for women but had made them wary of investing all their emotions in only one.

All hid their dependency needs and narcissistic vulnerability behind a fairly primitive phallic chauvinism; they symbolically controlled their women through phallic mastery and supremacy. The underlying dependence was revealed only in symptomatic outbreaks of anxiety, depression, or impotence when the relationships were on the verge of rupture.

All relied on their wives' (or girlfriends') accounts when reporting their problems to the analyst. There was an explicit belief that the wife was a better observer and reporter. However, the faithful repetition of the women's complaints, delivered in the most rational way imaginable, only gave lip-service to their powers of perception; the emotional significance of the female partner's accusations was denied, giving the lie to their cool, rational façade of fair-mindedness.

None of these men had intimate friendships with other men; the emotional reference points of their lives were women. In fact, they had excluded not only "fathers" from their emotional lives but "brothers" as well.

In treatment there was an attempt to establish the same covertly needy, manifestly dismissive or controlling relationship they maintained with their wives. These patients had relatively strong needs to negotiate and switch times, to stop and restart analysis, and to retaliate for the analyst's vacations. Simultaneously, they regarded the (female) analyst as powerful and phallic, though not sexual. All four analyses were distinguished by the marked absence of any well-developed erotic transference (Person, 1985, reprinted here as Chapter 15).

Development Sources of Feelings of Sexual Inadequacy and Fears of Female Unavailability

What is the source of the male's sense of sexual deficiency and potential "starvation"? Theories of male sexuality are somewhat skewed, focusing, as they do almost exclusively, on the resolution of the positive oedipal complex. In the standard formulation, the boy avoids the threat of castration by the father by renouncing his mother; he chooses the narcissistic cathexis of his penis over the libidinal cathexis of his mother, thereby preserving and strengthening his phallic narcissism. The fundamental sexual problem for boys is viewed as the struggle to achieve phallic strength and power vis-à-vis other men. And indeed, oedipal themes and fears are explicit in male fantasy life; they are copiously revealed in conscious fantasies, dreams, and analytic associations, leaving little doubt of their centrality to the male experience.

This formulation is accurate so far as it goes, but by focusing predominately on the father-son struggle, the threat of castration at the hands of the father, and the resolution through a powerful paternal identification, it minimizes the importance of other developmental components of male sexuality.

Castration anxiety is itself obviously affected by factors other than fear of the father. It is difficult to accept a direct and exclusive link between castration anxiety (at the hands of the father) and fears of female rejection and genital inferiority. There are clearly other sources that accentuate and contribute to these anxious preoccupations.

What is missing in traditional formulations is the impact of the mother-son relationship on sexuality at different developmental stages and the nature of the male's sexual realities at different points in the life cycle. Too often, the female is portrayed more as a prize than as a protagonist in the boy's sexual development. The psychoanalytic literature contains important contributions that focus on the effects of the mother-son relationship on male sexuality (Horney's 1932 paper, for example), but these discussions tend to be relegated to the footnotes (the exception being studies on perversion, in which some focus on preoedipal issues is inescapable). Even so, the ample evidence of everyday life emphasizes their importance. Another variable relates to the ambiguous masculine identification seen in some men and the degree of feminine identification that may be present.

Freud (1920a), Horney (1932), and, more recently, some of the French theorists (McDougall, 1980; Chasseguet-Smirgel, 1984) have suggested that the first blow to the boy's sexual narcissism is his inability to secure his mother's sexual love. In other words, the boy's fear of his father and the threat of castration at the hands of his father are not the only factors in the boy's renunciation of his mother. As Freud (1920a) suggests, the boy also withdraws his libidinal investment from his mother because he feels he does not have the genital endowment to compete with his father. His sense is that his mother rejects him in favor of his father because his penis is too small. Brenner (1979) has made a similar point. He stresses both the narcissistic injury and the depressive affect that may be generated in the phallic-oedipal period and their connection to castration anxiety. Many men never recover from this literal sense of genital inadequacy. It appears that many men are therefore destined to suffer lifelong penis envy.

It was Horney (1932) who most fully elaborated this formulation of male sexuality:

> The anatomical differences between the sexes lead to a totally different situation in girls and in boys, and really to understand both their anxiety and the diversity of their anxiety we must take into account first of all *the*

> *children's real situation* in the period of their early sexuality. The girl's nature as biologically conditioned gives her the desire to receive, to take into herself; she feels or knows that her genital is too small for her father's penis and this makes her react to her own genital wishes with direct anxiety: she dreads that if her wishes were fulfilled, she herself or her genital would be destroyed.
>
> The boy, on the other hand, feels or instinctively judges that his penis is much too small for his mother's genital and reacts with the dread of his own inadequacy, of being rejected and derided. Thus he experiences anxiety which is located in quite a different quarter from the girl's; his original dread of women is not castration-anxiety at all, but a reaction to the menace to his self-respect (pp. 355–356).

As Horney notes, the boy suffers a blow to his sense of genital adequacy and consequently to his masculine self-regard. At the same time, he is reminded of earlier frustrations (oral, anal) at the hands of that same mother. Consequently, in accordance with the talion principle, "The result is that his phallic impulses to penetrate merge with his anger at frustration, and the impulses take on a sadistic tinge" (p. 356). This might be regarded as nearly universal, but essentially transient. If the anger and sadism are great, the female genital (again, by virtue of the talion principle) will itself become the source of castration anxiety, and the mother, along with the father, will be seen as a potential castrator.

However, Horney observed that sexual sadism and fear of the female as castrator were not invariable among her male patients, whereas the anxiety connected to masculine self-regard was almost universal. As she puts it, "According to my experience the dread of being rejected and derided is a typical ingredient in the analysis of every man, no matter what his mentality or the structure of his neurosis" (p. 357). Horney (p. 358) quotes Freud (1923b) to the effect that the boy "behaves as if he had a dim idea that his member might be and should be larger." She points to the continuity between the narcissistic blow to the oedipal boy and the adult man's ongoing anxiety about the size and potency of his penis. This mental set has several components: fear that his genitals are inadequate, the corollary fear of female rejection, and a sense of the superior endowment of his rivals.

In addition to the castration anxiety engendered by the paternal rivalry, men suffer from a sense of inadequacy vis-à-vis the mother and from fear of her as well. The male's fear of the female, of his inability to please her (and his anger at her), stem from different developmental levels: fear of the preoedipal mother who abandons/engulfs, of the anal mother who intrudes/indulges, of the phallic-narcissistic-level mother who falsely seduces/denigrates masculinity, of the oedipal mother who cannot be fulfilled, rejects, and falsely seduces. From these potential fears arises the male propensity to compensate through sexual fantasies of power and control and through denial of his dependence on female sexual acceptance and participation.

I believe that this formulation delineates one important developmental strand in male sexuality. Yet it remains difficult to substantiate the continuity between these hypothetical childhood events and adult fears.[3] We do know, though, that the conjectured events are recapitulated in adolescence by the male and female adolescent's real situations, and again by the adult's real situation.

The boy's narcissistic wound—his inability to secure the object of his childhood sexual desire—is recapitulated in adolescence by the hypersexuality of the adolescent male compared to his female counterpart. The typical male adolescent experience is one of perpetual arousal with masturbation as his primary outlet. His arousal and desire come at a time when he is not equipped to easily maintain a secure sexual relationship. This discrepancy reinforces his fears about securing a sexual object and his own genital adequacy. Yet he resents the unavailability of a female partner. Since he assumes that other males are doing better (a derivative of his oedipal defeat), his feelings of inferiority vis-à-vis other men are intensified.

Furthermore, the ambivalence about his control over his genital equipment and sexuality can be traced to physical aspects of the adolescent induction into genitality. In adolescence, the male is overcome with a sexual arousal over which he feels he has little control. While spontaneous erection and ejaculation are best understood as release phenomena, the subjective experience is an ambivalent one: pride in the pleasure and power of the phallus, but the simultaneous sense that the phallus is not really under his control.

The idea that the penis has a separate life is reflected in the tendency of young men to personify the penis by giving it pet names. Adolescent boys feel dread and shame at inopportune erections. One middle-aged man described himself as still being led around by his "joint." The young man's tragedy has been described as having a gun and ammunition but no control; by the time control is achieved, the ammunition has been taken away. Wet dreams betray the boy's sexuality to his parents, particularly his mother. He feels he has no privacy.

Partly because self-control is crucial to mastery and partly out of gender training, control over his penis—and, through it, over the outside world—has

3. Although men in analysis offer many associations that demonstrate the male's sense of inadequacy vis-à-vis their sense of inadequate endowment, it is difficult to definitively establish the genetic source of the anxiety.

high priority for the boy. Sexuality becomes imbued with issues of control and dominance. Yet the adolescent's sense of lack of control over the penis is never completely resolved. It becomes a locus for symbolic elaboration and predisposes men to fears of impotence or premature ejaculation, the subjective evidence that they may not be fully in charge of their members.

Insecurity about his sexual adequacy and his ability to please the female are reinforced by another of the vagaries of sexual reality—a lifelong distinction between the sexes. Sexual excitement (or lack of it) is visible in only one.

How do men cope with these anxieties about performance and female rejection? Collectively and individually, men submerge their fears in an overestimation of male sexuality. Horney speculates, and I concur, that the boy's remedy for the narcissistic mortification implicit in the renunciation of his mother is a defensive phallic narcissism. Identification with the phallic father and his power and subsequent identification with male sexual strength and independence form the psychological core of the collective male ideal of male sexuality—macho sexuality. The boy's phallic narcissism, intensified by his adolescent pride in the erectile power of the penis, coalesces with the magical sexual properties with which he has endowed his father and other rivals. Out of this emerges the individual and collective male pride in some version of macho sexuality. (This solution is no doubt reinforced by male gender socialization, or "male bonding.")

Men attempt to assuage their sexual self-doubts through active sexuality (or fantasies of it), in which control over the penis is sought through sexual mastery and control over the sexual object. In his wishful fantasies, the male reverses his self-doubts and anxieties by endowing his penis with supernatural powers (those he once attributed to his all-powerful father).

The fear of female unavailability and rejection leads to compensatory fantasies featuring a cornucopia of sexually available women. We too often take fantasies of the omni-available woman and their enactments at face value, requiring no further understanding. The male interest in multiple or simultaneous partners is accepted as part of his sexual voraciousness (rapaciousness?). These sexual enthusiasms enter into the collective male ego ideal as part of an idealized macho sexuality. Yet there is something haunting in the fantasies—a denial and reversal of the realities of female sexuality, a magically exaggerated picture of male sexual prowess, and a wistful desire for a different sexual world. In fact, the male appears to project his own sexual desires onto his fantasy females. It is they who are forever randy, perpetually aroused and ready. Most important, they are always available and never reject him.

Fantasies of the omni-available woman reveal not only the pressing desire for female availability but the simultaneous desire to erase any one woman's individuality or importance. This obliteration provides reassurance about virility, the "on-call" availability of the sexual object, and the inherent importance of the man vis-à-vis the woman. While the fantasies may sometimes be contaminated by the need to discharge aggression, they are not fueled by it. These are not domination fantasies per se; they are more subtle, revealing the need to bolster the male's subjective sense of control and command, They counter the dread of personal inadequacy, male subordination, and female rejection. The assumption is that women are automatically satisfied and require no special stimulation; they take their pleasure from his pleasure. But the fact that the omni-available female (even in fantasy) is often viewed with condescension, contempt, or even sadism is evidence of the resentment caused by the experience of frustration at the hands of the rejecting mother (and subsequent female objects).

Consequently, men may be internally driven to conquer women, to possess them, and to do so repeatedly. They may also split their sexual desires among a number of women, usually those seen to be in an inferior position and therefore easily dominated. Men can thereby control the source of sexual gratification and insure the availability of one sexual object if another vanishes. In fantasy, it will be the woman, not the man, who is humiliated. It is she who will serve him, admire his penis, and submit.

Control of the sexual object serves as a compensatory device that defends against the male child's sense of inadequacy and inferiority vis-à-vis both parents and the humiliation of the unavailability of a sexual object at different points in his life. Out of revenge, the man reverses the humiliation implicit in both his infantile and his adolescent experience: he stands ready to demand sexual availability and fidelity of his partners while disavowing it for himself.

Normal Resolution Versus Power Resolution

I have suggested a series of developmental issues intended not as alternatives to castration anxiety in understanding male sexuality but as factors that may modify the intensity of castration anxiety and interfere with its resolution. Intense and persistent castration anxiety can be the end result of a number of contingent factors. One such factor, beyond the scope of this chapter, is the strong female identification seen in some men, usually a result of early separation anxiety (see Ovesey and Person, 1973). Once it has developed, it may serve as an inhibitory force (one sees here the various forms of sexual inhibitions) or as a stimulus to a variety of reactive solutions, among these the development of a macho sexuality.

By and large, in normal development, castration anxiety, envy and fear of both parents, and fear of female rejection will be largely resolved. However, even in "normal" male sexuality there will remain some latent or moderately active interest in multiple partners and lesbian sex. In those instances in which there is failure of an adequate father identification or intense preoedipal rage (particularly directed against the mother), the heterosexual male has a propensity to develop a sexuality imbued with power concerns and preoccupations.[4] These may easily revolve around sadomasochistic interactions. In extreme cases they may find expression in sexual sadism, either fantasied or enacted. Consequently, it is probably accurate to say that the male tendency to sexual aggression and sadism has preoedipal roots related to the fact or fear of loss of the object or loss of love. But sadism should not be considered the norm among men any more than masochism is viewed as the norm among women.

At the same time, there do appear to be specific problems inherent in male development that predispose to the centrality of concerns over control and power among the majority of men. The impulse to solve these problems through sexual domination grows out of the conviction that only possession and domination will guarantee fulfillment and surcease to the endless wheel of desire. Ultimately the power of sexual domination is (mistakenly) invoked to preserve a precarious sense of self, most readily in any cultural milieu that glorifies such domination, takes its apparent strength at face value, and minimizes its compensatory functions.

4. This is not to say that the male homosexual's sexuality is not just as imbued with issues of power, but that topic is beyond the scope of this chapter. (Footnote added, 1998.)

19

The Omni-Available Woman and Lesbian Sex: Two Fantasy Themes and Their Relationship to the Male Developmental Experience

1986

ETHEL S. PERSON

THE FEMINIST movement's demand for a reevaluation of psychoanalytic sexual theories correctly pointed to erroneous concepts regarding female sexuality. However, the tacit and mistaken assumption was that these same theories exhaustively and accurately portrayed male sexuality. We are now beginning to see that theories of male sexuality are incomplete if not skewed, as described in Person, 1986a, reprinted as Chapter 18.

In this chapter I propose to examine two sets of widespread male heterosexual fantasies—the omni-available woman and lesbian sex—the meaning of which draws our attention to an enlarged scheme of male psychosexual development. These fantasies are popularly acknowledged but largely unexplored in the psychoanalytic literature. At first glance, their meaning appears to be self-evident, no more than an expression of macho sexuality. Yet they are not so simple as their manifest content would initially lead one to believe.

Psychological exploration of the omni-available woman fantasy reveals traces of desires and frustrations directly referable to the boy's mother and his subsequent female sexual objects. It thereby draws our attention to prephallic factors in castration anxiety, to the narcissistic vulnerability of the sexual self, and to the impact of the adolescent experience. The lesbian fantasy frequently

The first half of this chapter draws on and elaborates themes in my paper "Male Sexuality and Power" (1986), reprinted here as Chapter 18.

I would like to express my thanks to Drs. Gerald Fogel, William Grossman, and Eleanor Schuker, for reading an earlier version of this chapter and offering many valuable comments.

incorporates maternal envy and the wish for a feminine identification. It suggests certain parallels between homosexual and transvestite solutions as trial resolutions of the oedipal conflict anterior to "normal" resolution. Might these two groups of fantasies have been neglected precisely because they focus on aspects of male sexuality at variance with the cultural ideal of the "macho"?

The Omni-Available Woman

The omni-available woman is totally sexually accessible. The fantasizer pictures her awaiting his arrival, forever lubricated, forever ready, forever desiring. He assumes he is in her thoughts at all times. From my patients' reports and my reading of the popular and scientific reports of fantasies, I conclude that, for men, it is the woman's availability, ready sexuality, and unqualified approval that is a major common thread. She never says "no." Her availability and enthusiasm bolster his virility.

Shaved pudenda are a surprisingly regular feature of male sexual fantasies. (Comparable fantasies in women are extremely rare.) This may reflect one variant of the wish for the woman to be completely exposed, to conceal nothing whatsoever. In fantasy, men can have all the girls they want and possess them fully—visually as well as sexually.[1]

The male preoccupation with the omni-availability of the sexual female, irrespective of his own availability, is enacted by men in myriad small ways. There is the legendary example (fact or fantasy) of the business magnate famed in his industry for having a woman perform fellatio on him under the desk while he does business, or examples of men who idly fondle women while conducting business on the phone. The fantasy of the omni-available women is also actualized in the phenomena of the "kept" woman. (The great courtesans generally play to this fantasy.) Furthermore, the repetitive recourse to naked, erotic women in advertising appears to speak to the male's unconscious need to be surrounded by sexually available and willing females. One could even argue that it is this need that provides a good deal of the market for prostitution.

A man with this fantasy preoccupation may ask a woman not to wear panties or a brassiere under her regular clothes, an obvious symbol of her sexual readiness and availability. However, the most common translation of such fantasies into real life is the obsessive urgency with which some men fill every spare evening with an erotic encounter, even when they have ongoing

1. The meaning of the fantasies of shaved pudenda is often more complex. For example, it also substitutes a nonthreatening little girl in the place of a grown, dangerous, potentially castrating woman. It may also be counterphobic.

satisfactory or superior emotional and sexual relationships (as self-reported). I have heard many businessmen boast that they have a wife on one coast and a girlfriend on the other.

These fantasies and their enactments are often taken at face value, and such sexual enthusiasms enter into the collective male ego ideal as part of an idealized macho sexuality. But a darker and more problematic reality underlies. There is something haunting in the fantasies—a denial and reversal of the realities of female sexuality, a magically exaggerated picture of male sexual prowess, and a wistful desire for a different sexual world.

Fantasies of the omni-available woman reveal not only the pressing desire for female availability but the simultaneous desire to erase any one woman's individuality or importance. This provides reassurance about virility, the "on-call" availability of the sexual object, and the inherent importance of the man to a woman. The omni-available woman fantasy counters the dread of personal inadequacy, male subordination, and female rejection or harm. It suggests an overabundance of women whose primary interest and sole function is sexual, ensuring that the man will never be humiliated by the absence of a sexual object.

Fantasies of the omni-available woman are reassuring insofar as they guarantee female sexual availability and approval—a state of affairs somewhat at variance with Everyman's actual experience. These fantasies also paint a picture at variance with the actuality of female sexuality. They portray unusually sexually energetic women. Such women cannot accuse men of being beasts, barbarians, or dirty; they are female versions of the man's own sexual self-image. (Consequently this set of fantasies denies the meaning of sexual differences.) And such women are ready to be sexually satisfied. Through their easy excitability they foster a male's excitement and assuage his sexual self-doubts. Because they are easy to please and experience great pleasure, these women are not viewed as potential castrators.

Ultimately, the fantasies focus on female complicity. The women do not surrender to their own desires; their desires are seen simply as extensions and mirrors of male desire and, therefore, essentially irrelevant and nonthreatening. The woman's voraciousness is seen as in the service of his needs, not in opposition to them and not primarily as a means to her own gratification.

But the reality is different. In fact, I have heard many women complain that men are frightened by active female sexuality. And men have confirmed that observation. Some men resent the "work" sometimes needed to arouse women and also resent women they regard as voracious in their demands, women who require "servicing." Sexually active women sometimes find themselves in the position of having "withholding" partners, men who would prefer to think that what pleases them is exactly what pleases (or should please) the woman, as it is in the fantasy of the omni-available woman. It is this wish that, in part, fuels the fantasy of simultaneous orgasm as the sine qua non of successful sex—the complete mutuality or mirroring that is effected in fantasy. At one level, such a wish serves simply as a denial of the sexual distinction (Brunswick, 1943; Person, 1983). At another level, the strength of this wish suggests some psychic continuity with the longing for a preoedipal ministering and "feeding" mother.

My clinical impression is that men for whom behavioral derivatives of the omni-available woman fantasy are urgent (for example, those men who never permit their wives to wear underpants) often camouflage intense oral and dependent needs in the guise of sexual ones. These men fear the loss of the object. In addition, the narcissistic use of the object may bolster phallic narcissism as a defense against a sense of phallic vulnerability. Clinically, one observes that when such men are sexually frustrated by their wives, their fantasies and dreams frequently veer to images of degradation of women or vengeance and violence directed against them.

On the one hand, fantasies of the omni-available woman appear to be continuous with earlier demands for instant gratification. On the other hand, the fantasies appear compensatory to specific anxieties engendered in the normative crises of male psychosexual development: anxieties about virility, the availability of female objects for sexual gratification, and the sexual difference.

Because these fantasies and their enactments reflect desires and counteract anxieties that appear to be widespread among men, one must look for their antecedents in common male experiences, not in the idiosyncratic experiences of a few. (For an account of their developmental sources, see Chapter 18.)

How do men cope with their anxieties about performance and female rejection and potential sexual starvation? Collectively and individually, men submerge their fears into an overestimation of male sexuality. Horney (1932) speculates, and I concur, that the boy's remedy for the narcissistic mortification that fuels his renunciation of his mother is a defensive phallic narcissism. (In part, he renounces her because he has a boy's penis not a man's penis.) His narcissism is reinforced by his compensatory identification with the phallic power of his father. His phallic narcissism, later intensified by his adolescent pride in the erectile power of the penis, coalesces with the magical sexual properties with which he has endowed his father and other rivals. Out of this emerges the individual and collective male pride in some version of "macho" sexuality, no doubt reinforced by male gender socialization or "male bonding."

In his fantasies, the male reverses his self-doubts and anxieties (Goldberg, 1976; Zilbergeld, 1978). The omni-available woman fantasy assuages the fear of female rejection. Because of that same fear of rejection, men may be internally driven to conquer women, to possess them, and to do so repeatedly. They may split their sexual desires among a number of women, usually those seen in a somewhat inferior position, who can therefore be readily dominated. This allows men to control the source of sexual gratification and ensures the availability of one sexual object if another vanishes. In fantasy, it will be the woman, not the man, who is possibly abandoned and humiliated. It is she who will serve him, admire his penis, and submit.

Control of the sexual object serves as a compensatory device that defends against the male child's sense of inadequacy and inferiority in relation to both parents and the humiliation of the unavailability of a sexual object at different points in his life. Out of revenge, the man reverses the humiliation implicit in both his infantile and his adolescent experience: he stands ready to demand sexual availability and fidelity while disavowing it himself.

Thus far I have focused on the male need to fantasize the availability of sexually available women ready to submit to his needs, wishes, and demands, and its relationship to anxieties about his genital adequacy and to his dread of female rejection. I have suggested in passing that the fantasy of the omni-available woman reveals the male wish to disavow any sexual distinction. The centrality of this latter dynamic—and the feminine identification that may be related to it—appears more dramatically in the underlying structure of the lesbian fantasy.

Lesbian Sex

As previously reported, the erotic fantasy life of many heterosexual men contains lesbian themes (Chapter 18). Although heterosexuals of both sexes fantasize participating in homosexual sex with members of their own sex, usually only heterosexual men also fantasize homosexual sex involving the opposite sex. Some heterosexual women may be aroused by male homosexual sex, but these are relatively few.

Fantasies of lesbian sex have two major variants. In the first, the sexual encounter is exclusively between the women; in the second, the women are joined either by a male onlooker or a male participant. These fantasies appear to be on a continuum; the transitional fantasy between lesbian sex and threesome sex is the fantasy in which the male is initially an onlooker, then joins in the sex play.

In the second variant (in which a male is present), what is remarkable is the cooperation among the players. Jealousy and possessiveness are nowhere in evidence. There is sexual sharing of the highest degree, plenty to go around, and no one feels excluded.

Lesbian sex is almost a convention of pornographic movies intended for heterosexual men. Some men are surprised by their arousal in response to a film sequence of female lovemaking. In other words, the visual depiction of lesbian sex arouses some men who do not generate the fantasy independently.

Even though the lesbian fantasy does not appear to occupy as prominent or conscious a place in the typical man's fantasy life as the omni-available woman, a study by Mavissakalian and associates (1975) revealed that heterosexual male arousal by lesbian images was as high as the response to either female autoerotic or heterosexual erotic images. (Homosexual men were not aroused by lesbian sexual encounters.) In a significant minority of men, it is not only a fantasy preoccupation but a major pursuit.

Lesbian fantasies, like those of the omni-available woman, are often enacted in derivative forms. The most common way to introduce a second woman into the bedroom is in conversation—in love talk, not in the flesh—though watching two women make love and threesome sex have become more popular practices (or so it seems from the reports of my patients). Another derivative of the fantasy is a man's insistence that his different lovers know of one another's existence, though the women may decline to meet.

One of my former patients, a call girl, reported that call girls were frequently requested in pairs. They may be required to make love to one another while the client looks on and masturbates, or the three may engage in sex together. (The irony within this configuration is that often the call girls are thereby allowed to satisfy their real homosexual proclivities.)

The most facile exploration of the meaning of lesbian sex as a fantasy theme is that the heterosexual male has concocted a fantasied harem for himself. This explanation obscures the subtler and deeper meanings of the lesbian fantasy behind the façade of a voracious macho sexuality. In order to understand the fantasy, one must consider why the women need to make love to each other rather than simply awaiting the man (the omni-available fantasy) and why so often the male subject is not himself ostensibly part of the conscious fantasy.

In part, the male preoccupation with sex with two women simultaneously is probably frequently related to an underlying anxiety about potency. Although there may be the lurking fear that women can do without him (as in the lesbian film sequence), in the fantasy the male feels powerful because he controls two women and believes, despite their mutual erotic involvement, that only he can satisfy them. At another level, the women protect him. They do part of the erotic work for him (with each other), even satisfy each other, so that the performance burden on him is lessened. To some degree, a voyeuristic impulse is obviously implicated, though the question remains as to why "lesbianism" is favored. From clinical data, it appears that the lesbian image is often linked to residual incestual impulses and to an unconscious female self-identification.

Desire, Envy, and Identification

One woman is often significantly older than the other in the lesbian fantasy, perhaps suggesting the simultaneous satisfaction of the man's desire for a teacher/nurturer and his wish for someone to initiate, the virgin he can claim as his conquest and who will be eternally grateful to him. In pornographic films, the older woman often initiates the younger in the wonders of lesbian sex. When the male appears, however, the attention is focused primarily on him. The presence of the two women together suggests superabundance and a connection with the omni-available fantasy vis-à-vis compensatory male dominance.

But insofar as one woman appears to represent a powerful maternal figure whose presence lends potency, these fantasies appear to reflect incestual fantasies and oedipal desires. The older woman appears to be a representation of his own mother, sometimes represented in his fantasy life as his mother-in-law. For some men, the incest theme is disguised by their unconscious identification with the younger woman in the lesbian fantasy, though I have been surprised that some male patients have an intuition of the meaning of the identification even prior to any analytic work.

In the course of her analysis of K., McDougall uncovered the existence of "a powerful and immutable fantasy whose meaning eluded him" (1980, p. 26). "The cast of characters frequently included two women [of whom] the elder, perhaps the mother, was beating her daughter on her bare buttocks." This took place in front of an unnamed spectator. K. also engaged in sex in which he beat his young mistress's buttocks and sometimes beat himself in front of a mirror. In her extended analysis of these fantasies and behaviors, it appeared to McDougall that K. identified both with the mother with the whip (the phallic woman who possessed the paternal phallus) and the girl who eroticized the welt marks (representing castration). For McDougall, the presence of the unknown onlooker established the transformation of the primal scene and of the oedipal constellation. That is, it undid the boy's discovery of his parents' sexual pleasure together.

Although McDougall's patient reports a perverse elaboration of the lesbian fantasy, I believe that some of the dynamic elements may have more widespread applicability. What is especially remarkable in lesbian fantasies is the absence of the oedipal rival of childhood. In some, the triad becomes a dyad. Insofar as there is a triangular configuration, there is a reversal in the makeup of that triangle. Two males and one female have been replaced by two females and one male. In both dyadic and triadic lesbian fantasies, the rival father has simply vanished.

An important, common dynamic function of the fantasy is that the boy solves the oedipal competition by disavowing his father. In part, he disavows the genital distinction as well. In analysis, however, it is often revealed that one or the other woman in the lesbian fantasy is phallic, thereby symbolically preserving the man's own hidden phallus. Whether the man identifies with the woman viewed as phallic (and thereby incorporates her phallus) or whether the phallic female is the disguised man himself (disguised to elude the castrating father), the oedipal constellation has been rearranged. The boy has solved the problem of his envy of one or both parents. He usurps his mother as libidinal object and incorporates her power as well.

Both these dynamics—identification with the phallic female and self-disguise—resonate with those found in the full-blown transvestitic syndrome (Ovesey and Person, 1976; Person and Ovesey, 1978). But it should not be assumed that these fantasies have reference just to evasion of the competitive and castrating father. Importantly, they also reveal a feminine identification, originating in the preoedipal period, that persists or is reinvoked for dynamic and defensive reasons.

The lesbian preoccupation appears to be restricted to heterosexual men; some researchers even consider the erotic response to lesbian sex as diagnostic of male heterosexuality. The fantasy life of transvestic men, in contrast to homosexual men, is known to be permeated with lesbian imagery. Consequently, the lesbian fantasy promises to shed some light on the divergence and convergence of sexual development among "normal" heterosexual men, homosexuals, and transvestites.

Freud (1924a) argued that the sexual distinction was not a matter of grave consequence for the boy until he had entered into the positive oedipal constellation. Only then does he conceive the idea that castration might be the punishment for coveting his mother. It is then that the sexual distinction appears to have personal meaning for him. In response to the imagined threat, he renounces his mother and identifies with his father.

However, the transvestite and homosexual resolutions allow different solutions to the problem of two sexes and its inevitable concomitant problem, sexual rivalry. Both homosexuals and transvestites are uncomfortable in a world made up of two sexes, but they react in diametrically opposed ways. Homosexuals eliminate women, living their intimate lives in a world of men, whereas transvestites eliminate men—to some degree in reality and to an extensive degree in fantasy. Both resolve the dilemma of oedipal competition by eliminating one sex; if there is no sexual distinction, there can be no oedipal competition.

The homosexual solution is familiar analytic territory, but I will elaborate somewhat on the transvestic solution. It is traditionally understood as a simultaneous identification with and love for a phallic woman (Fenichel, 1930). In transvestites (heterosexual cross-dressers) there is evidence of an unusually intense and ultimately unresolved oedipal struggle in which the incestual object persists and oedipal rivalry is perpetuated. The female clothes symbolize the mother as a simultaneously transitional and incestual object (Ovesey and Person, 1976; Person and Ovesey, 1978).

The transvestite's fantasy (two women, albeit with penises, making love together) symbolically destroys the father. At the same time, clothes (or feminine self-identification) represent a defensive posture in the oedipal constellation (Ovesey and Person, 1973; Person and Ovesey, 1978). They magically protect the transvestite in two ways: (1) they symbolize an autocastration, a token submission to his male competitors, which wards off their retaliation; and (2) they disguise his masculinity and serve to disarm his rivals. The clothes conceal his penis, the symbol of masculine power, and deny his hostile intent. He therefore feels safe because his rivals do not know that secretly he is plotting their demise. He avoids detection by passing as a woman, which makes it possible for him to risk assertion and thus validate himself as a man.

I would suggest that on the route to the "normal" resolution of the oedipal complex, most (all?) boys transiently attempt anterior (prior) solutions. It is here that the boy's penis envy (sense of inferior genital endowment) plays a role. Insofar as he feels he must renounce his mother because of his meager endowment, he has three choices.

The first alternative, of course, rests on the boy's temporary renunciation of his erotic ambitions, his projection of his ego ideal onto his father, identification with his father and the promise that identification will eventually prove its own reward (Chasseguet-Smirgel, 1985). Second, he can assume the feminine role and hope to incorporate the paternal phallus in a homosexual resolution. Last, he can declare the father's penis nonexistent; that is, he can construct a world made up solely of women—or a world of women in which he is the only male. This is a solution that eliminates oedipal rivalry and is clearly related to the transvestic solution. I would suspect that the lesbian fantasy, pronounced as it is in heterosexual men, reflects back to a transient transvestic resolution (analogous to the transient homosexual resolution found alongside "normal" oedipal resolution in so many analyses). The weaker the boy's authentic father-identification, the more pronounced the transvestic solution appears to be.

In part, female identification reflects envy of women and their prerogatives, but it also masks the negative oedipal constellation. The boy, in essence, envies both parents. Though I have stressed transient female identification as a solution to oedipal anxiety, there is, of course, a deeper layer. Regression to preoedipal roots, particularly merger or incorporation fantasies with mother that are reparative to separation anxiety, may be the more important dynamic.

Ovesey and Person (1973, 1976) have reported such fantasies as prominent in studies of transvestites and the cross-gender disorders. These same fantasies, to a lesser degree, are regularly seen in the psychoanalysis of male patients. The lesbian fantasy becomes a way of achieving security through incorporation or merger while preserving (hetero) sexuality.

Person and Ovesey (1978) reported transient transvestic episodes in adolescence (similar to transient homosexual episodes in adolescence) that resolve without clinical sequelae, though distinctive unconscious conflicts and constellations persist. The lesbian fantasy remains as the residue from an attempted transvestic resolution of the threat posed by the fact of two sexes, a resolution that is anterior to the conventional oedipal resolution and that may persist alongside it.

Discussion

That the theoretical discussion of male sexuality has been limited by its emphasis on the male reaction to oedipal castration anxiety is somewhat startling. Male fears in this model are almost exclusively restricted to castration anxiety related to the all-powerful father. Some theoretical attention has been paid to the threat of female castration, but little to the boy's subjective sense of female rejection. The boy's sense of genital inadequacy in relation to both mother and father has been inadequately explored. Yet pervasive conscious and unconscious fears of inadequate size are frequently seen in the clinical situation.

The theoretical neglect of the influence of the mother-son interaction at different developmental stages insofar as it impinges on male sexuality seems to me quite strange. In its way, it parallels the male's fantasy solution to his sexual fears. In fantasy, women are available, and their nonavailability cannot therefore constitute the problem. In theory as well, the problematic relationship to men is stressed. That females do not figure prominently in the developmental theory men write about male sexuality is another way of negating the importance of females.

As is well known, both in theory and in life, male psychology dictates a misunderstanding of the female as being the same, neither separate nor different from the male. In fantasy she is lusty, which seems a clear projection of male adolescent sexuality onto the fantasied woman and a denial of any sexual distinction. To the extent that such dynamics have influenced our theories, they have obscured a full appreciation of male development. It is not strictly true, as some have claimed, that psychoanalytic theories of sexuality accurately describe male sexuality (even while falling short of elucidating female sexuality). *Not just castration anxiety but penis envy is pivotal in the mental life of men.*

Men's insistence on penis envy as a central dynamic in women seems to be partly a projection of their own feelings toward stronger and more powerful men.

In addition, men commonly suffer from a sense of inadequacy in relation to the mother and from fear of her as well. Maternal identification, stemming from envy or separation anxiety or both, plays a role in the underlying concerns in male sexuality. It sometimes dictates an attempted transvestite resolution to the oedipal conflict in place of its "normal" resolution. Phallic narcissim, reinforced by the male cultural ideal of macho sexuality, tends to obscure these underlying dynamics. The fantasies of the omni-available woman and lesbian sex are "windows" on that buried world.

PART V

The Impact of Culture

20

Harry Benjamin and the Birth of a Shared Cultural Fantasy

1972/1997

ETHEL S. PERSON

Part I, 1972
Creative Maverick

Between Madison and Park, in the heart of boutiquedom, is the ground-floor office of a doctor with one of the strangest clienteles in Manhattan. If one sits in the sedate waiting room long enough, one will see recognizable New York politicos coming for their periodic testosterone injections to ward off impotence or a Buccellati-bejeweled woman seeking advice about how to confront her lover with his homosexual liaison, just uncovered by her private detective. But there is another group of patients too: in one corner sits a man with longish hair and a mild swelling of breasts under his shirt; in the leather lounge chair is someone who at first glance appears to be a showgirl but who on closer scrutiny is seen to have an Adam's apple and man-sized feet. The doctor in this office presides over the transformation of men into women—or

This chapter was written in two parts, the first part in 1972, when I was researching transsexualism and became fascinated with the background of the father of transsexualism. Benjamin wanted me to write about him after his death, and I was eager to do so. I interviewed him formally a dozen times and came to know him more informally too as I was spending hours in his office interviewing transsexual patients. Other sources for this chapter can be found in the references. The second part of the chapter originated in 1997 as a presentation I gave at the IPA Congress in Barcelona designed to illustrate the origin of a shared cultural fantasy.

I want to thank Dr. Charles L. Ihlenfeld, Harry Benjamin's long-time associate, for reading this chapter for me. He supplied some additional information, which I have incorporated in footnotes to the text. I also want to thank Dr. Ihlenfeld for his cooperation and kindnesses during those long-ago years when we were both working in the field of transsexualism.

chris-crosses, as they are called, in honor of Christine Jorgensen. His name is Harry Benjamin.

Harry Benjamin discovered the syndrome we call transsexualism, named it, helped devise the treatment, and breathed messianic intensity into its study and management. Since he first delineated the syndrome, Benjamin has diagnosed, treated, and befriended at least a thousand of the ten thousand Americans known to be so afflicted. He has come to be regarded not only as the discoverer but also as the patron saint of transsexuals.

What sort of doctor is it who gives female hormones to men to quiet their disturbing male sexuality, to diminish body hair, to create breasts, to prepare them ultimately for surgical sex conversion? Harry Benjamin is an eighty-eight-year-old charmer, possibly the last European gentleman in New York, a man who lights a lady's cigarette, quotes Goethe when pertinent (and politely translates the quote into English), annually travels to Milan to leave a rose on Verdi's grave ("no one has given me more pleasure"), and is always ready to buy a woman researcher interested in transsexuals a bloody Mary at the Polo Room around the corner.

When Benjamin was already in his late sixties, his good friend Alfred Kinsey referred a most unusual patient to him. Kinsey told Benjamin that among all his interviews, this man's history was unique. This patient believed he was a woman trapped in a man's body, and his desire was to live as a woman. Although cross-dressers were well known to sexologists and psychologists, they were always classified as homosexual cross-dressers (drag queens) or heterosexual cross-dressers (transvestites). In both these categories the men enjoy their sex and identify themselves as men who sometimes like to dress as women. In contrast, Kinsey's subject desired above all to live full time as a woman and, if possible, to be rid of all his male insignia, including his facial hair and his genitals, which he found disgusting. In fact, insofar as medical science permitted, he wished to be physically converted so that his body would conform to his identity of himself as woman. Benjamin, who had traveled the sexologists' circle and had always been peripherally interested in sexual problems, recognized that this man was neither a homosexual nor a transvestite. He had an intuition that he was seeing a new and third category of cross-dresser, a problem not previously delineated in the psychological literature. Another physician might well have dismissed the patient as homosexual or psychotic or both and thus missed the whole point.

Shortly after his initial meeting with Kinsey's patient, Benjamin learned of Christine Jorgensen. Benjamin suspected that Kinsey's subject and Jorgensen had the same problem. He made it his business to contact Jorgensen (they are now fast friends) and confirmed his suspicion. A few similar cases were discovered. By 1953, Benjamin had delineated a new syndrome, which he called transsexualism.[1]

The story of Benjamin and the transsexuals is one of the more interesting chapters in the history of sexology. A man presents himself as a woman trapped in a man's body and is not viewed as delusional; instead, a distinguished endocrinologist/geriatrician, by then in his sixties, listens sympathetically and weighs the truth of what the man is saying. Shall he label the patient's plaint "delusion" and attempt to change the mind to fit the body, or shall he honor the patient's feelings and change the body to fit the mind? Benjamin tentatively decided on the latter course. Albert Ellis, the well-known psychologist, thought it insane; even Kinsey, perhaps the most tolerant of all the sex researchers, backed off. But Benjamin persevered. Was this so different from what he had heard before? As a geriatrician, he had responded to the grief of the old who wanted to be young and gave them hormones. Now he responded to the grief of the man who wanted to be a woman and gave him hormones.

Benjamin not only delineated a syndrome and devised a treatment; he also forcibly turned the attention of sexologists to problems of gender. The study of transsexualism, once regarded as a fringe pursuit, is today receiving serious academic attention at major institutions around the country, including the gender identity clinics at Johns Hopkins and UCLA. In fact, the study of transsexualism has helped clarify a basic distinction between sex (male and female) and gender (masculinity and femininity).

Since the Jorgensen story and Benjamin's delineation of the syndrome, many thousands of transsexuals have surfaced. There have been 1,500 transsexual inquiries, chiefly from within the United States, to the Johns Hopkins Gender Identity Clinic alone since 1966 [to 1972]. Curiously, transsexualism is still little known to the public although it has received wide coverage in the sensational tabloids, particularly the *National Inquirer*. The general public became intrigued with the disorder when the Paula (Paul) Grossman story broke in 1971. Prior to his sex-reassignment operation, Grossman was a music teacher at a school in New Jersey. While the school board was deliberating on the question of her continued employment, Paula Grossman continued to reside with her (his) wife of more than nineteen years and their children.

1. The term 'transsexualism" was first coined in 1949 by the sexologist Cauldwell, who described a case of "psychopathia transsexualism" in which a girl wanted to be a boy. But Cauldwell did not describe transsexualism as it was later elaborated by Harry Benjamin.

A transsexual is defined as a biologically normal person who insistently requests hormonal and surgical sex reassignment. There are male transsexuals—that is, anatomic men who wish to become women (indeed, they often believe they are literally women trapped in men's bodies)—and female transsexuals—that is, anatomic females who wish to become men.

Sex reassignment involves hormonal and surgical procedures that permit a physical approximation of the sex of choice. In the man, administration of estrogenic hormones acts on the body by producing both partial chemical castration and hormonal feminization. Over many months breast development takes place with an increase in the size of the nipples and the areola surrounding them. Body hair decreases, except for pubic and axillary (underarm) hair. The beard is not affected, but most transsexuals have it removed by electrolysis. Fat assumes a more feminine distribution. Erections become hard to elicit, and ejaculation may disappear.

The surgical intervention consists of three principal steps: castration, penis amputation, and plastic surgery to create an artificial vagina and external female genitalia. Results vary, but some are very good. One well-known male transsexual was photographed naked and spread-legged for *Screw* Magazine and was indistinguishable in the photograph from a genetic woman. Although the newly created woman may function sexually and socially as a woman, she can never procreate and remains a genetic male. The success of the transformation depends on many variables; an effeminate, small-boned man will generally have a better physical result than a heavily bearded six-foot mesomorph. Breast implants and facial surgery are often utilized to improve the image.

In women, androgens are administered, resulting in an increased hair growth on face and body and a deepening voice. The conversion operation may include mastectomy and hysterectomy. The vagina is not usually closed. Sometimes the clitoris enlarges and appears as a small penis. The limitation in the female-to-male conversion is the impossibility of creating a really functional penis, though there have been some attempts. The most advanced surgery of this kind is being performed in Russia and Eastern Europe. The technique was highly developed during World War II because of the large number of injuries to the male organ from land mines. After treatment the female transsexual passes easily as a man when clothed since almost no one will question the sex of a bearded person. The illusion is shattered when the female transsexual removes her clothes, revealing the absence of a penis. The male transsexual has the option of "passing" completely, whereas the female transsexual must generally let her sexual partners know the truth, depending on the kind of sex in which they engage.[2]

Transsexuals by and large believe that their condition is biological and that any emotional problems they have derive from their transsexualism. Consequently, they seek treatment from endocrinologists rather than from psychia-

2. The recent biography of the female transsexual and jazz musician Billy Tipton reports that none of his wives suspected the truth (Middlebrook, 1998). (Footnote added, 1998.)

trists. In fact, transsexuals have forced some physicians to provide sex reassignment, both hormonal and surgical, by their frequent attempted suicides and self-mutilations when denied such treatment. Sex reassignment is legally available in this country, though with difficulty and with considerable resistance from the medical profession. The full force of the controversy has probably not yet surfaced.[3]

A group of professionals has arisen who work primarily with transsexuals. These include not only endocrinologists, surgeons, sociologists, and psychologists but also lawyers, cosmetologists, electrolysis experts, and others. Many of these professionals are explicit in their belief that transsexuals are discriminated against, that they are the stepchildren of medicine. In the civil-libertarian view of transsexualism, an individual has the right to be the sex of his choice, just as in the civil libertarian view of homosexuality, an individual has the right to a sexual partner of the same sex.

Benjamin himself is both a puzzle and a delight. I was at first surprised that the delineation of the syndrome as well as the radical treatment proposed for it should emanate from a man of his age. But as I came to know him, I saw his deanship of transsexualism as the natural culmination of a maverick life in science. Since the turn of the century, Benjamin has been at the frontier or the fringe of the medical mainstream, depending upon one's point of view and has been at the center of at least three major maelstroms—the tuberculosis cure scandal of the 1910s, the rejuvenation craze of the 1930s, and in the 1970s, the dispute over transsexualism.

Born in Berlin on January 12, 1884, Benjamin was the oldest child of stockbroker Julius Benjamin and Bertha Hoffmann Benjamin. Benjamin says his father was extremely elegant and lived like a millionaire although he wasn't one. He claims to be "psychologically pure Aryan," though when pressed he admits that "racially I am a true mixture." (Bertha, both anti-Semitic and anti-Catholic, was asked by young Harry why she had married a Jew—though

3. The etiology of transsexualism is unknown although both psychological and biological etiologies have been suggested. On the one hand, there are no known laboratory tests available today that show transsexuals as a group to be consistently different chromosomally, hormonally, or morphologically from the normal population; on the other hand, there are no observations that show them to be consistently different in terms of psychological history. Some investigators attempt to mediate these polar etiologies and suggest that there may be a biologic predisposition or vulnerability toward transsexualism that is triggered by postnatal psychological events. Treatment recommendations vary according to the theoretical formulation of the physicians. Physicians who hold the psychogenic theory favor psychotherapy, those who favor the theory of organic etiology favor sex-reassignment therapy. There are exceptions—for example, one gynecologist who is insistently opposed to sex conversion despite his belief in the endocrine etiology. There are also several psychiatrists who recommend sex conversion despite their belief in the psychogenic etiology. In fact, there are no instances on record of permanent remission of the transsexual impulse in psychotherapy, whereas some subjects report relief from anxiety and depression after sex reassignment.

converted—and replied that Papa was different.) Harry was brought up a Lutheran. Religion did not play a dominant role at home, though at school "Papa's Jewishness was a problem."

School was the Wilhelm Gymnasium, where half the students were from the German nobility and 10 percent were sons of the richest Jews. The gymnasium was nicknamed "very shiny leather shoes" (in German), which is the rough equivalent of our "white shoe." The Gentiles thought Benjamin Jewish and the Jews thought him Gentile. He does not remember that this caused him any pain, but he was a behavior problem at school until age fifteen, when his father permitted him to switch schools. Thus he was deprived of or spared (depending on your point of view) the dueling scars that distinguished the German aristocracy of his generation. Throughout his long life, his stint at the Wilhelm Gymnasium was the single instance in which he experienced himself as a complete outsider.

From earliest life, Benjamin wanted to be a physician; his mother claimed he was sketching doctors by the age of three. Where this desire came from is a mystery to Benjamin; there was no intellectual tradition on either side of the family. But his parents were well-to-do and devoted to art and music (they owned the first phonograph on the block). His mother's passion for opera, along with her great "ear," were transmitted to Benjamin, who spent most of his youth haunting the opera houses of Berlin. His first great crush was on Geraldine Farrar, who at nineteen sang Marguerite in *Faust* at the Royal Opera House. He collected her photographs, amassing a large number from which he has never parted. Many a day he kept vigil before her house to catch a glimpse of her.

When he was still a teenager, Benjamin devised a method of bridging his disparate interests in medicine and opera: he attached himself to the house physician of a privately owned opera house. This friendship afforded him many privileges. Benjamin's "opera days" spanned many decades, and in due course he came to know most of the great stars of the German opera and musical comedy (and to make love to some of them).

His premedical studies were undertaken in Berlin and Restock and were followed by a short stint in a Prussian Guard regiment. He did his medical studies at Tübingen, from which he graduated cum laude in 1912. He soon was as successful in attaching himself to the famous physicians of the day as he was in meeting the leading opera stars. After graduation, Benjamin did a year's postgraduate work with one of these famous physicians, Ernst von Romberg, who stimulated his interest in tuberculosis, an interest that was to have far-reaching consequences for his future.

In Berlin, Benjamin met Karl Ludwig Schleich, a well-known surgeon, physician, and philosopher and the original discoverer of local anesthesia. A fatherly man of middle age, very German with a bushy mustache and a love of beer, Schleich, knowing Benjamin's work in tuberculosis, urged him to accept a position as clinical assistant to Dr. F. F. Friedmann, who was working with a new remedy for tuberculosis. Benjamin accepted the position with Friedmann to do the clinical examinations, keep his records, and organize a private clinic for the exclusive use of his remedy, later known as "turtle vaccine." (A strain of tubercle bacilli had been "weakened" by passing it through turtles, and a suspension of these living nonvirulent bacilli in sterile water was used for injections that were claimed to arrest tuberculosis.) Some striking results occurred, particularly in joint and bone tuberculosis. Friedmann's announcement of his discovery and its endorsement by prominent physicians in Germany aroused a widespread interest in turtle vaccine. By accepting the position with Friedmann, Benjamin projected himself into a situation that was to develop into a scandal perhaps unparalleled in the annals of modern medicine[4] and that was to transplant him from Germany to the United States.

Then as now, newspapers often printed sensationalized versions of scientific reports culled from medical journals and meetings. Several American correspondents relayed the news of Friedmann's spectacular tuberculosis cure to the United States. As a result, a New York banker invited Dr. Friedmann to come to the United States to treat his tubercular son-in-law for a fee of a million dollars. Friedmann accepted. He was accompanied by Benjamin as well as a former reporter for the Hearst papers, an American who gave up his job in Berlin to act as Friedmann's secretary and press agent. They sailed for New York in 1913. Benjamin believed he was on a grand scientific mission.

They landed in late February and were ensconced in the Waldorf Astoria. The first few days were passed in a whirlwind of visitors, conferences, reporters, photographers. Daily, more and more prospective patients arrived at the hotel, filling the sidewalks in front of it. Once the police had to clear the lobby because there was a near-riot following an order that nobody was to be allowed access to Friedmann's suite. Then a sick man collapsed in the lobby, and an ambulance had to be called. Within a week, the Waldorf Astoria management asked the Friedmann party to leave the premises. The party moved to the Ansonia Hotel on Broadway and 73rd Street, and the work began.

Friedmann, attractive, slender, and taller than average, was forever fussing with his dark blond hair, his mustache, his necktie; in front of a mirror he would continuously invite admiring comments. He prepared the vaccine behind locked doors from a culture he had brought from Germany, never allowing another physician to have access to either culture or vaccine. When

4. I wrote this before the *real* medical scandal of the century: the laxity in insuring that blood was free of the AIDS virus. (Footnote added, 1998.)

patients were treated in various hospitals, he gave all the injections himself, usually intramuscularly, into the buttocks, rarely intravenously. If watched by another physician, he varied the dose. When Benjamin asked why, Friedmann whispered in German, "Let them break their heads over something." Meanwhile publicity was kept at a peak by the press agent.

The U.S. government sent physicians from Washington to investigate the "cure." The governor of Rhode Island gave Friedmann an honorary license so that he could accept fees from patients in that state. The results were initially reported as good, but they proved to be transitory. Friedmann chided Benjamin for not finding clinical improvement, but Benjamin was too honest to fudge his findings. Fearing public condemnation of both Friedmann and his cure, Benjamin, on the advice of friends, resigned, but offered to return to the Institute in Berlin to assist Schleich, who had been left in charge. Because Benjamin had resigned, Friedmann refused to pay his return passage, and he was stranded in New York—for the next sixty years, as it turned out.

Friedmann meanwhile found an American assistant, a hotel physician later revealed as an illegal abortionist, who was willing to substantiate his claims. The Friedmann "cure" was ultimately condemned by most of the American investigators, but not before Friedmann, profiting from the enormous publicity, had sold his remedy to a drug company for $125,000 and over a million dollars in stock. The "Friedmann Institute" opened on West End Avenue and 103rd Street but was closed after a few weeks by order of the New York Board of Health. Even before the closing of the Institute, the "turtle camp" was pretty well broken up. The press agent was happy to sever connections, and Friedmann himself had secretly left the country. A cartoon in the *Times* depicted a sad turtle crawling down the steps from the barred institute. "Back to the soup," said the legend.

This left Benjamin alone in New York. An apparent opportunity for him to take charge of a new tuberculosis sanitarium came to naught. The summer months were filled with new contacts and repetitive disappointments. Finally, in the spring of 1914, he found a job in a lab in a New York hospital; soon the physician in charge asked that Benjamin go to Germany for a few months to report on the current status of the Friedmann cure there. Notwithstanding his recent experiences, Benjamin still believed in the efficacy of the Friedmann cure in certain instances. (His infatuations in medicine often proved as durable as his infatuations with women, a few of whom he has maintained contact with for fifty or sixty years.) He agreed to go to Germany, hoping to bring back a report that would permit him to continue in tuberculosis research.

Benjamin boarded the *Kronprinzessin Caecilie* on July 25, 1914, but the ship was intercepted when war broke out and docked in England. Benjamin's official status was prisoner of war, although he was not incarcerated; at the time he was still a member of the German army on leave. He was denied permission to return to Germany but after several months was allowed to return to the United States. By the time the war ended, when he could have returned to Germany, he had already sunk his roots in America; so, as it turned out, he was spared army service, the killing inflation, and Hitler. Although Friedmann had done him in, Friedmann also saved him. When Benjamin thinks of Friedmann now, he quotes Mephisto's lines in Goethe's *Faust:* "Part of that power not understood, which always wills the Bad and always works the Good."

It was not until the 1920s and 1930s that Benjamin came into his own, as a leader in the controversial field of rejuvenation. The year 1916, when Benjamin began his private practice, saw the beginnings of the field of endocrinology. Benjamin was invited by Dr. Josef Frankle, founder of the Neurological Institute in New York, to participate in Wednesday-evening seminars on endocrine problems. Again Benjamin's interest was sparked by the new. Naturally, it was intensified by the widespread belief that endocrine constitutional medicine was quackery. In 1920, there was an enormous amount of publicity about Sergei Voronoff, who claimed he could rejuvenate old men with monkey glands. Harry, reading about Voronoff, became excited, "Since it was glands, it interested me."

Born in Russia, Voronoff became director of experimental surgery at the physiological laboratory of the College de France. He had done basic experiments with sheep and goats but achieved notoriety with the implantation of chimpanzee glands into a seventy-four-year-old-man. At the height of the monkey-gland craze, Voronoff had hundreds of African natives scouring the continent to supply him with live monkeys. His personal career helped validate his claims in the public eye. In 1934, when he was sixty-eight, he married his third wife, a twenty-year-old cousin of the wife of the former King Carol of Romania. Voronoff died in Lausanne on December 4, 1951, at the age of eighty-five.

Benjamin wanted to meet Voronoff and soon expressed his interest to Dr. Herz, the great heart specialist of Vienna (affectionately known as the Hertz-herz, or the heart-heart). Dr. Herz thought Voronoff sounded like a swindler and instead suggested a meeting with the "real pioneer" of rejuvenation, Dr. Eugen Steinach, who was said to effect rejuvenation "scientifically," without transplantation. A meeting between Steinach and Benjamin took place in 1921, and finally Benjamin, then thirty-seven, was launched on the pursuit that has engaged him, in one way or another, ever since.

Steinach at the time was already in his sixties. (Like Voronoff, he lived productively into his eighties, dying in 1944 at the age of eighty-four.) A short man with an impressive head and an abundant reddish-gray beard, Steinach was born in 1861 in a small town in the Austrian Alps into a family of physicians (Harms, 1969). He served as assistant to Ewald Hering, chief of the department of physiology at the German University of Prague in Czechoslovakia. He remained in Prague for two decades, advancing finally to full professor. After ten years of work following Hering's interest in the human senses, Steinach developed an interest in the physiology of reproduction and came to recognize the role of endocrines in human sexuality. He was called to Vienna in 1912 to become director of the famous Physiological Department of the Biological Institute of the Academy of Sciences, known as the Vivarium.[5] (This is the same Vivarium that housed Paul Kammerer, the last advocate of Lamarckian inheritance, memorialized by Arthur Koestler in "The Case of the Mid-Wife Toad," as well as von Frisch, discoverer of the dance language of bees, and Paul Weiss, who did limb transplants on amphibians. In fact, the Vivarium was a center for the newly burgeoning interest in actual animal experimentation and, as such, the center of much publicity, controversy, and singular scientific achievement.)

In the heady atmosphere of the Vivarium, Steinach engaged in "sex-changing" experiments with guinea pigs through castration and gland transplantations. He noted that the signs of castration in the male guinea pig were similar to signs of aging in the unoperated guinea pig. Therefore, he concluded, aging might be mitigated by administration of the male substance from the testes. This was pioneer work, and, in fact, Steinach was proposed several times for the Nobel Prize. Steinach also put forward the ingenious proposition that ligation of the vas deferens in the human male would produce atrophy of the spermatogenic tissue and that this tissue would be replaced by the interstitial cells, which would produce additional testosterone (the normal function of the interstitial cells). This operation, vasoligation, was extremely effective, at least from the point of view of the patients, who reported increased vigor and sexual power.

Benjamin's meeting with Steinach in 1921 had a major impact on him, and he became Steinach's American disciple. Their professional involvement lasted until Steinach's death twenty-three years later. The correspondence between them spanning more than twenty years was donated to the New York Academy of Medicine by Benjamin and was reviewed by Ernest Harms in its *Bulletin* (1969). Harms concludes that the relationship was that of student to professor. Steinach was erratic, eager for recognition in America, desirous even of the addition of a Steinach section to the Rockefeller Institute, but fearful of being "sold" in America and of being exploited by Harry. Benjamin,

5. Steinach stayed at the Vivarium until the Nazis invaded Austria.

on his side, managed Steinach with psychological skill, tolerance, and tact—qualities that came easily to him.

Benjamin was generally interested in meeting physicians with major innovative ideas, and so it was that a few years into their relationship he asked Steinach to arrange a meeting for him with Freud. Although Steinach was anti-psychoanalytic, he did so and Benjamin went to meet Freud sometime between 1928 and 1930. Benjamin describes his reception by Freud as friendly but not overly cordial. At one point, according to Benjamin, Freud "told me that he himself had undergone a 'Steinach operation,' a vasoligation (for the purpose of reactivation), performed by Professor Blum, the chief-urologist at the University and that he was very satisfied with the result. His general health and vitality had improved and he also thought that the malignant growth of his jaw had been favorably influenced" (Benjamin, 1970, p. 7). Freud asked Benjamin not to disclose this information as long as he was alive, and Benjamin kept his promise. (Steinach and Benjamin had both had the operation as well, which indicates their own belief in the procedure.)

At one point in the conversation, they discussed the body-mind relationship, and a joke occurred to Benjamin, which he shared with Freud: "that the disharmony of the emotions may well be caused by a *dishormony* of the endocrines" (p. 7). Freud agreed and asked whether Benjamin had ever been analyzed. Benjamin replied that he had been in a brief analysis by Kronfeld in Berlin, but Freud angrily retorted that Kronfeld had a very bad character.

Their conversation soon took a turn that made Benjamin unrelentingly hostile to Freud and his ideas. Benjamin revealed to Freud that he suffered from a form of impotence, particularly with his wife. Freud, as was sometimes his practice, given his uncanny access to the unconscious, leaped to the interpretation that Benjamin was a latent homosexual. This premature interpretation, correct or incorrect, infuriated Benjamin, who considered himself something of a ladies' man. Benjamin forever after deplored psychoanalysis as unscientific. Just as Freud had asked Benjamin not to report his Steinach operation until after his death, so Benjamin asked me not to report this aspect of his conversation with Freud until after *his* death.

In the 1920s and 1930s, before synthetic testosterone made the operation obsolete, Benjamin performed five hundred Steinach operations in the United States. (Apparently Steinach himself never performed the operation that was named for him but had it done by surgeons [Harms, 1929]). The operation was well received in Europe, though it was in disrepute in America from the beginning. It met with vitriolic opposition, largely owing to the efforts of Dr. Morris Fishbein, long-time influential figure in the A.M.A.

The proposition that vasoligation produced increased testosterone could never be scientifically tested since no procedure existed for detecting circulatory blood levels of testosterone. By the time such procedures became available, testosterone had been synthetically produced and could be administered directly, so there was no longer any need for the Steinach operation. Consequently, the actual blood levels of testosterone following the Steinach operation were never measured, and statements either repudiating or extolling the procedure are based on speculation. Curiously, the means to test Steinach's proposition are now at hand for the first time, since the current vasoligation for purposes of male sterilization (vasectomy) is the same as Steinach's procedure (although the Steinach operation was performed on one side only to allow for continued fertility).

Irrespective of the opposition, Benjamin's list of patients read like a who's who of the rich, the powerful, and the famous. During these years, Harry became a celebrity; he was the leading specialist in reactivation, a term that replaced "rejuvenation," and in gerontotherapy, a term he invented (and which was officially defined in the twentieth edition of Dorland's medical dictionary, a fact of which he was proud), and he was published widely and frequently quoted in the popular press.

Benjamin, along with Steinach, helped pioneer an equivalent treatment for women, diathermy, applied to the area of the ovaries. They also experimented with X-ray treatment of that area. Nowadays Benjamin thinks there was nothing to these treatments except the powers of suggestion, though he still believes in the efficacy of the Steinach operation. Nonetheless, his personal reputation was helped along by the patronage of a celebrated lady novelist who believed Benjamin had saved her life with X-ray treatment of the ovaries.

Gertrude Horn was born in 1857. At age seventeen, she met George Atherton, scion of a prominent California family, who was courting her widowed mother. George switched the object of his affection and vigorously pursued Gertrude. She finally eloped with him, though with some misgivings about the effect this might have on her mother. Before she was thirty, she, too, was widowed, but, given her zest for life and considerable wealth, she did not grieve for long.

She wrote and traveled continuously, became one of the leading female novelists of her time, and socialized with the great literary lights of the day—Sir James Barrie, Arnold Bennett, H. G. Wells, and Ambrose Bierce. When she was eighty-five, she wrote her fiftieth novel. Nonetheless, in her early sixties, she had a year-long work block. She read a newspaper account of an interview with Dr. Benjamin in which he stated that women all over Europe were going to the Steinach clinic for treatments to restore their exhausted energies. She sought out Benjamin, who prescribed X-ray stimulation. The outcome of the treatment was the novel *Black Oxen,* written in 1923 and subsequently made into a movie, in which the heroine (a stand-in for Atherton) received a youth-restoring treatment from a renowned scientist (a composite of Steinach and Benjamin). Twenty-five years later, at the age of ninety, Gertrude Atherton believed that the rejuvenation treatments were still effective, and, indeed, she was universally described as a handsome middle-aged woman (Davidson, 1948). Naturally, Mrs. Atherton became a devoted patron of Benjamin and introduced him to the social leaders of San Francisco. Through her, he established a summertime practice in San Francisco which he maintained for thirty-seven years. As long as Mrs. Atherton lived, Benjamin's first dinner in San Francisco was always with her.

Meanwhile, in New York in the 1920s and 1930s Benjamin developed a deluxe clientele; one patient paid him a thousand dollars for an hour's consultation. His twelve-room suite of offices at 71st Street and Park Avenue was dominated by a life mask of Goethe at age eighty. He lived in a deluxe duplex apartment with a sweeping marble staircase. He had servants, a chauffeur, and an energetic social life.

But there was blight in his life, both romantic and sexual. He describes his love life as always tragic, beginning from the time he was fifteen and fell in love with a thirty-year-old actress. It was love at a distance since she was engaged to a German officer. His second great love was a lesbian, a musical comedy star, and their relationship lasted ten years with never a kiss. He describes himself as having long relationships and staying in love with hopeless cases. He married Gretchen, a woman he never fell in love with but whom he felt responsible for, when he was forty and she was twenty.[6] While she attracted him sexually and was a great beauty, his interest in her declined after their marriage. Much to Benjamin's sorrow, Gretchen began to withdraw from social life.

Moreover, a golden practice such as his could not last. New physicians crowded into the field in the late 1930s and early 1940s, particularly with the advent of synthetic hormones. Ironically, Benjamin helped create his own demise; through three wealthy clients he raised the money with which Kosimar Funke, a biochemist, built a laboratory in Paris and first isolated the male hormone. Then, too, in the 1940s, psychoanalytic intervention into sexual problems replaced rejuvenation in the popular imagination. In essence, the field in which Benjamin was preeminent disappeared. With it vanished Benjamin's lifestyle, since he was no more conservative in money matters than in scientific ones. One might have been tempted to count Benjamin—close to

6. Dr. Ihlenfeld told me that they were married December 23, 1925, and that Gretchen had revealed to him that about six months after they were married Harry brought his mother from Germany to live with them. She also told Dr. Ihlenfeld that from then on their bedroom door remained open. (Footnote added, 1998.)

fifty by this time—down and out. But the final and perhaps strangest chapter in his medical life was yet to come.

Though primarily known as a geriatrician and an endocrinologist, Benjamin was always peripherally a sexologist. After all, many of the problems of aging were in fact potency problems. In addition to men with potency disturbances, Benjamin had always seen some homosexuals. He had made it a point to meet all the leading sexologists of this century, and some of them became good friends. He met August Forel in Berlin. He was introduced to Magnus Hirschfeld by the well-known Dr. Kopp, who was in charge of the section for sex offenses in the Berlin Police Department, and with them toured the gay bars of Berlin. Hirschfeld's sex institute in Berlin was promptly destroyed when the Nazis took power since so many Nazis had been his patients and since prevailing German opinion equated sexology with pornography. Benjamin knew Oscar Riddle, F. A. Crew, Herbert Lewandowski, Robert L. Dickinson, Hugo Gernsbach, Alfred Kinsey, Havelock Ellis, and Albert Ellis. He also knew many of the leading psychoanalysts, including Alfred Adler.

Given his familiarity with the field of sexology, it is not surprising that Benjamin turned his attention to patients with sexual problems. Nonetheless, his ability to develop transsexualism as such rather than consign it to the wastepaper-basket designation "psychotic," and his capacity to formulate so radical a treatment program as sex conversion are remarkable, particularly in a man who was by then approaching seventy. Apparently such daring innovations do not always spring from the young.

One might regard Benjamin's career in medicine as both deviant and creative. Although he has periodically been widely acclaimed and handsomely remunerated, he has never had a major academic appointment and, until recently, never received recognition from the medical establishment. Now, however, he is credited with establishing transsexualism as a major investigative area for leading researchers from several disciplines. One can only speculate on the complexities of mind that set Benjamin apart from his colleagues.

From Benjamin's point of view, his originality is mediated by a profound commitment to nonconformity, an attitude originally culled from Forel's *The Sexual Question,* which made a profound impression on him in his youth and found fertile soil in his early social ostracism. His nonconformism has been consolidated over the years. He scorns establishment doctors with their "standard thoughts, their standard equipment, their standard prescriptions and standard fees." He is a believer in scientific progress. He is constantly searching the outermost limits of knowledge. At age eighty-eight, he is still using himself as guinea pig to test out new drugs. Despite his belief in scientific progress, he feels an essential hopelessness about the human condition. He has never had children and explains this by pointing to the meaninglessness of life. This pessimistic bent, coupled with his rebelliousness, not overt since childhood but active nonetheless, leavens his other convictions and ultimately leads him to view absolutist positions of the establishment as absurd. He is always ready to abandon the entrenched position and move on.

Benjamin takes his role of physician very seriously. I have seen him insist on looking down the throat of a colleague who suddenly came down with fever at a dinner party, over general protestations that an eighty-eight-year-old man should not expose himself to the flu. The plight of the deviant has always touched him; today he identifies with the deviant condition himself, since he believes that attaining his advanced age confers freak status.

Benjamin's unruffled demeanor conceals a mind that unites some ideas of the nineteenth century with extreme twentieth-century values. He believes that the transsexual suffers from a biological disorder, that his brain was probably "feminized" in utero. He eschews any psychological explanation. His ideas stand in logical progression from the notion of deviance held by Krafft-Ebing.

The idea that a female brain may be trapped in a male body entered the scientific literature initially, not via any complaint of a patient, but via the early sexologists' hypothesis about the origins of homosexuality. The definitive nineteenth-century work on sexology was Krafft-Ebing's *Psychopathia Sexualis,* which first appeared in 1887 and was in its twelfth edition when Krafft-Ebbing died in 1902. He believed that the sex drive originated in the brain and the sex glands and that sexual disorders must have their origins in either or both of those parts of the body.[7]

Benjamin believed that deviance was neither degenerate nor psychological but that it was biological. His certainty can be attributed in part to the damaging interchange that took place in his meeting with Freud. Had the outcome of that meeting been different, so, too, might the history of transsexualism. In some sense, then, it is accidental (or, more accurately, psychological) that Benjamin's intellectual convictions on transsexualism remain rooted in a belief in biologic predilection, although, in fairness, one must add that

7. Krafft-Ebing presented literally hundreds of case histories of the perversions. He believed that "perverts," because of genetic flaws, had not differentiated correctly at the time of fetal bisexuality, resulting in physical and mental feminization in men and masculinization in women. The majority of innate male homosexuals were not manifestly effeminate; only their brains had been feminized.

By the turn of the century, most sexologists concurred that homosexuality was congenital, caused by hereditary damage; some believed that the predisposition to homosexuality could be exacerbated by masturbation. In homosexuals, for reasons unspecified, the embryonic bisexual stage had never been surmounted. The condition was congenital and therefore incurable. Nonetheless, homosexuality was still equated with moral degeneracy.

For the next fifty years there were rigorous attempts by scientists to establish criteria for both mental illness and mental health and to separate both more fully from moral judgment. Concurrently, the psychoanalytic hypothesis that deviance is rooted in psychological conflict engendered in childhood experience was formulated. (See Chapter 1.)

biological psychiatrists have entered a major intellectual heyday.[8] Then, too, it is typical for people to retain the scientific convictions they held when they came of age, and Benjamin came of age when Krafft-Ebing was the last word in scientific modernism. Despite his anti-analytic bias, Benjamin does have uncanny psychological perceptiveness; his observations on certain aspects of deviance are as shrewd and insightful as anyone is likely to hear.

Co-existing with his nineteenth-century intellectual roots, Benjamin has a value system congruent with one extreme form of twentieth-century modernism. In today's world, one is expected to shape not only one's life but also one's nose. The Countess Castiglione, mistress to Napoleon III, locked herself into a darkened apartment at the age of thirty-nine, not wishing to face the world with her legendary beauty gone; during the remainder of her long life she chose to receive few visitors. Today the current view is that every woman is capable of being attractive, if not beautiful, and the achievement of this capability becomes an obligation.

In the twentieth century, science, medicine, surgery, and technology offer unprecedented means of changing one's appearance and apparent age.[9] Rejuvenation is fashionable again, as exemplified by the fashionable Swiss retreat where the treatment is injection of embryo cells. Scientific innovations not only provide the technologic means for such intimate changes but place enormous pressure on the individual to effect them.

The cultural bias for endless self-modification sets the framework for the transsexual's insistence that his real self is female and that it is his innate right to express his true self. It also predisposes nontranssexuals to listen to the plea of transsexuals (to be who they really are) with sympathy. This twentieth-century attitude, the belief in the individual's right to fulfill his nature and find self-expression, makes possible the burgeoning number of conversion operations. In some sense, the historical shape of transsexualism simply reflects a basic attitudinal change toward the "self" over the past century.

Benjamin shares the ultimate belief in self-fulfillment, a belief that takes priority in his vision, since he is basically pessimistic. This belief was the underpinning of his commitment to the field of reactivation and rejuvenation, in which he achieved preeminence, and his work in offering sex conversion to transsexuals is a natural progression from this work in rejuvenation. He is someplace on the continuum between eccentric and genius but is moved above all by his compassion for the ultimate outsider.

8. This intellectual heyday involves not only the treatment of certain psychiatric conditions with drugs but also research indicating that there may be predispositions to sexual orientation and gender attributes that are "wired-in." This field is still in its early stages and heavily debated. See for example, Friedmann,1988. (Footnote added, 1998.)

9. It is somewhat ironic that science, presumably on the basis of "objective" reality, offers the means of attaining such an effective illusion.

Part II, 1997
The Shared Cultural Fantasy of Transsexualism

The "discovery" or "invention" of transsexualism took place in the context of an encounter between Harry Benjamin and the "first" transsexual, George (Christine) Jorgensen, which gave rise to the diagnosis of transsexualism as a distinct entity. This diagnosis has shaped the way in which both society and the medical profession view cross-gender identifications and disorders and has ultimately led to the postmodernist endorsement of (if not injunction to) gender-bending. The sequence of events that permitted a shared culture fantasy to emerge could take place only in the context of a unique constellation of cultural attitudes, values, and technological inventions (Person, 1996).

This is the first historical period in which endocrinological, medical, and surgical technology enables the transsexual to modify his or her physical body to match the psychological predilection. In earlier years, such patients were viewed quite differently. Krafft-Ebing described a patient who would now be described as transsexual as representing a "stage of transition to change of sex delusion" (1969, pp. 240–256). In 1890 a correspondent sent him a "unique" autobiography in that a physical sensation was transformed into a sense of change of sex (recorded as Case 29, pp. 240–256). The correspondent, a physician, reported that from earliest childhood he tried to be like a boy but felt like a girl and was described as "not intended for a boy." By the age of twelve or thirteen he had "a definite feeling of preferring to be a young lady" and says that if he could have become female "I am sure that I should not have shrunk from the castration-knife, could I thus have attained my desire."

What is of particular interest to my thesis is the conclusion in the physician's accompanying letter. He wrote that "after reading your work, I hope that, if I fulfill my duties as physician, citizen, father, and husband, I may still count myself among human beings who do not deserve merely to be despised. Finally I wish to lay the results of my recollection and reflection before you, in order to show that one thinking and feeling like a woman can still be a physician. I consider it a great injustice to debar woman from Medicine." (p. 255).

Krafft-Ebing's comments about the patient's "autobiography" show the different "scientific" mindset a hundred years ago: "In 1893, three years later [after the first communication], this unhappy colleague sent me a new account of his present state. This corresponded essentially with the former. His physical and psychical feelings were absolutely those of a woman; but his intellectual powers were intact, and he was thus saved from *paranoia*" (p. 256).

Krafft-Ebing was describing an individual whom most of us would today diagnose as transsexual, but who had no option at the time but to continue his life as a man. And this was true of other potential transsexuals, who had little choice but to renounce, minimize, or live with the agony of an obsessive but unrealizable wish/fantasy.

The wish to transform one's sex is rooted in an individual's ability to fantasize; to consider actually transforming one's (apparent) sex requires the technological means of transforming that fantasy into reality. What the sources of the core sex-change fantasy are is, of course, the central question in trying to decipher the etiology of transsexualism. Whatever its etiology, the current widespread acceptance of the transsexual wish as more than fantasy—or paranoia—depends on several twentieth century trends in addition to the technological advances that make the fantasy realizable.

Self-Realization as a Cultural Ideal: Once upon a time, an individual accepted certain external realities as unalterable. These realities determined his place in society. As historical changes, both technological and social, accelerated, the individual began to believe more in the alterability of his circumstances and ultimately of his person. The question was not whether to adjust to or rebel against reality but how to discriminate between those realities that needed to be recognized as unalterable and those one might change. We now assume that little of external reality is unalterable, an assumption derived in part from our increasingly astonishing scientific advances.

The Civil-Libertarian Point of View: Many of the first professionals who worked with transsexuals, including endocrinologists, surgeons, sociologists, psychologists, and lawyers, were explicit about their belief that transsexuals were being deprived of their civil liberties. Many of these professionals share the messianic intensity that characterizes many civil-rights workers and public-interest lawyers. Many focus on helping transsexuals change their sex designation on their birth records and passports or mediate disputes about what bathrooms they may use. They regard transsexuals as the newest minority group to be defended from the repressive elements in society.

Preexisting Ideas about Being Trapped in the Body of the Opposite Sex: In the nineteenth century, deviance was classified with crime (and even poverty) as a sign of a hereditary degenerative failure, but later, as I have described, the theory that the homosexual was not criminal or insane but a female soul in a male body, a condition deriving from an error in embryonic differentiation, emerged and was picked up by major sexologists.

It was the idea of a female soul in a male body that George Jorgensen creatively elaborated. Like many others confused about their sex or gender, Jorgensen immersed himself in books that might help him understand his feelings. By chance, he happened upon *The Male Hormone,* by Paul de Kruif (1945). De Kruif wrote, "There's an uncanny ability in one of the pure female hormones to alter the lives and fate of man, and the pure male hormone—testosterone—to bring about deep changes in the sex lives of women" (quoted in Jorgensen, 1967, p. 79). Reading this, Jorgensen believed he had proof that he was victim of a small but powerful biological error, and that the remedy was to take female hormones. After all, according to de Kruif, "the chemical difference between testosterone and estradiol is four atoms of hydrogen and one atom of carbon" (quoted in Jorgensen, pp. 84–5). Jorgensen discovered that sex operations were being done in Scandinavia, probably on pseudo-hermaphrodites. He found his way to Dr. Christian Hamburger in Denmark and, serving as an experimental subject, became the first operated transsexual (Hamburger et al., 1953).

Enter Harry Benjamin. By 1953, Benjamin had codified Jorgensen's wish/fantasy/belief/enactment into a new medical entity that he called transsexualism. Benjamin was ideally suited to play this role. Like many others of his generation, he was firmly committed to the ideology of sexual tolerance. Moreover, he was primed to accept transsexuals' stories at face value, biased as he was against psychology and psychoanalysis. Even so, in the 1970s and 1980s, he gave me permission—despite my profession—to conduct interviews with all his transsexual patients.

Over some years, Benjamin and I became friends, and he asked me to write about him after his death. I interviewed him over many months, and the story he told me about his encounter with Freud, which he asked me to keep to myself until after his death, surely shaped his profound aversion to psychoanalytic thinking. (Given what I now know about the lesbian fantasy and my belief that an interest in lesbians is so closely associated with heterosexuality, I doubt that Freud's interpretation was correct. As I discussed in Chapter 19, such preoccupations are almost diagnostic of heterosexuality. But I hold no theories as to the causes of Benjamin's potency problems.)

Of course, we do not know that Benjamin was wrong in his ideas about transsexualism. No biological or psychological etiology of transsexualism has yet been definitively proved by either sexologists or psychoanalysts. In the popular imagination, a biological explanation seems to be favored. Nor do we know the outcome of conversion surgery with any certainty. While some patients achieve relief, many others devote their lives to an unending attempt to perfect their new gender roles. Most are lost to follow-up, by suicide or other causes.

My interest here, however, is not in etiology or treatment but in the way the disorder came to be recognized. It gained standing in the scientific community only because a group of doctors—Benjamin foremost among them—gave their imprimature to sex conversion. The diagnosis itself served to name and organize the discomfort and pain of a group of patients with specific gender problems.

Paradoxically, while the general public often romanticizes transsexualism as an extreme demand for liberation, transsexuals themselves, although they make extraordinary demands for their "freedom" to pursue sex conversion, almost invariably favor extremely conservative gender stereotypes, so much so that they have been called the "Uncle Toms" of the sexual movement. They subscribe to social values fundamentally at odds with the liberationist demands of either feminists or gays. Ironically, then, while transsexualism found acceptance as part of our liberationist ideals, most transsexuals themselves are among the gender reactionaries of our century.

While the diagnosis of transsexualism is based on specific clinical findings, the diagnosis could emerge only when many different cultural strands came together: the ideology of the sexual liberation movements, new research into hormones, new surgical technologies, the creative imagination of Christine (George) Jorgensen, and the perceptivity, open mindedness, and scientific background of Harry Benjamin, and perhaps his encounter with Freud as well. In essence, the identification of transsexualism as a separate entity took place in the context of an ongoing liberalization of sex practices and increasing fascination with studies of sex. In turn, the very discovery (or invention) of transsexualism fostered a change in the way we regard gender.[10] Thus, the discovery (or invention) of transsexualism is both a product of and a contribution to our shared cultural fantasy (project) of extending life, of changeability, of living without limits, a fantasy wish that draws what credibility it possesses from our technological wizardry.

Harry Benjamin died in 1986, six months short of 102. To some degree, longevity is found in certain family trees. (Benjamin's father died at sixty-seven, his mother at ninety-seven.)[11] Even so, given the long and productive lives of Voronoff, Steinach, and Benjamin, the longevity doctors may have been onto something.

10. Our notions of a strict gender dichotomy have been challenged in recent years, not only by advocates of the women's movement and investigators of pseudo-hermaphrodism but also by students of transsexualism. All three groups have lent their authority to an endorsement of more fluid conceptions of gender role and to a growing appreciation that beneath the sometimes rigid dichotomization of gender, each of us harbors many unexpressed cross-gender impulses and identities. This knowledge has found expression in the popular culture through enactments of cross-gender traits, a practice referred to colloquially as gender-bending.

11. Dr. Ihlenfeld reminded me that Benjamin was the eldest of three children. His brother Walter, the next oldest, and Edith, the youngest, were both married and in their nineties when they died. But like Harry, neither had children. As Ihlenfeld points out, the line, notwithstanding the longevity of its individual members, perished.

REFERENCES

Achenbach, T. M. 1978. The Child Behavior Profile: I. Boys aged 6–11. *J. Consult. Clin. Psychol.* 46:478–488.

——. 1979. The Child Behavior Profile: II. Boys aged 12–16 and girls aged 6–11 and 12–16. *J. Consult. Clin. Psychol.* 47:223–233.

Achenbach, T. M., and Edelbrock, C. 1983. *Manual for the Child Behavior Checklist and Revised Child Behavior Profile.* Burlington, Vt.: Queen City Printers, Inc.

Aminoff, M. J. 1993. *Brown-Sequard: A Visionary of Science.* New York: Raven Press.

Arafat, I. S., and Cotton, W. L. 1979. Masturbation practices of college males and females. In *Human Autoerotic Practices,* ed. M. F. DeMartino. New York: Human Sciences Press.

Arlow, J. 1954. Perversions: Theoretical and therapeutic aspects. *JAPA (Journal of the American Psychoanalytic Association)* 2:336–345.

——. 1969. Unconscious fantasy and disturbances of conscious experience. *Psychoanal. Q.* 38:1–27.

Awad, G. 1992. A fantasy penis: Development, multiple meanings, and resolution. *IJPA (International Journal of Psycho-Analysis)* 73:691–674.

Bak, R. 1968. The phallic woman: The ubiquitous fantasy in perversion. *PSOC (The Psychoanalytic Study of the Child)* 23:15–36.

Bak, R., and Stewart, W. 1974. Fetishism, transvestism, and voyeurism: A psychoanalytic approach. *Am. Handbook Psychiatry.* 2nd ed. 3:352–363.

Baker, S. 1980. Biological influences on human sex and gender. *Signs: Journal of Women in Culture and Society* 6:1.

——. 1981. Biological influences on human sex and gender. In *Women: Sex and Sexuality,* eds. C. Stimpson and E. Person. Chicago: University of Chicago Press.

Bancroft, J. 1989. *Human Sexuality and Its Problems.* New York: Churchill Livingstone.

Barclay, A. M. 1973. Sexual fantasies in men and women. *Medical Aspects of Human Sexuality* 7:205–216.

Barglow, P., and Schaefer, M. 1976. A new female psychology? *JAPA* 24:305–350.

Bassin, Donna. 1996. Beyond the he and the she: Toward the reconciliation of masculinity and femininity in the post-oedipal female mind. *JAPA* 44 (Suppl.):157–187.

Bates, J. E., Bentler, P. M., and Thompson, S. K. 1979. Gender deviant boys compared with normal and clinical control boys. *J. Abnorm. Child Psychol.* 7:243–259.

——. 1973. Measurement of deviant gender development in boys. *Child Develpm.* 44:591.

Bates, J. E. et al. 1974. Gender role abnormalities in boys: An analysis of clinical ratings. *J. Abnorm. Child Psychol.*, 2:1–16.

Beach, F. A. 1956. Characteristics of masculine "sex drive." In *Nebraska Symposium on Motivation*, ed. M. R. Jones. Lincoln: University of Nebraska Press.

——. 1976. Cross-species comparisons and the human heritage. In *Human Sexuality in Four Perspectives*, ed. F. A. Beach. Baltimore: Johns Hopkins University Press.

Beigel, H. 1969. A weekend in Alice's Wonderland. *J. Sex Res.* 5:108.

Biegel, H., and Feldman, R. 1963. The male transvestite's motivation in fiction, research, and reality. In *Advances in Sex Research*, ed. H. Beigel, 198–210. New York: Norton.

Bell, A., and Weinberg, M. 1978. *Homosexualities: A Study of Diversity Among Men and Women*. New York: Simon and Schuster.

Bemporad, J. 1975. Sexual deviation: A critical review of psychoanalytic theory. In *Sexuality and Psychoanalysis*, ed. E. Adelson, 267–290. New York: Brunner/Mazel.

Benjamin, H. 1953. Transvestism and transsexualism. *Int. J. Sexology* 7:12–14.

——. 1954. Transsexualism and transvestism as psychosomatic and somatopsychic syndromes. *Amer. J. Psychotherapy* 8:219–230.

——. 1966. *The Transsexual Phenomenon*. New York: Julian Press.

——. 1970. Reminiscences. *J. of Sex Research* 6(1):3–9.

Bieber, I. et al. 1962. *Homosexuality: A Psychoanalytic Study of Male Homosexuals*. New York: Basic Books.

Bergmann, M. S. 1971. Psychoanalytic observations on the capacity to love. In *Separation-Individuation: Essays in Honor of Margaret S. Mahler*, eds. J. B. McDevitt and C. F. Settlage, 15–40. New York: International Universities Press.

——. 1980. On the intrapsychic function of failing in love. *Psychoanal. Q.* 49:56–77.

——. 1982. Platonic love, transference love, and love in real life. *JAPA* 30:87–111.

Bibring, G. 1936. A contribution to the subject of transference resistance. *IJPA* 17:181–189.

Birksted-Breen, D. 1996. Phallus, penis, and mental space. *IJPA* 77:650–657.

Blos, P. 1979. *The Adolescent Passage: Developmental Issues*. New York: International Universities Press.

Blum, H. P. 1971. On the conception and development of the transference neurosis. *J. Am. Psychoanal. Assoc.* 19:41–53.

——. 1973. The concept of eroticized transference. *JAPA* 21:61–76.

——. 1976. Masochism, the ego ideal, and the psychology of women. *JAPA* 24:157–191.

Bolan, A. 1994. Transcending and transgendering: Male-to-female transsexuals dichotomy and diversity. In *Third Sex, Third Gender: Beyond Sexual Dimorphism in Culture and History*, ed. G. Herdt, pp. 447–486. New York: Zone Books.

Boswell, J. 1980. *Christianity, Social Tolerance and Homosexuality*. Chicago: University of Chicago Press.

Bradley, F. et al. 1980. Assessment of the gender/disturbed child: A comparison to sibling and psychiatric controls. In *Childhood and Sexuality*, ed. J. Sampson. Montreal: Editions Etudes Vivantes, pp. 554–568.

Brecher, S. 1969. *The Sex Researchers*. Boston: Little Brown.

Brenner, C. 1979. Depressive affect, anxiety, and psychic conflict in the phallic-oedipal phase. *Psychoanal. Q.* 48:177–197.

Broverman, I. K. et al. 1970. Sex-role stereotypes and clinical judgements of mental health. *J. Consult. Clin. Psychol.* 34:1–7.

Brown, N. 1959. *Life Against Death: The Psychoanalytic Meaning of History*. Middletown, Conn.: Wesleyan University Press.

Brownmiller, S. 1976. *Against Our Will: Men, Women and Rape*. New York: Bantam Books.

Brunswick, R. M. 1943. The accepted lie. *Psychoan. Q.* 11:458–464.

Bullough, V. 1994. *Science in the Bedroom: A History of Sex Research*. New York: Basic Books.

Campbell, B. 1980. A feminist sexual politics: Now you see it, now you don't. In *Feminist Review*. No. 5. London, England.

Cauldwell, D. C. 1949. Psychopathia transsexualis. *Sexology* 16:274–280.

Chasseguet-Smirgel, J. 1984. *Creativity and Perversion*. New York: Norton.

——. 1985. *The Ego Ideal: A Psychoanalytic Essay on the Malady of the Ideal*. New York: Norton.

——. 1995. "Creative Writers and Day-dreaming": A Commentary. In *On Freud's "Creative Writers and Day-dreaming*, eds. E. S. Person, P. Fonagy, and S. A. Figueira, 107–121. New Haven: Yale University Press.

Cherfas, J., and Gribbin, J. 1984. *The Redundant Male*. London: The Bodley Head.

Chesler, E. 1992. *Woman of Valor: Margaret Sanger and the Birth Control Movement in America*. New York: Simon and Schuster.

Chodorow, N. 1974. Family structure and feminine personality. In *Women, Culture and Society*, eds. M. Z. Rosaldo L. Lamphere, 43–66. Stanford: Stanford University Press.

——. 1978. *The Reproduction of Mothering: Psychoanalysis and the Sociology of Gender*. Berkeley: University of California Press.

——. 1994. *Femininities, Masculinities, Sexualities: Freud and Beyond*. Lexington: University of Kentucky Press.

Christgau, R. 1997. The pleasure seekers: A survey of the issues and players in the world of modern sex. *New York Times Book Review*, April 27, 1997.

Cixous, H. 1979. Presentation at the Columbia University Seminar on "Women and Society," October 8.

Coates, S., and Tuber, S. 1985. Representations of object relations in the Rorschach's of feminine boys. In *Primitive Mental States and the Rorschach*, eds. P. Lerner and H. Lerner. New York: International Universities Press.

Coates, S. W., and Wolfe, S. M. 1995. Gender identity in boys: The interface of constitution and early experience. *Psychoanalytic Inquiry* 15:6–38.

Coen, S. 1992. *The Misuse of Persons: Analyzing Pathological Dependency*. Hillsdale, N.J.: Analytic Press.

Colapinto, J. 1997. The true story of John/Joan. *Rolling Stone* Dec. 11.

Coons, F. W. 1971. The developmental tasks of the college student. In *Adolescent Psychiatry*, eds. S. C. Feinstein, P. Giovacchini, and A. A. Miller, Vol. I: Development and Clinical Studies. New York: Basic Books.

Dahl, E. K. 1993. Play and the construction of gender in the oedipal child. In *The Many Meanings of Play: A Psychoanalytic Perspective*, eds. A. J. Solnit, D. J. Cohen, and P. B. Neubauer, 117–134. New Haven: Yale University Press.

Davidson, M. H. 1948. Young at 90: Gertrude Atherton's surprising story. *The American Weekly* Jan. 4, 1948.

de Kruif, P. 1945. *The Male Hormone*. New York: Harcourt, Brace.

Derogatis, L. 1978. *Derogatis Sexual Functioning Inventory*. Rev. ed. Baltimore: Clinical Psychometric Research.

Deutsch, H. 1964. Cited by Burness Moore, Panel Report, "Frigidity in Women." *JAPA* 9:571–584.

——. 1925. The psychology of women in relation to the functions of reproduction. *IJPA* 6:405–418.

Diamond, M., and Sigmundson, H. K. 1997. Sex reassignment at birth: Long-term review and clinical implications. *Arch. Pediatr. Adolesc. Med.* 151:298–304.

Dinnerstein, D. 1976. *The Mermaid and the Minotaur: Sexual Arrangements and Human Malaise*. New York: Harper & Row.

Douvan, E., and Adelson, J. 1960. *The Adolescent Experience*. New York: John Wiley.

Dowling, I. 1969. *Attachment and Love*. New York: Basic Books.

Druss, R. 1973. Changes in body image following augmentation breast surgery. *Int. J. Psychanal. Psychother.* 2:248.

Ehrenreich, B., Hess, E., and Jacobs, G. 1982. A report on the sex crisis. *Ms* 61–88, March.

Eissler, K. 1958a. Notes on problems of technique in the psychoanalytic treatment of adolescents: With some remarks on perversions. *PSOC* 13:223–254.

——. 1958b. Problems of identity. *JAPA* 6:131–142.

Ellis, H. 1936. *Studies in the Psychology of Sex*. 7 Vols. 1896–1928. New York: The Modern Library.

——. 1939. *My Life: An Autobiography*. Boston: Houghton Mifflin.

Fairbairn, W. R. D. 1952. *An Object-Relations Theory of Personality*. New York: Basic Books.

Fenichel, O. 1930. The psychology of transvestism. In *Collected Papers*, Vol. 1, 167–180. New York: W. W. Norton (1953).

——. 1945. *The Psychoanalytic Theory of Neurosis*. New York: Norton.

Ferenczi, S. 1908. The analytic interpretation and treatment of psychosexual impotence. In *First Contributions to Psycho-Analysis*. Hogarth: London (1952).

Fineman, J. 1979. Psychoanalysis, bisexuality, and the difference before the sexes. In *Psychosexual*

Imperatives: Their Roles in Identity Formation, eds. M. C. Nelson and J. Ikenberry. New York: Human Sciences Press.

Fleiss, J. L. 1981. *Statistical Methods for Rates and Proportions.* 2nd edition. New York: John Wiley.

Fliegel, Z. 1973. Feminine psychosexual development in Freudian theory: A historical reconstruction. *Psychoanal. Q.* 42:385–408.

Ford, C. S., and Beach, F. A. 1951. *Patterns of Sexual Behavior.* New York: Harper & Bros.

Foucault, M. 1978. *The History of Sexuality. Vol. 1: An Introduction.* New York: Random House.

Freud, S. 1900. The interpretation of dreams. *S.E.* 4–5.

——. 1905a. Fragment of an analysis of a case of hysteria. *S.E.* 7.

——. 1905b. Three essays on sexuality. *S.E.* 7:125–248.

——. 1908a. "Civilized" sexual morality and modern nervousness. In *Collected Papers,* Vol. 2, trans. J. Riviere. New York: Basic Books (1959).

——. 1908b. Creative writers and day-dreaming. *S.E.* 9:143–153.

——. 1908c. *Three Contributions to the Theory of Sex,* trans. A. A. Brill. New York: E. P. Dutton (1962).

——. 1912. On the universal tendency to debasement in the sphere of love (Contributions to the psychology of love II). *S.E.* 11.

——. 1915. Observations of transference love. *S.E.* 12.

——. 1917. Introductory lectures on psychoanalysis. *S.E.* 15.

——. 1920a. Beyond the pleasure principle. *S.E.* 18.

——. 1920b. *A General Introduction to Psychoanalysis,* trans. Joan Riviere. New York: Washington Square Press (1960).

——. 1923a. The ego and the id. *S.E.* 19.

——. 1923b. The infantile genital organization. *S.E.* 19.

——. 1924a. The dissolution of the Oedipus complex. *S.E.* 19:173–179.

——. 1924b. The economic problem in masochism. *S.E.* 19:157–170.

——. 1925. Some psychical consequences of the anatomical distinction between the sexes. *S.E.* 19:248–258.

——. 1927. Fetishism. *S.E.* 21.

——. 1931. Female sexuality. *S.E.* 21:221–243.

——. 1933a. Civilization and its discontents. *S.E.* 21:59–151.

——. 1933b. Femininity. *S.E.* 22:112–135.

——. 1940 (1938). Splitting of the ego in the process of defense. *S.E.* 23:271–228.

Friday, N. 1977. *My Mother/My Self.* New York: Delacorte.

——. 1980. *Men in Love: Male Sexual Fantasies: The Triumph of Love Over Rage.* New York: Delacorte.

Friedman, R. C. 1988. *Male Homosexuality.* New Haven: Yale University Press.

Friedman, R. C., and Downey, J. 1995. Biology and the Oedipus complex. *Psychoanal. Q.* 64:234–264.

FTM International Newsletter. 1360 Mission Street, Suite 200, San Francisco, Calif. 94103.

Gagnon, J., and Simon, W. 1973. *Sexual Conduct. The Social Sources of Human Sexuality.* Chicago: Aldine.

Gershman, H. 1970. The role of core gender identity in the genesis of perversions. *Am. J. Psychoanal.* 30:58–65.

Giambra, L. M. 1979. Sex differences in daydreaming and related mental activity: Daydreaming. *Int. J. of Aging and Human Dev.* 10:80.

Gill, M. 1979. Analysis of the transference. *JAPA* 27 (Suppl.):263–288.

Gillespie, W. H. 1952. Notes on the analysis of sexual perversions. *IJPA* 3:397–402.

Gilligan, C. 1982. *In a Different Voice: Psychological Theory and Women's Development.* Cambridge: Harvard University Press.

Goldberg, H. 1976. *The Hazards of Being Male: Surviving the Myth of Masculine Privilege.* New York: New American Library.

Golosow, N., and Weitzman, E. L. 1969. Psychosexual and ego repression in the male transsexual. *J. Nerv. Ment. Dis.* 49:328–336.

Gorski, R. A. 1974. The neuroendocrine regulation of sexual behavior. In *Advances in Psychobiology,* Vol. 2, eds. G. Newton and A. H. Riesen, New York: John Wiley.

Green, R. 1968a. Childhood cross-gender identification. In *Transsexualism and Sex Reassignment,* eds. R. Green and J. Money, 23–35. Baltimore: Johns Hopkins University Press.

——. 1968b. Sex reassignment surgery. *Am. J. Psychiat.,* 124.

——. 1974. *Sexual Identity Conflict in Children and Adults.* New York: Basic Books.

——. 1976. One-hundred feminine and masculine boys: Behavioral contrasts and demographic similarities. *Arch. Sex. Behav.* 5:425–446.

——. 1979. Childhood cross-gender behavior and subsequent sexual preference. *Amer. J. Psychiat.* 36:106–108.

Greenacre, P. C. 1953. Certain relationships between fetishism and faulty development of the body image. *PSOC* 8:78–98.

——. 1958. Early physical determinants in the development of the sense of identity. *JAPA* 6:612–627.

——. 1959. Certain technical problems in the transference relationship. *JAPA* 7:484–502.

Greenson, R. R. 1966. A transvestite boy and a hypothesis. *IJPA* 47:396–403.

——. 1967. *The Technique and Practice of Psychoanalysis.* New York: International Universities Press.

——. 1968. Dis-identifying from mother: Its special importance for the boy. *IJPA* 49:370.

Greenwald, H. 1958. *The Call Girl: A Social and Psychoanalytic Study.* New York: Ballantine.

Grinker, R., Werble, B., and Drye, R. 1968. *The Borderline Syndrome.* New York: Basic Books.

Gross, M. 1978. *The Psychological Society.* New York: Random House.

Grossman, W. I., and Stewart, W. A. 1976. Penis envy: From childhood wish to developmental metaphor. *JAPA* 24:193–212.

Gutheil, E. 1930. Analysis of a case of transvestism. In *Sexual Aberrations,* ed. W. Stekel. New York: Liverwright.

Guze, H. 1968. Psychosocial adjustment of transsexuals: An evaluation and theoretical formulation. In *Transsexualism and Sex Reassignment,* eds. R. Green and J. Money, 171–181. Baltimore: Johns Hopkins University Press.

Hamburger, C., Stürup, G., and Dahl-Iversen, E. 1953.Transvestism. *JAMA* 152:391–396.

Hamer, D. et al. 1993. A linkage between DNA markers on the X chromosome and male sexual orientation. *Science,* July 16, 321–323.

Hampson, J. G. 1955. Hermaphroditic genital appearance, rearing and eroticism in hyperadrenocorticism. *Johns Hopkins Hospital Bulletin* 96:265–273.

Hardy, K. R. 1964. An appetitional theory of sexual motivations. *Psychological Review* 71(1):1–18.

Hare, R. 1981. The philosophical basis of psychiatric ethics. In *Psychiatric Ethics,* ed. S. Block and P. Chodoff. New York: Oxford University Press.

Hariton, E. B., and Singer, J. L. 1974. Women's fantasies during sexual intercourse and theoretical implications. *J. Consulting and Clin. Psych.* 42:313–322.

Harms, E. 1969. *Bull. New York Academy of Medicine* 45(8):761–766.

Hasselund, H. 1975. Masturbation and sexual fantasies in married couples. *Arch. of Sexual Behavior* 133–147.

Heath, R. G. 1972. Pleasure and brain activity in man: Deep and surface electroencephalograms during orgasm. *J. Nervous and Mental Disease* 154:3–18.

Heath, S. 1986. Joan Rivière and the masquerade. In *Formations of Fantasy,* eds. Burgin et al. London: Methuen.

Heidenry, J. 1997. *What Wild Ecstasy: The Rise and Fall of the Sexual Revolution.* New York: Simon and Schuster.

Herdt, G. 1994. *Third Sex, Third Gender: Beyond Sexual Dimorphism in Culture and History.* New York: Zone Books.

Hogan, R. T., and Emler, N. T. 1978. The biases in contemporary social psychology. *Social Research: An International Quarterly in the Social Sciences* 45(3):478–534.

Hollingshead, A. B. 1975. Four-factor index of social status. Unpublished manuscript (available from the Dept. of Sociology, Yale University, New Haven, Conn. 06510).

Horney, K. 1924. On the genesis of the castration complex in women. *IJPA* 5:50–65.

——. 1926. The flight from womanhood: The masculinity-complex in women, as viewed by men and by women. *IJPA* 7:324–339.

——. 1932. The dread of women, observations on a specific difference in the dread felt by men and by women respectively for the opposite sex. *IJPA* 13:348–360.

——. 1933. The denial of the vagina, a contribution to the problem of the genital anxieties specific to women. *IJPA* 14:57–70.

Howell, E. 1981. Women: From Freud to the present. In *Women and Mental Health,* eds. E. Howell and M. Bayes. New York: Basic Books.

Hoyer, N., ed. 1933. *Man Into Woman. An Authentic Story of a Change of Sex.* New York: Dutton.

Hunt, M. 1974. Changes in masturbatory attitudes and behavior. In *Human Autoerotic Practices,* ed. M. F. DeMartino. New York: Human Sciences Press.

——. 1984. *Sex in the 1970s*. Chicago: Playboy Press.
Imperato-McGinley, J. et al. 1979. Androgens and the evolution of male gender identity among male pseudohermaphrodites with 5a-redutase deficiency. *N. Eng. J. Med.* 300:1233–1237.
Inderbitzin, L. B., and Levy, S. T. 1990. Unconscious fantasy: A reconsideration of the concept. *JAPA* 38:113–130.
Jacobson, E. 1954. Contributions to the metapsychology of psychotic identifications. *JAPA* 2:239–262.
——. 1964. *The Self and the Object World*. New York: International Universities Press.
Johnson, A. G. 1980. On prevalence of rape in the U.S. *Signs* 6:136–146.
Jones, E. 1927. The early development of female sexuality. In *Papers on Psychoanalysis*, 438–451. Boston: Beacon Press.
——. 1933. The phallic phase. In *Papers on Psychoanalysis*, 452–484. Boston: Beacon Press.
——. 1935. Early female sexuality. In *Papers on Psychoanalysis*, 485–495. Boston: Beacon Press.
——. 1953. *The Life and Work of Sigmund Freud*. Vol. 1. New York: Basic Books.
——. 1955. *The Life and Work of Sigmund Freud*. Vol. 2. New York: Basic Books.
Jones, J. 1997. Panels of Sexology: Dr. Yes. *The New Yorker*, August 25 and September 1.
Jorgensen, C. 1967. *Christine Jorgensen: A Personal Autobiography*. New York: Paul G. Eriksson.
Jucovy, M. 1976. Initiation fantasies and transvestism. *JAPA* 24:525–546.
Kalogerakis, M. G. 1975. The effect on ego development of sexual experience in early adolescence. In *Sexuality and Psychoanalysis*, ed. E. T. Adelson. New York: Brunner/Mazel.
Kaplan, H. S. 1979. *Disorders of Sexual Desire*. New York: Brunner/Mazel.
——. 1995. *The Sexual Desire Disorders: Dysfunctional Regulation of Sexual Motivation*. New York: Brunner/Mazel.
Kaplan, L. 1990. *Female Perversions: The Temptations of Emma Bovary*. New York: Doubleday.
Kardiner, A. 1939. *The Individual and His Society*. New York: Columbia University Press.
——. 1977. *My Analysis with Freud: Reminiscences*. New York: Norton.
Kardiner, A., Karush, A., and Ovesey, L. 1959. A methodological study of Freudian theory. *Journal of Nervous and Mental Disease* 129(1). Republished in *Int. J. Psychiatry* 2(5):489–542 (1966).
Karlen, A. 1971. *Sexuality and Homosexuality*. New York: Norton.
Karme, L. 1979. The analysis of a male patient by a female analyst: The problem of the negative oedipal transference. *IJPA* 60:253–261.
Karush, A., and Ovesey, L. 1961. Unconscious mechanisms of magical repair. *Arch. Gen. Psychiatry*. 5:55–69.
Kastrup, M. (1976), Psychic disorders among pre-school children in a geographically delimited area of Aarhus County, Denmark. *Acta Psychiat. Scand.*, 54:29–42.
Kern, S. 1975. *Anatomy and Destiny: A Cultural History of the Human Body*. New York: Bobbs-Merrill.
Kernberg, O. 1967. Borderline personality organization. *JAPA* 15:641.
——. 1991a. Aggression and love in the relationship of the couple. *JAPA* 39(1):45–70.
——. 1991b. Sadomasochism, sexual excitement, and perversion. *JAPA* 39(2):333–360.
——. 1995. *Love Relations: Normality and Pathology*. New Haven: Yale University Press.
Kestenbaum, C. J. 1975. Some effects of the "sexual revolution" on the mid-adolescent girl. In *Sexuality and Psychoanalysis*, ed. E. T. Adelson. New York: Brunner/Mazel.
Keyes, E. 1977. *Scarlett O'Hara's Younger Sister: My Lively Life in and out of Hollywood*. Secaucus, N.J.: Lyle Stuart.
Khan, M. M. R. 1966. Foreskin fetishism and its relation to ego pathology in a male homosexual. In *Psychoanalysis and Male Sexuality*, ed. H. Ruitenbeek, 235–268. New Haven: College and University Press.
Kinsey, A. C., Pomeroy, W. B., and Martin, C. E. 1948. *Sexual Behavior in the Human Male*. Philadelphia: W. B. Saunders.
Kinsey, A., Pomeroy, W. B., Martin, C. E., and Gebhard, P. H. 1953. *Sexual Behavior in the Human Female*. Philadelphia: W. B. Saunders.
Klebanow, S. 1975. Developmental readiness and dependency in adolescent sexuality. In *Sexuality and Psychoanalysis*, ed. E. T. Adelson. New York: Brunner/Mazel.
Kleeman, J.1976. Freud's views on early female sexuality in the light of direct childhood observation. *JAPA* 24 (Suppl. 5):3–27.
Klein, G. S. 1976. Freud's two theories of sexuality. *Psychological Issues* 9(4):14–70, monograph 36. New York: International Universities Press.
Klerman, G. L. 1982. Testing analytic hypotheses: Are personality attributes predisposed to depres-

sion? In *Psychoanalysis: Critical Explorations in Contemporary Theory and Practice*, eds. A. M. Jacobson and D. X. Parmalee. New York: Brunner/Mazel.
Knorr, N., Wolf, S., and Meyer, E. 1968. Psychiatric evaluation of male transsexuals for surgery. In *Transsexualism and Sex Reassignment*, eds. R. Green and J. Money. Baltimore: Johns Hopkins University Press. 271–279.
Kohlberg, L. 1966. Cognitive-developmental analysis of children's sex role concepts and attitudes. In *The Development of Sex Differences*, 82–173. Stanford: Stanford University Press.
Kohut, H. 1971. *The Analysis of the Self.* New York: International Universities Press.
——. 1977. *The Restoration of the Self.* New York: International Universities Press.
Koss, M., Gidyez, C., and Wisniewsky, N. 1987. Scope of rape. *J. of Consulting and Clin. Psych.* 55(2):162–170.
Krafft-Ebing. R. 1969. *Psychopathia Sexualis.* 12th edition. trans. F. S. Klaf. New York: Bantam.
Kubie, L. S. 1948. Instincts and homeostasis. *Psychosomatic Medicine* 10: 15–29.
——. 1956. Influence of symbolic processes on the role of instincts in human behavior. *Psychosomatic Medicine* 18:189–208.
Kubie, L. S. , and Mackie, J. B. 1968. Critical issues raised by operations for gender transmutations. *J. Nerv. Ment. Dis.* 147: 431–444.
Kuhn, T. S. 1962. *The Structure of Scientific Revolutions. Chicago*: University of Chicago Press.
Laplanche, J., and Pontalis, J. -B. 1973. *The Language of Psycho-Analysis.* New York: W. W. Norton.
Lapouse, R., and Monk, M. A. 1978. An epidemiologic study of behavior characteristics in children. *Amer. J. Public Hlth.*, 48:1134–1144.
Lebowitz, P. S. 1972. Feminine behavior in boys: Aspects of its outcome. *Amer. J. Psychiat.*, 128: 1283–1289.
Lerner, H. 1980. Penis envy: Alternatives in conceptualization. *Bull. Menninger Clin.* 44:39–48.
Lester, E. 1983. The female analyst and the eroticized transference. *IJPA* 66:283–293.
Lichtenstein, H. 1961. Identity and sexuality. *JAPA* 9:179–260.
——. 1970. The changing concept of psychosexual development. *JAPA* 18:300–318.
——. 1977. Identity and sexuality. In *The Dilemma of Human Identity.* New York: Jason Aronson.
Litman, R., and Swearingen, C. 1972. Bondage and suicide. *Arch. Gen. Psychiatry* 27:80–85.
Lorber, J. 1994. *Paradoxes of Gender.* New Haven: Yale University Press.
Lothstein, L. M. 1983. *Female-to-Male Transsexualism: Historical, Clinical, and Theoretical Issues.* Boston: Routledge and Kegan Paul.
Lukianowicz, N. 1960. Imaginary sexual partner and visual masturbatory fantasies. *Arch. Gen. Psychiat.* 3:429–449.
McDougall, J. 1980. *Plea for a Measure of Abnormality.* New York: International Univervities Press.
Macklin, R. 1973. Values in psychoanalysis and psychotherapy: A survey and analysis. *JAPA* 33:133–150.
MacLean, P. D. 1975. Brain mechanisms of primal sexual functions and related behavior. In *Sexual Behavior: Pharmacology and Biochemistry*, eds. M. Sander and G. L. Gessa. New York: Raven Press.
Mahler, M. 1968. *On Human Symbiosis and the Vicissitudes of Individuation.* New York: International Universities Press.
——. 1972. On the first three subphases of the separation-individuation Process. *IJPA* 53:333.
——. 1975. Discussion of "Healthy parental influences on the earliest development of masculinity in baby boy," by R. Stoller. In *Psychoanalytic Forum*, Vol. 5. New York: International Universities Press.
Malamuth, N. 1988. A multi-dimensional approach to sexual aggression: Combining measures of past behavior and present likelihood. In *Human Sexual Aggression: Current Perspectives*, eds. R. A. Prentky and V. L. Quinsey. Annals of the N.Y. Academy of Sciences.
Marantz, S. 1984. Mothers of extremely feminine boys: Child rearing practices and psychopathology. Doctoral dissertation, New York University.
Marcus, S. 1964. *The Other Victorians: A Study of Sexuality in Pornography in Mid-Nineteenth-Century England.* New York: Basic Books.
——. 1975. Freud's "Three Essays on the Theory of Sexuality." *Partisan Review* 42:517–534.
——. 1982. Culture and psychoanalysis. *Partisan Review* 2:224–252.
Marcuse, H. 1955. *Eros and Civilization.* Boston: Beacon Press.
Marmor, J. 1973. Changing patterns of femininity: Psychoanalytic implications. In *Psychoanalysis and Women*, ed. J. B. Miller. New York: Brunner/Mazel.

Maslow, A. 1939. Dominance, personality and social behavior in women. *J. of Social Psychology* 10:3–39.

——. 1942. Self-esteem (dominance-feeling) and sexuality in women. *J. of Social Psychology* 16:259–94.

Masters, W. H., and Johnson, V. E. 1966. *Human Sexual Response*. Boston: Little, Brown.

——. 1970. *Human Sexual Inadequacy*. Boston: Little Brown.

Masterson, J. 1972. *Treatment of the Borderline Adolescent: A Developmental Approach*. New York: John Wiley.

Mavissakalian, M. et al. 1975. Responses to complex erotic stimuli in homosexual and heterosexual males. *Brit. J. Psychiatry* 126:252–257.

May, R. 1980. *Sex and Fantasy: Patterns of Male and Female Development*. New York: Norton.

Meerloo, J. A. M. 1967. Changes of sex and collaboration with the psychosis. *Am. J. Psychiat.* 124:263.

Meyer-Bahlburg, H. F. L. 1997. The role of prenatal estrogens in sexual orientation. In *Sexual Orientation: Toward Biological Understanding*, eds. L. Ellis and L. Ebertz, pp. 41–51. Westport, Conn.: Praeger.

——. 1998. Commentary: Gender assignment and intersexuality. *Journal of Psychology and Human Sexuality*, 10 (2):1–21.

——. 1999 (in press). Variance of Gender Differentiation. In *Risks and Outcomes in Developmental Psychopathology*, eds. Steinhausen and Verhulst. New York: Oxford University Press.

Middlebrook, D. W. 1998. *Suits Me: The Double Life of Billy Tipton*. Boston: Houghton Mifflin.

Millett, K. 1970. *Sexual Politics*. New York: Doubleday.

Mitchell, J. 1974. *Psychoanalysis and Feminism: Freud, Reich, Laing, and Women*. New York: Pantheon.

Mitchell, S. A. 1988. *Relational Concepts in Psychoanalysis*. Cambridge: Harvard University Press.

Modell, A. H. 1978. Affects and the complementarity of biologic and historical meaning. In *The Annual of Psychoanalysis*, Vol. 6. New York: International Universities Press.

Money, J. 1956. Sexual incongruities and psychopathology: The evidence of human hermaphroditism. *Bull. Johns Hopkins Hosp.* 98:43–57.

——. 1968a. Sex reassignment as related to hermaphroditism and transsexualism. In *Transsexualism and Sex Reassignment*, eds. R. Green and J. Money. Baltimore: Johns Hopkins University Press.

——. 1968b. Sexual dimorphism and dissociation in the psychology of male transsexuals. In *Transsexualism and Sex Reassignment*, eds. R. Green and J. Money, 115–136.

——. 1970–71. Sex Reassignment. *Int. J. Psychiat.* 9:249.

——. 1973. Gender role, gender identity, core gender identity: Usage and definition of terms. *J. Am. Acad. Psychoanal.* 1:397–402.

——. 1974. Two names, two wardrobes, two personalities. *J. of Homosexuality* 1:65–70.

——. 1975. Ablatio penis: Normal male infant sex-reassigned as a girl. *Archives of Sexual Behavior* 4(1):65–71

Money, J., ed. 1965. *Sex Research: New Developments*. New York: Holt, Rinehart & Winston.

Money, J., and Dalery, J. 1977. Hyperadrenocortical 46XX hermaphroditism with penile urethra: Psychological studies in seven cases, three reared as boys, four as girls. In *Congenital Adrenal Hyperphasia*, ed. P. A. Lee et al. Baltimore, Md.: University Park Press.

Money, J., and Gaskin, R. J. 1970–71. Sex reassignment. *Int. J. Psychiatry* 9:249–282.

Money, J., Hampson, J. G., and Hampson, J. L. 1955a. An examination of some basic sexual concepts: The evidence of human hermaphroditism. *Bulletin of the Johns Hopkins Hospital.* 97:301–319.

——. 1955b. Hermaphroditism: Recommendations concerning assignment, change of sex, and psychological management. *Bull. Johns Hopkins Hospital.* 97:284–330.

Money, J., and Russo, A. J. 1979. Homosexual outcome of the discordant gender identity/role in childhood: Longitudinal followup. *J. Pediat. Psychol.*, 4:29–41.

Money, J., and Schwartz, F. 1968. Public opinion and social issues in transsexualism. In *Transsexualism and Sex Reassignment*, eds. R. Green and J. Money, 253–269. Baltimore: Johns Hopkins University Press.

Money, J., Schwartz, F. , and Davis, V. G. 1984. Adult erotosexual status and fetal hormonal masculinization and de-masculinization: 46, XX congenital virilizing adrenal hyperplasia and 46, XY androgen-insensitivity syndrome compared. *Psychoneuroendochrinology* 9:405–415.

Moore, B., and Fine, B., eds. 1990. *Psychoanalytic Terms and Concepts.* New Haven: Yale University Press.

Morgenthau, H., and Person, E. 1978. The roots of narcissism. *Partisan Review* 3:337–347.

Mosher, D. L., and Anderson, R. D. 1986. Masochistic personality, sexual aggression, and reactions to guided imagery of realistic rape. *J. of Research in Personality* 20:77–94.

Moulton, R. 1966. Multiple factors in frigidity. In *Science and Psychoanalysis,* ed. Jules Masserman, Vol. 10. New York: Grune & Stratton.

——. 1973. A survey and re-evaluation of the concept of penis envy. In *Psychoanalysis and Women,* ed. J. B. Miller. New York: Brunner/Mazel.

Orvaschel, H., and Weissman, M. M. 1985. Epidemiology of anxiety disorders in children: A review. In *Anxiety Disorders in Children,* ed. R. Gittelman. New York: Guilford.

Ott, L. 1984. *An Introduction to Statistical Methods and Data Analysis.* Boston: Duxbury Press.

Ovesey, L. 1955. The pseudohomosexual anxiety. *Psychiatry* 18:17–25.

——. 1956. Masculine aspirations in women. *Psychiatry* 19:341–51.

——. 1969. *Homosexuality and Pseudohomosexuality.* New York: Science House.

Ovesey, L., and Meyers, H. 1968. Retarded ejaculation. *Am. J. of Psychother.* 22:185–201.

Ovesey, L., and Person. E. 1973. Gender identity and sexual psychopathology in men: A psychodynamic analysis of homosexuality, transsexualism and transvestism. *J. Amer. Acad. Psychoanal.* 1:53–72.

——. 1976. Transvestism: A disorder of the sense of self. *Int. J. Psychoanal. Psychother.* 5:219–235.

Pace, E. 1986. Harry Benjamin dies at 101, specialist in transsexualism. Obituary in *The New York Times,* August 27, D18.

Perper, T. 1985. *Sex Signals: The Biology of Love.* Philadelphia: ISI Press.

Person, E. 1974. Some new observations on the origins of femininity. In *Women and Analysis, Psychoanalytic Views of Femininity,* ed. J. Strouse. New York: Grossman.

——. 1975. The treatment of male homosexuality. Presented at meetings of the American Psychoanalytic Assoc., May. Reported in Panel 1977. "The psychoanalytic treatment of male sexuality," E. Payne, reporter. *JAPA* 25:183–199.

——. 1976. Discussion of "initiation fantasies and transvestism" by M. Jucovy. *JAPA* 24:547–551.

——. 1980. Sexuality as the mainstay of identity: Psychoanalytic perspectives. *Signs: J. of Women in Culture and Society* 5:605–630.

——. 1982. Women working: Fears of failure, deviance and success. *J. Am. Acad. Psychoanal.* 10:67–84.

——. 1983. Women in therapy: Therapist gender as a variable. *Int. Rev.Psycho-Anal.* 10:193–204.

——. 1985a. Female sexual identity: The impact of the adolescent experience. In *Sexuality: New Perspectives,* 71–88. Westport, Conn.: Greenwood.

——. 1985b. The erotic transference in women and in men: Differences and consequences. *J. Amer. Acad. Psychoanal.* 13 (2):159–180.

——. 1986a. Male sexuality and power. *Psychoanalytic Inquiry* 6:3–25.

——. 1986b. The omni-available woman and lesbian sex: Two fantasy themes and their relationship to the male developmental experience. In *The Psychology of Men,* eds. G. Fogel, F. M. Lane, and R. S. Liebert. New York: Basic Books.

——. 1988. *Dreams of Love and Fateful Encounters/The Power of Romantic Passion.* New York: W. W. Norton & Co.

——. 1993 [1996]. The "construction" of femininity: Its influence throughout the life cycle. In *The Course of Life,* eds. S. Greenspan and G. Pollock. Rockville, Md.: NIMH. Reprinted and revised in *The Textbook of Psychoanalysis,* eds. E. Nersessian and R. Kopff. Washington D.C.: American Psychiatric Press, 1996.

——. 1995. *By Force of Fantasy: How We Live Our Lives.* New York: Basic Books.

Person, E. S., ed. 1997. *On Freud's "A Child Is Being Beaten."* New Haven: Yale University Press.

Person, E. S. et al. 1989. Gender differences in sexual behaviors and fantasies in a college population. *Journal of Sex and Marital Therapy* 15(3):187–198 (1989).

Person, E. S. et al. 1992. Associations between sexual experiences and fantasies in a non-patient population: A preliminary study. *Journal of the American Academy of Psychoanalysis* 20(1):75–90.

Person, E., and Ovesey, L. 1974a. The transsexual syndrome in males: Part I: Primary transsexualism. *Amer. J. Psychother.* 28(1):4–20.

——. 1974b. The transsexual syndrome in males: Part II: Secondary transsexualism. *Amer. J. Psychother.* 28(2):174–193.

——. 1974c. Psychodynamics of male transsexualism. In *Sex Differences in Behavior,* eds. R. C. Friedman, R. M. Richart, and R. L.Vande Wiele, 315–326. New York: John Wiley & Sons.
——. 1978. Transvestism: New perspectives. *J. Amer. Acad. Psychoanal.* 6(3):301–323.
——. 1983. Psychoanalytic theories of gender identity. *J. Amer. Acad. Psychoanal.* 11(2):203–226.
——. 1984. Homosexual cross-dressers. *J. Amer. Acad. of Psychoanal.* 12(2):167–186.
"Poll shows decline in sex by high-school students." *New York Times,* September 18, 1998, A26.
Pomeroy, W. B. 1968. Transsexualism and sexuality: Sexual behavior of pre- and postoperative male transsexuals. In *Transsexualism and Sex Reassignment,* ed. R. Green and J. Money, 183–188. Baltimore: Johns Hopkins University Press.
Rado, S. 1956. An adaptational view of sexual behavior. In *Psychoanalysis of Behavior.* New York: Grune & Stratton.
Rekers, G. A. et al. 1977. Child gender disturbance: a clinical rationale for intervention. *Psychother. Theory Res. Pract.* 14:1–8.
——.1979. Genetic and physical studies of male children with psychological gender disturbances. *Psychol. Med.* 9:373–375.
Rich, A. 1980. Compulsory heterosexuality and lesbian existence. *Signs,* Special Issue, eds. C. Stimpson and E. Person 5:631–60. Reprinted in *Women: Sex and Sexuality.* 1980. Eds. C. Stimpson and E. Person. Chicago: University of Chicago Press.
Rieff, P. 1961. *Freud: The Mind of the Moralist.* New York: Doubleday Anchor.
——. 1966. *The Triumph of the Therapeutic: Uses of Faith After Freud.* New York: Harper & Row.
Rivière, J. 1929. Womanliness as a masquerade. *IJPA* 10:303–313.
Robinson, P. 1976. *The Modernization of Sex.* New York: Harper and Row.
Rohrbaugh, J. B. 1979. *Women: Psychology's Puzzle.* New York: Basic Books/Harper Colophon Books.
Rosen, A. C., Rekers, G. A., and Friar, L. R. 1977. Theoretical and diagnostic issues in child gender disturbances. *J. Sex Res.,* 13:89–103.
Ross, N. 1970. The primacy of genitality in the light of ego psychology. *J. Am. Psychoanal. Assoc.* 18:267–284.
——. 1979. On the significance of infantile sexuality. In *On Sexuality: Psychoanalytic Observations,* eds. T. Karasu and C. Socarides. New York: International Universities Press.
Ross, N. 1970. The primacy of genitality in the light of ego psychology. *JAPA* 18(2):265–284.
——. 1979. On the significance of infantile sexuality. In *On Sexuality: Psychoanalytic Observations,* eds. T. Karasu and C. Socarides. New York: International Universities Press.
Sandler, J., and Sandler, A. M. 1978. On the development of object relationships and affects. *IJPA* 59:277–296.
——.1987. The past unconscious, the present unconscious, and the vicissitudes of guilt. *IJPA* 68:331–341.
Schacter, S., and Singer, J. E. 1962. Cognitive, social and physiological determinants of emotional state. *Psychological Review* 69:379–399.
Schafer, R. 1968. *Aspects of Internalization.* New York: International Universities Press.
——. 1974. Problems in Freud's psychology of women. *JAPA* 22:459–489.
——. 1976. Discussion of "Transvestism: A disorder of the sense of self," by L. Ovesey and E. Person at The Association for Psychoanalytic Medicine.
——. 1977. The interpretation of transference and the conditions of loving. *JAPA* 25:335–362.
——. 1978. *Language and Insight.* New Haven: Yale University Press.
Scruton, R. 1986. *Sexual Desire: A Moral Philosophy of the Exotic.* New York: Free Press.
Segal, M. M. 1965. Transvestism as an impulse and as a defense. *IJPA* 46:209–217.
Shulman, A. K. 1980. Sex and power: Sexual bases of radical feminism. In *Women—Sex and Sexuality,* eds. C. R. Stimpson and E. S. Person. Chicago: University of Chicago Press.
Singer, J. 1966. *Day-dreaming: An Introduction to the Experimental Study of Inner Experience.* New York: Random House.
——. 1975. *The Inner World of Daydreaming.* New York: Harper and Row.
Singer, J., and Antrobus, J. S. 1963. A factor-analytic study of daydreaming and conceptually related cognitive and personality variables. *Perceptual and Motor Skills* 3 (Monograph Suppl.):17.
Socarides, C. W. 1968. *The Overt Homosexual.* New York: Grune & Stratton.
——. 1970. A psychoanalytic study of the desire for sexual transformation ("transsexualism"): The plaster of paris man. *IJPA* 51:341–349.
——. 1975. Discussion of "Healthy parental influences on the earliest development of masculinity

in baby boys," by R. Stoller, in *Psychoanalytic Forum*, ed. J. Lindon, Vol. 5:241–243. New York: International Universities Press.

——. 1977. Transsexualism and the first law of medicine. *Psychiatr. Opinion* 14:20–24.

——. 1978. *Homosexuality*. New York: Jason Aronson.

Sorensen, R. C. 1973. *Adolescent Sexuality in Contemporary America*. New York: World.

Sperling, M. 1947. The analysis of an exhibitionist. *IJPA* 28:32–45.

Spitz, R. 1945. Hospitalism: An inquiry into the genesis of psychiatric conditions in early childhood. In *PSOC* 1:53–74. New York: International Universities Press.

——. 1946. Hospitalism: A follow-up report. In *PSOC* 2:111–13.

Stekel, W. 1940. *Impotence in the Male: The Psychic Disorders of Sexual Dysfunction in the Man*. Trans. Oswald Boltz. London: John Lane the Bodley Head.

Stimpson, C., and E. Person, eds. 1980. *Women: Sex and Sexuality*. Chicago: University of Chicago Press.

Stoller, R. J. 1968a. *Sex and Gender*. New York: Science House.

——. 1968b. Parental influences in male transsexualism. In *Transsexualism and Sex Reassignment*, eds. R. Green and J. Money, 153–169. Baltimore: Johns Hopkins University Press.

——. 1970. Pornography and perversion. *Arch. Gen.Psychiat.* 22:490.

——. 1974. Facts and fancies: An examination of Freud's concept of bisexuality. In *Women and Analysis: Dialogues on Psychoanalytic Views of Femininity*, ed. J. Stouse, 343–364. New York: Grossman (1974).

——. 1975a. *Perversion—The Erotic Form of Hatred*. New York: Pantheon.

——. 1975b. *The Transsexual Experiment*. Vol. 2. New York: Jason Aronson.

——. 1976. *Sex and Gender, Vol. 2: The Transsexual Experiment*. New York: Jason Aronson.

——. 1979. *Sexual Excitement: Dynamics of Erotic Life*. New York Pantheon.

——. 1985a. *Observing the Erotic Imagination*. New Haven: Yale University Press.

——. 1985b. *Presentations of Gender*. New Haven: Yale University Press.

Stone, L. 1967. The psychoanalytic situation and transference. *JAPA* 15:3–57.

Sulcov, M. 1973. Transsexualism: Its social reality. Unpublished doctoral thesis, Indiana University.

Sulloway, F. 1979. *Freud, Biologist of the Mind*. New York: Basic Books.

Symonds, D. 1979. *The Evolution of Human Sexuality*. New York: Oxford Univserity Press.

Szasz, T. 1963. The concept of transference. *IJPA* 44:432–443.

Thompson, C. 1943. Penis envy in women. In *Psychoanalysis and Women*, ed. J. B. Miller. New York: Brunner/Mazel (1973).

——. 1950. Some effects of the derogatory attitude towards female sexuality. *Psychiatry* 13:349–354.

Thorne, E. 1971. *Your Erotic Fantasies*. New York: Ballantine Books.

Toolan, J. 1975. Sexual behavior in high school and college students. In *Sexuality and Psychoanalysis*, ed. E. T. Adelson. New York: Brunner/Mazel.

TransFag Rag: Information and Networking for Gay/Bi Transmen. Elessar Press, 1259 El Camino Real, Suite 151, Menlo Park, Calif. 94025.

Tripp, C. A. 1975. *The Homosexual Matrix*. New York: New American Library.

Tuber, S., and Coates, S. 1985. Interpersonal phenomena in the Rorschachs of feminine boys. *Psychoanal. Psychol.* 2:251–265.

Tyson, P. 1982. A developmental line of gender identity, gender role, and choice of love object. *JAPA* 30:61–86.

van Lustbader, E. 1984. *The Miko*. New York: Villard Books.

Vaughter, R. M. 1976. Review essay on psychology. *Signs: J. of Women in Culture and Society* 2:120–146.

Weeks, J. 1979. Movements of affirmation: Sexual meaning and homosexual identity. *Radical Hist. Rev.* 20.

——. 1986. *Sexuality*. New York: Routledge.

Weitzman, E. L., Shamoian, C. A., and Golosow, N. 1970. Identity diffusion and the transsexual resolution. *J. Nervous and Mental Diseases* 51:295–302.

Whalen, R. E. 1966. Sexual motivation. *Psychol. Rev.* 73(2):151–63.

White, E. 1980. *States of Desire: Travels in Gay America*. New York: E. P. Dutton.

Zilbergeld, B. 1978. *Male Sexuality*. New York: Bantam Books.

Zucker, K. J. 1982. Childhood gender disturbances: Diagnostic issues. *Journal of the American Academy of Child Psychiatry* 21(3):274–284.

Zuger, B. 1978. Effeminate behavior in boys in childhood: Ten additional years of follow-up. *Comp. Psychiat.*, 19:363–369.

INDEX

Abortion, 21–22
Adelson, J., 281
Adler, Alfred, 84, 360
Aggression (and hostility), 28, 169, 170–71, 192–93, 218–19, 220, 222, 298
AIDS, 2, 12, 28, 29, 242, 291
American Psychiatric Association, 21
Antrobus, J. S., 244
Appetitional theory, 33, 36–38
Arafat, I. S., 288
Arlow, Jacob, 244
Atherton, George, 358
Atherton, Gertrude, 358–59

Bak, R., 163, 167
Baldwin, James, 317
Barclay, A. M., 320
Barglow, P., 76
Bassin, Donna, 313–14
Bates, J. E., 197
Beach, F. A., 32, 33, 36
Beigel, H., 150
Bell, A., 26
Bemporad, J., 167
Benjamin, Gretchen, 359
Benjamin, Harry: and sexology, 16, 360; and transsexualism, 19–20, 106, 112, 115, 347–51, 360–63, 365–66; family background of, 351–53; and tuberculosis work, 352–55; and rejuvenation work, 355–60, 362, 366
Bergmann, M. S., 263
Bias: and female sexuality, 2–3; in Freud's sexuality theories, 3, 82, 84; and sex and gender, 3, 297; theoretical bias against women, 3, 74–77, 82–83, 86, 87; and culture, 8, 14, 75; and sexology, 19, 20; and essentialist/constructionist integration, 28; and libido theory, 34; and psychoanalysis, 73, 76. *See also* Values
Bibring, G., 269
Bieber, I., 100, 101, 122, 133
Birth control, 12, 21–22, 29
Bisexuality: and gender role, 8; and Kinsey, 20; and Freud, 22, 24, 26; and sex print, 45, 227; and transvestism, 170; and erotic transference, 270; and sexual development, 300
Bloch, Iwan, 15
Blos, P., 281
Blum, H. P., 80–81, 83, 261, 264
Boredom. *See* Sexual boredom
Boswell, J., 27
Boyhood femininity: and separation anxiety, 5, 194, 197, 200, 201–2, 205–7; and transsexualism, 5, 66, 195–96; and cross-gender disorders, 65, 206; and gender identity, 194–98, 200–1, 207; and developmental history, 199–200; and clinical findings, 201–4
Brenner, C., 327
Breuer, Josef, 259, 260
Broverman, I. K., 74
Brown, Norman, 13, 24, 51
Brownmiller, Susan, 318
Bullough, Vern, 16
Burroughs, William, 317

Campbell, B., 286
Castration anxiety: and cross-gender disorders, 4, 68; and male sexuality, 50, 163, 172, 240, 319, 326–27, 328, 331, 342; and gender theory, 58–59, 70; and sexual disorders, 98–99; and homosexuality, 99, 100, 163; and transsexualism, 108, 134; and transvestism, 154, 159, 168, 170, 172; and psychoanalysis, 163, 164; and omni-available woman fantasy, 333
Chasseguet-Smirgel, J., 221, 222–23
Child Behavior Checklist, 196, 199–201, 205
Childhood Gender Identity Project, 198
Chodorow, Nancy, 26, 69, 77
Christgau, R., 12n1
Clarke group, 196, 197, 207
Coates, S., 198, 204
Coen, Stanley, 219
Conformity, 301–2
Constructionism (constructivism), 14, 19, 25, 26–30, 298, 299
Core gender identity: and gender role identity, 3, 25, 32, 57, 70, 92–93; lack of fluidity, 8; and gender, 32, 42, 53, 69, 71; and cross-gender disorders, 66, 68, 68n10; and transsexualism, 68, 93, 107–9, 111, 113–14, 141, 142, 300; and changing theories, 79; as biological self-image, 92; development of, 92, 298; and transvestism, 93, 111; and primary transsexualism, 114, 125, 126, 133, 144; and secondary transsexualism, 114, 133, 139, 144; and boyhood femininity, 206; and intersexed children, 298–300; biological impact on, 299
Cotton, W. L., 288
Countertransference, 76–77, 260, 266, 267, 272
Crew, F. A., 360
Cross-gender disorders: and fantasy, 4, 68, 98, 342; and separation anxiety, 5, 62, 68, 68n10, 98, 158, 197; as disorders, 7–8; and boyhood femininity, 65, 206; psychoanalytic theories of, 65–69; and preoedipal period, 158, 166; cross-gender identifications as, 312–13. *See also* Homosexual cross-dressing; Transsexualism; Transvestism
Cross-gender identifications: conflictual nature of, 6, 297, 298, 314; and women, 6, 297–98, 303–12; and culture, 12, 314; and conformity, 301–2; and masculine identifications in heterosexual women, 304–9; and fantasy, 305–8; and neuter women, 309–11; as cross-gender disorders, 312–13
Culture: and sex and gender, 2, 6, 30, 297; and sexual mores, 2, 11; and conformity, 3, 8, 28; and social norms, 3; and bias, 8, 14, 75; and sexuality, 11, 13–14, 24, 31, 32, 33, 38, 43, 51, 87; and cross-gender identifications, 12, 314; and sexual-liberation movements, 14, 24, 291; and sexual behavior, 17; and heterosexuality, 25–26; and homosexuality, 27; and sexual desire, 29, 213, 215, 219–20, 228n14; and female sexuality, 31, 37, 49, 53, 77, 78, 278, 289, 291; and sexual identity, 46, 291; and fantasy, 54, 223, 272, 366; and values, 72–73, 82–83; and psychoanalytic theory, 73, 86; and masturbation, 78–79; and gender theory, 80; and gender role identity, 93, 302, 315; and gender stereotypes, 230, 241, 314–15; and erotic transference, 272, 274, 275, 276; and femininity, 273–74, 276, 281, 286, 297, 301, 303–4; and masculinity, 273–74, 275, 276, 281, 286, 301; and sexual role, 280; and male sexuality, 316, 317–18, 319; and domination, 332; and transsexualism, 362, 363–66; and self-realization, 364

Dalery, J., 71
de Kruif, Paul, 114–15, 364–65
Desire, 29; and heterosexual desire, 60. *See also* Sexual desire
Desired object, 6, 93, 280, 281, 289, 295
Desiring subject, 6, 280
Deutsch, H., 80
Dickinson, Robert L., 360
Dimen, Muriel, 314
Dinnerstein, Dorothy, 49
Disidentification, 62–63
Domination: and female sexuality, 31; and male sexuality, 50, 54, 316, 318, 330, 332; and masculinity, 94, 96, 101; and fantasy, 319, 320, 321, 322
Douvan, E., 281
Dumas, Alexandre, 224

Eissler, K., 41–42, 44
Ellis, Albert, 349, 360
Ellis, Henry Havelock, 16–17, 20, 22, 360
Emler, N. T., 72
Enactment: and transvestism, 4, 148, 149–53, 156–58, 175; and fantasy, 5, 223; and sexual desire, 220; and erotic transference, 263, 269n4; and sexual identity, 282; and male sexuality, 335, 336
Envy, 63, 156, 156n, 319, 330. *See also* Penis envy
Erickson Educational Foundation, 112, 124
Erotic stimuli: and sex print, 32, 44, 45, 280; and transvestism, 148; and homosexual cross-dressing, 191; and sexual desire, 216, 225; and sexual development, 300
Erotic transference: and psychoanalysis, 259–60; definition of, 260–61; and men, 260, 269–72, 270n5, 273–74, 275, 276; and resistance, 260, 262, 266, 267, 268, 270–71, 272, 276; and women, 260, 263, 266–68, 272, 273–74, 275, 276; therapeutic potential and liabilities of, 262–64, 267–68; and enactment, 263, 269n4; and homosexuality, 263, 269, 270, 272, 272n6; and four treatment dyads, 264–72; female patient-male analyst dyad, 266–68, 269, 276; female patient-female analyst dyad, 269, 275; male patient-female analyst dyad, 269–72, 275, 276, 326; and culture, 272, 274, 275, 276; male patient-male analyst dyad, 272
Erotogenic zones, 16, 22, 23, 34, 162
Essentialism, 13, 14, 25, 26, 28

Fairbairn, W. R. D., 220
Fantasy: and power, 1, 50–51; and conscious fantasy, 4, 5, 217, 243–44, 319–22; and cross-gender disorders, 4, 68, 98, 342; and imaginative limitation, 4; initiation fantasies, 4, 150–51, 159, 181; and substitute gratification, 4, 5–6; and nonsexual themes, 5, 218, 219, 221–23, 226; and sexual behavior, 5, 22, 243–56; and sexual desire, 5, 7, 16, 211, 213, 214, 215–17, 218, 220, 224, 225–29; and reality experiences, 6, 255; and male sexuality, 7, 230, 240–41, 318, 319–22, 320n1, 333–43; and Freud, 13, 22, 224, 244, 255–56, 307; and sexology, 19; and object relations, 40, 221; and sex print, 45, 226–27, 280; and culture, 54, 223, 272, 366; and merger fantasies, 68, 68n9, 189, 190, 192; and penis envy, 83; incorporative fantasies, 96–97; and neuroses, 97; and homosexuality, 100; and transvestism, 103, 146, 147, 148–58, 167, 170, 171, 174, 175, 176, 340–41, 342; and transsexualism, 108, 111, 114, 141–42, 364; and primary transsexualism, 116, 117, 122, 124, 125, 144; and secondary transsexualism, 131–32, 133, 138, 139; and homosexual cross-dressing, 179, 180–82, 184, 185, 186–88; transformation fantasies, 186–88; and unconscious, 217, 221, 226, 244, 319; and hostility, 219; multiple uses of, 219, 220; and bodily sensations, 221–22, 226, 228; and idealization, 222–23; and sexual boredom, 223–24, 224n8, 255; and perversions, 225, 225n10, 226; and gender identity, 229, 301; and female sexuality, 230, 241–42, 320, 320n1; and gender, 230, 232, 236–42, 314; role of, 244; and masturbation, 255; and erotic transference, 270, 271; and sexual identity, 280; and orgasm, 285, 286, 336; and sexual development, 300; and cross-gender identifications, 305–8. *See also* Lesbian sex fantasy; Omni-available woman fantasy
Fantasy Project of the Columbia Psychoanalytic Center, 243–44, 321
Father: and castration anxiety, 7, 58–59, 342; and gender theory, 58–59, 60, 61n3, 64; and penis envy, 77; and fantasy, 98; and homosexuality, 100, 101; and transvestism, 103–4, 105, 148, 159, 160, 166, 171, 341; and transsexualism, 118, 120, 128, 130, 132, 136, 238; and erotic transference, 267–68, 273, 274–75; and women's loss of love fear, 274–75; and sexual identity, 292, 294; and cross-gender identifications, 303–9; and male sexuality, 326–27, 328, 330, 332, 339, 340, 341
Feldman, R., 150
Female sexuality: and bias, 2–3; and male sexuality, 2–3, 31, 43–44, 47, 48, 53–54; and hyposexuality, 6, 31, 37, 50, 77, 279, 285; and masturbation, 6, 47–48, 78–79, 284–85, 287–88, 291, 295; and sexual identity, 6, 44, 279, 292, 295; and orgasmic sex, 18, 46–49, 77–78, 279, 283, 284–88, 292, 295, 322; and sexology, 21; changes in theory of, 28, 77–78; and culture, 31, 37, 49, 53, 77, 78, 278, 289, 291; and psychoanalysis, 31, 333; and libido theory, 34; and sexual motivation theory, 34; and inhibition of sexuality, 40, 44, 46–47, 49, 53, 78; and identity, 42, 53; and relevance of sexual paradigms, 46–53; and sexual-liberation movements, 51–53, 54, 278, 283; and penis envy, 59, 70n13, 77, 80–81, 293, 295, 343; and values, 81, 82; and fantasy, 230, 241–42, 320, 320n1; and adolescent development, 281; nonsexual purposes for, 282; clinical examples of sexual problems, 283–86; and deference in sexual interaction, 289–90; and omni-available woman fantasy, 335–36
Female-to-male transsexuals (FMT), 312–13
Femininity: as parallel construct, 3, 62, 64, 69, 80; changes in attitudes towards, 11–12, 28, 74, 75–76, 85; re-evaluation of, 12, 24; and sexology, 21; and Freud, 25, 26, 55, 69, 74, 77; and gender identity, 25, 55–62, 69; development of, 55; and cross-gender disorders, 65–68; and bias, 74, 87; and values, 81, 82, 93–94; and homosexual cross-dressing, 101, 176, 178, 188, 189–90; and transvestism, 155–56, 170, 189; and transsexualism, 190; and culture, 273–74, 276, 281, 286, 297, 301, 303–4; and sexual identity, 292; and professional aspirations, 297; and cross-gender identification, 303. *See also* Boyhood femininity
Feminism: and sexual-liberation movement, 12, 53; and Masters and Johnson, 19; and sex and gender, 30, 297; and female sexuality, 31, 46, 51; and power, 51; and sexism in psychotherapy, 74; and penis envy, 80, 82; and psychoanalytic theory, 85, 333; and cultural analysis, 297; and male sexuality, 316, 318
Feminist theory, 53
Fenichel, O., 151
Film, 290–91
Fine, B., 211
Fineman, J., 43
Fishbein, Morris, 357
Fliegel, Z., 61
Ford, C. S., 36
Forel, August, 360
Foucault, Michel, 14, 37
Four-Factor Index of Social Status, 198
Frankle, Josef, 355
Free love movement, 12
Freud, Martha, 259
Freud, Sigmund: and sexuality, 2, 12–13, 26, 27; gender theory of, 3, 25, 55, 58–59, 60, 63, 64, 69, 70, 70n13, 71, 77, 314; sexual theories of, 3, 16, 19, 22–24, 23n9, 25, 162–63; and fantasy, 13, 22, 224, 244, 255–56, 307; and sexual desire, 13, 211–13, 214, 215; and interpretation of dreams, 22; three essays on sexuality, 22–24; and homosexuality, 23, 164; and unconscious, 30; and libido theory, 33–36, 52; and object relations theory, 38–40; and core gender identity, 43; and sex print, 44, 45; pessimism

Freud, Sigmund (*continued*)
of, 51; and values, 73, 74; and female psychology, 77, 79, 84–86, 87; and penis envy, 77–78, 80, 81, 83; patriarchal bias of, 82–83; and biological assumptions, 85; and ego split, 154, 160; and sexual boredom, 223; and erotic transference, 259–60, 262, 262n2, 263, 268; and transference, 262; and men's oedipal development, 275; and women's preoedipal tie to mother, 275; and masochism, 320; and male sexuality, 327, 328, 340; and Benjamin, 357, 361, 365, 366
Friday, Nancy, 321
Friedmann, F. F., 353–54, 355
Full Scale Wechsler IQ, 198
Funke, Kosimar, 359

Gagnon, John, 14, 37, 48–49
Gay liberation, 12
Gender: sexuality distinguished from, 2, 21, 25, 43–44, 55–56, 70, 171, 349; and Freud, 3, 25, 55, 58–59, 60, 63, 64, 69, 70, 70n13, 71, 77, 314; and gender differentiation, 19, 25, 26, 61, 69–70, 80; and core gender identity, 32, 42, 53, 69, 71; and third gender, 43, 43n6, 315n12; and male sexuality, 50; and bias, 74; and fantasy, 230, 232, 236–42, 314; and sexual behavior, 230, 232, 233–35, 240; and transference, 264; and oedipal transference, 265; fluidity of, 297, 314–15, 363; and psychoanalysis, 298; and sexual preferences, 301; and unconscious, 301, 314; and female sexuality, 313; and transsexualism, 366, 366n10
Gender Behavior Inventory for Boys, 196
Gender bending, 12
Gender identity: independence-interdependence of, 3; development of, 25, 297; and sexuality, 43, 53; psychoanalytic theories of, 55–71, 71n16, 297; definitions of, 56–58; changing theories of, 79–80; and homosexuality, 91, 97, 99–102; and men, 91–109, 171, 278; and transsexualism, 91, 113–15, 177, 189; and transvestism, 91, 146, 154, 160, 171, 172–73, 177, 189; disorders of, 97–109, 171–72; and secondary transsexualism, 137; and women, 171, 297–98; and homosexual cross-dressing, 177, 184–85, 189–90; and boyhood femininity, 194–98, 200–1, 207; and fantasy, 229, 301; and sexual identity, 279–81, 282, 289; and male sexuality, 289; and desired object, 296; and conformity, 301–2
Gender role identity: and core gender identity, 3, 25, 32, 57, 70, 92–93; and psychoanalytic theory, 71, 79; development of, 92–93; as psychological self-image, 92; and culture, 93, 302, 315; and unconscious, 93; pathological disturbances of, 94; and sexual disorders, 99; and homosexuality, 100, 111; and homosexual cross-dressing, 101, 102, 179; and transvestism, 102, 111, 302; and transsexualism, 109; and primary transsexualism, 126; and sexual identity, 289; biological impact on, 298; fluidity in, 302
Gender roles: fluidity of, 8; reevaluation of, 12, 29; and sexology, 19; and Money, 56–57; shaping of, 71; and sexism, 75; polarity of, 80, 298; and unconscious, 91, 93, 94; stereotypes of, 291; and cross-gender identifications, 297–98, 301
Genet, Jean, 37
Genital herpes, 2, 12, 291
Gernsbach, Hugo, 360
Gill, M., 260, 266, 271
Green, André, 224
Green, R., 195, 207
Greenacre, P. C., 62, 265
Greenson, R. R., 56, 62–63, 67, 140, 156, 172
Grinker, R., 126
Griswold v. Connecticut (1965), 21
Grossman, Paula, 349
Grossman, W. I., 83
Guze, H., 120, 155

Hamburger, Christina, 365
Hampson, J. G., 298
Hampson, J. L., 298
Hardy, K. R., 36–37, 39
Harms, Ernest, 356
Hartmann, Ernest, 12
Heindenry, John, 18
Hering, Ewald, 356
Hermaphroditism, 56, 91
Heterosexual desire, 60. *See also* Sexual desire
Heterosexuality: and boyhood femininity, 5, 195; and cross-gender identifications, 6; changes in attitudes towards, 11; and reproduction, 13; and sexology, 17–18, 19; re-evaluation of, 24–26; and culture, 25–26; and sex print, 45; and gender theory, 60, 62, 63, 64, 69, 79; and gender identity, 91; and pseudohomosexuality, 94, 95–96; and transvestism, 102, 146, 147, 159, 161, 166, 174; and secondary transsexualism, 139, 144; and erotic transference, 263, 272, 273; and female sexuality, 279, 286; and male sexuality, 286–87, 291; and masculine identifications in heterosexual women, 304–9; and lesbian sex fantasy, 340
Hirschfeld, Magnus, 360
Hogan, R. T., 72
Homosexual cross-dressing: field study of, 4; and imaginative limitation, 4, 190; and men, 65; and merger fantasies, 68; and femininity, 101, 176, 178, 188, 189–90; and gender role identity, 101, 102, 179; and secondary transsexualism, 122, 123, 127–35; and transsexualism, 123, 127–28, 133, 179, 181, 182, 189, 190; as perversion, 165; and preoedipal period, 166; and separation anxiety, 166, 192; and transvestism, 173–76, 189, 190; and gender identity, 177, 184–85, 189–90; definition of, 178–79; and object relations, 179, 190–92; developmental history of, 180–88, 192–93; and sense of self, 184, 187–88, 190, 192; and personality structure, 188–89; and boyhood femininity, 206; and sexology, 348

Homosexualities: as term, 3, 26, 92n2, 164, 314; and boyhood femininity, 5; and homosexual cross-dressing, 193
Homosexuality: changes in attitudes towards, 11–12, 21, 28, 30, 51; and sex reformers, 13; and sexology, 15, 17–18, 19, 21, 25, 361, 361n7, 364; and Freud's theories, 23, 164; re-evaluation of, 24–26; and culture, 27; and sexual identity, 27, 279, 281; and sex print, 45; and andrenogenital syndrome, 70–71, 300; women's issues compared to, 74; and gender identity, 91, 97, 99–102; and core gender identity, 93, 111; and separation anxiety, 98, 100, 111; and attitude towards women, 99–100, 175–76, 340; and castration anxiety, 99, 100, 163; and pleasure facilitators, 99; and dependency needs, 100–1; and transsexualism, 108, 112, 113; and transvestism, 137, 139, 147, 151, 154, 167, 174–75; homosexual women, 151, 161n1, 227, 269, 285, 296, 312–13; and potency disorders, 169; and boyhood femininity, 195; and erotic transference, 263, 269, 270, 272, 272n6; masculine identification in homosexual women, 313; and homosexual dread, 319; transient homosexual resolution, 341, 342
Horney, Karen: gender theory of, 3, 55–56, 59–62, 64, 69, 71, 79–80; and adult masculinity complex, 60–61, 61n3; and Freud's bias, 82, 84; and male sexuality, 327–28, 330, 336
Howell, E., 79
Hunt, M., 288
Hyposexuality, 31

Identity: and sexuality, 41–42. *See also* Sexual identity
Impotence: psychogenic, 212–13
Inhibited sexual desire (ISD), 214–16
Intersexuality, 70–71, 298–300, 315
Introjective identification, 155, 156, 165, 173, 176, 177, 191

Jacobson, E., 62, 192
Johns Hopkins University Gender Identity Clinic, 144, 349
Johnson, Virginia E., 16, 18–19, 28, 78, 214, 285
Jones, Ernest: gender theory of, 3, 55, 59–62, 64, 69, 71, 79; and libido theory, 34; and erotic transference, 259
Jorgensen, Christine: autobiography of, 107, 114–15; and transsexualism, 117, 124, 130, 348, 349, 366; and Benjamin, 363; and female soul in male body, 364–65
Jucovy, M., 150

Kaplan, Helen Singer, 213, 214–15, 223–24
Kardiner, Abram, 35, 38, 212–13
Karme, L., 264–65, 269
Karush, A., 35
Kastrup, M., 205
Kernberg, Otto, 218, 222, 224
Kinsey, Alfred: and sexology, 16; and homosexuality, 17–18; and sexual liberation, 20; and perversions, 28; and masturbation, 47, 288; and fantasy, 240, 320n1; and adolescent sexuality, 283; and Benjamin, 348, 360; and transsexualism, 349
Kinsey Scale, 17
Kleeman, J., 61, 64–65
Klein, George, 38–40, 226, 304
Klein, Melanie, 314
Klerman, G. L., 84
Kohut, H., 160, 172
Krafft-Ebing, Richard, 15, 22, 131, 361, 362, 363
Kubie, L. S., 35
Kuhn, T. S., 72

Lacan, Jacques, 314
Laplanche, J., 211
Lapouse, R., 205
Lawrence, D. H., 316–17
Lebowitz, P. S., 195
Lerner, H., 81
Lesbians, 151, 161n1, 227, 269, 285, 296, 312–13
Lesbian sex fantasy: and male sexuality, 7, 320, 321–22, 323, 325, 332, 333, 337–40, 343; and transvestism, 7, 151, 174; and feminine identification, 334, 337
Lester, E., 269, 275
Lewandowski, Herbert, 360
Libido, 2, 13, 13n2, 33–34, 211, 214
Libido theory (sexual instinct), 13, 32–36, 41, 49, 51, 52, 86, 163
Lichtenstein, H., 39, 41, 42, 86
Lorber, Judith, 296
Lorenz, Konrad, 67

McDougall, J., 339
Macklin, R., 73
Mahler, M., 206
Mailer, Norman, 317
Male sexuality: and female sexuality, 2–3, 31, 43–44, 47, 48, 53–54; development of, 6, 326–31, 333–43; and masturbation, 6, 48, 49, 78–79, 232, 240, 287–88, 291, 295, 329; and power, 6, 50, 54, 240, 316–32; and sexual identity, 6, 44; and fantasy, 7, 230, 240–41, 318, 319–22, 320n1, 333–43; re-evaluation of, 28; and libido theory, 34, 35; and identity, 42, 53; and compulsive sexuality, 49–50; and castration anxiety, 50, 163, 172, 240, 319, 326–27, 328, 331, 342; and domination, 50, 54, 316, 318, 330, 332; and heterosexuality, 286–87, 291; and gender identity, 289; and culture, 316, 317–18, 319; and loss of love fear, 319, 332; and conscious fears, 322–23, 326–31, 342; clinical examples of macho sexuality, 323–26
Marantz, S., 200
Marcus, Steven, 22–23, 86
Marcuse, Herbert, 13, 24
Marmor, J., 76
Masculinity: as parallel construct, 3, 62, 64, 69, 80; changes in attitudes towards, 11–12, 28; re-

Masculinity (*continued*)
evaluation of, 12, 24; and sexology, 21; and Freud, 25, 26; and gender identity, 25, 55–58, 62–64, 69; development of, 55; and disidentification, 62–63, 67, 67n7; and cross-gender disorders, 65; and masculine identifications in heterosexual women, 65, 304–9, 311; and values, 93–94; and sexual disorders, 99; and homosexuality, 100–2; and transvestism, 104, 105, 147, 157, 166–67, 176, 189; and transsexualism, 109, 122; and secondary transsexualism, 140; and homosexual cross-dressing, 178, 185, 191; and culture, 273–74, 275, 276, 281, 286, 301; and cross-gender identification, 303, 312
Masochism: and female sexuality, 5, 46, 241, 316, 319, 320; and male sexuality, 5, 320, 332; and sexology, 16, 28; and Kinsey, 20; and castration anxiety, 99; and transvestism, 103, 105–6, 150, 152, 156, 169–71; and pleasure facilitators, 164; and homosexual cross-dressing, 188; and sexual excitement, 218; and sexual desire, 219; and fantasy, 220, 227, 242, 320, 321; and cross-gender identification, 308–9
Masters, William H., 16, 18–19, 28, 78, 214, 285
Masterson, J., 132
Masturbation: and female sexuality, 6, 47–48, 78–79, 284–85, 287–88, 291, 295; and male sexuality, 6, 48, 49, 78–79, 232, 240, 287–88, 291, 295, 329; and sex differences, 48; and sex reformers, 13; and sexology, 15, 17, 18, 21; acceptance of, 28; and autonomy, 41, 47–48; and transvestism, 102, 103, 147, 148, 152, 167, 176; and transsexualism, 108; and primary transsexualism, 117, 119, 122, 125; and secondary transsexualism, 136, 139; and sex print, 226; and fantasy, 255
Mavissakalian, M., 338
May, Rollo, 28, 281, 317–18
Medical advances, 2, 12, 14, 29–30, 297, 362
Men: and reproductive technology, 29; and sexuality, 43; and cross-gender disorders, 65; and transvestism, 65, 161; and gender identity, 91–109, 171, 278; competitive relationships between, 94–95, 103, 104; and erotic transference, 260, 269–72, 270n5, 273–74, 275, 276; and self-identity, 277; and desiring subject, 280; and adolescent development, 281; feminine identification in, 331, 334, 337, 340, 341. *See also* Male sexuality
Meyer-Bahlburg, H. F. L., 299
Miller, Henry, 316
Millett, Kate, 82, 316
Misogyny, 84, 85, 87
Mitchell, J., 61
Mitchell, Stephen, 221–22
Money, John: and gender, 2, 14, 69, 298, 299; and sex/gender distinctions, 3, 56; and sexology, 16; and intersexed patients, 19, 298, 299; and gender differentiation, 25, 56, 80; and gender identity, 57, 91; and andrenogenital syndrome, 70–71, 300; and transsexualism, 106, 116; and transvestism, 153; and boyhood femininity, 195
Monk, M. A., 205
Moore, B., 211
Mother: and male sexuality, 7, 275, 327–30, 331, 333, 336, 339, 340, 341, 342, 343; and protofemininity, 56; and gender theory, 58, 59, 62–64; and cross-gender disorders, 65, 68; and transsexualism, 66, 68, 107–8, 111, 114, 115–16, 118–20, 122, 128–29, 130, 132–33, 135–36, 138, 141, 148, 148n1, 166, 168; and penis envy, 77; and gender role identity, 95–96; and fantasy, 98, 225; and homosexuality, 100, 101, 111n2, 166, 175–76; and transvestism, 102, 103–4, 105, 111n2, 158–59, 160, 166, 167, 170, 171, 175, 341; and homosexual cross-dressing, 180–82; and boyhood femininity, 196, 198–99, 200, 202, 206; and erotic transference, 267, 268, 273, 274–75; and women's loss of love fear, 274–75; and sexual identity, 292–95; and cross-gender identifications, 304, 305–11; and castration anxiety, 328, 340
Moulton, R., 85

Neuroses: and Freud, 23; and gender role, 94–95; definition of, 97; and separation anxiety, 97–98; perversions distinguished from, 162, 163, 164, 165; transference neurosis, 264

Object relations: and sexuality, 3, 23, 24, 27, 41; and theory, 6, 38–40; and sexual motivation, 33, 38–40, 53; and fantasy, 40, 221; and identity, 42; and female sexuality, 49; and nonsexual motives, 52; and gender identity, 56; and gender theory, 60–61, 70, 80, 81; and psychoanalytic theory, 86–87, 164, 165; and transvestism, 154–56, 157, 173, 191; and homosexual cross-dressing, 179, 190–92; and transsexualism, 190–91; and sexual desire, 220, 221, 228; and women, 274; and masculine identification, 311; and penis envy, 311–12
Oedipus complex, 26, 34, 49, 58–59, 99, 104–5, 158–59, 167, 172, 212, 223, 260, 261, 264–265, 268, 270, 274–75, 292–93, 301, 305, 311, 326–28, 339–441
Omni-available woman fantasy: and male sexuality, 7, 320, 321, 325, 330–31, 332, 333, 334–37, 343; and lesbian sex fantasy, 338, 339
Orgasm: and female sexuality, 18, 46–49, 77–78, 279, 283, 284–88, 292, 295, 322; and Masters and Johnson, 18; and function of sexuality, 40–42; and male sexuality, 43, 48, 49; and sex difference, 48–50; and perversions, 163; and sexual cycle, 214; and fantasy, 285, 286, 336
Orvaschel, H., 205
Ovesey, Lionel, xi–xiii, 3, 35, 85, 113, 206, 342

Penis envy: and female sexuality, 59, 70n13, 77, 80–81, 293, 295, 343; and Horney, 59–61, 61n3, 79–80, 82; and gender theory, 70; and

psychoanalytic theory, 75, 76, 77, 83, 85, 313; and gender role identity, 79; changing theories of, 80–81; feminist criticism of, 80, 82; primary and secondary, 85; and cross-gender identification, 309; as multidetermined compromise formation, 311, 312n8; and object relations, 311–12; and male sexuality, 327, 341, 342–43
Perversion: and sexology, 16, 25, 26, 28, 162; and Freud, 23, 24; and Stoller, 26, 168, 170; and object relations, 41; and male sexuality, 43, 171–72, 327; and sex print, 44, 45, 280; and psychoanalysis, 162–65, 162n2, 168–69, 177, 213, 219; and fantasy, 225, 225n10, 226
Pincus, Gregory, 21
Pomeroy, W. B., 121
Pontalis, J. -B., 211
Postmodernism, 6, 8, 297, 363
Power: and fantasy, 1, 50–51; and male sexuality, 6, 50, 54, 240, 316–32; and sexuality, 7, 14, 29, 37, 50–51, 271–72; and sexual masochism, 46; and men, 94; and homosexuality, 101; and secondary transsexualism, 140; and transvestism, 156, 159, 170, 173; and homosexual cross-dressing, 187, 191, 193; and impotence, 212; and sexual desire, 219, 222; and women, 297
Powerlessness, 1; and Adler's concept of the masculine protest, 84; and male sexuality, 318–19; 322–23
Pregenital sexuality, 39–40
Primary transsexualism: as classification, 3, 112, 127; and core gender identity, 114, 125, 126, 133, 144; case studies of, 115–26; and treatment, 144; and femininity, 190
Projective identification, 155, 156, 165, 173, 176, 177, 191
Pseudohomosexuality, 91, 94, 95–97, 100
Psychoanalysis: paradigms within, 2, 86–87; and sexual mores, 2; new formulations in, 14, 24–26, 176–77; and sexual object choice, 27; and constructionism, 28; and female sexuality, 31, 333; and sexual identity, 31–54; and gender identity, 55–71, 71n16, 297; and cross-gender disorders, 65–69; influence of values in, 72–88; and bias, 73, 76; and sexism, 74; verification of psychoanalytic theory, 83–84; biological assumptions of, 84–86, 87; and perversions, 162–65, 162n2, 168–69, 177, 213, 219; and sexuality, 162–64, 245; and subjectivity/intersubjectivity, 211; and sexual desire, 213, 216–17; and fantasy, 216; and erotic transference, 259–60; and gender, 298

Queer theory, 14

Rado, S., 38
Reich, Wilhelm, 51
Reproduction and reproductive technologies, 13, 29–30, 32
Rich, Adrienne, 25
Riddle, Oscar, 360
Rieff, P., 73, 84
Rivière, Joan, 303–4, 309
Robbins, Harold, 317
Robinson, Paul, 12–13, 17, 22, 28
Rock, John, 21
Roe v. Wade (1973), 21–22
Rohrbaugh, J. B., 82, 85
Romberg, Ernest von, 352
Rosen, A. C., 197
Ross, N., 86
Russo, A. J., 195
Rycroft, Charles, 262

Sadism: and sexology, 16, 28; and transvestism, 152, 169; and pleasure facilitators, 164; and sexual excitement, 218; and sexual desire, 219; and fantasy, 220, 240, 242, 320, 321; and male sexuality, 241, 316, 318, 328, 331, 332; and cross-gender identification, 304
Sandler, Anne-Marie, 301
Sandler, Joseph, 301
Sanger, Margaret, 16, 21
Schacter, S., 37
Schaefer, M., 76
Schafer, R., 82, 85, 167, 192, 221, 262–63
Schleich, Karl Ludwig, 352–53, 354
Schuker, Eleanor, 298
Secondary transsexualism: as classification, 3, 112; and core gender identity, 114, 133, 139, 144; and homosexuality, 122, 123, 127–35; and transvestism, 123, 127, 135–40, 167; definition of, 127
Segal, M. M., 174
Separation anxiety: and transsexualism, 3–4, 68, 98, 107–8, 111, 113–14, 120–21, 123, 125, 141, 166, 192; and boyhood femininity, 5, 194, 197, 200, 201–2, 205–7; and cross-gender disorders, 5, 62, 68, 68n10, 98, 158, 197; and neuroses, 97–98; and homosexuality, 98, 100, 111; and transvestism, 98, 111, 148n1, 158, 160, 166, 170, 192; and primary transsexualism, 120–21, 123, 125, 126, 144; and secondary transsexualism, 138, 144; and homosexual cross-dressing, 166, 192; and adolescent development, 282; and male sexuality, 331, 341, 343
Separation-individuation: and transsexualism, 3–4, 111, 141–42; and object relations, 42; and cross-gender disorders, 65–66, 68, 69, 111, 166; and merger fantasies, 68, 68n9, 68n10; and gender identity, 172; and homosexual cross-dressing, 192, 193; and masculine identification, 311
Sex and gender: and symbolic meanings, 1; conceptualization of, 2, 14, 55, 349; and culture, 2, 6, 30, 297; and bias, 3, 297; development of, 7; and unconscious, 13, 30; and reproductive techniques, 29–30
Sexism, 52–53, 74–77, 297
Sexologists (sex researchers), 2, 15–21
Sexology: origins of, 2; shifts within, 2, 14; and homosexuality, 15, 17–18, 19, 21, 25, 361,

Sexology (*continued*)
361n7, 364; and masturbation, 15, 17, 18, 21; and Benjamin, 16, 360; and perversions, 16, 25, 26, 28, 162; and sexual-liberation movements, 20–21; and reproduction, 29; and sex print, 44; and sexual desire, 213, 215, 216, 217; and transsexualism, 348–49
Sex print: and erotic stimuli, 32, 44, 45, 280; and identity, 42; and sexuality, 44–46, 53; and sexual preferences, 44–45, 228; and fantasy, 226, 226–27, 280; definition of, 280
Sex reformers, 13, 14, 16, 21–22
Sex therapy, 18–19, 214–16
Sexual abuse, 12, 29
Sexual arousal, 32, 214, 217
Sexual attitudes, 11–14, 54
Sexual behavior: symbolic meaning of, 1; and fantasy, 5, 22, 243–56; and sexual desire, 13; and culture, 17; and sexology, 21; and AIDS, 29; and technology, 30; and sexual object choice, 32; and libido theory, 35, 36; and female sexuality, 78, 283; and gender identity, 91; and gender role identity, 93; defensive use of, 219; and gender, 230, 232, 233–35, 240; and sex print, 280
Sexual boredom, 5, 212, 223–25, 224n8
Sexual cycle: Kaplan, 214; Masters and Johnson, 217
Sexual desire: and fantasy, 5, 7, 16, 29, 211, 213, 214, 215–17, 218, 220, 224, 225–29; and sexual excitement, 5, 214; and Freud, 13, 211–13, 214, 215; and women, 13; and culture, 29, 213, 215, 219–20, 228n14; and sexual motivation, 32; disorders of, 214–16; triggers of, 217–21, 222, 228; and hostility, 218–19; and narcissism, 222; and sex print, 280; and sexual identity, 280; fluidity of, 297; and omni-available woman fantasy, 333, 335
Sexual diseases, 12, 28; and antibiotics, 12
Sexual disorders: and transsexualism, 3; and gender identity disorders, 97, 98–99; and castration anxiety, 98–99; groups of, 164–65
Sexual excitement, 5, 213–14, 216–19, 218–19n6, 220, 222, 228
Sexual experiences, 246–47, 254–56; male-female difference in adolescence, 47–48
Sexual harassment, 29
Sexual identity: independence-interdependence of, 3; and female sexuality, 6, 44, 279, 292, 295; and homosexuality, 27, 279, 281; and psychoanalysis, 31–54; and culture, 46, 291; and gender identity, 279–81, 282, 289; and adolescent development, 281; normative problems in consolidation of, 282–83; and intrapsychic impediments, 291–95; fluidity of, 297
Sexual instinct. *See* Libido theory
Sexual Inventory, 231–32
Sexuality: gender distinguished from, 2, 21, 25, 43–44, 55–56, 70, 171, 349; and object relations, 3, 23, 24, 27, 41; and power, 7, 14, 29, 37, 50–51, 271–72; and culture, 11, 13–14, 24, 31, 32, 33, 38, 43, 51, 87; and constructionism, 14, 26–30; and medical advances, 14, 29–30; and childhood, 22, 23–24, 34, 35, 39, 162, 163, 226, 280; and adolescence, 47–48; and aggression, 26, 28, 101; and identity, 31, 41–42, 43; and hormone level, 35–36; function and value of, 40–46; and sex print, 44–46, 53; and individual development, 46–50; changing theories of, 77–79; and psychoanalytic theory, 86; and transvestism, 146, 173; and perversions, 162–64; development of, 171, 212, 300; and fantasy, 223; and film, 290–91
Sexual liberation, 2, 11, 12, 13–14, 24, 51–53, 78, 291; and sexology, 20–21; and women, 21, 297; contraction of movement, 28–29; and female sexuality, 51–53, 54, 278, 283; and transsexualism, 366
Sexual modernism, 12–13, 15, 17, 28
Sexual motivation, 2, 32–40, 51, 53, 223–25; and libido theory, 33–36; and appetitional theory, 38–40
Sexual object choice: and sexology, 19; and Freud, 23; hormonal influence on, 25, 300; and psychoanalysis, 27; and sexual behavior, 32; and sex print, 44; and gender theory, 60, 69; and homosexuality, 99–100, 99–100n6, 193; fluidity in choice of, 226–27; and gender identity, 296; and sexual development, 300; and cross-gender identification, 312–13
Sexual preferences: lack of fluidity, 8; and self-identity, 14; and perversions, 23; etiology of, 26; conflicts concerning, 28; and sex print, 44–45, 228; and gender, 301
Sexual repression, 13
Sexual role, 280
Sexualization, 219
Shared cultural fantasy, 124n, 363–66
Shulman, Alix Kates, 278
Simon, William, 14, 37, 48–49
Singer, Jerome E., 37, 244
Socarides, C. W., 206
Sodomy statutes, 20
Sorensen, R. C., 283, 287, 288
Spillane, Mickey, 317
Steinach, Eugen, 355–58, 366
Stewart, W. A., 83
Stoller, Robert: gender theory of, 3, 55, 56, 57, 62–65, 69, 71; and perversions, 26, 168, 170; and cross-gender disorders, 65–66, 69; and gender identity, 91; and transsexualism, 91, 106, 107, 113, 116, 120, 121–22, 132–33, 143, 168; and transvestism, 91, 138, 148n1, 168, 170; and boyhood femininity, 195–96, 206; and sexual desire, 213, 216, 218; and sexual excitement, 213, 216, 218, 219, 220
Sulcov, M., 113
Supreme Court, 20; and *Roe versus Wade*, 21; and *Griswold versus Connecticut*
Szasz, T., 260, 262

Technological advances, 2, 29–30, 362, 363, 364
Thompson, Clara, 77, 85

Thorne, E., 320
Toolan, J., 284
Transference: and psychoanalysis, 259–60; definitions of, 260–61; erotic versus eroticized, 261; erotic compared with other types, 263; and gender influence, 264; and oedipal transference, 264–65, 268, 269; and transference neurosis, 264. *See also* Erotic transference
Transference love, 260–61
Transgender movement, 300
Transsexualism: classification of, 3, 111–13; etiology of, 3–4, 19–20, 64, 66, 67, 106–7, 141–42, 351n3, 364, 365; as gender disorder, 3; and separation anxiety, 3–4, 68, 98, 107–8, 111, 113–14, 120–21, 123, 125, 141, 166, 192; and boyhood femininity, 5, 66, 195–96; and shared fantasy, 7; and sexual-liberation movements, 12; and sex print, 44; and men, 65; women as transsexuals, 65, 112, 312–13, 350; and protofemininity, 66, 69; conflictual basis for, 67; and core gender identity, 68, 93, 107–9, 111, 113–14, 141, 142, 300; and merger fantasy, 68; and gender identity, 91, 113–15, 177, 189; and gender identity disorders, 97, 106–9; and pleasure inhibitors, 99; and fantasy, 108, 111, 114, 141–42, 364; and transvestism, 108, 112, 113, 120, 146, 151, 152, 155, 158, 160, 167–69, 173; definition of, 110, 349n1; and preoedipal period, 111, 166; and homosexual cross-dressing, 123, 127–28, 133, 179, 181, 182, 189, 190; treatment of, 142–45; and sense of self, 192, 193; and Benjamin, 347–51; and culture, 362, 363–66; and gender, 366, 366n10. *See also* Primary transsexualism; Secondary transsexualism
Transvestism: and imaginative limitation, 4–5; and boyhood femininity, 5, 195; and male sexuality, 7; transient transvestic resolution, 7, 341, 342; and sexual-liberation movements, 12; and sex print, 44; and men, 65, 161; and gender identity, 91, 146, 154, 160, 171, 172–73, 177, 189; and core gender identity, 93, 111; and gender identity disorders, 97, 102–6; and separation anxiety, 98, 111, 148n1, 158, 160, 166, 170, 192; and pleasure facilitators/inhibitors, 99, 164; and gender role identity, 102, 111, 302; and fantasy, 103, 146, 147, 148–58, 167, 170, 171, 174, 175, 176, 340–41, 342; and transsexualism, 108, 112, 113, 120, 146, 151, 152, 155, 158, 160, 167–69, 173; and preoedipal period, 111, 158, 166, 170; and secondary transsexualism, 123, 127, 135–40, 167; and homosexuality, 137, 139, 147, 151, 154, 167, 174–75; definition of, 146, 161; and sense of self, 146–47, 153–54, 163, 172–73, 176, 192, 193; and developmental history, 147; and relationships with women, 154–55, 160, 175; etiology of, 160, 161–62; and aggression, 169; and homosexual cross-dressing, 173–76, 189, 190; and sexology, 348
Treatment goals: and women, 75–77
Tripp, C. A., 44, 45
Tyson, Phyllis, 81

UCLA Gender Identity Unit, 196, 197, 207
Ulrichs, Carl Heinrich, 15, 19
Unconscious: and sex and gender, 13, 30; and core gender identity, 42, 69; and values, 72; and female sexuality, 78; and gender differentiation, 80; and psychoanalytic theory, 86; and gender role, 91, 93, 94; and gender role identity, 93; and transsexualism, 108; and transvestism, 162, 170, 174; and perversions, 164; and fantasy, 217, 221, 226, 244, 319; and erotic transference, 260; and cross-gender indentifications, 297, 298, 303–4, 313; and gender, 301, 314; and male sexuality, 334, 339, 342

Values: and sexual modernism, 15, 17; and sexology, 20; influence of, in psychoanalysis, 72–88; and science, 72; and femininity, 81, 82, 93–94; and transsexualism, 363, 366. *See also* Bias
van Lustbader, Eric, 317
Victorianism, 11, 12
Vivarium, 356
Voronoff, Sergei, 355, 366

Weeks, Jeffrey, 14, 26–27
Weinberg, M., 26
Weissman, M. M., 205
Weitzmann, E. L., 206
White, Edmund, 178
Wish fulfillment, 5, 13, 33–34, 244, 255–56
Women: theoretical bias against, 3, 74–77, 82–83, 86, 87; and cross-gender identifications, 6, 297–98, 303–12; and sexual desires, 13; and Kinsey, 18; and birth control reformers, 21–22; and sexual-liberation movements, 12, 21, 297; and sexuality, 43; and cross-gender disorders, 65; and masculine identifications in heterosexual women, 65, 304–9, 311, 313; as transsexuals, 65, 112, 312–13, 350; and loss of love fear, 70n13, 81, 269, 274–75, 293; homosexuals' issues compared to, 74; and role dissatisfaction, 74; homosexual women, 151, 161n1, 227, 269, 285, 296, 312–13; transvestites' relationships with, 154–56, 160, 175; as transvestites, 161n1; and gender identity, 171, 297–98; and perversions, 171–72; and erotic transference, 260, 263, 266–68, 272, 273–74, 275, 276; men's envy of, 272; and self-identity, 277; and adolescent development, 281; and power, 297; and neuter women, 309–11. *See also* Female sexuality
Women's movement. *See* Feminism
Women's studies, 14, 298

Zilbergeld, B., 316, 317
Zuger, B., 195